# Of God and His Creatures

# Of God and His Creatures

## St. Thomas Aquinas

# Of God and His Creatures

© Lighthouse Publishing 2019

Written by: St. Thomas Aquinas (1225 – March 7, 1274)
By Joseph Rickaby S.J, M.A. Lond B.Sc. Oxon . (1845-1932)
Updated into Modern U.S English by A.M. Overett, B.A., REL.
(b. 1960)

All rights reserved. Without limiting the rights under copyright reserved above, no part of this publication may be reproduced, stored in a retrieval system, or transmitted, in any form or by any means (electronic, mechanical, photocopying, recording or otherwise), without the prior written permission of the copyright owner of this book.

Published by
Lighthouse Christian Publishing
SAN 257-4330
5531 Dufferin Drive
Savage, Minnesota, 55378
United States of America

www.lighthousechristianpublishing.com

Preface

SOME years ago, a priest of singularly long and varied experience urged me to write "a book about God." He said that wrong and imperfect notions of God lay at the root of all our religious difficulties. Professor Lewis Campbell says the same thing in his own way in his work, Religion in Greek Literature, where he declares that the age needs "a new definition of God." Thinking the need over, I turned to the Summa contra Gentiles. I was led to it by the Encyclical of Leo XIII, Aeterni Patris, urging the study of St Thomas. A further motive, quite unexpected, was supplied by the University of Oxford in 1902 placing the Summa Contra Gentiles on the list of subjects which a candidate may at his option offer in the Final Honor School of Literae Humaniores, -- a very unlikely book to be offered so long as it remains simply as St Thomas wrote it. Lastly I remembered that I had in 1892 published under the name of Aquinas Ethicusa translation of the principal portions of the second part of St Thomas's Summa Theologica: thus I might be reckoned something of an expert in the difficult art of finding English equivalents for scholastic Latin. There are two ways of behaving towards St Thomas's writings, analogous to two several treatments of a church still standing, in which the saint might have worshipped. One way is to hand the edifice over to some Society for the Preservation of Ancient Monuments: they will keep it locked to the vulgar, while admitting some occasional connoisseur: they will do their utmost to preserve every stone identically the same that the mediaeval builder laid. And the Opera Omnia of St Thomas, handsomely bound, may fill a library shelf, whence a volume is occasionally taken down for the sole purpose of knowing what St Thomas said and no more. Another thirteenth-century church may stand, a parish church still, in daily use; an ancient monument, and something besides; a present-day house of prayer, meeting the needs of a twentieth-century congregation; and for that purpose refitted, repainted, restored, repaired and modernized; having had that done to it which its mediaeval architects would have done, had they lived in our time. Nothing is more remarkable in our old English churches than the sturdy self-confidence, and the good taste also lasting for some centuries, with which each successive age has superimposed its own style upon the architecture of its predecessors. If St Thomas's works are to serve modern uses, they must pass from their old Latinity into modern speech: their conclusions must be tested by all the subtlety of present day science, physical, psychological, and historical; maintained, wherever maintainable, but altered, where tenable no longer. Thus only can St Thomas keep his place as a living teacher of mankind. For the history of the Contra Gentiles I refer the reader to the folio edition printed at the Propaganda Press in 1878 cura et studio Petri Antonii Uccell ii, pp. xiii-xxxlx. Thomas Aquinas (1225-1274) came to the University of Paris in 1245, and there for three years heard the lectures of Albertus Magnus, taking his Bachelor's degree in 1248. He returned to the University in 1253, took his Master's degree in 1257, and thereupon lectured in theology for two or three years, leaving the University in 1259 or 1260. He wrote the Summa contra Gentiles in Italy, under the pontificate of Urban IV (1261-1264), at the request of St Raymund of Pennafort. He went for the third time to the University of Paris in 1269, finally returning

Viii to Italy in 1271. Though the Summa contra Gentiles was written in Italy, there is reason to believe that the substance of it was got together during the Saint's second residence at Paris, and formed the staple of his lectures in the University. The more celebrated Summa Theologica was a later work. The Summa contra Gentiles is in the unique position of a classic whereof the author's manuscript is still in great part extant. It is now in the Vatican Library. The manuscript consists of strips of parchment, of various shades of color, contained in an old parchment cover to which they were originally stitched. The writing is in double columns, minute and difficult to decipher, abounding in abbreviations, often passing into a kind of shorthand. Through many passages a line is drawn in sign of erasure: but these remain not less legible than the rest, and are printed as foot notes in the Propaganda edition: they do not appear in the present translation. To my mind, these erasures furnish the best proof of the authenticity of the autograph, which is questioned by S. E. Fretté, editor of Divi Thomae Opera Omnia (Vivès, Paris, 1874), vol. XII, preface iv-vi. An inscription on the cover states that the manuscript is the autograph of St Thomas, and that it was brought from Naples to the Dominican convent at Bergamo in 1354: whence its name of the 'Bergamo autograph.' Many leaves were lost in the sack of the convent by the armies of the first French Revolution; and the whole of Book IV is missing. The frequent erasures of the Saint himself lend some countenance to the omissions of his translator. Re-reading his manuscript in the twentieth century, St Thomas would have been not less ready than he showed himself in the thirteenth century to fulfil the Horatian precept, saepe stylum vertas. J. R. Pope's Hall, Oxford, Michaelmas 1905

Nihil obstat: T. M. TAAFFE S.J., Censor deputatus
Imprimatur: GULIELMUS PRAEPOSITUS JOHNSON, Vicarius Generalis Westmonasterii, die 12 Septembris 1905

BOOK 1

CHAPTER I—The Function of the Wise Man

My mouth shall discuss truth, and my lips shall detest the ungodly (Prov. vii, 7).

ACCORDING to established popular usage, which the Philosopher considers should be our guide in the naming of things, they are called 'wise' who put things in their right order and control them well. Now, in all things that are to be controlled and put in order to an end, the measure of control and order must be taken from the end in view; and the proper end of everything is something good. Hence we see in the arts that art A governs and, as it were, lords it over art B, when the proper end of art B belongs to A. Thus the art of medicine lords it over the art of the apothecary, because health, the object of medicine, is the end of all drugs that the apothecary's art compounds. These arts that lord it over others are called 'master-building,' or 'masterful arts'; and the 'master-builders' who practice them arrogate to themselves the name of 'wise men.' But because these persons deal with the ends in view of certain particular things, without attaining to the general end of all things, they are called 'wise in this or that particular thing,' as it is said, 'As a wise architect I have laid the foundation' (1 Cor. iii, 10); while the name of 'wise' without qualification is reserved for him alone who deals with the last end of the universe, which is also the first beginning of the order of the universe. Hence, according to the Philosopher, it is proper to the wise man to consider the highest causes.

Now the last end of everything is that which is intended by the prime author or mover thereof. The prime author and mover of the universe is intelligence, as will be shown later (B. II, Chap. XXIII, XXIV). Therefore the last end of the universe must be the good of the intelligence, and that is truth. Truth then must be the final end of the whole universe; and about the consideration of that end wisdom must primarily be concerned. And therefore the Divine Wisdom, clothed in flesh, testifies that He came into the world for the manifestation of truth: *For this was I born, and unto this I came into the World, to give testimony to the truth* (John xvii, 37). The Philosopher also rules that the first philosophy is the science of truth, not of any and every truth, but of that truth which is the origin of all truth, and appertains to the first principle of the being of all things; hence its truth is the principle of all truth, for things are in truth as they are in being.

It is one and the same function to embrace either of two contraries and to repel the other. Hence, as it is the function of the wise man to discuss truth, particularly of the first beginning, so it is his also to impugn the contrary error. Suitably therefore is the double function of the wise man displayed in the words above quoted from the Sapiential Book, namely, to study, and upon study to speak out the truth of God, which of all other is most properly called truth, and this is referred to in the words, *My mouth shall discuss truth,* and to impugn error contrary to truth, as referred to in the words, *And my lips shall detest the ungodly.*

## CHAPTER II—Of the Author's Purpose

OF all human pursuits, the pursuit of wisdom is the more perfect, the more sublime, the more useful, and the more agreeable. The more perfect, because in so far as a man gives himself up to the pursuit of wisdom, to that extent he enjoys already some portion of true happiness. Blessed is the man that shall dwell in wisdom (Ecclus xiv, 22). The more sublime, because thereby man comes closest to the likeness of God, who hath made all things in wisdom (Ps. ciii, 24). The more useful, because by this same wisdom we arrive at the realm of immortality. The desire of wisdom shall lead to an everlasting kingdom (Wisd. vi, 21). The more agreeable, because her conversation hath no bitterness, nor her company any weariness, but gladness and joy (Wisd. viii, 16).

But on two accounts it is difficult to proceed against each particular error: first, because the sacrilegious utterances of our various erring opponents are not so well known to us as to enable us to find reasons, drawn from their own words, for the confutation of their errors: for such was the method of the ancient doctors in confuting the errors of the Gentiles, whose tenets they were readily able to know, having either been Gentiles themselves, or at least having lived among Gentiles and been instructed in their doctrines. Secondly, because some of them, as Mohammedans and Pagans, do not agree with us in recognizing the authority of any scripture, available for their conviction, as we can argue against the Jews from the Old Testament, and against heretics from the New. But these receive neither: hence it is necessary to have recourse to natural reason, which all are obliged to assent to. But in the things of God natural reason is often at a loss.

CHAPTER III—That the Truths which we confess concerning God fall under two Modes or Categories

BECAUSE not every truth admits of the same mode of manifestation, and "a well-educated man will expect exactness in every class of subject, according as the nature of the thing admits," as is very well remarked by the Philosopher (Eth. Nicom.I, 1094b), we must first show what mode of proof is possible for the truth that we have now before us. The truths that we confess concerning God fall under two modes. Some things true of God are beyond all the competence of human reason, as that God is Three and One. Other things there are to which even human reason can attain, as the existence and unity of God, which philosophers have proved to a demonstration under the guidance of the light of natural reason. That there are points of absolute intelligibility in God altogether beyond the compass of human reason, most manifestly appears. For since the leading principle of all knowledge of any given subject matter is an understanding of the thing's innermost being, or substance — according to the doctrine of the Philosopher, that the essence is the principle of demonstration — it follows that the mode of our knowledge of the substance must be the mode of knowledge of whatever we know about the substance. Hence if the human understanding comprehends the substance of anything, as of a stone or triangle, none of the points of intelligibility about that thing will exceed the capacity of human reason. But this is not our case with regard to God. The human understanding cannot go so far of its natural power as to grasp His substance, since under the conditions of the present life the knowledge of our understanding commences with sense; and therefore objects beyond sense cannot be grasped by human understanding except so far as knowledge is gathered of them through the senses. But things of sense cannot lead our understanding to read in them the essence of the Divine Substance, inasmuch as they are effects inadequate to the power that caused them. Nevertheless our understanding is thereby led to some knowledge of God, namely, of His existence and of other attributes that must necessarily be attributed to the First Cause. There are, therefore, some points of intelligibility in God, accessible to human reason, and other points that altogether transcend the power of human reason.

The same thing may be understood from consideration of degrees of intelligibility. Of two minds, one of which has a keener insight into truth than the other, the higher mind understands much that the other cannot grasp at all, as is clear in the 'plain man' (in rustico), who can in no way grasp the subtle theories of philosophy. Now the intellect of an angel excels that of a man more than the intellect of the ablest philosopher excels that of the plainest of plain men (rudissimi idiotae). The angel has a higher standpoint in creation than man as a basis of his knowledge of God, inasmuch as the substance of the angel, whereby he is led to know God by a process of natural knowledge, is nobler and more excellent than the things of sense, and even than the soul itself, whereby the human mind rises to the knowledge of God. But the Divine Mind exceeds the angelic much more than the angelic the human. For the Divine Mind of its own comprehensiveness covers the whole extent of its substance, and therefore perfectly understands its own essence, and knows all that is knowable about itself; but an angel of his natural knowledge does not know the essence of God, because the angel's own substance, whereby it is led to a knowledge of God, is an effect inadequate to the power of the cause that created it. Hence not all things that God understands in Himself can be grasped by the natural knowledge of an angel; nor is human reason competent to take in all that an angel understands of his own natural ability. As therefore it would be the height of madness in a 'plain man' to declare a philosopher's propositions false, because he could not understand them, so and much more would a man show exceeding folly if he suspected of falsehood a divine revelation given by the ministry of angels, on the mere ground that it was beyond the investigation of reason.

The same thing manifestly appears from the incapacity which we daily experience in the observation of nature. We are ignorant of very many properties of the things of sense; and of the properties that our senses do apprehend, in most cases we cannot perfectly dis cover the reason. Much more is it beyond the competence of human reason to investigate all the points of intelligibility in that supreme excellent and transcendent substance of God. Consonant with this is the saying of the Philosopher, that "as the eyes of bats are to the light of the sun, so is the intelligence of our soul to the things most manifest by nature" (Aristotle, Metaphysics I, min. l).

To this truth Holy Scripture also bears testimony. For it is said: Perchance thou wilt seize upon the traces of God, and fully discover the Almighty (Job xi, 7). And, Lo, God is great, and surpassing our knowledge (Job xxxvi, 26). And, We know in part (I Cor. xiii, 9). Not everything, therefore, that is said of God, even though it be beyond the power of reason to investigate, is at once to be rejected as false.

CHAPTER IV—That it is an advantage for the Truths of God, known by Natural Reason, to be proposed to men to be believed on faith

IF a truth of this nature were left to the sole enquiry of reason, three disadvantages would follow. One is that the knowledge of God would be confined to few. The discovery of truth is the fruit of studious enquiry. From this very many are hindered. Some are hindered by a constitutional unfitness, their natures being ill-disposed to the acquisition of knowledge. They could never arrive by study to the highest grade of human knowledge, which consists in the knowledge of God. Others are hindered by the needs of business and the ties of the management of property. There must be in human society some men devoted to temporal affairs. These could not possibly spend time enough in the learned lessons of speculative enquiry to arrive at the highest point of human enquiry, the knowledge of God. Some again are hindered by sloth. The knowledge of the truths that reason can investigate concerning God presupposes much previous knowledge. Indeed almost the entire study of philosophy is directed to the knowledge of God. Hence, of all parts of philosophy, that part stands over to be learnt last, which consists of metaphysics dealing with points of Divinity. Thus, only with great labor of study is it possible to arrive at the searching out of the aforesaid truth; and this labor few are willing to undergo for sheer love of knowledge.

Another disadvantage is that such as did arrive at the knowledge or discovery of the aforesaid truth would take a long time over it, on account of the profundity of such truth, and the many prerequisites to the study, and also because in youth and early manhood, the soul, tossed to and fro on the waves of passion, is not fit for the study of such high truth: only in settled age does the soul become prudent and scientific, as the Philosopher says. Thus, if the only way open to the knowledge of God were the way of reason, the human race would dwell long in thick darkness of ignorance: as the knowledge of God, the best instrument for making men perfect and good, would accrue only to a few, and to those few after a considerable lapse of time.

A third disadvantage is that, owing to the infirmity of our judgement and the perturbing force of imagination, there is some admixture of error in most of the investigations of human reason. This would be a reason to many for continuing to doubt even of the most accurate demonstrations, not perceiving the force of the demonstration, and seeing the divers judgements of divers persons who have the name of being wise men. Besides, in the midst of much demonstrated truth there is sometimes an element of error, not demonstrated but asserted on the strength of some plausible and sophistic reasoning that is taken for a demonstration. And therefore it was necessary for the real truth concerning divine things to be presented to men with fixed certainty by way of faith. Wholesome therefore is the arrangement of divine clemency, whereby things even that reason can investigate are commanded to be held on faith, so that all might easily be partakers of the knowledge of God, and that without doubt and error.

Hence it is said: Now ye walk not as the Gentiles walk in the vanity of their own notions, having the understanding darkened (Eph. iv, 17, 18); and, I will make all thy sons taught of the Lord (Isa. liv, 1, 5).

CHAPTER V—That it is an advantage for things that cannot he searched out by Reason to be proposed as Tenets of Faith

SOME may possibly think that points which reason is unable to investigate ought not to be proposed to man to believe, since Divine Wisdom provides for every being according to the measure of its nature; and therefore we must show the necessity of things even that transcend reason being proposed by God to man for his belief.

1. One proof is this. No one strives with any earnestness of desire after anything, unless it be known to him beforehand. Since, then, as will be traced out in the following pages (B. III, Chap. CXLVIII), Divine Providence directs men to a higher good than human frailty can experience in the present life, the mental faculties ought to be evoked and led onward to something higher than our reason can attain at present, learning thereby to desire something and earnestly to tend to something that transcends the entire state of the present life. And such is the special function of the Christian religion, which stands alone in its promise of spiritual and eternal goods, whereas the Old Law, carrying temporal promises, proposed few tenets that transcended the enquiry of human reason.

2. Also another advantage is thence derived, to wit, the repression of presumption, which is the mother of error. For there are some so presumptuous of their own

genius as to think that they can measure with their understanding the whole nature of the Godhead, thinking all that to be true which seems true to them, and that to be false which does not seem true to them. In order then that the human mind might be delivered from this presumption, and attain to a modest style of enquiry after truth, it was necessary for certain things to be proposed to man from God that altogether exceeded his understanding.

3. There is also another evident advantage in this, that any knowledge, however imperfect, of the noblest objects confers a very high perfection on the soul. And therefore, though human reason cannot fully grasp truths above reason, nevertheless it is much perfected by holding such truths after some fashion at least by faith. And therefore it is said: Many things beyond the understanding of man are shown to thee (Ecclus iii, 23). And, The things that are of God, none knoweth but the Spirit of God: but to us God hath revealed them through his Spirit (1 Cor. ii, 10, 11).

CHAPTER VI—That there is no lightmindedness in assenting to Truths of Faith, although they are above Reason

THE Divine Wisdom, that knows all things most fully, has deigned to reveal these her secrets to men, and in proof of them has displayed works beyond the competence of all natural powers, in the wonderful cure of diseases, in the raising of the dead, and what is more wonderful still, in such inspiration of human minds as that simple and ignorant persons, filled with the gift of the Holy Ghost, have gained in an instant the height of wisdom and eloquence. By force of the aforesaid proof, without violence of arms, without promise of pleasures, and, most wonderful thing of all, in the midst of the violence of persecutors, a countless multitude, not only of the uneducated but of the wisest men, flocked to the Christian faith, wherein doctrines are preached that transcend all human understanding, pleasures of sense are restrained, and a contempt is taught of all worldly possessions. That mortal minds should assent to such teaching is the greatest of miracles, and a manifest work of divine inspiration leading men to despise the visible and desire only invisible goods. Nor did this happen suddenly nor by chance, but by a divine disposition, as is manifest from the fact that God foretold by many oracles of His prophets that He intended to do this. The books of those prophets are still venerated amongst us, as bearing testimony to our faith. This argument is touched upon in the text: Which(salvation) having begun to be uttered by the Lord, was confirmed by them that heard him even unto us, God joining in the testimony by signs and portents and various distributions of the Holy Spirit (Heb. ii, 3, 4). This so wonderful conversion of the world to the Christian faith is so certain a sign of past miracles, that they need no further reiteration, since they appear evidently in their effects. It would be more wonderful than all other miracles, if without miraculous signs the world had been induced by simple and low-born men to believe truths so arduous, to do works so difficult, to hope for reward so high. And yet even in our times God ceases not through His saints to work miracles for the confirmation of the faith.

## CHAPTER VII—That the Truth of reason is not contrary to the Truth of Christian Faith

THE natural dictates of reason must certainly be quite true: it is impossible to think of their being otherwise. Nor a gain is it permissible to believe that the tenets of faith are false, being so evidently confirmed by God. Since therefore falsehood alone is contrary to truth, it is impossible for the truth of faith to be contrary to principles known by natural reason.

2. Whatever is put into the disciple's mind by the teacher is contained in the knowledge of the teacher, unless the teacher is teaching dishonestly, which would be a wicked thing to say of God. But the knowledge of principles naturally known is put into us by God, seeing that God Himself is the author of our nature. Therefore these principles also are contained in the Divine Wisdom. Whatever therefore is contrary to these principles is contrary to Divine Wisdom, and cannot be of God.

3. Contrary reasons fetter our intellect fast, so that it cannot proceed to the knowledge of the truth. If therefore contrary information were sent us by God, our intellect would be thereby hindered from knowledge of the truth: but such hindrance cannot be of God.

4. What is natural cannot be changed while nature remains. But contrary opinions cannot be in the same mind at the same time: therefore no opinion or belief is sent to man from God contrary to natural knowledge.

And therefore the Apostle says: The word is near in thy heart and in thy mouth, that is, the word of faith which we preach (Rom. x, 8). But because it surpasses reason it is counted by some as contrary to reason, which cannot be. To the same effect is the authority of

Augustine (Gen. ad litt. ii, 18): "What truth reveals can nowise be contrary to the holy books either of the Old or of the New Testament." Hence the conclusion is evident, that any arguments alleged against the teachings of faith do not proceed logically from first principles of nature, principles of themselves known, and so do not amount to a demonstration; but are either probable reasons or sophistical; hence room is left for refuting them.

CHAPTER VIII—Of the Relation of Human Reason to the first Truth of Faith

THE things of sense, from whence human reason takes its beginning of knowledge, retain in themselves some trace of imitation of God, inasmuch as they are, and are good; yet so imperfect is this trace that it proves wholly insufficient to declare the substance of God Himself. Since every agent acts to the producing of its own likeness, effects in their several ways bear some likeness to their causes: nevertheless the effect does not always attain to the perfect likeness of the agent that produces it. In regard then to knowledge of the truth of faith, which can only be thoroughly known to those who behold the substance of God, human reason stands so conditioned as to be able to argue some true likenesses to it: which likenesses however are not sufficient for any sort of demonstrative or intuitive comprehension of the aforesaid truth. Still it is useful for the human mind to exercise itself in such reasonings, however feeble, provided there be no presumptuous hope of perfect comprehension or demonstration. With this view the authority of Hilary agrees, who says (De Trinitate, ii, 10), speaking of such truth: "In this belief start, run, persist;

and though I know that you will not reach the goal, still I shall congratulate you as I see you making progress. But intrude not into that sanctuary, and plunge not into the mystery of infinite truth; entertain no presumptuous hope of comprehending the height of intelligence, but understand that it is incomprehensible."

## CHAPTER IX—The Order and Mode of Procedure in this Work

THERE is then a twofold sort of truth in things divine for the wise man to study: one that can be attained by rational enquiry, another that transcends all the industry of reason. This truth of things divine I do not call twofold on the part of God, who is one simple Truth, but on the part of our knowledge, as our cognitive faculty has different aptitudes for the knowledge of divine things. To the declaration therefore of the first sort of truth we must proceed by demonstrative reasons that may serve to convince the adversary. But because such reasons are not forthcoming for truth of the second sort, our aim ought not to be to convince the adversary by reasons, but to refute his reasonings against the truth, which we may hope to do, since natural reason cannot be contrary to the truth of faith. The special mode of refutation to be employed against an opponent of this second sort of truth is by alleging the authority of Scripture confirmed from heaven by miracles. There are however some probable reasons available for the declaration of this truth, to the exercise and consolation of the faithful, but not to the convincing of opponents, because the mere insufficiency of such reasoning would rather confirm them in their error, they thinking that we assented to the truth of faith for reasons so weak.

According then to the manner indicated we will bend our endeavor, first, to the manifestation of that truth which faith professes and reason searches out, alleging reasons demonstrative and probable, some of which we have gathered from the books of philosophers and saints, for the establishment of the truth and the confutation of the opponent. Then, to proceed from what is more to what is less manifest in our regard, we will pass to the manifestation of that truth which transcends reason, solving the arguments of opponents, and by probable reasons and authorities, so far as God shall enable us, declaring the truth of faith.

Taking therefore the way of reason to the pursuit of truths that human reason can search out regarding God, the first consideration that meets us is of the attributes of God in Himself; secondly of the coming forth of creatures from God; thirdly of the order of creatures to God as to their last end.

CHAPTER X—Of the Opinion of those who say that the Existence of God cannot he proved, being a Self-evident Truth

THIS opinion rests on the following grounds:

1. Those truths are self-evident which are recognized at once, as soon as the terms in which they are expressed are known. Such a truth is the assertion that God exists: for by the name 'God' we understand something greater than which nothing can be thought. This notion is formed in the understanding by whoever hears and understands the name 'God,' so that God must already exist at least in the mind. Now He cannot exist in

the mind only: for what is in the mind and in reality is greater than that which is in the mind only; but nothing is greater than God, as the very meaning of the name shows: it follows that the existence of God is a self-evident truth, being evidenced by the mere meaning of the name.

2. The existence of a being is conceivable, that could not be conceived not to exist; such a being is evidently greater than another that could be conceived not to exist. Thus then something greater than God is conceivable if He could be conceived not to exist; but anything 'greater than God' is against the meaning of the name 'God.' It remains then that the existence of God is a self-evident truth.

3. Those propositions are most self-evident which are either identities, as 'Man is man,' or in which the predicates are included in the definitions of the subjects, as 'Man is an animal.' But in God of all beings this is found true, that His existence is His essence, as will be shown later (Chap. XXII); and thus there is one and the same answer to the question 'What is He?' and 'Whether He is.' Thus then, when it is said 'God is,' the predicate is either the same with the subject or at least is included in the definition of the subject; and thus the existence of God will be a self-evident truth.

4. Things naturally known are self-evident: for the knowledge of them is not attained by enquiry and study. But the existence of God is naturally known, since the desire of man tends naturally to God as to his last end, as will be shown further on (B. III, Chap. XXV).

5. That must be self-evident whereby all other things are known; but such is God; for as the light of the sun is the principle of all visual perception, so the divine light is the principle of all intellectual cognition.

CHAPTER XI—Rejection of the aforesaid Opinion, and Solution of the aforesaid Reasons

THE above opinion arises partly from custom, men being accustomed from the beginning to hear and invoke the name of God. Custom, especially that which is from the beginning, takes the place of nature; hence notions wherewith the mind is imbued from childhood are held as firmly as if they were naturally known and self-evident. Partly also it owes its origin to the neglect of a distinction between what is self-evident of itself absolutely and what is self-evident relatively to us. Absolutely indeed the existence of God is self-evident, since God's essence is His existence. But since we cannot mentally conceive God's essence, his existence is not self-evident relatively to us.

1. Nor is the existence of God necessarily self-evident as soon as the meaning of the name 'God' is known. First, because it is not evident, even to all who admit the existence of God, that God is something greater than which nothing can be conceived, since many of the ancients said that this world was God. Then granting that universal usage understands by the name 'God' something greater than which nothing can be conceived, it will not follow that there exists in rerum naturasomething greater than which nothing can be conceived. For 'thing' and "notion implied in the name of the thing" must answer to one another. From the conception in the mind of what is declared by this name 'God' it does not follow that God exists otherwise than in the mind. Hence there will be no necessity either of that something, greater than which nothing can be conceived, existing otherwise than in the mind; and from this it does not follow that there is

anything in rerum natura greater than which nothing can be conceived. And so the supposition of the nonexistence of God goes untouched. For the possibility of our thought outrunning the greatness of any given object, whether of the actual or of the ideal order, has nothing in it to vex the soul of anyone except of him alone who already grants the existence in rerum natura of something than which nothing can be conceived greater.

2. Nor is it necessary for something greater than God to be conceivable, if His non-existence is conceivable. For the possibility of conceiving Him not to exist does not arise from the imperfection or uncertainty of His Being, since His Being is of itself most manifest, but from the infirmity of our understanding, which cannot discern Him as He is of Himself, but only by the effects which He produces; and so it is brought by reasoning to the knowledge of Him.

3. As it is self-evident to us that the whole is greater than its part, so the existence of God is most self-evident to them that see the divine essence, inasmuch as His essence is His existence. But because we cannot see His essence, we are brought to the knowledge of His existence, not by what He is in Himself but by the effects which He works.

4. Man knows God naturally as he desires Him naturally. Now man desires Him naturally inasmuch as he naturally desires happiness, which is a certain likeness to the divine goodness. Thus it is not necessary that God, considered in Himself, should be naturally known to man, but a certain likeness of God. Hence man must be led to a knowledge of God through the likenesses of Him that are found in the effects which He works.

5. God is that wherein all things are known, not as

though other things could not be known without His being known first, as happens in the case of self-evident principles, but because through His influence all knowledge is caused in us.

CHAPTER XII—Of the Opinion of those who say that the Existence of God is a Tenet of Faith alone and cannot be demonstrated

THE falseness of this opinion is shown to us as well by the art of demonstration, which teaches us to argue causes from effects, as also by the order of the sciences, for if there be no knowable substance above sensible substances, there will be no science above physical science; as also by the efforts of philosophers, directed to the proof of the existence of God; as also by apostolic truth asserting: The invisible things of God are clearly seen, being understood by the things that are made(Rom. i, 20).23

The axiom that in God essence and existence are the same is to be understood of the existence whereby God subsists in Himself, the manner of which is unknown to us, as also is His essence; not of the existence which signifies an affirmative judgement of the understanding. For in the form of such affirmative judgement the fact that there is a God falls under demonstration; as our mind is led by demonstrative reasons to form such a proposition declaratory of the existence of God. In the reasonings whereby the existence of God is demonstrated it is not necessary to assume for a premise the essence or quiddity of God: but instead of the quiddity the effect is taken for a premise, as is done in demonstrations a posterior from effect to cause. All the names of God are imposed either on the principle of denying of God Himself certain effects of His power, or from some habitude of God towards those effects. Although God transcends sense and the objects of sense, nevertheless sensible effects are the basis of our demonstration of the existence of God. Thus the origin of our own knowledge is in sense, even of things that transcend sense.

CHAPTER XIII—Reasons in Proof of the Existence of God

WE will put first the reasons by which Aristotle proceeds to prove the existence of God from the consideration of motion as follows.

Everything that is in motion is put and kept in motion by some other thing. It is evident to sense that there are beings in motion. A thing is in motion because something else puts and keeps it in motion. That mover therefore either is itself in motion or not. If it is not in motion, our point is gained which we proposed to prove, namely, that we must posit something which moves other things without being itself in motion, and this we call God. But if the mover is itself in motion, then it is moved by some other mover. Either then we have to go on to infinity, or we must come to some mover which is motionless; but it is impossible to go on to infinity, therefore we must posit some motionless prime mover. In this argument there are two propositions to be proved: that everything which is in motion is put and kept in motion by something else; and that in the series of movers and things moved it is impossible to go on to infinity.

The Philosopher also goes about in another way to show that it is impossible to proceed to infinity in the series of efficient causes, but we must come to one first cause, and this we call God. The way is more or less as follows. In every series of efficient causes, the first term is cause of the intermediate, and the intermediate is cause of the last. But if in efficient causes there is a process to infinity, none of the causes will be the first: therefore all the others will be taken away which are intermediate. But that is manifestly not the case; therefore we must posit the existence of some first efficient cause, which is God.

Another argument is brought by St John Damascene (De Fid. Orthod.I, 3), thus: It is impossible for things contrary and discordant to fall into one harmonious order always or for the most part, except under some one guidance, assigning to each and all a tendency to a fixed end. But in the world we see things of different natures falling into harmonious order, not rarely and fortuitously, but always or for the most part. Therefore there must be some Power by whose providence the world is governed; and that we call God.

CHAPTER XIV—That in order to a Knowledge of God we must use the Method of Negative Differentiation

AFTER showing that there is a First Being, whom we call God, we must enquire into the conditions of His existence. We must use the method of negative differentiation, particularly in the consideration of the divine substance. For the divine substance, by its immensity, transcends every form that our intellect can realize; and thus we cannot apprehend it by knowing what it is, but we have some sort of knowledge of it by knowing what it is not. The more we can negatively differentiate it, or the more attributes we can strike off from it in our mind, the more we approach to a knowledge of it: for we know each thing more perfectly, the fuller view we have of its differences as compared with other things; for each thing has in itself a proper being, distinct from all others. Hence in dealing with things that we can define, we first place them in some genus, by which we know in general what the thing is; and afterwards we add the differentias whereby the thing is distinguished from other things; and thus is achieved a complete knowledge of the substance of the thing. But because in the study of the divine substance we cannot fix upon anything for a genus (Chap. XXV), nor can we mark that substance off from other things by affirmative differentias, we must determine it by negative differentias. In affirmative differentias one limits the extension of another, and brings us nearer to a complete designation of the thing under enquiry, inasmuch as it makes that thing differ from more and more things. And the same holds good also of negative differentias. For example, we may say that God is not an accident, in that He is distinguished from all accidents; then if we add that He is not a body, we shall further distinguish Him from some substances; and so in order by such negations He will be further distinguished from everything besides Himself; and then there will be a proper notion of His substance, when He shall be known as distinct from all. Still it will not be a perfect knowledge, because He will not be known for what He is in Himself.

To proceed therefore in the knowledge of God by way of negative differentiation, let us take as a principle what has been shown in a previous chapter, that God is altogether immovable, which is confirmed also by the authority of Holy Scripture. For it is said: I am the Lord and change not (Mal. iii, 6); With whom there is no change (James i, 17); God is not as man, that he should change (Num. xxiii, 19).

## CHAPTER XV—That God is Eternal

THE beginning of anything and its ceasing to be is brought about by motion or change. But it has been shown that God is altogether unchangeable: He is therefore eternal, without beginning or end.

2. Those things alone are measured by time which are in motion, inasmuch as time is an enumeration of motion. But God is altogether without motion, and therefore is not measured by time. Therefore in Him it is impossible to fix any before or after: He has no being after not being, nor can He have any not being after being, nor can any succession be found in His being, because all this is unintelligible without time. He is therefore without beginning and without end, having all His being at once, wherein consists the essence of eternity.

3. If at some time God was not, and afterwards was, He was brought forth by some cause from not being to being. But not by Himself, because what is not cannot do anything. But if by another, that other is prior to Him. But it has been shown that God is the First Cause; therefore He did not begin to be: hence neither will He cease to be; because what always has been has the force of being always.

4. We see in the world some things which are possible to be and not to be. But everything that is possible to be has a cause: for seeing that of itself it is

open to two alternatives, being and not being; if being is to be assigned to it, that must be from some cause. But we cannot proceed to infinity in a series of causes: therefore we must posit something that necessarily is. Now everything necessary either has the cause of its necessity from elsewhere, or not from elsewhere, but is of itself necessary. But we cannot proceed to infinity in the enumeration of things necessary that have the cause of their necessity from elsewhere: therefore we must come to some first thing necessary, that is of itself necessary; and that is God. Therefore God is eternal, since everything that is of itself necessary is eternal.

Hence the Psalmist: But thou, O Lord, abides forever: thou art the self-same, and thy years shall not fail (Ps. ci, 13-28).

CHAPTER XVI—That in God there is no Passive Potentiality

EVERYTHING that has in its substance an admixture of potentiality, to the extent that it has potentiality is liable not to be: because what can be, can also not be. But God in Himself cannot not be, seeing that He is everlasting; therefore there is in God no potentiality.
2. Although in order of time that which is sometimes in potentiality, sometimes in actuality, is in potentiality before it is in actuality, yet, absolutely speaking, actuality is prior to potentiality, because potentiality does not bring itself into actuality, but is brought into actuality by something which is already in actuality. Everything therefore that is any way in potentiality has something else prior to it. But God is the First Being and the First Cause, and therefore has not in

Himself any admixture of potentiality.

4. Everything acts inasmuch as it is in actuality. Whatever then is not all actuality, does not act by its whole self, but by something of itself. But what does not act by its whole self, is not a prime agent; for it acts by participation in something else, not by its own essence. The prime agent then, which is God, has no admixture of potentiality, but is pure actuality.

6. We see that there is that in the world which passes from potentiality to actuality. But it does not educe itself from potentiality to actuality, because what is in potentiality is not as yet, and therefore cannot act. Therefore there must be some other prior thing, whereby this thing may be brought out from potentiality to actuality. And again, if this further thing is going out from potentiality to actuality, there must be posited before it yet some other thing, whereby it may be reduced to actuality. But this process cannot go on forever: therefore we must come to something that is only in actuality, and nowise in potentiality; and that we call God.

CHAPTER XVIII—That in God there is no Composition

IN every compound there must be actuality and potentiality. For a plurality of things cannot become one thing, unless there be actuality and potentiality. For things that are not one absolutely, are not actually united except by being in a manner tied up together or driven together: in which case the parts thus got together are in potentiality in respect of union; for they combine actually, after having been potentially combinable. But in God there is no potentiality: therefore there is not in Him any

composition.
3. Every compound is potentially soluble in respect of its being compound, although in some cases there may be some other fact that stands in the way of dissolution. But what is soluble is in potentiality not to be, which cannot be said of God, seeing that He is of Himself a necessary Being.

CHAPTER XX—That God is Incorporeal

EVERY corporeal thing, being extended, is compound and has parts. But God is not compound: therefore He is not anything corporeal.
5. According to the order of objects is the order and distinction of powers: therefore above all sensible objects there is some intelligible object, existing in the nature of things. But every corporeal thing existing in nature is sensible: therefore there is determinable above all corporeal things something nobler than they. If therefore God is corporeal, He is not the first and greatest Being.

With this demonstrated truth divine authority also agrees. For it is said: *God is a spirit* (John iv, 24): *To the King of ages, immortal, invisible, only God* (1 Tim. i, 17): *The invisible things of God are understood and discerned by the things that are made* (Rom. i, 29). For the things that are discerned, not by sight but by understanding, are incorporeal. Hereby is destroyed the error of the first natural philosophers, who posited none but material causes. The Gentiles also are refuted, who set up the elements of the world, and the powers therein existing, for gods; also the follies of the Anthropomorphite heretics, who figured God under bodily lineaments; also of the

Manicheans, who thought God was an infinite substance of light diffused through infinite space. The occasion of all these errors was that, in thinking of divine things, men came under the influence of the imagination, which can be cognizant only of bodily likeness. And therefore we must transcend imagination in the study of things incorporeal.

CHAPTER XXI—That God is His own Essence

IN everything that is not its own essence, quiddity, or nature, there must be some composition. For since in everything its own essence is contained, — if in anything there were contained nothing but its essence, the whole of that thing would be its essence, and so itself would be its own essence. If then anything is not its own essence, there must be something in that thing besides its essence, and so there must be in it composition. Hence also the essence in compound things is spoken of as a part, as humanity in man. But it has been shown that in God there is no composition. God therefore is His own essence.

2. That alone is reckoned to be beyond the essence of a thing, which does not enter into its definition: for the definition declares what the thing essentially is. But the accidents of a thing are the only points about it which fall not within the definition: therefore the accidents are the only points about a thing besides its essence. But in God there are no accidents, as will be shown (Chap. XXIII): therefore there is nothing in Him besides His essence.

3. The forms that are not predicable of subsistent things, whether in the universal or in the singular, are forms that do not of themselves subsist singly, individualized in themselves. It is not said that Socrates or

man or animal is whiteness; because whiteness is not anything subsisting singly in itself, but is individualized by the substance in which it exists. Also the essences or quiddities of genera or species are individualized according to the definite matter of this or that individual, although the generic or specific quiddity includes form and matter in general: hence it is not said that Socrates or man is humanity. But the Divine Essence is something existing singly by itself, and individualized in itself, as will be shown (Chap. XLII). The Divine Essence therefore is predicated of God in such a way that it can be said: 'God is His own essence.'

CHAPTER XXII—That in God Existence and Essence is the same

IT has been shown above (Chap. XV, n. 4) that there is an Existence which of itself necessarily is; and that is God. If this existence, which necessarily is, is contained in some essence not identical with it, then either it is dissonant and at variance with that essence, as subsistent existence is at variance with the essence of whiteness; or it is consonant with and akin to that essence, as existence in something other than itself is consonant with whiteness. In the former case, the existence which of itself necessarily is will not attach to that essence, any more than subsistent existence will attach to whiteness. In the latter case, either such existence must depend on the essence, or both existence and essence depend on another cause, or the essence must depend on the existence. The former two suppositions are against the idea of a being which of itself necessarily is; because, if it depends on another thing, it no longer is necessarily. From the third supposition it follows that that essence is accidental and adventitious to the thing which of itself necessarily is; because all that follows upon the being of a thing is accidental to it; and thus the supposed essence will not be the essence at all. God therefore has no essence that is not His existence.

2. Everything is by its own existence. Whatever then is not its own existence does not of itself necessarily exist. But God does of Himself necessarily exist: therefore God is His own existence.

4. 'Existence' denotes a certain actuality: for a thing is not said to 'be' for what it is potentially, but for what it is actually. But everything to which there attaches an actuality, existing as something different from it, stands to the same as potentiality to actuality. If then the divine essence is something else than its own existence, it follows that essence and existence in God stand to one another as potentiality and actuality. But it has been shown that in God there is nothing of potentiality (Chap. XVI), but that He is pure actuality. Therefore God's essence is not anything else but His existence.

5. Everything that cannot be except by the concurrence of several things is compound. But nothing in which essence is one thing, and existence another, can be except by the concurrence of several things, to wit, essence and existence. Therefore everything in which essence is one thing, and existence another, is compound. But God is not compound, as has been shown (Chap. XVIII). Therefore the very existence of God is His essence.

This sublime truth was taught by the Lord to Moses (Exod. iii, 13, 14) If they say to me, What is his name? what shall I say to them? Thus shalt thou say to the children of Israel: He who is hath sent me to you: showing this to be His proper name, He who is. But every name is given to show the nature or essence of something. Hence it remains that the very existence or being of God is His essence or nature.

CHAPTER XXIII—That in God there is no Accident

EVERYTHING that is in a thing accidentally has a cause for its being therein, seeing that it is beside the essence of the thing wherein it is. If then there is anything in God accidentally, this must be by some cause. Either therefore the cause of the accident is the Divinity itself, or something else. If something else, that something must act upon the divine substance: for nothing induces any form, whether substantial or accidental, in any recipient, except by acting in some way upon it, because acting is nothing else than making something actually be, which is by a form. Thus God will be acted upon and moved by some agent, which is against the conclusions of Chapter XIII. But if the divine substance itself is the cause of the accident supposed to be in it, then, — inasmuch as it cannot possibly be the cause of it in so far as it is the recipient of it, because at that rate the same thing in the same respect would actualize itself, — then this accident, supposed to be in God, needs must be received by Him in one respect and caused by Him in another, even as things corporeal receive their proper accidents by the virtue of their matter, and cause them by their form. Thus then God will be compound, the contrary of which has been above proved. &gt;

4. In whatever thing anything is accidentally, that

thing is in some way changeable in its nature: for accident as such may be and may not be in the thing in which it is. If then God has anything attaching to Him accidentally, it follows that He is changeable, the contrary of which has above been proved (Chap. XIII, XV).
5. A thing into which an accident enters, is not all and everything that is contained in itself: because accident is not of the essence of the subject. But God is whatever He has in Himself. Therefore in God there is no accident. — The premises are proved thus. Everything is found more excellently in cause than in effect. But God is cause of all: therefore whatever is in Him is found there in the most excellent way possible. But what most perfectly attaches to a thing is the very thing itself. This unity of identity is more perfect than the substantial union of one element with another, e.g., of form with matter; and that union again is more perfect than the union that comes of one thing being accidentally in another. It remains therefore that God is whatever He has.

Hence Augustine (De Trinitate, v, c. 4, n. 5): "There is nothing accidental in God, because there is nothing changeable or perishable." The showing forth of this truth is the confutation of sundry Saracen jurists, who suppose certain "ideas" superadded to the Divine Essence.

CHAPTER XXIV—That the Existence of God cannot he characterized by the addition of any Substantial Differentia

IT is impossible for anything actually to be, unless all things exist whereby its substantial being is characterized. An animal cannot actually be without being either a rational or an irrational animal. Hence the

Platonists, in positing Ideas, did not posit self-existent Ideas of genera, seeing that genera are characterized and brought to specific being by addition of essential differentias; but they posited self-existent Ideas of species alone, seeing that for the (further) characterizing of species (in the individuals belonging to it) there is no need of essential differentias. If then the existence of God is characterized and receives an essential characteristic by the addition of something else, that existence will not of itself actually be except by having that other thing superadded to it. But the existence of God is His own very substance, as has been shown. It would follow that the substance of God could not actually be except by something supervening upon it; and thence the further conclusion would ensue that the substance of God is not of itself necessarily existent, the contrary of which has been shown above (Chap. XV, n. 4)

2. Everything that needs something superadded to enable it to be, is in potentiality in respect of that addition. Now the divine substance is not in any way in potentiality, as has been shown (Chap. XVI), but God's own substance is God's own being. Therefore His existence cannot be characterized by any superadded substantial characteristic.

CHAPTER XXV—That God is not in any Genus

EVERYTHING that is in any genus has something in it whereby the nature of the genus is characterized and reduced to species: for there is nothing in the genus that is not in some species of it. But this is impossible in God, as has been shown in the previous chapter.

2. If God is in any genus, He is either in the genus of accident or the genus of substance. He is not in the genus of accident, for an accident cannot be the first being and the first cause. Again, He cannot be in the genus of substance: for the substance that is a genus is not mere existence: otherwise every substance would be its own existence, since the idea of the genus is maintained in all that is contained under the genus: at that rate no substance would be caused by another, which is impossible (Chap. XIII, XV). But God is mere existence: therefore He is not in any genus.

3. Whatever is in a genus differs in point of existence from other things that are in the same genus: otherwise genus would not be predicated of several things. But all things that are in the same genus must agree in the quiddity, or essence, of the genus: because of them all genus is predicated so as to answer the question what (quid) each thing is. Therefore the existence of each thing that exists in a genus is something over and above the quiddity of the genus. But that is impossible in God.

4. Everything is placed in a genus by reason of its quiddity. But the quiddity of God is His own mere (full) existence. Now a thing is not ranked in a genus on the score of mere (bare) existence: otherwise 'being,' in the sense of mere (bare) existence, would be a genus. But that 'being' cannot be a genus is proved in this way. If 'being' were a genus, some differentia would have to be found to reduce it to species. But no differentia participates in its genus: I mean, genus is never comprehended in the idea of the differentia: because at that rate genus would be put twice over in the definition of the species. Differentia then must be something over and above what is understood in the idea of genus. Now nothing can be over and above

what is understood by the idea of 'being'; since 'being' enters into the conceivability of all things whereof it is predicated, and thus can be limited by no differentia. Hence it is also apparent that God cannot be defined, because every definition is by genus and differentias. It is apparent also that there can be no demonstration of God except through some effect of His production: because the principle of demonstration is a definition of the thing defined.

CHAPTER XXVI—That God is not the formal or abstract being of all things

THINGS are not distinguished from one another in so far as they all have being, because in this they all agree. If therefore things do differ from one another, either 'being' itself must be specified by certain added differentias, so that different things have a different specific being; or things must differ in this that 'being' itself attaches to specifically different natures. The first alternative is impossible, because no addition can be made to 'being,' in the way that differentia is added to genus, as has been said (Chap. XXV, n. 4). It remains therefore that things differ in that they have different natures, to which 'being' accrues differently. But the divine being is not something accessory to any nature, but is the very nature or essence of God (Chap. XXII). If therefore the divine being were the formal and abstract being of all things, all things would have to be absolutely one.

4. What is common to many is not anything over and above the many except in thought alone. For example, 'animal' is not anything over and above

## St. Thomas Aquinas

Socrates and Plato and other animals, except in the mind that apprehends the form of 'animal' despoiled of all individualizing and specifying marks: for what is really animal is man: otherwise it would follow that in Plato there were several animals, to wit, animal in general, and man in general, and Plato himself. Much less then is bare being in general anything over and above all existing things, except in the mind alone. If then God be being in general, God will be nothing more than a logical entity, something that exists in the mind alone.

This error is set aside by the teaching of Holy Scripture, which confesses God lofty and high (Isa. vi, 1), and that He is above all (Rom. ix, 5). For if He is the being of all, then He is something of all, not above all. The supporters of this error are also cast out by the same sentence which casts out idolaters, who gave the incommunicable name of God to stocks and stones (Wisd. xiv, 8, 21). For if God were the being of all, it would not be more truly said, 'A stone is a being,' than 'A stone is God.'

What has led men into this error is a piece of faulty reasoning. For, seeing that what is common to many is specialized and individualized by addition, they reckoned that the divine being, to which no addition is made, was not any individual being, but was the general being of all things: failing to observe that what is common or universal cannot really exist without addition, but merely is viewed by the mind without addition. 'Animal' cannot be without 'rational' or 'irrational' as a differentia, although it may be thought of without these differentias. Moreover, though the universal be thought of without addition, yet not without susceptibility of addition. 'Animal' would not be a genus if no differentia could be added to it; and so of other generic names. But the divine being is without addition, not only in thought, but also in rerum natura; and not only without addition, but without even susceptibility of addition. Hence from this very fact, that He neither receives nor can receive addition, we may rather conclude that God is not being in general, but individual being: for by this very fact His being is distinguished from all other beings, that nothing can be added to it. (Chap. XXIV).

## CHAPTER XXVIII—That God is Universal Perfection

AS all perfection and nobility is in a thing inasmuch as the thing is, so every defect is in a thing inasmuch as the thing in some manner is not. As then God has being in its totality, so not-being is totally removed from Him, because the measure in which a thing has being is the measure of its removal from not-being. Therefore all defect is absent from God: He is therefore universal perfection.

2. Everything imperfect must proceed from something perfect: therefore the First Being must be most perfect.

3. Everything is perfect inasmuch as it is in actuality; imperfect, inasmuch as it is in potentiality, with privation of actuality. That then which is nowise in potentiality, but is pure actuality, must be most perfect; and such is God.

4. Nothing acts except inasmuch as it is in actuality: action therefore follows the measure of actuality in the agent. It is impossible therefore for any effect that is brought into being by action to be of a nobler actuality

than is the actuality of the agent. It is possible though for the actuality of the effect to be less perfect than the actuality of the acting cause, inasmuch as action may be weakened on the part of the object to which it is terminated, or upon which it is spent. Now in the category of efficient causation everything is reducible ultimately to one cause, which is God, of whom are all things. Everything therefore that actually is in any other thing must be found in God much more eminently than in the thing itself; God then is most perfect. Hence the answer given to Moses by the Lord, when he sought to see the divine face or glory: I will show thee all good (Exod. xxxiii, 19).

CHAPTER XXIX—How Likeness to God may be found in Creatures

EFFECTS disproportionate to their causes do not agree with them in name and essence. And yet some likeness must be found between such effects and their causes: for it is of the nature of an agent to do something like itself. Thus also God gives to creatures all their perfections; and thereby He has with all creatures a likeness, and an unlikeness at the same time. For this point of likeness, however, it is more proper to say that the creature is like God than that God is like the creature. For that is said to be like a thing, which possesses its quality or form. Since then that which is found to perfection in God is found in other beings by some manner of imperfect participation, the said point of likeness belongs to God absolutely, but not so to the creature. And thus the creature has what belongs to God, and is rightly said to be like to God: but it cannot be said that God has what belongs to the creature, nor is it fitting to say that God is like the creature; as we do not say that a man is like his picture, and yet his picture is rightly pronounced to be like him.

## CHAPTER XXX—What Names can be predicated of God

WE may further consider what may be said or not said of God, or what may be said of Him only, what again may be said of God and at the same time also of other beings. Inasmuch as every perfection of the creature may be found in God, although in another and a more excellent way, it follows that whatever names absolutely denote perfection without defect, are predicated of God and of other beings, as for instance, 'goodness,' 'wisdom,' 'being,' and the like. But whatever names denote such perfection with the addition of a mode proper to creatures, cannot be predicated of God except by way of similitude and metaphor, whereby the attributes of one thing are wont to be adapted to another, as when a man is called a 'block' for the denseness of his understanding. Of this sort are all names imposed to denote the species of a created thing, as 'man,' and 'stone': for to every species is due its own proper mode of perfection and being. In like manner also whatever names denote properties that are caused in things by their proper specific principles, cannot be predicated of God otherwise than metaphorically. But the names that express such perfections with that mode of supereminent excellence in which they appertain to God, are predicated of God alone, as for instance, 'Sovereign Good,' 'First Being,' and the like. I say that some of the aforesaid names imply perfection without defect, if we consider that which the name was imposed to signify. But if we consider the mode of signification, every name is attended with defect: for by a name we express things as we conceive them in our understanding: but our understanding, taking its beginning of knowledge from sensible objects, does not transcend that mode which it finds in such sensible objects. In them the form is one thing, and that which has the form another. The form, to be sure, is simple, but imperfect, as not subsisting by itself: while that which has the form subsists, but is not simple — nay, is concrete and composite. Hence whatever our understanding marks as subsisting, it marks in the concrete: what it marks as simple, it marks, not as something that is, but as that whereby something is. And thus in every name that we utter, if we consider the mode of signification, there is found an imperfection that does not attach to God, although the thing signified may attach to God in some eminent way, as appears in the name 'goodness' and 'good.' 'Goodness' denotes something as not subsisting by itself: 'good,' something as concrete and composite. In this respect, then, no name befits God suitably except in respect of that which the name is imposed to signify. Such names therefore may be both affirmed and denied of God, affirmed on account of the meaning of the name, denied on account of the mode of signification. But the mode of supereminence, whereby the said perfections are found in God, cannot be signified by the names imposed by us, except either by negation, as when we call God 'eternal' or 'infinite,' or by reference or comparison of Him to other things, as when He is called the 'First Cause' or the 'Sovereign Good.' For we cannot take in (capere) of God what He is, but what He is not, and how other beings stand related to Him.

## CHAPTER XXXI—That the Plurality of divine Names is not inconsistent with the Simplicity of the Divine Being predicated of God and of other Beings

THE perfections proper to other things in respect of their several forms must be attributed to God in respect of His productivity alone, which productivity is no other than His essence. Thus then God is called 'wise,' not only in respect of His producing wisdom, but because, in so far as we are wise, we imitate in some measure His productivity, which makes us wise. But He is not called 'stone,' though He has made stones, because in the name of 'stone' is understood a determinate mode of being wherein a stone is distinguished from God. Still a stone is an imitation of God its cause, in being, in goodness, and other such respects. Something of the sort may be found in the cognitive and active powers of man. The intellect by its one power knows all that the sentient part knows by several powers, and. much more besides. Also, the higher the intellect, the more it can know by one effort, to which knowledge an inferior intellect does not attain without many efforts. Again, the royal power extends to all those particulars to which the divers powers under it are directed. Thus also God by His one simple being possesses all manner of perfection, all that other beings compass by divers faculties — yea, much more. Hereby the need is clear of many names predicated of God: for as we cannot know Him naturally otherwise than by arriving at Him from the effects which He produces, the names whereby we denote His perfections must be several and diverse, answering to the diverse perfections that are found in things. But if we could understand His essence as it is in itself, and adapt to it a name proper to it, we should express it by one name only, as is promised to those who shall behold Him in essence: *In that day there shall be one Lord, and his name shall be one*(Zach. xiv, 9).

## CHAPTER XXXII—That nothing is predicated of God and other beings synonymously

AN effect that does not receive a form specifically like the form whereby the agent acts, is incapable of receiving in synonymous predication the name taken from that form. But, of the things whereof God is cause, the forms do not attain to the species of the divine efficacy, since they receive piecemeal and in particular what is found in God simply and universally.

3. Everything that is predicated of several things synonymously, is either genus species, differentia, accidens, or proprium. But nothing is predicated of God as genus, as has been shown (Chap. XXV); and in like manner neither as differentia; nor again as species, which is made up of genus and differentia; nor can any accident attach to Him, as has been shown (Chap. XXIII); and thus nothing is predicated of God either as accident or as proprium, for propriumis of the class of accidents. The result is that nothing is predicated synonymously of God and other beings.

6. Whatever is predicated of things so as to imply that one thing precedes and the other is consequent and dependent on the former, is certainly not predicated synonymously. Now nothing is predicated of God and of other beings as though they stood in the same rank, but it is implied that one precedes, and the other is consequent

and dependent. Of God all predicates are predicated essentially. He is called 'being' to denote that He is essence itself; and 'good,' to denote that He is goodness itself. But of other beings predications are made to denote participation. Thus Socrates is called 'a man,' not that he is humanity itself, but one having humanity. It is impossible therefore for any predicate to be applied synonymously and in the same sense to God and other beings.

CHAPTER XXXIII—That it is not at all true that the application of common Predicates to God and to Creatures involves nothing beyond a mere Identity of Name

WHERE there is a mere accidental identity of name, there is no order or respect implied of one thing to another, but quite by accident one name is applied to several different things. But this is not the case with the names applied to God and to creatures: for in such a community of names we have regard to the order of cause and effect (Chap. XXIX, XXXII).

2. Moreover, there is some manner of likeness of creatures to God (Chap. XXIX).

3. When there is no more than a mere identity of name between several things, we cannot be led from one of them to the knowledge of another; but from the attributes found in creatures we are led to a knowledge of the attributes of God (Chap. XXX, XXXI).

5. There is no use predicating any name of anything unless by the name we come to understand something about the thing. But if names are predicated of God and creatures by a mere coincidence of sound, we

understand by those names nothing whatever about God, seeing that the significations of those names are known to us only inasmuch as they apply to creatures: there would at that rate be no use in saying or proving of God that God is a good being, or anything else of the sort.

If it is said that by such names we only know of God what He is not — in that, e.g., He is called 'living' as not being of the genus of inanimate things — at least it must be allowed that the predicate 'living,' applied to God and to creatures, agrees in the negation of the inanimate, and thus will be something more than a bare coincidence of name.

CHAPTER XXXIV—That the things that are said God and Creatures are said analogously

THUS then from the foregoing arguments the conclusion remains that things said alike of God and of other beings are not said either in quite the same sense, or in a totally different sense, but in an analogous sense, that is, in point of order or regard to someone object. And this happens in two ways: in one way inasmuch as many things have regard to one particular, as in regard to the one point of health an animal is called 'healthy' as being the subject of health medicine is called 'healthful' as being productive of health; food is 'healthy,' being preservative of health; urine, as being a sign of health: in another way, inasmuch as we consider the order or regard of two things, not to any third thing, but to one of the two, as 'being' is predicated of substance and accident inasmuch as accident is referred to substance, not that substance and accident are referred to any third thing. Such names then as are predicated of God and of other beings are not predicated analogously in the former way of analogy — for then we should have to posit something before God — but in the latter way. In this matter of analogous predication we find sometimes the same order in point of name and in point of thing named, sometimes not the same. The order of naming follows the order of knowing, because the name is a sign of an intelligible concept. When then that which is prior in point of fact happens to be also prior in point of knowledge, there is one and the same priority alike in point of the concept answering to the name and of the nature of the thing named. Thus substance is prior to accident by nature, inasmuch as substance is the cause of accident; and prior also in knowledge, inasmuch as substance is put in the definition of accident; and therefore 'being' is predicated of substance before it is predicated of accident, alike in point of the nature of the thing and in point of the concept attaching to the name. But when what is prior in nature is posterior in knowledge, in such cases of analogy there is not the same order alike in point of the thing named and in point of the concept attaching to the name. Thus the power of healing, that is in healing remedies, is prior by nature to the health that is in the animal, as the cause is prior to the effect: but because this power is known from its effect, it is also named from its effect: hence, though 'healthful' or 'health- producing,' is prior in order of fast, yet the application of the predicate 'healthy' to the animal is prior in point of the concept attaching to the name. Thus then, because we arrive at the knowledge of God from the knowledge of other realities, the thing signified by the names that we apply in common to God and to those other realities — the thing signified, I say, is by priority in God, in the mode proper to God: but the concept attaching to the name is posterior in its application to Him: hence He is said to be named from the effects which He causes.

CHAPTER XXXV—That the several Names predicated of God are not synonymous

THOUGH the names predicated of God signify the same thing, still they are not synonymous, because they do not signify the same point of view. For just as divers realities are by divers forms assimilated to the one simple reality, which is God, so our understanding by divers concepts is in some sort assimilated to Him, inasmuch as, by several different points of view, taken from the perfections of creatures, it is brought to the knowledge of Him. And therefore our understanding is not at fault in forming many concepts of one thing; because that simple divine being is such that things can be assimilated to it in many divers forms. According to these divers conceptions the understanding invents divers names, an assigns them to God — names which, though they denote one and the same thing, yet clearly are not synonymous, since they are not assigned from the same point of view. The same meaning does not attach to the name in all these cases, seeing that the name signifies the concept of the understanding before it signifies the thing understood.

CHAPTER XXXVI—That the Propositions which our Understanding forms of God are not void of meaning

FOR all the absolute simplicity of God, not in vain does our understanding form propositions concerning

Him, putting together and putting asunder. For though our understanding arrives by way of divers concepts to the knowledge of God, still it understands the absolute oneness of the object answering to all those concepts. Our mind does not attribute the manner of its understanding to the object is understood: thus it does not attribute immateriality to a stone, though it knows the stone immaterially. And therefore it asserts unity of the object by an affirmative proposition, which is a sign of identity, when it says, 'God is good': in which case any diversity that the composition shows is referable to the understanding, but unity to the thing understood. And on the same principle sometimes our mind forms a statement about God with some mark of diversity by inserting a preposition, as when it is said, 'Goodness is in God.' Herein is marked a diversity, proper to the understanding; and a unity, proper to the thing.

### CHAPTER XXXVIII—That God is His own Goodness

EVERY good thing, that is not its own goodness, is called good by participation. But what is called good by participation presupposes something else before itself, whence it has received the character of goodness. This process cannot go to infinity, as there is no processus in infinitum in a series of final causes: for the infinite is inconsistent with any end, while good bears the character of an end. We must therefore arrive at some first good thing, which is not good by participation in reference to anything else, but is good by its own essence; and that is God.

4. What is, may partake of something; but sheer

being can partake of nothing. For that which partakes, is potentiality: but being is actuality. But God is sheer being, as has been proved (Chap. XXII): He is not then good by participation, but essentially so.
5. Every simple being has its existence and what it is, in one: if the two were different, simplicity would be gone. But God is absolute simplicity, as has been shown (Chap. XVIII): therefore the very goodness that is in Him is no other than His own very self.

The same reasoning shows that no other good thing is its own goodness: wherefore it is said: None is good but God alone (Mark x, 18; Luke xviii, 19).

CHAPTER XXXIX—That in God there can be no Evil

ESSENTIAL being, and essential goodness, and all other things that bear the name of 'essential,' contain no admixture of any foreign element; although a thing that is good may contain something else besides being and goodness, for there is nothing to prevent the subject of one perfection being the subject also of another. Everything is contained within the bounds of its essential idea in such sort as to render it incapable of containing within itself any foreign element. But God is goodness, not merely good. There cannot therefore be in Him anything that is not goodness, and so evil cannot be in Him at all.

3. As God is His own being, nothing can be said of God that signifies participation. If therefore evil could be predicated of Him, the predication would not signify participation, but essence. Now evil cannot be predicated of any being so as to be the essence of any: for to an

essentially evil thing there would be wanting being, since being is good. There cannot be any extraneous admixture in evil, as such, any more than in goodness. Evil therefore cannot be predicated of God.

5. A thing is perfect in so far as it is in actuality: therefore it will be imperfect inasmuch as it is failing in actuality. Evil therefore is either a privation, or includes a privation, or is nothing. But the subject of privation is potentiality; and that cannot be in God: therefore neither can evil.

This truth also Holy Scripture confirms, saying: *God is light, and there is no darkness in Him,* (1 John i, 5) *Far from God impiety, and iniquity from the Almighty* (Job xxxiv, 10).

CHAPTER XL—*That God is the Good of all Good*

GOD in His goodness includes all goodnesses, and thus is the good of all good.

2. God is good by essence: all other beings by participation: therefore nothing can be called good except inasmuch as it bears some likeness to the divine goodness. He is therefore the good of all good.

Hence it is said of the Divine Wisdom: *There came to me all good things along with it* (Wisd. vii, 11).

From this it is further shown that God is the sovereign good (Chap. XLI.

CHAPTER XLII—*That God is One*

THERE cannot possibly be two sovereign goods. But God is the sovereign good. Therefore there is but one

## St. Thomas Aquinas

God.

2. God is all-perfect, wanting in no perfection. If then there are several gods, there must be several thus perfect beings. But that is impossible: for if to none of them is wanting any perfection, nor is there any admixture of imperfection in any, there will be nothing to distinguish them one from another.

7. If there are two beings, each necessarily existent, they must agree in point of necessary existence. Therefore they must be distinguished by some addition made to one only or to both of them; and thus either one or both must be composite. But no composite being exists necessarily of itself, as has been shown above (Chap. XVIII). Therefore there cannot be several necessary beings, nor several gods.

9. If there are two gods, this name 'God' is predicated of each either in the same sense or in different senses. If in different senses, that does not touch the present question: for there is nothing to prevent anything from being called by any name in a sense different from that in which the name is ordinarily borne, if common parlance so allows. But if the predication is in the same sense, there must be in both a common nature, logically considered. Either then this nature has one existence in both, or it has two different existences. If it has one existence, they will be not two but one being: for there is not one existence of two beings that are substantially distinct. But if the nature has a different existence in each possessor, neither of the possessors will be his own essence, or his own existence, as is proper to God (Chap. XXII): therefore neither of them is that which we understand by the name of God.

12. If there are many gods, the nature of godhead

cannot be numerically one in each. There must be therefore something to distinguish the divine nature in this and that god: but that is impossible, since the divine nature does not admit of addition or difference, whether in the way of points essential or of points accidental (Chap. XXIII, XXIV).

13. Abstract being is one only: thus whiteness, if there were any whiteness in the abstract, would be one only. But God is abstract being itself, seeing that He is His own being (Chap. XXII). Therefore there can be only one God.

This declaration of the divine unity we can also gather from Holy Writ. For it is said: Hear, O Israel, the Lord thy God is one Lord (Deut. vi, 4) And, One Lord, one faith (Eph. iv, 5).

By this truth the Gentiles are set aside in their assertion of a multitude of gods. Yet it must be allowed that many of them proclaimed the existence of one supreme God, by whom all the other beings to whom they gave the name of gods had been created. They awarded the name of godhead to all everlasting substances, chiefly on the score of their wisdom and felicity and their government of the world. And this fashion of speech is found even in Holy Scripture, where the holy angels, or even men bearing the office of judges, are called gods: There is none like thee among gods, O Lord(Ps. lxxxv, 8.); and, I have said, Ye are gods (Ps. lxxxi, 6). Hence the Manicheans seem to be in greater opposition to this truth in their maintenance of two first principles, the one not the cause of the other.

## CHAPTER XLIII—That God is Infinite

INFINITY cannot be attributed to God on the score of multitude, seeing there is but one God. Nor on the score of quantitative extension, seeing He is incorporeal. It remains to consider whether infinity belongs to Him in point of spiritual greatness. Spiritual greatness may be either in power or in goodness (or completeness) of nature. Of these two greatnesses the one follows upon the other: for by the fact of a thing being in actuality it is capable of action. According then to the completeness of its actuality is the measure of the greatness of its power. Thus it follows that spiritual beings are called great according to the measure of their completeness, as Augustine says: "In things in which greatness goes not by bulk, being greater means being better" (De Trinit. vi, 9). But in God infinity can be understood negatively only, inasmuch as there is no term or limit to His perfection. And so infinity ought to be attributed to God.

2. Every actuality inhering in another takes limitation from that wherein it is: for what is in another is therein according to the measure of the recipient. An actuality therefore that is in none, is bounded by none: thus, if whiteness were self-existent, the perfection of whiteness in it would have no bounds till it attained all the perfection of whiteness that is attainable. But God is an actuality in no way existent in another: He is not a form inherent in matter; nor does His being inhere in any form or nature; since He is His own being, His own existence (Chap. XXI). The conclusion is that He is infinite.

4. Actuality is more perfect, the less admixture it has of potentiality. Every actuality, wherewith potentiality

is blended, has bounds set to its perfection: while that which is without any blend of potentiality is without bounds to its perfection. But God is pure actuality without potentiality (Chap. XVI), and therefore infinite.

6. There cannot be conceived any mode in which any perfection can be had more perfectly than by him, who is perfect by his essence, and whose being is his own goodness. But such is God: therefore anything better or more perfect than God is inconceivable. He is therefore infinite in goodness.

7. Our intellect, in understanding anything, reaches out to infinity; a sign whereof is this, that, given any finite quantity, our intellect can think of something greater. But this direction of our intellect to the infinite would be in vain, if there were not something intelligible that is infinite. There must therefore be some infinite intelligible reality, which is necessarily the greatest of realities; and this we call God.

8. An effect cannot reach beyond its cause: now our understanding cannot come but of God, who is the First Cause. If then our understanding can conceive something greater than any finite being, the conclusion remains that God is not finite.

9. Every agent shows greater power in action, the further from actuality is the potentiality which it reduces to actuality, as there is need of greater power to warm water than to warm air. But that which is not at all, is infinitely distant from actuality, and is not in any way in potentiality: therefore if the world was made a fact from being previously no fact at all, the power of the Maker must be infinite.

This argument avails to prove the infinity of the divine power even to the mind of those who assume the eternity of the world. For they acknowledge God to be the cause of the substantial being of the world, although they think that substance to have been from eternity, saying that the eternal God is the cause of an ever-existing world in the same way that a foot would be the cause of an everlasting foot-print, if it had been from eternity stamped on the dust. Still, even accepting the position thus defined, it follows that the power of God is infinite. For whether He produced things in time, according to us, or from eternity, according to them, there can be nothing in the world of reality that He has not produced, seeing that He is the universal principle of being; and thus He has brought things to be, without presupposition of any matter or potentiality. Now the measure of active power must be taken according to the measure of potentiality or passivity; for the greater the pre-existing or preconceived passivity, the greater the active power required to reduce it to complete actuality. The conclusion remains that, as finite power in producing an effect is conditioned on the potentiality of matter, the power of God, not being conditioned on any potentiality, is not finite, but infinite, and so is His essence infinite.

To this truth Holy Scripture bears witness: Great is the Lord and exceedingly to he praised, and of his greatness there is no end (Ps. cxliv, 3).

CHAPTER XLIV—That God has Understanding

IN no order of causes is it found that an intelligent cause is the instrument of an unintelligent one. But all causes in the world stand to the prime mover, which is God, as instruments to the principal agent. Since then in the world there are found many intelligent causes, the prime mover cannot possibly cause unintelligently.

5. No perfection is wanting in God that is found in any kind of beings (Chap. XXVIII): nor does any manner of composition result in Him for all that (Chap. XVIII). But among the perfections of creatures the highest is the possession of understanding: for by understanding a thing is in a manner all things, having in itself the perfections of all things.

6. Everything that tends definitely to an end, either fixes its own end, or has its end fixed for it by another: otherwise it would not tend rather to this end than to that. But the operations of nature tend to definite ends: the gains of nature are not made by chance: for if they were, they would not be the rule, but the exception, for chance is of exceptional cases. Since then physical agents do not fix their own end, because they have no idea of an end, they must have an end fixed for them by another, who is the author of nature. But He could not fix an end for nature, had He not Himself understanding.

7. Everything imperfect is derived from something perfect: for perfection is naturally prior to imperfection, as actuality to potentiality. But the forms that exist in particular things are imperfect, for the very reason that they do exist in particular, and not in the universality of their idea, or the fullness of their ideal being. They must therefore be derived from some perfect forms, which are not under particular limitations. Such forms cannot be other than objects of understanding, seeing that no form is found in its universality or ideal fullness, except in the understanding. Consequently such forms must be endowed with understanding, if they are to subsist by themselves: for only by that endowment can they be operative. God therefore, who is the first actuality

existing by itself, whence all others are derived, must be endowed with understanding.

This truth also is in the confession of Catholic faith: for it is said: He is wise of heart and mighty of power (Job ix, 4): With him is strength and wisdom (Ibid. xii, 16): Thy wisdom is made wonderful to me (Ps. cxxxviii, 6): O depth of riches, of wisdom and of knowledge of God (Rom. vi, 33).

CHAPTER XLV—That in God the Understanding is His very Essence

TO understand is an act of an intelligent being, existing in that being, not passing out to anything external, as the act of warming passes out to the object warmed: for an intelligible object suffers nothing from being understood, but the intelligence that understands it is perfected thereby. But whatever is in God is the divine essence. Therefore the act of understanding in God is the divine essence.

5. Every substance is for the sake of its activity. If therefore the activity of God is anything else than the divine substance, His end will be something different from Himself; and thus God will not be His own goodness, seeing that the good of every being is its end.

From the act of understanding in God being identical with His being, it follows necessarily that the act of His understanding is absolutely eternal and invariable, exists in actuality only, and has all the other attributes that have been proved of the divine being. God then is not potentially intelligent, nor does He begin anew to understand anything, nor does He undergo any change or composition in the process of understanding.

55

CHAPTER XLVI—That God understands by nothing else than by His own Essence

UNDERSTANDING is brought actually to understand by an impression made on the understanding, just as sense comes actually to feel by an impression made on sense. The impression made on the understanding then is to the understanding as actuality to potentiality. If therefore the divine understanding came to understand by any impression made on the understanding other than the understanding itself, the understanding would be in potentiality towards that impression, which, it has been shown, cannot be (Chap. XVI, XVII).

3. Any impression on the understanding that is in the understanding over and above its essence, has an accidental being: by reason of which fact our knowledge reckons as an accident. But there can be no accident in God. Therefore there is not in His understanding any impression besides the divine essence itself.

CHAPTER XLVII—That God perfectly understands Himself

WHEN by an impression on the understanding that power is brought to bear on its object, the perfection of the intellectual act depends on two things: one is the perfect conformity of the impression with the thing understood: the other is the perfect fixing of the impression on the understanding: which perfection is the greater, the greater the power of the understanding to understand. Now the mere divine essence, which is the intelligible representation whereby the divine understanding understands, is absolutely one and the same with God Himself and with the understanding of God. God therefore knows Himself most perfectly.

6. The perfections of all creatures are found at their best in God. But of perfections found in creatures the greatest is to understand God: seeing that the intellectual nature is pre-eminent above other natures, and the perfection of intellect is the act of understanding, and the noblest object of understanding is God. God therefore understands Himself perfectly.

This also is confirmed by divine authority, for the Apostle says: *The spirit of God searches into even the deep things of God* (1 Cor. ii, 10).

CHAPTER XLVIII—*That God primarily and essentially knows Himself alone*

THE Understanding is in potentiality in regard of its object, in so far as it is a different thing from that object. If therefore the primary and essential object of divine understanding be something different from God, it will follow that God is in potentiality in respect of some other thing, which is impossible (Chap. XVI).

5. A thing understood is the perfection of him who understands it: for an understanding is perfected by actually understanding, which means being made one with the object understood. If therefore anything else than God is the first object of His understanding, something else will be His perfection, and will be nobler than He, which is impossible.

CHAPTER XLIX—That God knows other things besides Himself

WE are said to know a thing when we know its cause. But God Himself by His essence is the cause of being to others. Since therefore He knows His own essence most fully, we must suppose that He knows also other beings.
3. Whoever knows anything perfectly, knows all that can be truly said of that thing, and all its natural attributes. But a natural attribute of God is to be cause of other things. Since then He perfectly knows Himself, He knows that He is a cause: which could not be unless He knew something also of what He has caused, which is something different from Himself, for nothing is its own cause. Gathering together these two conclusions, it appears that God knows Himself as the primary and essential object of His knowledge, and other things as seen in His essence.

CHAPTER L—That God has a particular Knowledge of all things

EVERY agent that acts by understanding has a knowledge of what it does, reaching to the particular nature of the thing produced; because the knowledge of the maker determines the form of the thing made. But God is cause of things by His understanding, seeing that in Him to be and to understand are one. But everything acts inasmuch as it is in actuality. God therefore knows in particular, as distinct from other things, whatever He causes to be.
3. The collocation of things, distinct and separate,

cannot be by chance, for it is in regular order. This collocation of things, then, distinct and separate from one another, must be due to the intention of some cause. It cannot be due to the intention of any cause that acts by physical necessity, because physical nature is determined to one line of acton. Thus of no agent, that acts by physical necessity, can the intention reach to many distinct effects, inasmuch as they are distinct. The distinct arrangement and collocation of things must proceed from the intention of some knowing cause. Indeed it seems the proper function of intellect to remark the distinction of things. It belongs therefore to the First Cause, which of itself is distinct from all others, to intend the distinct and separate collocation of all the materials of the Universe.

4. Whatever God knows, He knows most perfectly: for there is in Him all perfection (Chap. XXVIII). Now what is known only in general is not known perfectly: the main points of the thing are not known, the finishing touches of its perfection, whereby its proper being is completely realized and brought out. Such mere general knowledge is rather a perfectible than a perfect knowledge of a thing. If therefore God in knowing His essence knows all things in their universality, He must also have a particular knowledge of things.

8. Whoever knows any nature, knows whether that nature be communicable: for he would not know perfectly the nature of 'animal,' who did not know that it was communicable to many. But the divine nature is communicable by likeness. God therefore knows in how many ways anything may exist like unto His essence. Hence arises the diversity of types, inasmuch as they imitate in divers ways the divine essence. God therefore has a knowledge of things according to their several

particular types. This also we are taught by the authority of canonical Scripture. God saw all things that he had made, and they were very good (Gen. i, 31). Nor is there any creature invisible in his sight, but all things are naked and open to his eyes (Heb. iv, 13).

CHAPTER LI—Some Discussion of the Question how there is in the Divine Understanding a Multitude of Objects

THIS multitude cannot be taken to mean that many objects of understanding have a distinct being in God. For these objects of understanding would be either the same with the divine essence, and at that rate multitude would be posited in the essence of God, a doctrine above rejected on many grounds (Chap. XXXI); or they would be additions made to the divine essence, and at that rate there would be in God some accident, which we have above shown to be an impossibility (Chap. XXXIII). Nor again can there be posited any separate existence of these intelligible forms, which seems to have been the position of Plato, who, by way of avoiding the above inconveniences, introduced the doctrine of Ideas. For the forms of physical things cannot exist without matter, as neither can they be understood without matter. And even supposing them so to exist, even this would not suffice to explain God understanding a multitude of objects. For, assuming the aforesaid forms to exist outside the essence of God, and that God could not understand the multitude of things without them, such understanding being requisite to the perfection of His intellect, it would follow that God's perfection in understanding depended on another being than Himself, and consequently His perfection in being, seeing that His being is His understanding: the contrary of all which has been shown (Chap. XL). Moreover, assuming what shall be proved hereafter (Bk II, Chap. XV), that whatever is beyond the essence of God is caused by God, the above forms, if they are outside of God, must necessarily be caused by Him. But He is cause of things by His understanding, as shall be shown (Bk II, Chap. XXIII, XXIV). Therefore God's understanding of these intelligible forms is a natural prerequisite for the existence of such forms. God's understanding then of the multitude of creatures is not to be explained by the existence of many intelligible abstract forms outside of God.

CHAPTER LII—Reasons to show how the Multitude of intelligible Ideal Forms has no Existence except in the Divine Understanding

IT is not to be supposed that the multitude of intelligible ideal forms is in any other understanding save the divine, say, the understanding of an angel. For in that case the divine understanding would depend, at least for some portion of its activity, upon some secondary intellect, which is impossible: for as substances are of God, so also all that is in substances: hence for the being of any of these forms in any secondary intellect there is prerequired an act of the divine intelligence, whereby God is cause.

2. It is impossible for one intellect to perform an intellectual operation by virtue of another intellect being disposed to that operation: that intellect itself must operate, which is disposed so to do. The fact then of many intelligible forms being in some secondary intellect

cannot account for the prime intellect knowing the multitude of such forms.

## CHAPTER LIII—How there is in God a Multitude of Objects of Understanding

AN external object, coming to be an object of our understanding, does not thereby exist in our understanding in its own proper nature: but the impression (species) of it must be in our understanding, and by that impression our understanding is actualized, or comes actually to understand. The understanding, actualized and 'informed' by such an impression, understands the 'thing in itself.' The act of understanding is immanent in the mind, and at the same time in relation with the thing understood, inasmuch as the aforesaid 'impression,' which is the starting-point of the intellectual activity, is a likeness of the thing understood. Thus informed by the impression (species) of the thing, the understanding in act goes on to form in itself what we may call an 'intellectual expression' (intentio) of the thing. This expression is the idea (ratio, λόγος) of the thing, and so is denoted by the definition. So it must be, for the understanding understands alike the thing absent and the thing present; in which respect imagination and understanding agree. But the understanding has this advantage over the imagination, that it understands the thing apart from the individualizing conditions without which the thing exists not in rerum natura. This could not be except for the understanding forming to itself the aforesaid 'expression.'

This 'expression' (intentio) in the understanding, being, we may say, the term of the intellectual activity, is different from the 'intellectual impression' (species intelligibilis), which actualizes the understanding and which must be considered the starting-point of intellectual activity; and yet both the one and the other, both the 'impression' (species) and the 'expression' (intentio), are likenesses of the 'thing in itself,' which is the object of the understanding. From the fact of the intellectual impression, which is the form of the intellect and the starting-point of intellectual knowledge, being a likeness of the external thing, it follows that the expression, or idea, formed by the understanding, is also like the thing: for as an agent is, so are its activities. And again, from the fact of the expression, or idea, in the understanding being like to its object, it follows that the understanding in the act of forming such an idea understands the said object.

But the divine mind understands by virtue of no impression other than its own essence (Chap. XLVI). At the same time the divine essence is the likeness of all things. It follows therefore that the concept of the divine understanding itself, which is the Divine Word, is at once a likeness of God Himself understood, and also a likeness of all things whereof the divine essence is a likeness. Thus then by one intelligible impression (species intelligibilis), which the divine essence, and by one intellectual recognition (intentio intellecta), which is the Divine Word, many several objects may be understood by God.

CHAPTER LIV—That the Divine Essence, being One, is the proper Likeness and Type of all things Intelligible

BUT again it may seem to some difficult or impossible that one and the same simple being, as the divine essence, should be the proper type (propria ratio) and likeness of different things. For as different things are distinguished by means of their proper forms, it needs must be that what is like one thing according to its proper form should be found unlike to another.

True indeed, different things may have one point of likeness in so far as they have one common feature, as man and ass, inasmuch as they are animals. If it were by mere discernment of common features that God knew things, it would follow that He had not a particular but only a general knowledge of things (contrary to Chap. L). To return then to a proper and particular knowledge, of which there is here question.

The act of knowledge is according to the mode in which the likeness of the known object is in the knowing mind: for the likeness of the known object in the knowing mind is as the form by which that mind is set to act. If therefore God has a proper and particular knowledge of many different things, He must be the proper and particular type of each. We have to enquire how that can be.

As the Philosopher says, the forms of things, and the definitions which mark such forms, are like numbers, in which the addition or subtraction of unity varies the species of the number. So in definitions: one differentia subtracted or added varies the species: thus 'sentient substance' varies in species by the addition of 'irrational' or 'rational.' But in instances of 'the many in one' the condition of the understanding is not as the condition of concrete nature. The nature of a concrete being does not admit of the severance of elements, the union of which is requisite to the existence of that being: thus animal nature will not endure if the soul be removed from the body. But the understanding can sometimes take separately elements that in actual being are united, when one of them does not enter into the concept of the other; thus in 'three' it may consider 'two' only, and in 'rational animal' the 'sentient' element alone. Hence the understanding may take what is inclusive of many elements for a proper specimen of many, by apprehending some of them without others. It may take 'ten' as a proper specimen of nine by subtraction of one unit, and absolutely as a proper specimen of all the numbers included in 'ten.' So also in 'man' it might recognize a proper type of 'irrational animal' as such, and of all the species of 'irrational animal,' unless these species involved some positive differentias. Therefore a certain philosopher, named Clement, said that in the scale of beings the nobler are types and patterns of the less noble. Now the divine essence contains in itself the noble qualities of all beings, not by way of a compound but by way of a perfect being (Chap. XXXI). Every form, as well particular as general, is a perfection in so far as it posits something; and involves imperfection only in so far as it falls short of true being. The divine understanding then can comprehend whatever is proper to each in its essence, by understanding wherein each thing imitates the divine essence, and wherein it falls short of the perfection proper to that essence. Thus, by understanding its own essence as imitable in the way of life without consciousness, it gathers the proper form of a plant, by understanding the same essence as imitable in the way of consciousness without intellect, the proper form of an animal; and so of the rest. Evidently then the divine essence, inasmuch as it is absolutely perfect, may be taken as the proper type of each entity; and hence by it God may have a particular knowledge of all. But because the proper type of one is distinct from the proper type of another — and distinction is the principle of plurality — there must be observable in the divine intellect a distinction and plurality of recognized types, in so far as the content of the divine mind is the proper type of different things. And as it is in this way that God is cognizant of the special relation of likeness that each creature bears to Him, it follows that the types (rationes) of things on the divine mind are not several or distinct, except in so far as God knows things to be in several divers ways capable of assimilation to Himself.

And from this point of view Augustine says that God has made man in one plan and horse on another; and that the plans or types of things exist severally in the divine mind (Dediv. quaest., LXXXIII, 46). And herein also is defensible in some sort the opinion of Plato, who supposes Ideas, according to which all beings in the material world are formed.

CHAPTER LV—That God understands all things at once and together

THE reason why our understanding cannot understand many things together in one act is because in the act of understanding the mind becomes one with the object understood; whence it follows that, were the mind to understand many things together in one act, it would be many things together, all of one genus, which is impossible. Intellectual impressions are all of one genus: they are of one type of being in the existence which they have in the mind, although the things of which they are impressions do not agree in one type of being: hence the contrariety of things outside the mind does not render the impressions of those things in the mind contrary to one another. And hence it is that when many things are taken together, being anyhow united, they are understood together. Thus a continuous whole is understood at once, not part by part; and a proposition is understood at once, not first the subject and then the predicate: because all the parts are known by one mental impression of the whole. Hence we gather that whatever several objects are known by one mental presentation, can be understood together: but God knows all things by that one presentation of them, which is His essence; therefore He can understand all together and at once.

2. The faculty of knowledge does not know anything actually without some attention and advertence. Hence the phantasms, stored in the sensorium, are at times not actually in the imagination, because no attention is given to them. We do not discern together a multitude of things to which we do not attend together: but things that necessarily fall under one and the same advertence and attention, are necessarily understood together. Thus whoever institutes a comparison of two things, directs his attention to both and discerns both together. But all things that are in the divine knowledge must necessarily fall under one advertence; for God is attentive to behold His essence perfectly, which is to see it to the whole reach of its virtual content, which includes all things. God

therefore, in beholding His essence, discerns at once all things that are.

6. Every mind that understands one thing after another, is sometimes potentially intelligent, sometimes actually so; for while it understands the first thing actually, it understands the second potentially. But the divine mind is never potentially intelligent, but always actually: it does not, then, understand things in succession, but all at once. Holy Scripture witnesses to this truth, saying that with God there is no change nor shadow of vicissitude (James i, 17).

CHAPTER LVI—That there is no Habitual Knowledge in God

IN whatever minds there is habitual knowledge, not all things are known together: but some things are known actually, others habitually. But in God all things are known actually (Chap. LV). 2. He who has a habit of knowledge, and is not adverting to what he knows, is in a manner in potentiality, although otherwise than as he was before he understood at all: but the divine mind is nowise in potentiality.

3. In every mind that knows anything habitually, the mind's essence is different from its intellectual activity, which is the act of attentive thought. To such a mind, in habitual knowledge, activity is lacking, though the essence of the mind itself cannot be lacking. But in God His essence is His activity (Chap. XLV).

4. A mind that knows habitually only, is not in its ultimate perfection: hence that best of goods, happiness, is not taken to be in habit but in act. If then God is habitually knowing, He will not be all-perfect (contrary to

Chap. XXVIII).
5. As shown in chapter XLVI, God has understanding by His essence, not by any intelligible forms superadded to His essence. But every mind in habitual knowledge understands by some such forms: for a habit is either a predisposition of the mind to receive mental impressions, or forms, whereby it comes actually to understand; or it is an orderly aggregation of such forms, existing in the mind, not in complete actuality, but in some manner intermediate between potentiality and actuality.
6. A habit is a quality: but in God there can be neither quality nor any other accident (Chap. XXIII): habitual knowledge therefore is not proper to God.

Because the mental state of thinking, or willing, or acting habitually only, is like the state of a sleeper, David says, by way of removing all habitual states from God: Lo, he shall not slumber or sleep who keepeth Israel (Ps. cxx, 4). And again it is said: The eyes of the Lord are far brighter than the sun (Ecclus xxiii, 28), for the sun is always in the act of shining.

CHAPTER LVII—That the Knowledge of God is not a Reasoned Knowledge

OUR thought is then reasoned, when we pass from one object of thought to another, as in making syllogisms from principles to conclusions. Reasoning or arguing does not consist in seeing how a conclusion follows from premises by inspection of both together. That is not argument, but judging of argument. Now God does not think of one thing after another in any sort of succession, but of all things at once (Chap. LV). His knowledge therefore is not reasoned or argumentative, although He knows the argument and reason of all things.

2. Every reasoner intues principles with one thought, and the conclusion with another. There would be no need to proceed to a conclusion from the consideration of premises, if the mere consideration of the premises at once laid the conclusion bare. But God knows all things by one act which is His essence (Chap. LV). His knowledge therefore is not argumentative.

3. All argumentative knowledge has something of actuality and something of potentiality, for conclusions are potentially in premises. But in the divine mind potentiality has no place.

5. Things that are known naturally are known without reasoning, as appears in the case of first principles. But in God there can be no knowledge that is not natural, nay, essential: for His knowledge is His essence.

7. Only in its highest advance does the inferior touch upon the superior. But the highest advance of our knowledge is not reasoning, but intuition (intellectus), which is the starting point of reasoning. God's knowledge then is not 'rational,' in the sense of 'argumentative,' but intuitive only.

8. Reasoning means a lack of intuition: the divine knowledge therefore is not reasoned.

If any should take it amiss that God cannot make a syllogism, let them mark that He has the knowledge how to make syllogisms as one judging of them, not as one arguing syllogistically.

To this there is witness of Holy Scripture in the text: *All things are naked and open to his eyes*(Heb. iv, 13): whereas things that we know by reasoning are not of themselves naked and open to us, but are opened out and laid bare by reason.

CHAPTER LVIII—That God does not understand by Combination and Separation of Ideas

THINGS mentally combinable and separable are naturally considered by the mind apart from one another: for there would be no need of their combination and separation, if by the mere apprehension of a thing as being it were at once understood what was in it or not in it. If therefore God understood by a mental process of combination and separation, it would follow that He did not take in all things at one glance, but each thing apart, contrary to what has been shown above (Chap. LV).

3. A mind that combines and separates, forms different judgements by different combinations. For a mental combination does not go beyond the terms of the combination. Hence, in the combination, or affirmative judgement (compositione), whereby the mind judges that man is an animal, it does not judge that a triangle is a figure. Now combination or separation is an operation of the mind. If God therefore views things by mentally combining and separating them, His mental act will not be one only but manifold; and so His essence will not be one only.

Not for this however must we say that He is ignorant of tenable propositions: for His one and simple essence is the pattern of all things manifold and compound; and so by it God knows the whole multitude and complexity as well of actual nature as of the ideal world (tam naturae quam rationis).

This is in consonance with the authority of Holy

Scripture: for it is said, For my thoughts are not your thoughts (Isa. lv, 8); and yet, The Lord knoweth the thoughts of men (Ps. xciii, 11), which certainly proceed by combination and separation of ideas.

CHAPTER LIX—That the Truth to be found in Propositions is not excluded from God

THOUGH the knowledge of the divine mind is not after the manner of combination and separation of ideas in affirmative and negative propositions, nevertheless there is not excluded from it that truth which, according to the Philosopher, obtains only in such combinations and separations. For since the truth of the intellect is an equation of the intellect and the thing, inasmuch as the intellect says that to be which is, or that not to be which is not, truth belongs to that in the intellect which the intellect says, not to the act whereby it says it; for it is not requisite to the truth of the intellect that the mere act of understanding be equated to the thing, but what the mind says and knows by understanding must be equated to the thing, so that the case of the thing shall be as the mind says it is. But God by his simple understanding, in which there is no combination and separation of ideas, knows not only the essence of things, but also the propositions that are tenable concerning them (Chap. LVII, LVIII). Thus what the divine mind says by understanding is affirmation and negation. Therefore the simplicity of the divine mind does not import the shutting out from it of truth.

CHAPTER LX—That God is Truth

TRUTH is a perfection of the understanding and of its act. But the understanding of God is His substance; and the very act of understanding, as it is the being of God, is perfect as the being of God is perfect, not by any superadded perfection, but by itself. It remains therefore that the divine substance is truth itself.

4. Though truth is properly not in things but in the mind, nevertheless a thing is sometimes called true, inasmuch as it properly attains the actuality of its proper nature. Hence Avicenna says that the truth of a thing is a property of the fixed and appointed being of each thing, inasmuch as such a thing is naturally apt to create a true impression of itself, and inasmuch as it expresses the proper idea of itself in the divine mind. But God is His own essence: therefore, whether we speak of truth of the intellect or truth of the object, God is His own truth.

This is also confirmed by the authority of our Lord saying of Himself: I am the way and the truth and the life (John xiv, 6).

## CHAPTER LXI—That God is pure Truth

THE understanding is not liable to error in its knowledge of abstract being, as neither is sense in dealing with the proper object of each sense. But all the knowledge of the divine mind is after the manner of a mind knowing abstract being (Chap. LVIII): it is impossible therefore for error or deception or falsehood to creep into the cognitive act of God.

3. The intellect does not err over first principles, but over reasoned conclusions from first principles. But the divine intellect is not reasoning or argumentative (Chap. LVII), and is therefore not liable to deception.

4. The higher any cognitive faculty is, the more universal and far-reaching is its proper object: hence what sight is cognizant of accidentally, general sensibility or imagination seizes upon as a content of its proper object. But the power of the divine mind is the acme of cognitive power: therefore all things knowable stand to it as proper and ordinary objects of knowledge, not as accidental objects. But over proper and ordinary objects of knowledge a cognitive faculty never makes a mistake.

5. An intellectual virtue is a perfection of the understanding in knowing. It never happens that the understanding utters anything false, but its utterance is always true, when prompted by any intellectual virtue; for it is the part of virtue to render an act good, and to utter truth is the good act of the understanding. But the divine mind, being the acme of perfection, is more perfect by its nature than the human mind by any habit of virtue.

6. The knowledge of the human mind is in a manner caused by things: hence it comes to be that things knowable are the measure of human knowledge: for the judgement of the mind is true, because the thing is so. But the divine mind by its knowledge is the cause of things. Hence God's knowledge must be the measure of things, as art is the measure of products of art, whereof the perfection of each varies according to its agreement with art. Thus the divine mind stands to things as things stand to the human mind. But any error that arises out of any inequality between the human mind and the thing is not in things, but in the mind. If therefore there were not an absolutely perfect correspondence of the divine mind with things, the error would be in the things, not in the divine mind. There is however no error in the things that be: because each has so much of truth as it has of being.

There is then no failure of correspondence between the divine mind and the things that be.

Hence it is said: God is truthful (Rom. iii, 4): God is not like man, that he should lie (Num. xxiii, 19): God is light, and there is no darkness in him (1 John i, 5).

CHAPTER LXII—That the Truth of God is the First and Sovereign Truth

THE standard in every genus is the most perfect instance of the genus. But the divine truth is the standard of all truth. The truth of our mind is measured by the object outside the mind: our understanding is called true, inasmuch as it is in accordance with that object. And again the truth of the object is measured by its accordance with the divine mind, which is the cause of all things (B. II, Chap. XXIV), as the truth of artificial objects is measured by the art of the artificer. Since then God is the first understanding and the first object of understanding, the truth of every understanding must be measured by His truth, as everything is measured by the first and best of its kind.

CHAPTER LXIII—The Arguments of those who wish to withdraw from God the Knowledge of Individual Things

THE first argument is drawn from the very condition of individuality. For as matter (materia signata) is the principle of individuality, it seems that individuals cannot be known by any immaterial faculty, inasmuch as all knowledge is a certain assimilation, and hence even in us those powers alone apprehend individual objects, that make use of material organs, as do the imagination and senses, but our understanding, which is immaterial, does not recognize individuals as such: much less then is the divine understanding apt to take cognizance of individuals, being, as it is, the furthest removed from matter.

2. The second argument is that individual things do not always exist. Either then they will always be known by God, or they will sometimes be known and sometimes not known. The former alternative is impossible, because there can be no knowledge of that which is not: for knowledge is only of things true, and things that are not cannot be true. The second alternative is also impossible, because the knowledge of the divine mind is absolutely invariable (Chap. XLV).

3. The third argument is from the consideration that not all individual things come of necessity, but some are by contingency: hence there can be no certain knowledge of them except when they exist. For that knowledge is certain, which is infallible: but all knowledge of contingent being is fallible while the thing is still in the future; for the opposite may happen of that which is held in cognition: for if the opposite could not happen, the thing would be a necessity: hence there can be no science in us of future contingencies, only a conjectural reckoning. On the other hand we must suppose that all God's knowledge is most certain and infallible (Chap. LXI). It is also impossible for God to begin to know anything, by reason of His immutability. From this it seems to follow that He does not know

individual contingencies.

4. The fourth argument is from this, that some individual effects have their cause in will. Now an effect, before it is produced, can be known only in its cause: for so only can it have being before it begins to have being in itself. But the motions of the will can be known with certainty by none other than the willing agent, in whose power they are. It is impossible therefore that God should have certain knowledge of such individual effects as derive their causation from a created will.

5. The fifth argument is from the infinite multitude of individual things. The infinite as such is unknown: for all that is known is measured in a manner by the comprehension of the knower, measurement being nothing else than a marking out and ascertaining of the thing measured: hence every art repudiates infinities. But individual existences are infinite, at least potentially.

6. The sixth argument is from the vileness of individual things. As the nobility of knowledge is weighed according to the nobility of the thing known, so the vileness also of the thing known seems to redound to the vileness of the knowledge. Therefore the excellent nobility of the divine mind does not permit of God knowing sundry most vile things that have individual existence.

7. The seventh argument is from the evil that is found in sundry individual things. Since the object known is in some manner in the knowing mind, and evil is impossible in God, it seems to follow that God can have no knowledge at all of evil and privation: only the mind that is in potentiality can know that, as privation can be only in potentiality.

**CHAPTER LXIV**—A list of things to be said concerning the Divine Knowledge

TO the exclusion of the above error we will show first that the divine mind does know individual things; secondly, that it knows things which actually are not; thirdly, that it knows future contingencies with infallible knowledge; fourthly, that it knows the motions of the will; fifthly, that it knows infinite things; sixthly, that it knows the vilest and least of things that be; seventhly, that it knows evils and all manner of privations or defects.

**CHAPTER LXV**—That God Knows Individual Things

GOD knows things in so far as He is the cause of them. But the substantial effects of divine causation are individual things, universals not being substantial things, but having being only in individuals.

2. Since God's cognitive act is His essence, He must know all that is in any way in His essence; and as this essence is the first and universal principle of being and the prime origin of all, it virtually contains in itself all things that in any way whatsoever have being.

5. In the gradation of faculties it is commonly found that the higher faculty extends to more terms, and yet is one; while the range of the lower faculty extends to fewer terms, and even over them it is multiplied, as we see in the case of imagination and sense, for the single power of the imagination extends to all that the five senses take cognizance of, and to more. But the cognitive faculty in God is higher than in man: whatever therefore man knows by the various faculties of understanding,

imagination and sense, God is cognizant of by His one simple intuition. God therefore is apt to know the individual things that we grasp by sense and imagination.

6. The divine mind, unlike ours, does not gather its knowledge from things, but rather by its knowledge is the cause of things; and thus its knowledge of things is a practical knowledge. But practical knowledge is not perfect unless it descends to individual cases: for the end of practical knowledge is work, which is done on individuals.

9. As the Philosopher argues against Empedocles, God would be very wanting in wisdom, if He did not know individual instances, which even men know. This truth is established also by the authority of Holy Scripture, for it is said: There is no creature invisible in his sight: also the contrary error is excluded by the text: Say not, I shall be hidden from God; and from the height of heaven who shall mind me? (Ecclus xvi, 16). From what has been said it is evident how the objection to the contrary (Chap. LXIII, 1) is inconclusive: for though the mental presentation whereby divine understanding understands is immaterial, it is still a type both of matter and form, as being the prime productive principle of both.

CHAPTER LXVI—That God knows things which are not

THE knowledge of the divine mind stands to things as the knowledge of the artificer to the products of his art. But the artificer by the knowledge of his art knows even those products of it which are not yet produced.

3. God knows other things besides Himself by His essence, inasmuch as His essence is the type of other

things that come forth from Him (Chap. LIV). But since the essence of God is infinitely perfect (Chap. XLIII), while of every other thing the being and perfection is limited, it is impossible for the whole sum of other things to equal the perfection of the divine essence. Therefore the representative power of that essence extends to many more things than the things that are. As then God knows entirely the power and perfection of His essence, His knowledge reaches not only to things that are, but also to things that are not.

6. The understanding of God has no succession, as neither has His being: it is all together, ever abiding, which is the essential notion of eternity, whereas the duration of time extends by succession of before and after. The proportion of eternity to the whole duration of time is as the proportion of an indivisible point to a continuous surface, — not of that indivisible point which is a term of the surface, and is not in every part of its continuous extent: for to such a point an instant of time bears resemblance; but of that indivisible point which lies outside of the surface, and yet co-exists with every part or point of its continuous extent: for since time does not run beyond motion, eternity, which is altogether beyond motion, is no function of time. Again, since the being of the eternal never fails, eternity is present to every time or instant of time. Some sort of example of this may be seen in a circle: for a point taken on the circumference does not coincide with every other point; but the center, lying away from the circumference, is directly opposite to every point on the circumference. Whatever therefore is in any portion of time, co-exists with the eternal, as present to it, although in respect to another portion of time it be past or future. But nothing can co-exist in presence with the

eternal otherwise than with the whole of it, because it has no successive duration. Whatever therefore is done in the whole course of time, the divine mind beholds it as present throughout the whole of its eternity; and yet it cannot be said that what is done in a definite portion of time has always been an existing fact. The conclusion is that God has knowledge of things that in the course of time as yet are not.

By these reasons it appears that God has knowledge of nonentities. But all nonentities do not stand in the same regard to His knowledge. Things that neither are, nor shall be, nor have been, are known by God as possible to His power: hence He does not know them as being anywise in themselves, but only as being within the compass of divine power. These sort of things are said by some to be known by God with the 'knowledge of simple understanding' (notitia simplicis intelligentiae). But as for those things that are present, past, or future to us, God knows them as they are within the compass of His power; and as they are within the compass of their own several created causes; and as they are in themselves; and the knowledge of such things is called the 'knowledge of vision' (notitia visionis). For of the things that are not yet with us, God sees not only the being that they have in their causes, but also the being that they have in themselves, inasmuch as His eternity is indivisibly present to all time. We must remember that God knows the being of everything through His own essence: for His essence is representable by many things that are not, nor ever shall be, nor ever have been. That same essence is the type of the power of every cause, in virtue of which power effects pre-exist in their causes. Again the being of everything, that it has in itself, is modelled upon the being of the divine essence. Thus then God knows nonentities inasmuch as in some way they have being, either in the power of God, or in their (creature) causes, or in themselves.

To this the authority of Holy Scripture also gives testimony: *All things are known to the Lord our God before their creation; as also, after they are fully made, he regarded all* (Ecclus xxiii, 29): and, *Before I formed thee in the womb, I knew thee* (Jer. i, 5).

CHAPTER LXVII—That God knows Individual Contingent Events

HENCE we may gather some inkling of how God has had an infallible knowledge of all contingent events from eternity, and yet they cease not to be contingent. For contingency is not inconsistent with certain and assured knowledge except so far as the contingent event lies in the future, not as it is present. While the event is in the future, it may not be; and thus the view of him who reckons that it still be may be mistaken: but once it is present, for that time it cannot but be. Any view therefore formed upon a contingent event inasmuch as it is present may be a certitude. But the intuition of the divine mind rests from eternity upon each and every [one] of the events that happen in the course of time, viewing each as a thing present. There is nothing therefore to hinder God from having from eternity an infallible knowledge of contingent events.

2. A contingent event differs from a necessary event in point of the way in which each is contained in its cause. A contingent event is so contained in its cause as that it either may not or may ensue therefrom: whereas a

necessary event cannot but ensue from its cause.

But as each of these events is in itself, the two do not differ in point of reality; and upon reality truth is founded. In a contingent event, considered as it is in itself, there is no question of being or not being, but only of being: although, looking to the future, a contingent event possibly may not come off. But the divine mind knows things from eternity, not only in the being which they have in their causes, but also in the being which they have in themselves.

3. As from a necessary cause the effect follows with certainty, with like certainty does it follow from a contingent cause, when the cause is complete, provided no hindrance be placed. But as God knows all things (Chap. L). He knows not only the causes of contingent events, but like-wise the means whereby they may be hindered from coming off. He knows therefore with certitude whether they are going to come off or not.

6. The knowledge of God would not be true and perfect, if things did not happen in the way that God apprehends them to happen. But God, cognizant as He is of all being of which He is the principle, knows every event, not only in itself, but also in its dependence on any proximate causes on which it happens to depend: but the dependence of contingent events upon their proximate causes involves their ensuing upon them contingently. God therefore knows sundry events to happen, and to happen contingently: thus the certitude and truth of divine knowledge does not remove the contingency of events.

7. When it is said, 'God knows, or knew, this coming event,' an intervening medium is supposed between the divine knowledge and the thing known, to wit, the time to which the utterance points, in respect to

which that which is said to be known by God is in the future. But really it is not in the future in respect of the divine knowledge, which existing in the instant of eternity is present to all things. In respect of such knowledge, if we set aside the time of speaking, it is impossible to say that so-and-so is known as non-existent; and the question never arises as to whether the thing possibly may never occur. As thus known, it should be said to be seen by God as already present in its existence. Under this aspect, the question of the possibility of the thing never coming to be can no longer be raised: what already is, in respect of that present instant cannot but be. The fallacy then arises from this, that the time at which we speak, when we say 'God knows,' co-exists with eternity; or again the last time that is marked when we say 'God knew'; and thus a relation of time, past or present, to future is attributed to eternity, which attribution does not hold; and thus we have fallacia accidentis.

8. Since everything is known by God as seen by Him in the present, the necessity of that being true which God knows is like the necessity of Socrates's sitting from the fact of his being seen seated. This is not necessary absolutely, 'by necessity of the consequent,' as the phrase is, but conditionally, or 'by necessity of the consequence.' For this conditional proposition is necessary: 'He is sitting, if he is seen seated.' Change the conditional proposition into a categorical of this form: 'What is seen sitting, is necessarily seated': it is clear that the proposition is true as a phrase, where its elements are taken together (compositam), but false as a fact, when its elements are separated (divisam). All these objections against the divine knowledge of contingent facts are fallacia compositionis et divisionis.

That God knows future contingencies is shown also by the authority of Holy Scripture: for it is said of Divine Wisdom, It knows signs and portents beforehand, and the issues of times and ages (Wisd. viii, 8): and, There is nothing hidden from his eyes: from age to age he regarded (Ecclus xxxix, 24, 25).

## CHAPTER LXVIII—That God knows the Motions of the Will

GOD knows the thoughts of minds and the volitions of hearts in virtue of their cause, as He is Himself the universal principle of being. All that in any way is, is known by God in His knowledge of His own essence (Chap. XLIX). Now there is a certain reality in the soul, and again a certain reality in things outside the soul. The reality in the soul is that which is in the will or thought. God knows all these varieties of reality.

3. As God by knowing His own being knows the being of everything, so by knowing His own act of understanding and will He knows every thought and volition.

5. God knows intelligent substances not less well than He knows or we know sensible substances, seeing that intelligent substances are more knowable, as being better actualized. This is confirmed by the testimony of Holy Scripture: — God searcher of hearts and reins (Ps. vii, 10): Hell and perdition are before the Lord: how much more the hearts of the sons of men? (Prov. xi, 11): He needed not that anyone should bear testimony of what was in man: for he himself knew what was in man (John ii, 25). The dominion of the will over its own acts, whereby it has it in its power to will and not to will, is

inconsistent with will-force being determined to one fixed mode of action: it is inconsistent also with the violent interference of any external agency; but it is not inconsistent with the influence of that Higher Cause, from whence it is given to the will both to be and to act. And thus in the First Cause, that is, in God, there remains a causal influence over the motions of the will, such that, in knowing Himself, God is able to know these motions.

CHAPTER LXIX—That God knows infinite things

BY knowing Himself as the cause of things, He knows things other than Himself (Chap. XLIX). But He is the cause of infinite things, if beings are infinite, for He is the cause of all things that are.

2. God knows His own power perfectly (Chap. XLIX). But power cannot be perfectly known, unless all the objects to which it extends are known, since according to that extent the amount of the power may be said to be determined. But His power being infinite (Chap. XLIII) extends to things infinite, and therefore also His knowledge.

3. If the knowledge of God extends to all things that in any sort of way are, He must not only know actual being, but also potential being. But in the physical world there is potential infinity, though not actual infinity, as the Philosopher proves. God therefore knows infinite things, in the way that unity, which is the principle of number, would know infinite species of number if it knew whatever is in its potentiality: for unity is in promise and potency every number.

4. God in His essence, as in a sort of exemplar

medium, knows other things. But as He is a being of infinite perfection, there can be modelled upon Him infinite copies with finite perfections, because no one of these copies, nor any number of them put together, can come up to the perfection of their exemplar; and thus there always remains some new way for any copy taken to imitate Him.

10. The infinite defies knowledge in so far as it defies counting. To count the parts of the infinite is an intrinsic impossibility, as involving a contradiction. To know a thing by enumeration of its parts is characteristic of a mind that knows part after part successively, not of a mind that comprehends the several parts together. Since then the divine mind knows all things together without succession, it has no more difficulty in knowing things infinite than in knowing things finite.

11. All quantity consists in a certain multiplication of parts; and therefore number is the first of quantities. Where then plurality makes no difference, no difference can be made there by anything that follows upon quantity. But in God's knowledge many things are known in one, not by many different presentations, but by that one species, or presentation, which is the essence of God. Hence a multitude of things is known by God all at once; and thus plurality makes no difference in God's knowledge: neither then does infinity, which follows upon quantity. In accordance with this is what is said in Psalm cxlvi: *And of his wisdom there is no telling*. From what has been said it is clear why our mind does not know the infinite as the divine mind does. Our mind differs from the divine mind in four respects; and they make all the difference. The first is that our mind is simply finite, the divine mind infinite. The second is that as our mind

knows different things by different impressions, it cannot extend to an infinity of things, as the divine mind can. The third results in this way, that as our mind is cognizant of different things by different impressions, it cannot be actually cognizant of a multitude of things at the same time; and thus it could not know an infinity of things except by counting them in succession, which is not the case with the divine mind, which discerns many things at once as seen by one presentation. The fourth thing is that the divine mind is cognizant of things that are and of things that are not (Chap. LXVI).

It is also clear how the saying of the Philosopher, that the infinite, as infinite, is unknowable, is in no opposition with the opinion now put forth: because the notion of infinity attaches to quantity; consequently, for infinite to be known as infinite, it would have to be known by the measurement of its parts, for that is the proper way of knowing quantity: but God does not know the infinite in that way. Hence, so to say, God does not know the infinite inasmuch as it is infinite, but inasmuch as, to His knowledge, it is as though it were finite.

It is to be observed however that God does not know an infinity of things with the 'knowledge of vision,' because infinite things neither actually are, nor have been, nor shall be, since, according to the Catholic faith, there are not infinite generations either in point of time past or in point of time to come. But He does know an infinity of things with the 'knowledge of simple understanding': for He knows infinite things that neither are, nor have been, nor shall be, and yet are in the power of the creature; and He also knows infinite things that are in His own power, which neither are, nor shall be, nor have been. Hence to the question of the knowledge of particular things it may be replied by denial of the major: for particular things are not infinite: if however they were, God would none the less know them.

## CHAPTER LXX—That God knows Base and Mean Things

THE stronger an active power is, to the more remote objects does it extend its action. But the power of the divine mind in knowing things is likened to active power: since the divine mind knows, not by receiving aught from things, but rather by pouring its influence upon things. Since then God's mind is of infinite power in understanding (Chap. XLIII), its knowledge must extend to the remotest objects. But the degree of nobility or baseness in all things is determined by nearness to or distance from God, who is the fullness of nobility. Therefore the very vilest things in being are known to God on account of the exceeding great power of His understanding.

2. Everything that is, in so far as it has place in the category of substance or quality, is in actuality: it is some sort of likeness of the prime actuality, and is ennobled thereby. Even potential being, from its reference to actuality shares in nobility, and so comes to have the name of 'being.' It follows that every being, considered in itself, is noble; and is only mean and vile in comparison with some other being, nobler still. But the noblest creatures are removed from God at a distance not less than that which separates the highest in the scale of

creation from the lowest. If then the one distance were to bar God's knowledge, much more would the other; and the consequence would be that God would know nothing beyond Himself.

3. The good of the order of the universe is nobler than any part of the universe. If then God knows any other noble nature, most of all must He know the order of the universe. But this cannot be known without taking cognizance at once of things nobler and things baser: for in the mutual distances and relations of these things the order of the universe consists.

4. The vileness of the objects of knowledge does not of itself redound on to the knower; for it is of the essence of knowledge that the knower should contain within himself impressions of the object known according to his own mode and manner. Accidentally however the vileness of the objects known may redound upon the knower, either because in knowing base and mean things he is withdrawn from the thought of nobler things, or because from the consideration of such vile objects he is inclined to some undue affections: which cannot be the case with God.

5. A power is not judged to be small, which extends to small things, but only that which is limited to small things. A knowledge therefore that ranges alike over things noble and things mean, is not to be judged mean; but that knowledge is mean, which ranges only over mean things, as is the case with us: for we make different studies of divine and of human things, and there is a different science of each. But with God it is not so; for with the same knowledge and the same glance He views Himself and all other beings. With this agrees what is said of the Divine Wisdom: It findeth place everywhere

on account of its purity, and nothing defiled stealeth in to corrupt it (Wisdom vii, 24, 25).

CHAPTER LXXI—That God knows Evil Things

WHEN good is known, the opposite evil is known. But God knows all particular good things, to which evil things are opposed: therefore God knows evil things.

2. The ideas of contraries, as ideas in the mind, are not contrary to one another: otherwise they could not be together in the mind, or be known together: the idea therefore whereby evil is known is not inconsistent with good, but rather belongs to the idea of good (ratio qua cognoscitur malum ad rationem boni pertinet). If then in God, on account of His absolute perfection, there are found all ideas of goodness (rationes bonitatis, as has been proved (Chap. XL), It follows that there is in Him the idea (ratio) whereby evil is known. 3. Truth is the good of the understanding: for an understanding is called good inasmuch as it knows the truth. But truth is not only to the effect that good is good, but also that evil is evil: for as it is true that what is, is, so it is true that what is not, is not. The good of the understanding therefore consists even in the knowledge of evil. But since the divine understanding is perfect in goodness, there cannot be wanting to it any of the perfections of understanding; and therefore there is present to it the knowledge of things evil.

4. God knows the distinction of things (Chap. L). But in the notion of distinction there is negation: for those things are distinct, of which one is not another: hence the first things that are of themselves distinct, mutually involve the exclusion of one another, by reason of which

fast negative propositions are immediately verified of them, e.g., 'No quantity is a substance.' God then knows negation. But privation is a sort of negation: He therefore knows privation, and consequently evil, which is nothing else than a privation of due perfection. 8. In us the knowledge of evil things is never blameworthy in mere point of knowledge, that is in the judgement that is passed about evil things, but accidentally, inasmuch as by the observation of evil things one is sometimes inclined to evil. But that cannot be in God; and therefore there is nothing to prevent His knowing evil.

With this agrees what is said, that Evil surpasses not [God's] wisdom (Wisd. vii, 30) and, Hell and perdition are before the Lord (Prov. xv, 11) and, My offences are not hidden from thee(Ps. lxviii, 6); and, He knoweth the vanity of men, and seeing doth he not consider iniquity?(Job xi, 11.)

It is to be observed however that if God's knowledge were so limited as that His knowledge of Himself did not involve His knowing other beings of finite and partial goodness, at that rate He would nowise know privation or evil: because to the good which is God Himself there is no privation opposed, since privation and its opposite are naturally about the same object; and so to that which is pure actuality no privation is opposed, and consequently no evil either. Hence on the supposition that God knows Himself alone, by knowing the excellences of His own being, He will not know evil. But because in knowing Himself He knows beings in which privations naturally occur, He must know the opposite privations, and the evils opposite to particular goods.

It must be further observed that as God, without any argumentative process, knows other beings by knowing Himself, so there is no need of His knowledge being argumentative in coming to the knowledge of evil things through good things: for good is as it were the ground of the knowledge of evil, evil being nothing else than privation of good: hence what is evil is known through what is good as things are known through their definitions, not as conclusions through their premises.

CHAPTER LXXII—That God has a Will

FROM the fact that God has understanding, it follows that He has a will. Since good apprehended in understanding is the proper object of the will, understood good, as such, must be willed good. But anything understood involves an understanding mind. A mind then that understands good, must, as such, be a mind that wills good.

3. What is consequent upon all being, is a property of being, as such. Such a property must be found in its perfection in the first and greatest of beings. Now it is a property of all being to seek its own perfection and the preservation of its own existence. Every being does this in its own way: intelligent beings, by their will: animals, by their sensitive appetite: unconscious nature, by a certain physical nisus. It makes a difference however whether the thing craved for is possessed or not. Where it is not possessed, the nisus of desire proper to each several kind goes out to seek what is wanting: where the thing is possessed, it is rested in and clung to. This characteristic of all being cannot be wanting in the first of beings, which is God. Since then God has understanding, He has also a will, whereby He takes complacency in His own being and His own goodness.

4. The more perfect the act of understanding is, the more delightful to the understanding mind. But God has understanding and a most perfect act thereof (Chap. XLIV): therefore that act yields Him the utmost delight. But as sensible delight is through the concupiscible appetite, so is intellectual delight through the will. God then has a will. This will of God the testimonies of Holy Scripture confess: All things whatsoever he hath willed, the Lord hath done (Ps. cxxxiv, 6): Who resisted his will? (Rom. ix, 19).

CHAPTER LXXIII—That the Will of God is His Essence

GOD has will inasmuch as He has understanding. But He has understanding by His essence (Chap. XLIV, XLV), and therefore will in like manner.
2. The act of will is the perfection of the agent willing. But the divine being is of itself most perfect, and admits of no superadded perfection (Chap. XXIII): therefore in God the act of His willing is the act of His being.
3. As every agent acts inasmuch as it is in actuality, God, being pure actuality, must act by His essence. But to will is an act of God: therefore God must will by His essence.
4. If will were anything superadded to the divine substance, that substance being complete in being, it would follow that will was something adventitious to it as an accident to a subject; also that the divine substance stood to the divine will as potentiality to actuality; and that there was composition in God: all of which positions have been rejected (Chap. XVI, XVIII, XXIII).

CHAPTER LXXIV—That the Object of the Will of God in the First Place is God Himself

GOOD understood is the object of the will. But what is understood by God in the first place is the divine essence: therefore the divine essence is the first object of the divine will.
3. The object in the first place willed is the cause of willing to every willing agent. For when we say, 'I wish to walk for the benefit of my health,' we consider that we are assigning a cause; and if we are further asked, 'Why do you wish to benefit your health?' we shall go on assigning causes until we come to the final end, which is the object willed in the first place, and is in itself the cause of all our willing. If then God wills anything else than Himself in the first place, it will follow that that 'something else' is to Him a cause of willing. But His willing is His being (Chap. LXXIII), Therefore something else will be the cause of His being, which is contrary to the notion of the First Being.

CHAPTER LXXV—That God in willing Himself wills also other things besides Himself

EVERY one desires the perfection of that which for its own sake he wills and loves: for the things which we love for their own sakes we wish to be excellent, and ever better and better, and to be multiplied as much as possible. But God wills and loves His essence for its own sake. Now that essence is not augmentable and multipliable in itself (Chap. XLII), but can be multiplied only in its likeness, which is shared by many. God therefore wills the multitude of things, inasmuch as He wills and loves His own perfection.

3. Whoever loves anything in itself and for itself, wills consequently all things in which that thing is found: as he who loves sweetness in itself must love all sweet things. But God wills and loves His own being in itself and for itself; and all other being is a sort of participation by likeness of His being.

6. The will follows the understanding. But God with His understanding understands Himself in the first place, and in Himself understands all other things: therefore in like manner He wills Himself in the first place, and in willing Himself wills all other things.

This is confirmed by the authority of Holy Scripture: *Thou loves all things that are, and hates nothing of the things that thou hast made* (Wisd. xi, 2)

CHAPTER LXXVI—*That with one and the same Act of the Will God wills Himself and all other Beings*

EVERY power tends by one and the same activity to its object and to that which makes the said object an object to such a power, as with the same vision we see light and the color which is made actually visible by light. But when we wish a thing for an end, and for that alone, that which is desired for the end receives from the end its character of an object of volition. Since then God wills all things for Himself (Chap. LXXIV), with one act of will He wills Himself and other things.

2. What is perfectly known and desired, is known and desired to the whole extent of its motive power. But a final end is a motive not only inasmuch as it is desired in

itself, but also inasmuch as other things are rendered desirable for its sake. He therefore who perfectly desires an end, desires it in both these ways. But it is impossible to suppose any volitional act of God, by which He should will Himself, and not will Himself perfectly: since there is nothing imperfect in God. By every act therefore by which He wills Himself, He wills Himself and other things for His own sake absolutely; and other things besides Himself He does not will except inasmuch as He wills Himself.

3. As promises are to conclusions in things speculative, so is the end to the means in things practical and desirable: for as we know conclusions by premises, so from the end in view proceeds both the desire and the carrying out of the means. If then one were to wish the end apart, and the means apart, by two separate acts, there would be a process from step to step in his volition (Chap. LVII). But this is impossible in God, who is beyond all movement.

7. To will belongs to God inasmuch as He has understanding. As then by one act He understands Himself and other beings, inasmuch as His essence is the pattern of them all, so by one act He wills Himself and all other beings, inasmuch as His goodness is the type of all goodness.

CHAPTER LXXVII—That the Multitude of the Objects of God's Will is not inconsistent with the Simplicity of His Substance

GOD wills other things inasmuch as He wills His own goodness (Chap. LXXV). Things then come under the will of God according as they are included in His goodness. But in His goodness all things are one: for they are in Him according to the mode that befits Him; material things, immaterially; and things many, in union (Chap. LV, LVIII). Thus the multitude of the objects of the divine will does not multiply the divine substance.

CHAPTER LXXVIII—That the Divine Will reaches to the good of Individual Existences

THE excellence of order in the universe appears in two ways, first, inasmuch as the whole universe is referred to something beyond the universe, as an army to its leader: secondly, inasmuch as the parts of the universe are referred to one another, like the parts of an army; and the second order is for the sake of the first. But God, in willing Himself as an end, wills other things in their reference to Him as an end. He wills therefore the excellence of order in the universe in reference to Himself, and the excellence of order in the universe in mutual reference of its parts to one another. But the excellence of order is made up of the good of individual existences.

This is confirmed by the authority of Scripture: God saw the light, that it was good (Gen. i, 4); and similarly of His other works; and lastly of them altogether: God saw all things that he had made, and they were very good (Gen. i, 31).

CHAPTER LXXIX—That God wills things even that as yet are not

## St. Thomas Aquinas

SOME one might perhaps think that God wills only the things that are: for correlatives go together; and if one perishes, the other perishes; if then willing supposes a relation of the willing subject to the object willed, none can will any but things that are. Besides, the will and its objects are to one another as Creator and creature: now God cannot be called Creator, or Lord, or Father, except of things that are: neither then can He be said to will any but things that are. And it may be further argued, that if the divine will is invariable, as is the divine being, and wills only actual existences, it wills nothing but what always is.

Let us say then in answer to these objections, that as good apprehended by the intellect moves the will, the act of the will must follow the condition of the mental apprehension. Now the mind apprehends the thing, not only as it is in the mind, but also as it is in its own nature: for we not only know that the thing is understood by us (for that is the meaning of its being 'in the mind'), but also that the thing exists, or has existed, or is to exist in its own nature. Though then at the time the thing has no being other than in the mind, still the mind stands related to it, not as it is in the mind, but as it is in its own nature, which the mind apprehends. Therefore the relation of the divine will to a non-existent thing is to the thing according as it is in its own nature, attached to some certain time, and not merely to the thing as it is in the knowledge of God. For God wills the thing, that is not now, to be in some certain time: He does not merely will it inasmuch as He Himself understands it.

Nor is the relation of the will to its object similar to the relation of Creator to creature, of Maker to made, of

Lord to subject. For will, being an immanent act, does not involve the actual external existence of the thing willed: whereas making and creating and governing do signify an action terminated to an external effect, such that without its existence such action is unintelligible.

CHAPTER LXXX—That God of necessity wills His own Being and His own Goodness

GOD wills His own being and His own goodness as His first object and reason for willing all other things (Chap. LXXIV), and this He wills in everything that He does will. Nor is it possible for Him to will it merely potentially: He must will it actually, as His willing is His being.

4. All things, in so far as they have existence, are likened to God, who is the first and greatest being. But all things, in so far as they have existence, cherish their own being naturally in such manner as they can. Much more therefore does God cherish His own being naturally.

CHAPTER LXXXI—That God does not of necessity love other things than Himself

A WILL does not of necessity tend to the means to an end, if the end can be had without those means. Since then the divine Goodness can be without other beings, — nay, other beings make no addition to it, — God is under no necessity of willing other things from the fact of His willing His own goodness.

2. Since good, understood to be such, is the proper object of the will, the will may fasten on any object conceived by the intellect in which the notion of good is

fulfilled. Hence though the being of anything, as such, is good, and its not-being, as such, is evil; still the very not-being of a thing may become an object to the will, though not of necessity, by reason of some notion of good fulfilled: for it is good for a thing to be, even though some other thing is not. The only good then which the will by the terms of its constitution cannot wish not to be, is the good whose non-existence would destroy the notion of good altogether. Such a good is no other than God. The will then by its constitution can will the non-existence of anything else except of God. But in God there is will according to the fullness of the power of willing. God then can will the non-existence of any other being besides Himself.

3. God in willing His own goodness wills also other things than Himself as sharing His goodness. But since the divine goodness is infinite, and partakable in infinite ways, if by the willing of His own goodness He of necessity willed the beings that partake of it, the absurdity would follow that He must will the existence of infinite creatures sharing His goodness in infinite ways: because, if He willed them, those creatures would exist, since His will is the principle of being to creatures.

We must consider therefore why God of necessity knows other beings than Himself, and yet does not of necessity will them to exist, notwithstanding that His understanding and willing of Himself involves His understanding and willing other beings. The reason of it is this: an intelligent agent's understanding anything arises from a certain condition of the understanding, — for by a thing being actually understood its likeness is in the mind: but a volitional agent's willing anything arises from a certain condition of the object willed, — for we will a thing either because it is an end, or because it is a means to an end. Now the divine perfection necessarily requires that all things should so be in God as to be understood in Him. But the divine goodness does not of necessity require that other things should exist to be referred to Him as means to an end; and therefore it is necessary that God should know other things, but not that He should will other things. Hence neither does He will all things that are referable to His goodness: but He knows all things which are in any way referable to His essence, whereby He understands.

CHAPTER LXXXII—*Arguments against the aforesaid Doctrine and Solutions of the same*

THESE awkward consequences seem to follow, if any things that God wills He does not will of necessity.

1. If the will of God in respect of certain objects of will is not determined by any of them, it seems to be indifferent. But every faculty that indifferent is in a manner in potentiality.

2. Since potential being, as such, is naturally changeable, — for what can be can also not be, — it follows that the divine will is variable.

4. Since what hangs loose, indifferent between two alternatives, does not tend to one rather than to the other, unless it be determined by one or other, either God wills none of the things to which He is indifferent, or He is determined by one or other of them, in which case there must be something antecedent to God to determine Him. But none of the above objections can stand.

1. The indifference, or indeterminateness, of a faculty may be attributable either to the faculty itself or to

its object. To the faculty itself, when its indeterminateness comes from its not having yet attained to its perfection. This argues imperfection in the faculty, and an unfulfilled potentiality, as we see in the mind of a doubter, who has not yet attained to premises sufficient to determine him to take either of two sides. To the object of the faculty, when the perfect working of the faculty does not depend on its adoption of either alternative, and yet either alternative may be adopted, as when art may employ different instruments to do the same work equally well. This argues no imperfection in the faculty, but rather its pre-eminent excellence, inasmuch as it rises superior to both opposing alternatives, and therefore is indifferent to both and determined by neither. Such is the position of the divine will with respect to things other than itself. Its perfection depends on none of them; being as it is intimately conjoined with its own last end and final perfection.

2. In the divine will there is no potentiality. Unnecessitated, it prefers one alternative to another respecting the creatures which it causes to be. It is not to be looked upon as being in a potential attitude to both alternatives, so as first to be potentially willing both, and then to be actually willing one. It is for ever actually willing whatever it wills, as well its own self as the creatures which are the objects of its causation. But whatever creature God wills to exist, that creature stands in no necessary relation to the divine goodness, which is the proper object of the divine will.

4. We cannot admit that either the divine will wills none of the effects of its causation, or that its volition is determined by some exterior object. The proper object of the will is good apprehended as such by the understanding. Now the divine understanding apprehends,

not only the divine being, or divine goodness, but other good things likewise (Chap. XLIX); and it apprehends them as likenesses of the divine goodness and essence, not as constituent elements of the same. Thus the divine will tends to them as things becoming its goodness, not as things necessary to its goodness. So it happens also in our will: which, when it inclines to a thing as absolutely necessary to its end, tends to it with a certain necessity; but when it tends to a thing solely on account of its comeliness and appropriateness, does not tend to it necessarily.

CHAPTER LXXXIII—That God wills anything else than Himself with an Hypothetical Necessity

IN every unchangeable being, whatever once is, cannot afterwards cease to be. Since then God's will is unchangeable, supposing Him to will anything, He cannot on that supposition not will it.
2. Everything eternal is necessary. But God's will for the causation of any effect is eternal: for, as His being, so His willing is measured by eternity. That will therefore is necessary, yet not absolutely so, since the will of God has no necessary connexion with this objection willed. It is therefore necessary hypothetically, on a supposition. 3. Whatever God once could do, He can still. His power does not grow less, as neither does His essence. But He cannot now not-will what He is already supposed to have willed, because His will cannot change: therefore He never could not-will whatever He once willed (nunquam potuit non velle quidquid voluit). It is therefore hypothetically necessary for Him to have willed whatever He has willed, as it is for Him to will whatever He does

will: but in neither case is the necessity absolute.

4. Whoever wills anything, necessarily wills all that is necessarily requisite to that purpose, unless there be some defect on his part, either by ignorance, or because his will sometimes is drawn away by some passion from a right choice of means to the end: nothing of which can be said of God. If God then in willing Himself wills anything else besides Himself, He needs must will all that is necessarily required to the effecting of the thing willed, as it is necessary that God should will the being of a rational soul, if He wills the being of a man.

CHAPTER LXXXIV—That the Will of God is not of things in themselves Impossible

THOSE things are in themselves impossible, which involve an inconsistency, as that man should be an ass, which involves the rational being irrational. But what is inconsistent with a thing, excludes some one of the conditions requisite to it, as being an ass excludes a man's reason. If therefore God necessarily wills the things requisite to that which by supposition He does will, it is impossible for Him to will what is inconsistent therewith.

2. God, in willing His own being, wills all other things, that He does will, in so far as they have some likeness to it. But in so far as anything is inconsistent with the notion of being as such, there cannot stand therein any likeness to the first or divine being, which is the fountain of being. God therefore cannot will anything that is inconsistent with the notion of being as such, as that anything should be at once being and not being, that affirmation and negation should be true together, or any other such essential impossibility, inconsistency, and

implied contradiction.
3. What is no object of the intellect, can be no object of the will. But essential impossibilities, involving notions mutually inconsistent, are no objects of intellect, except perchance through the error of a mind that does not understand the proprieties of things, which cannot be said of God.

CHAPTER LXXXV—That the Divine Will does not take away Contingency from things

HYPOTHETICAL necessity in the cause cannot lead to absolute necessity in the effect. But God's will about a creature is not absolutely necessary, but hypothetically so (Chap. LXXXIII). Therefore the divine will is no argument of absolute necessity in creatures. But only this absolute necessity excludes contingency: for even a contingent fact may be extended either way into a hypothetical necessity: thus it is necessary that Socrates moves, if he runs. It does not therefore follow that a thing happens of necessity, if God wills it: all that holds is the necessary truth of this conditional: 'If God wills anything, the thing will be': but the 'consequent' (as distinguished from the 'consequence') need not be a necessary truth.

CHAPTER LXXXVI—That Reason can be assigned for the Divine Will

THE end is a reason for willing the means. But God wills His own goodness as an end, and all things else as means thereto: His goodness therefore is a reason why He wills other things different from Himself.
2. The good of a part is ordained to the end of the

good of the whole, as the imperfect to the perfect. But things become objects of the divine will according as they stand in the order of goodness. It follows that the good of the universe is the reason why God wills every good of any part of the universe.

3. Supposing that God wills anything, it follows of necessity that He wills the means requisite thereto. But what lays on others a necessity for doing a thing, is a reason for doing it. Therefore the accomplishment of a purpose, to which such and such means are requisite, is a reason to God for willing those means.

We may therefore proceed as follows. God wishes man to have reason, to the end that he may be man: He wishes man to be, to the end of the completion of the universe: He wishes the good of the universe to be, because it befits His own goodness. The same proportion however is not observable in all three stages of this ratiocination. The divine goodness does not depend on the perfection of the universe, and receives no accession thereby. The perfection of the universe, though depending necessarily on the good of some particular components, which are essential parts of the universe, has no necessary dependence on others, although even from them some goodness or beauty accrues to the universe, such things serving solely for the fortification (munimentum) or embellishment of the rest. But any particular good depends absolutely on the elements that are requisite to it: and still even such goods have adjuncts that go merely to better their condition. Sometimes therefore the reason of the divine will involves mere becomingness, sometimes utility, sometimes also hypothetical necessity, but never absolute necessity, except when the object of God's volition is God Himself.

## CHAPTER LXXXVII—That nothing can be a Cause to the Divine Will

THOUGH some reason may be assigned for the divine will, yet it does not follow that there is any cause of that will's volition. For the cause of volition is the end in view: now the end in view of the divine will is its own goodness: that then is God's cause of willing, which is also His own act of willing. But of other objects willed by God none is to God a cause of willing, but one of them is cause to another of its being referred to the divine goodness, and thus God is understood to will one for the sake of another. But clearly we must suppose no passing from point to point of God's will, where there is only one act, as shown above of the divine intellect (Chap. LVII). For God by one act wills His own goodness and all other things, as His action is His essence.

By this and the previous chapter the error is excluded of some who say that all things proceed from God by sheer will, so that no reason is to be rendered of anything that He does beyond the fact that God so wills. Which position is even contrary to divine Scripture, which tells us that God has done all things according to the order of His wisdom: Thou hast done all things in wisdom(Ps. ciii, 24); and God has shed wisdom over all his works(Ecclus i, 10).

## CHAPTER LXXXVIII—That there is a Free Will in God

GOD does not necessarily will things outside

Himself (Chap. LXXXI). 3. Willis of the end: choice of the means. Since then God wills Himself as end, and other things as means, it follows that in respect of Himself He has will only, but in respect of other things choice. But choice is always an act of free will.
4. Man by free will is said to be master of his own acts. But this mastery belongs most of all to the Prime Agent, whose act depends on no other.

CHAPTER LXXXIX—That there are no Passions in God

PASSION is not in the intellectual appetite, but only in the sensitive. But in God there is no sensitive appetite, as there is no sensible knowledge.
2. Every passion involves some bodily alteration, a thing impossible in the incorporeal Deity.
3. In every passion the subject is more or less drawn out of his essential condition or connatural disposition: which is not possible in the unchangeable God.
4. Every passion fixes determinedly on someone object, according to the mode and measure of the passion. Passion, like physical nature, rushes blindly at some one thing: that is why passion needs repressing and regulating by reason. But the divine will is not determined of itself to any one object in creation: but proceeds according to the order of its wisdom (Chap. LXXXII).
5. Every passion is the passion of a subject that is in potentiality. But God is altogether free from potentiality, being pure actuality. Thus every passion, generically as such, is removed from God. But certain

passions are removed from God, not only generically, but also specifically. For every passion takes its species from its object: if then an object is altogether unbefitting for God, the passion specified by that object is removed from God also on specific grounds. Such a passion is Sadness and Grief, the object of which is evil already attaching to the sufferer. Hope, again, though it has good for its object, is not of good obtained, but to be obtained, a relation to good which is unbefitting for God by reason of His so great perfection, to which addition is impossible. Much more does that perfection exclude any potentiality in the way of evil. But Fear regards an evil that may be imminent. In two ways then Fear, specifically as such, is removed from God, both because it supposes a subject that is in potentiality, and because it has for its object some evil that may come to be in the subject. Regret again, or Repentance, is repugnant to God, as well because it is a species of sadness, as also because it involves a change of will.

Moreover, without an error of the intellectual faculty, it is impossible for good to be mistaken for evil. And only in respect of private advantages is it possible for the loss of one being to be the gain of another. But to the general good nothing is lost by the good of any private member; but every private good goes to fill in the public good. But God is the universal good, by partaking in whose likeness all other things are called good. No other being's evil then can possibly be good for God. Nor again, seeing that God's knowledge makes no mistakes, can He apprehend as evil that which is simply good, and no evil to Him. Envy therefore is impossible to God, specifically as Envy, not only because it is a species of sadness, but also because it is sadness at the good of another, and thus takes the good of another as evil to itself.

It is part of the same procedure to be sad at good and to desire evil. Such sadness arises from good being accounted evil: such desire, from evil being accounted good. Now Anger is desire of the evil of another for vengeance' sake. Anger then is far from God by reason of its species, not only because it is a species of sadness, but also because it is a desire of vengeance, conceived for sadness at an injury done one.

CHAPTER XC—That there is in God Delight and Joy

THERE are some passions which, though they do not befit God as passions, nevertheless, so far as their specific nature is considered, do not involve anything inconsistent with divine perfection. Of the number of these is Delight and Joy. Joy is of present good. Neither by reason of its object, which is good, nor by reason of the relation in which the object, good actually possessed, stands to the subject, does joy specifically contain anything inconsistent with divine perfection. Hence it is manifest that joy or Delight has being properly in God. For as good and evil apprehended is the object of the sensitive appetite, so also is it of the intellectual appetite, or will. It is the ordinary function of both appetites to pursue good and to shun evil, either real or apparent, except that the object of the intellectual appetite is wider than that of the sensitive, inasmuch as the intellectual appetite regards good and evil simply, while the sensitive appetite regards good and evil felt by sense; as also the object of intellect is wider than the object of sense. But the activities of appetite are specified by their objects. There exist therefore in the intellectual appetite, or will, activities specifically similar to the activities of the sensitive appetite, and differing only in this, that in the sensitive appetite they are passions on account of the implication of a bodily organ, but in the intellectual appetite they are simple activities. For as by the passion of fear, coming over the sensitive appetite, one shuns evil looming in the future, so the intellectual appetite works to the same effect without passion. Since then joy and Delight are not repugnant to God specifically, but only inasmuch as they are passions, it follows that they are not wanting even in the divine will.

2. Joy and Delight are a sort of rest of the will in its object. But God singularly rests in Himself as in the first object of His own will, inasmuch as He has all sufficiency in Himself. 3. Delight is the perfection of activity, perfecting activity as bloom does youth. But the activity of the divine understanding is most perfect. If therefore our act of understanding, coming to its perfection, yields delight, most delightful must be the act whereby God understands.

4. Everything naturally feels joy over what is like itself, except accidentally, inasmuch as the likeness hinders one's own gain, and 'two of a trade' quarrel. But every good thing is some likeness of the divine goodness, and nothing is lost to God by the good of His creature. Therefore God rejoices in good everywhere.

Joy and Delight differ in our consideration: for Delight arises out of good really conjoined with the subject; while Joy does not require this real conjunction, but the mere resting of the will on an agreeable object is sufficient for it. Hence, strictly speaking, Delight is at good conjoined with the subject: Joy over good external to the subject. Thus, in strict parlance, God takes delight in Himself: but has Joy both over Himself and over other things.

CHAPTER XCI—That there is Love in God.

IT is of the essential idea of love, that whoever loves wishes the good of the object loved. But God wishes His own good and the good of other beings (Chap. LXXV); and in this respect He loves Himself and other beings.

2. It is a requisite of true love to love the good of another inasmuch as it is his good. But God loves the good of every being as it is the good of that being, though He does also subordinate one being to the profit of another.

3. The essential idea of love seems to be this, that the affection of one tends to another as to a being who is in some way one with himself. The greater the bond of union, the more intense is the love. And again the more intimately bound up with the lover the bond of union is, the stronger the love. But that bond whereby all things are united with God, namely, His goodness, of which all things are imitations, is to God the greatest and most intimate of bonds, seeing that He is Himself His own goodness. There is therefore in God a love, not only true, but most perfect and strong.

But some might be of opinion that God does not love one object more than another; for a higher and a lower degree of intensity of affection is characteristic of a changeable nature, and cannot be attributed to God, from whom all change is utterly removed. Besides, wherever else there is mention of any divine activity, there is no question of more and less: thus one thing is not known by God more than another. In answer to this difficulty we must observe that whereas other activities of the soul are concerned with one object only, love alone seems to tend to two. For love wishes something to somebody: hence the things that we desire, we are properly said to 'desire,' not to 'love,' but in them we rather love ourselves for whom we desire them. Every divine act then is of one and the same intensity; but love may be said to admit of 'greater and less' in two ways, either in point of the good that we will to another, in which way we are said to love him more to whom we wish greater good; or again in point of the intensity of the act, in which way we are said to love him more to whom we wish, not indeed a greater good, but an equal good more fervently and effectually. In the former way then there is nothing to object to in the saying that God loves one more than another, inasmuch as He wishes him a greater good: but, understood of the second way, the saying is not tenable.

Hence it appears that of our affections there is none that can properly be in God except joy and love, though even these are in Him not by way of passion, as they are in us. That there is in God joy or delight is confirmed by the authority of Holy Scripture. I was delighted day by day playing before him, says the Divine Wisdom, which is God (Prov. viii, 30). The Philosopher also says that God ever rejoices with one simple delight. The Scripture also speaks of love in God: With everlasting love I have loved thee (Jer. xxxi, 3); For the Father himself loves you (John xvi, 27).

But even other affections (affectiones), which are specifically inconsistent with divine perfection, are predicated in Holy Writ of God, not properly but metaphorically, on account of likeness of effects. Thus sometimes the will in following out the order of wisdom tends to the same effect to which one might be inclined by a passion, which would argue a certain imperfection: for the judge punishes from a sense of justice, as an angry man under the promptings of anger. So sometimes God is said to be 'angry,' inasmuch as in the order of His wisdom He means to punish some one: *When his anger shall blaze out suddenly* (Ps. ii, 13). He is said to be 'compassionate,' inasmuch as in His benevolence He takes away the miseries of men, as we do the same from a sentiment of pity: *The Lord is merciful and compassionate, patient and abounding in mercy* (Ps. cli, 8). Sometimes also He is said to be 'repentant,' inasmuch as in the eternal and immutable order of His providence, He builds up what He had previously destroyed, or destroys what He had previously made, as we do when moved by repentance: *It repented me that I have made man* (Gen. vi, 6, 7). God is also said to be 'sad,' inasmuch as things happen contrary to what He loves and approves, as sadness is in us at what happens against our will: *And the Lord saw, and it seemed evil in his eyes, because judgement is not: God saw that there is no man, and he was displeased, because there was none to meet him* (Isa. lix, 15, 16).

CHAPTER XCII—In what sense Virtues can be posited in God

AS the divine goodness comprehends within itself in a certain way all goodnesses, and virtue is a sort of goodness, the divine goodness must contain all virtues after a manner proper to itself. But no virtue is predicated as an attribute of God after the manner of a habit, as virtues are in us. For it does not befit God to be good by anything superadded to Him, but only by His essence, since He is absolutely simple. Nor again does He act by anything superadded to His essence, as His essence is His being (Chap. XLV). Virtue therefore in God is not any habit, but His own essence.

2. A habit is an imperfect actuality, half-way between potentiality and actuality: hence the subjects of habits are compared to persons asleep. But in God actuality is most perfect. Virtue therefore in Him is not like a habit or a science, but is as a present act of consciousness, which is the extremest perfection of actuality.

Since human virtues are for the guidance of human life, and human life is twofold, contemplative and active, the virtues of the active life, inasmuch as they perfect this present life, cannot be attributed to God: for the active life of man consists in the use of material goods, which are not assignable to God. Again, these virtues perfect human conduct in political society: hence they do not seem much to concern those who keep aloof from political society: much less can they befit God, whose conversation and life is far removed from the manner and custom of human life. Some again of the virtues of the active life direct us how to govern the passions: but in God there are no passions.

CHAPTER XCIII—*That in God there are the Virtues which regulate Action*

THERE are virtues directing the active life of

man, which are not concerned with passions, but with actions, as truth, justice, liberality, magnificence, prudence, art. Since virtue is specified by its object, and the actions which are the objects of these virtues are not inconsistent with the divine perfection, neither is there in such virtues, specifically considered, anything to exclude them from the perfection of God.

3. Of things that come to have being from God, the proper plan of them all is in the divine understanding (Chap. LXVI). But the plan of a thing to be made in the mind of the maker is Art: hence the Philosopher says that Art is "the right notion of things to be made." There is therefore properly Art in God, and therefore it is said: Wisdom, artificer of all, taught me (Wisd. vii, 21).

4. Again, the divine will, in things outside God, is determined by His knowledge (Chap. LXXXII). But knowledge directing the will to act is Prudence: because, according to the Philosopher, Prudence is "the right notion of things to be done." There is therefore Prudence in God; and hence it is said: With him is prudence (Job xii, 13).

5. From the fact of God wishing anything, He wishes the requisites of that thing. But the points requisite to the perfection of each several thing are due to that thing: there is therefore in God Justice, the function of which is to distribute to each his own. Hence it is said: The Lord is just, and hath loved justice (Ps. x, 8).

6. As shown above (Chapp. LXXIV, LXXV), the last end, for the sake of which God wills all things, in no way depends on the means to that end, neither in point of being nor in point of well-being. Hence God does not wish to communicate His goodness for any gain that may accrue to Himself thereby, but simply because the mere

communication befits Him as the fountain of goodness. But to give, not from any advantage expected from the gift, but out of sheer goodness and the fitness of giving, is an act of Liberality. God therefore is in the highest degree liberal; and, as Avicenna says, He alone can properly be called liberal: for every other agent but Him is in the way of gaining something by his action and intends so to gain. This His liberality the Scripture declares, saying: As thou opens thy hand, all things shall be filled with goodness (Ps. ciii, 28); and, Who giveth to all abundantly, and reproached not (James i, 5).

7. All things that receive being from God, necessarily bear His likeness, in so far as they are, and are good, and have their proper archetypes in the divine understanding (Chap. LIV). But this belongs to the virtue of Truth, that everyone should manifest himself in his deeds and words for such as he really is. There is therefore in God the virtue of Truth. Hence, God is true (Rom. iii, 4); and, All thy ways are truth (Ps. cxviii, 151).

In point of exchange, the proper act of commutative justice, justice does not befit God, since He receives no advantage from any one; hence, Who hath first given to him, and recompense shall be made him?(Rom. xi, 35;) and, Who bath given to me beforehand, that I may repay him? (Job xli, 2.) Still, in a metaphorical sense, we are said to give things to God, inasmuch as He takes kindly what we have to offer Him. Commutative justice therefore does not befit God, but only distributive justice.

To judge of things to be done, or to give a thing, or make a distribution, is not proper to man alone, but belongs to any and every intellectual being. Inasmuch therefore as the aforesaid actions are considered in their generality, they have their apt place even in divinity: for as man is the distributer of human goods, as of money or honor, so is God of all the goods of the universe. The aforesaid virtues therefore are of wider extension in God than in man: for as the justice of man is to a city or family, so is the justice of God to the entire universe: hence the divine virtues are said to be archetypes of ours. But other virtues, which do not properly become God, have no archetype in the divine nature, but only, as is the case with corporeal things generally, in the divine wisdom, which contains the proper notions of all things.

CHAPTER XCIV—That the Contemplative (Intellectual) Virtues are in God

IF Wisdom consists in the knowledge of the highest causes; and God chiefly knows Himself, and knows nothing except by knowing Himself, as the first cause of all (Chap. XLVI), it is evident that Wisdom ought to be attributed to God in the first place. Hence it is said: He is wise of heart (Job ix, 4.); and, All wisdom is of the Lord God, and hath been with him always (Ecclus i, 1). The Philosopher also says at the beginning of his Metaphysics that Wisdom is a divine possession, not a human.
2. If Knowledge (Science) is an acquaintance with a thing through its proper cause, and God knows the order of all causes and effects, and thereby the several proper causes of individual things (Chapp. LXV, LXVII), it is manifest that Knowledge (Science) is properly in God; hence God is the Lord of sciences (1 Kings ii, 3)
3. If the immaterial cognition of things, attained without discussion, is Understanding (Intuition), God has

such a cognition of all things (Chap. L); and therefore there is in Him Understanding. Hence, He hath counsel and understanding (Job xii, 13).

### CHAPTER XCV—That God cannot will Evil

EVERY act of God is an act of virtue, since Ills virtue is His essence (Chap. XCII).

2. The will cannot will evil except by some error coming to be in the reason, at least in the matter of the particular choice there and then made. For as the object of the will is good, apprehended as such, the will cannot tend to evil unless evil be somehow proposed to it as good; and that cannot be without error. But in the divine cognition there can be no error (Chap. LXI).

3. God is the sovereign good, admitting no intermixture of evil (Chap. LXI).

4. Evil cannot befall the will except by its being turned away from its end. But the divine will cannot be turned away from its end, being unable to will except by willing itself (Chap. LXXV). It cannot therefore will evil; and thus free will in it is naturally established in good. This is the meaning of the texts: God is faithful and without iniquity (Deut. xxxii, 4); Thine eyes are clean, O Lord, and thou canst not look upon iniquity (Hab. i, 13).

### CHAPTER XCVI—That God hates nothing

AS love is to good, so is hatred to evil; we wish good to them whom we love, and evil to them whom we hate. If then the will of God cannot be inclined to evil, as has been shown (Chap. XCV), it is impossible for Him to hate anything.

2. The will of God tends to things other than Himself inasmuch as, by willing and loving His own being and goodness, He wishes it to be diffused as far as is possible by communication of His likeness. This then is what God wills in beings other than Himself, that there be in them the likeness of His goodness. Therefore God wills the good of everything, and hates nothing.

4. What is found naturally in all active causes, must be found especially in the Prime Agent. But all agents in their own way love the effects which they themselves produce, as parents their children, poets their own poems, craftsmen their works. Much more therefore is God removed from hating anything, seeing that He is cause of all.

Hence it is said: Thou loves all things that are, and hates nothing of the things that Thou hast made (Wisd. xi, 25).

Some things however God is said, to hate figuratively (similitudinarie), and that in two ways. The first way is this, that God, in loving things and willing their good to be, wills their evil not to be: hence He is said to have hatred of evils, for the things we wish not to be we are said to hate. So it is said: Think no evil in your hearts every one of you against his friend, and love no lying oath: for all these are things that I hate, saith the Lord (Zach. viii, 17). But none of these things are effects of creation: they are not as subsistent things, to which hatred or love properly attaches. The other way is by God's wishing some greater good, which cannot be without the privation of a lesser good; and thus He is said to hate, whereas it is more properly love. Thus inasmuch as He wills the good of justice, or of the order of the universe, which cannot be without the punishment or perishing of some, He is said to hate those beings whose punishment or perishing He wills, according to the text, *Esau I have hated* (Malachi. i, 3); and, *Thou hates all who work Iniquity, thou wilt destroy all who utter falsehood: the man of blood and deceit the Lord shall abominate* (Ps. v, 7).

## CHAPTER XCVII—That God is Living

IT has been shown that God is intelligent and willing: but to understand and will are functions of a living being only.

2. Life is attributed to beings inasmuch as they appear to move of themselves, and not to be moved by another. Therefore things that seem to move of themselves, the moving powers of which the vulgar do not perceive, are figuratively said to live, as we speak of the 'living' (running) water of a flowing stream, but not so of a cistern or stagnant pool; and we call 'quicksilver' that which seems to have a motion of its own. This is mere popular speech, for properly those things alone move of themselves, which do so by virtue of their composition of a moving force and matter moved, as things with souls; hence these alone are properly said to live: all other things are moved by some external force, a generating force, or a force removing an obstacle, or a force of impact. And because sensible activities are attended with movement, by a further step everything that determines itself to its own modes of activity, even though unattended with movement, is said to live; hence to understand and desire and feel are vital actions. But God, of all beings, is determined to activity by none other than Himself, as He is prime agent and first cause; to Him

therefore, of all beings, does it belong to live.

3. The divine being contains the perfection of all being (Chap. XXVIII). But living is perfect being; hence animate things in the scale of being take precedence of inanimate. With God then to be is to live.

This too is confirmed by authority of divine Scripture: I will raise to heaven my hand, and swear by my right hand, and say: I live forever (Deut. xxxii, 40): My heart and my flesh) have rejoiced in the living God (Ps. lxxiii, 3).

CHAPTER XCVIII—That God is His own Life

IN living things, to live is to be: for a living thing is said to be alive inasmuch as it has a soul; and by that soul, as by its own proper form, it has being: living in fact is nothing else than living being, arising out of a living form. But, in God, Himself is His own being (Chap. XXII): Himself therefore is His own life.

2. To understand is to live: but God is His own act of understanding (Chap. XLV).

3. If God is living, there must be life in Him. If then He is not His own life, there will be something in Him that is not Himself, and thus He will be compound, — a rejected conclusion (Chap. XVIII).

And this is the text: I am life (John xiv, 6).

CHAPTER XCIX—That the Life of God is everlasting

IT is impossible for God to cease to live, since Himself He is His own life (Chap. XCVIII).

2. Everything that at one time is and at another

time is not, has existence through some cause. But the divine life has no cause, as neither has the divine being. God is therefore not at one time living and at another not living, but always lives.
3. In every activity the agent remains, although sometimes the activity passes in succession: hence in motion the moving body remains the same in subject throughout the whole course of the motion, although not the same in our consideration. Where then the action is the agent himself, nothing there can pass in succession, but all must be together at once. But God's act of understanding and living is God Himself (Chapp. XLV, XCVIII): therefore His life has no succession, but is all together at once, and everlasting. Hence it is said: *This is the true God and life everlasting* (1 John v, 20).

CHAPTER C—That God is Happy

HAPPINESS is the proper good of every intellectual nature. Since then God is an intellectual being, happiness will be His proper good. But God in regard of His proper good is not as a being that is still tending to a proper good not yet possessed: that is the way with a nature changeable and in potentiality; but God is in the position of a being that already possesses its proper good. Therefore He not only desires happiness, as we do, but is in the enjoyment of happiness.
2. The thing above all others desired or willed by an intellectual nature is the most perfect thing in that nature, and that is its happiness. But the most perfect thing in each is its most perfect activity: for power and habit are perfected by activity: hence the Philosopher says that happiness is a perfect activity. Now the perfection of

activity depends on four conditions. First, on its kind, that it be immanent in the agent. I call an activity 'immanent in the agent,' when nothing else comes of it besides the act itself: such are the acts of seeing and hearing: such acts are perfections of the agents whose acts they are, and may have a finality of their own in so far as they are not directed to the production of anything else as an end. On the other hand, any activity from which there results something done besides itself, is a perfection of the thing done, not of the doer: it stands in the relation of a means to an end, and therefore cannot be the happiness of an intellectual nature. Secondly, on the principle of activity, that it be an activity of the highest power: hence our happiness lies not in any activity of sense, but in an activity of intellect, perfected by habit. Thirdly, on the object of activity; and therefore our happiness consists in understanding the highest object of understanding. Fourthly, on the form of activity, that the action be perfect, easy, and agreeable. But the activity of God fulfils all these conditions: since it is (1) activity in the order of understanding; and (2) His understanding is the highest of faculties, not needing any habit to perfect it; and (3) His understanding is bent upon Himself, the highest of intelligible objects; and (4) He understands perfectly, without any difficulty, and with all delight. He is therefore happy.

3. Boethius says that happiness is a state made perfect by a gathering of all good things. But such is the divine perfection, which includes all perfection in one single view (Chapp. XXVIII, LIV).

4. He is happy, who is sufficient for himself and wants nothing. But God has no need of other things, seeing that His perfection depends on nothing external to

Himself; and when He wills other things for Himself as for an end, it is not that He needs them, but only that this reference befits His goodness.

5. It is impossible for God to wish for anything impossible (Chap. LXXXIV). Again it is impossible for anything to come in to Him which as yet He has not, seeing that He is nowise in potentiality (Chap. XVI). Therefore He cannot wish to have what He has not: therefore He has whatever He wishes; and He wishes nothing evil (Chap. XCV). Therefore He is happy, according to the definition given by some, that "he is happy who has what he wishes and wishes nothing evil." His happiness the Holy Scriptures declare: *Whom he will show in his own time, the blessed and powerful one* (1 Tim. vi, 15).

CHAPTER CI—That God Is His own Happiness

GOD'S happiness is the act of His understanding (Chap. C). But that very act of God's understanding is His substance (Chap. XLV). He therefore is His own happiness.

CHAPTER CII—That the Happiness of God is most perfect, and exceeds all other happiness

WHERE there is greater love, there is greater delight in the attainment of the object loved. But every being, other things being equal, loves itself more than it loves anything else: a sign of which is that, the nearer anything is to oneself, the more it is naturally loved. God therefore takes greater delight in His happiness, which is Himself, than other blessed ones in their happiness, which is not what they are.

3. What is by essence, ranks above what is by participation. But God is happy by His essence, a prerogative that can belong to no other: for nothing else but God can be the sovereign good; and thus whatever else is happy must be happy by participation from Him. The divine happiness therefore exceeds all other happiness.

4. Perfect happiness consists in an act of the understanding. But no other act of understanding can compare with God's act: as is clear, not only from this that it is a subsistent act, but also because by this one act God perfectly understands Himself as He is, and all things that are and are not, good and evil; whereas in all other intellectual beings the act of understanding is not itself subsistent, but is the act of a subsistent subject. Nor can anyone understand God, the supreme object of understanding, so perfectly as He is perfect, because the being of none is so perfect as the divine being, nor can any act ever be more perfect than the substance of which it is the act. Nor is there any other understanding that knows even all that God can do: for if it did, it would comprehend the divine power. Lastly, even what another understanding does know, it does not know all with one and the same act. God therefore is incomparably happy above all other beings.

5. The more a thing is brought to unity, the more perfect is its power and excellence. But an activity that works in succession, is divided by different divisions of time: in no way then can its perfection be compared to the perfection of an activity that is without succession, all present together, especially if it does not pass in an instant but abides to eternity. Now the divine act of

understanding is without succession, existing all together for eternity: whereas our act of understanding is in succession by the accidental attachment to it of continuity and time. Therefore the divine happiness infinitely exceeds human happiness, as the duration of eternity exceeds the 'now in flux' of time (nunc temporis fluens).

6. The fatigue and various occupations whereby our contemplation in this life is necessarily interrupted, — in which contemplation whatever happiness there is for man in this life chiefly consists, — and the errors and doubts and various mishaps to which the present life is subject, show that human happiness, in this life particularly, can in no way compare with the happiness of God.

7. The perfection of the divine happiness may be gathered from this, that it embraces all happinesses according to the most perfect mode of each. By way of contemplative happiness, it has a perfect and perpetual view of God Himself and of other beings. By way of active life, it has the government, not of one man, or of one house, or of one city, or of one kingdom, but of the whole universe. Truly, the false happiness of earth is but a shadow of that perfect happiness. For it consists, according to Boethius, in five things, in pleasure, riches, power, dignity and fame. God then has a most excellent delight of Himself, and a universal joy of all good things, without admixture of contrary element. For riches, He has absolute self-sufficiency of all good. For power, He has infinite might. For dignity, He has primacy and rule over all beings. For fame, He has the admiration of every understanding that in any sort knows Him. To Him then, who is singularly blessed, be honor and glory for ever and ever, Amen.

## CHAPTER BOOK II

CHAPTER I—Connexion of what follows with what has gone before.

THERE can be no perfect knowledge of anything unless its activity be known: for from the mode of activity proper to a thing, and the species to which it belongs, the measure and quality of its power is estimated; and the power shows the nature of the thing, for each thing is naturally active according to the nature with which it is actually endowed. But there is a twofold activity: one immanent in the agent, and a perfection of his, as feeling, understanding and willing; the other passing out to an exterior thing, and a perfection of the thing made and constituted thereby, as warming, cutting and building. Both of these acts are proper to God: the first, inasmuch as he understands, wills, rejoices and loves; the second inasmuch as He produces and brings things into being, conserves and governs them. Of the first act of God we have spoken in the previous book, treating of the divine knowledge and will. It remains now to treat of the second action, whereby things are produced and governed by God.

CHAPTER IV—That the Philosopher and the Theologian view Creatures from Different Standpoints

HUMAN philosophy considers creatures as they are in themselves: hence we find different divisions of philosophy according to the different classes of things.

But Christian faith considers them, not in themselves, but inasmuch as they represent the majesty of God, and in one way or another are directed to God, as it is said: Of the glory of the Lord his work is full: hath not the Lord made his saints to tell of his wonders?(Ecclus xlii, 16, 17.) Therefore the philosopher and the faithful Christian (fidelis) consider different points about creatures: the philosopher considers what attaches to them in their proper nature: the faithful Christian considers about creatures only what attaches to them in their relation to God, as that they are created by God, subject to God, and the like. Hence it is not to be put down as an imperfection in the doctrine of faith, if it passes unnoticed many properties of things, as the configuration of the heavens, or the laws of motion. And again such points as are considered by philosopher and faithful Christian alike, are treated on different principles: for the philosopher takes his stand on the proper and immediate causes of things; but the faithful Christian argues from the First Cause, showing that so the matter is divinely revealed, or that this makes for the glory of God, or that God's power is infinite. Hence this speculation of the faithful Christian ought to be called the highest wisdom, as always regarding the highest cause, according to the text: This is your wisdom and understanding before the nations (Deut. iv, 6). And therefore human philosophy is subordinate to this higher wisdom; and in sign of this subordination divine wisdom sometimes draws conclusions from premises of human philosophy. Further, the two systems do not observe the same order of procedure. In the system of philosophy, which considers creatures in themselves and from them leads on to the knowledge of God, the first study is of creatures and the last of God; but in the system of faith, which studies creatures only in their relation to God, the study is first of God and afterwards of creatures; and this is a more perfect view, and more like to the knowledge of God, who, knowing Himself, thence discerns other beings. Following this latter order, after what has been said in the first book about God in Himself, it remains for us to treat of the beings that come from God.

### CHAPTER V—Order of Matters to be Treated

THE order of our treatise will be to deal first with the production and bringing of things into being (Chapp VI-XXXVIII); secondly with the distinction of things (Chapp. XXXIXXLV); thirdly, with the nature of things thus produced and distinct so far as it appertains to the truth of faith (Chapp. XLVI-CI).

### CHAPTER VI—That it belongs to God to be to other Beings the Principle of Existence

IN inferior agents it is a sign of attained perfection, when they can produce their own likeness. But God is sovereignly perfect (B.I. Chap. XXVIII). Therefore it belongs to Him to make some being like Himself in actual existence.

6. The more perfect any principle of activity is, the wider its sphere of action. But that pure actuality, which is God, is more perfect than actuality mingled with potentiality, such as is in us. Now actuality is the principle

of action. Since then by the actuality which is in us, we are not only capable of immanent acts, such as understanding and willing, but also of acts tending to exterior things and productive of effects, much more can God, by virtue of His actuality, not only understand and will, but also produce an effect.

Hence it is said: Who makes great and wonderful and inscrutable works without number (Job v. 9).

## CHAPTER VII—That there is in God Active Power

AS passive power, or passivity, follows upon being in potentiality, so active power follows upon being in actuality; for everything acts by being in actuality, and is acted upon by being in potentiality. But it belongs to God to be in actuality; and therefore there is suitably ascribed to Him active power, but not passive power.

Hence it is said: Thou art powerful, O Lord (Ps. lxxxviii, 9); and Thy power and thy justice, O God, are even to the highest heaven, in the wonders that thou hast made (Ps. lxx, 18, 19).

## CHAPTER VIII—That God's Power is His Substance

ACTIVE power belongs to the perfection of a thing. But every divine perfection is contained in God's own being (B. I, Chap. XXVIII). God's power therefore is not different from his being. But God is His own being (B. I, Chap. XXII); He is therefore His own power.

4. In things the powers of which are not their substance, the said powers are accidents.4 But there can be no accident in God (B. I, Chap. XXIII), who is therefore his own power.

### CHAPTER IX—That God's Power is His Action

GOD'S power is His substance, as has been shown in the previous chapter: also His action is His substance, as has been shown of His intellectual activity (B. I, Chap. XLV), and the same argument holds of His other activities. Therefore in God power and action are not two different things.

2. The action of any being is a complement of its power; for it stands to power as the second actuality to the first. But the divine power, being God's very essence, has no other complement than itself. And therefore in God action and power are not distinct.

4. Any action that is not the agent's very substance is in the agent as an accident in its subject. But in God there can be nothing accidental. Therefore in God His action is none other than His substance and His power.

### CHAPTER X—In what manner Power is said to be in God

SINCE the divine action is nothing else than the divine power, it is manifest that power is not said to be in God as a principle of His action (for nothing is the principle of itself), but as a principle of the thing made or done: also that when power is said to be in God in respect of the things made or done by Him, this is a predication of objective fact: but when it is said to be in Him in respect of His own action, such predication regards only our way of viewing things, inasmuch as our understanding views under two different concepts God's power and God's action. Hence if there be any actions proper to God, that do not pass into anything made or done, but are immanent in the agent, in respect of these actions there is not said to be power in God except in our way of viewing things, not in objective fact. There are such actions, namely, understanding and willing. Properly speaking, the power of God does not regard these actions, but only effects produced in the world external to Him. Intellect and will, then, are in God, not as 'faculties,' or 'powers,' but only as actions. It is also clear from the aforesaid that the multitude of actions which are attributed to God, as understanding, willing, producing creatures, and the like, are not different things, since each one of these actions in God is His own being, which is one and the same.

CHAPTER XI—That something is predicated of God in relation to Creatures

SINCE power is proper to God in respect of the effects of His production, and power ranks as a principle, and a principle is so called in relation to its derivative; it is clear that something may be predicated of God in relation to the effects of His production.

2. It is unintelligible how one thing can be made a subject of predication in relation to another thing, unless contrariwise the other thing be made a subject of predication in relation to it. But other beings are made subjects of predication in relation to God, as when it is said that they have their being from God and depend on Him. God therefore must be made a subject of predication

in relation to creatures.

3. Likeness is a relation. But God, as other agents, acts to the production of His own likeness.

4. Knowledge is predicated in relation to the thing known. But God has knowledge of other beings.

5. Whatever is first and sovereign, is so in relation to others, But God is the first being and the sovereign good.

CHAPTER XII—That the Relations, predicated of God in regard to Creatures, are not really in God

THESE relations cannot be in God as accidents in a subject, seeing that in God there is no accident (B. I, Chap XXIII). Nor again can they be in the very substance of God: for then the substance of God in its very essence would be referred to another; but what is referred to another for its very essence, in a manner depends on that other, as it can neither be nor be understood without it; but this would make the substance of God dependent on another being, foreign to itself.

2. God is the first measure of all beings (B. I, Chap. XXVIII). He is to them as the object is to our knowledge, that is to say, its measure. But though the object is spoken of in relation to the knowledge of it, nevertheless the relation really is not in the object known, but only in the knowledge of it. The object is said to be in relation, not because it is itself related, but because something else is related to it.

3. The aforesaid relations are predicated of God, not only in respect of things that actually are, but also in

respect of things that potentially are, because of them also He has knowledge, and in respect of them He is called both first being and sovereign good. But what actually is bears no real relation to what is not actually but potentially. Now God is not otherwise related to things that actually are than to things that potentially are, because he is not changed by producing anything.

4. To whatsoever is added anything fresh, the thing receiving that addition must be changed, either essentially or accidentally. Now sundry fresh relations are predicated of God, as that He is lord or ruler of this thing newly come into being. If then any relation were predicated as really existing in God, it would follow that something fresh was added to God, and therefore that He had suffered some change, either essential or accidental, contrary to what was shown above (B. I, Chapp. XXIII, XXIV)

CHAPTER XIII—How the aforesaid Relations are predicated of God

IT cannot be said that the aforesaid relations are things existing outside of God. For since God is first of beings and highest of excellencies, we should have to consider other relations of God to those relations, supposing them to be things; and if the second relations again were things, we should have to invent again a third set of relations, and so on to infinity. Again, there are two ways in which a denomination may be predicated. A thing is denominated from what is outside it, as from place a man is said to be 'somewhere,' and from time 'once'; and again a thing is denominated from what is within it, as 'white' from whiteness. But from relation nothing is found to bear a denomination as from something outside itself, but only as from something within itself: thus a man is not called 'father' except from the paternity that is in him. It is impossible therefore for the relations, whereby God has relation to the creature, to be anything outside God. Since then it has been shown that they are not in Him really and yet are predicated of Him, the only possible conclusion is that they are attributed to Him merely by our mode of thought, inasmuch as other beings are in relation to Him: for when our understanding conceives that A is related to B, it further conceives that B is related to A, even though sometimes B is not really so related.

Hence it is also clear that the aforesaid relations are not predicated of God in the same way that other things are predicated of God: for all other things, as wisdom or will, are predicated of His essence, while the aforesaid relations are by no means so predicated, but only according to our mode of thought. And yet our thought is not at fault: for, by the very fact of our mind knowing that the relations of effects of divine power have God himself for their term it predicates some things of Him relatively.

CHAPTER XIV—That the Predication of many Relations of God is no prejudice to the Simplicity and Singleness of His Being

IT is no prejudice to the simplicity of God's being that many relations are predicated of Him, not as denoting anything affecting His essence, but according to our mode of thought. For our mind, understanding many things, may very well be related in manifold ways to a being that is in itself simple; and so it comes to view that simple being under manifold relations. Indeed the more simple anything is, the greater is its power, and the more numerous the effects whereof it is the principle; and thus it is viewed as coming into relation in more manifold ways. The fact then that many things are predicated of God relatively is an attestation of the supreme simplicity and singleness of His being.

CHAPTER XV—That God is to all things the Cause of their being

HAVING shown (Chap VI) that God is to some things the cause of their being, we must further show that nothing out of God has being except of Him. Every attribute that attaches to anything otherwise than as constituting its essence, attaches to it through some cause, as whiteness to man. To be in a thing independently of causation is to be there primarily and immediately, as something ordinary (per se) and essential. It is impossible for anyone attribute, attaching to two things, to attach to each as constituting its essence. What is predicated as constituent of a thing's essence, has no extension beyond that thing: as the having three angles together equal to two right angles has no extension beyond 'triangle,' of which it is predicated, but is convertible with 'triangle.' Whatever then attaches to two things, cannot attach to them both as constituting the essence of each. It is impossible therefore for any one attribute to be predicated of two subjects without its being predicated of one or the other as something come there by the operation of some cause: either one must be the cause of the other, or some third thing must be cause of both. Now 'being' is predicated of everything that is. It is impossible therefore for there to be two things, each having being independently of any cause; but either these things must both of them have being by the operation of a cause, or one must be to the other the cause of its being. Therefore everything which in any way is, must have being from that which is uncaused; that is, from God (B. I, Chap. XV).

2. What belongs to a thing by its nature, and is not dependent on any causation from without, cannot suffer diminution or defect. For if anything essential is withdrawn from or added to nature, that nature, so increased or diminished, will give place to another. If on the other hand the nature is left entire, and something else is found to have suffered diminution, it is clear that what has been so diminished does not absolutely depend on that nature, but on some other cause, by removal of which it is diminished. Whatever property therefore attaches to a thing less in one instance than in others, does not attach to that thing in mere virtue of its nature, but from the concurrence of some other cause. The cause of all effects in a particular kind will be that whereof the kind is predicated to the utmost. Thus we see that the hottest body is the cause of heat in all hot bodies, and the brightest body the cause of brightness in all bright bodies. But God is in the highest degree 'being' (B. I, Chap. XIII). He then is the cause of all things whereof 'being' is predicated.

3. The order of causes must answer to the order of effects, since effects are proportionate to their causes. Hence, as special effects are traced to special causes, so

any common feature of those special effects must be traced to some common cause. Thus, over and above the particular causes of this or that generation, the sun is the universal cause of all generation; and the king is the universal cause of government in his kingdom, over the officials of the kingdom, and also over the officials of individual cities. But being is common to all things. There must then be over all causes some Cause to whom it belongs to give being.

4. What is by essence, is the cause of all that is by participation, as fire is the cause of all things fiery, as such. But God is being by His essence because He is pure being; while every other being is being by participation, because there can only be one being that is its own existence (B. I, Chapp. XXII, XLII). God therefore is cause of being to all other beings.

5. Everything that is possible to be and not to be, has some cause: because, looked at by itself, it is indifferent either way; and thus there must be something else that determines it one way. Hence, as a process to infinity is impossible, there must be some necessary being that is cause of all things which are possible to be and not to be.

6. God in His actuality and perfection includes the perfections of all things (B. I, Chap. XXVIII); and thus He is virtually all. He is therefore the apt producing cause of all.

This conclusion is confirmed by divine authority: for it is said: *Who made heaven and earth, the sea, and all things that are therein* (Ps. cxlv, 6). And, *All things were made by him, and without him was made nothing* (John i, 3). And *From whom are all things, by whom are all things, in (unto) whom are all things* (Rom. xi, 16).

## CHAPTER XVI—That God has brought things into being out of nothing

TO every effect produced by God there is either something pre-existent or not. If not, the thesis stands, that God produces some effect out of nothing pre-existent. If anything pre-exists, we either have a process to infinity, which is impossible, or we must come to something primitive, which does not presuppose anything else previous to it. Now this primitive something cannot be God Himself, for God is not the material out of which anything is made (B. I, Chap. XVI): nor can it be any other being, distinct from God and uncaused by God (Chap. XV).

3. The more universal the effect, the higher the cause: for the higher the cause, the wider its range of efficiency. Now being is more universal than motion. Therefore above any cause that acts only by moving and transmitting must be that cause which is the first principle of being; and that we have shown to be God (B. I, Chap. XIII). God therefore does not act merely by moving and transmuting: whereas every cause that can only bring things into being out of pre-existing material acts merely in that way, for a thing is made out of material by movement or some change.

4. It is not proper to the universal cause of being, as such, to act only by movement and change: for not by movement and change is being, as such, made out of not-being, as such, but 'being this' is made out of 'not being this.' But God is the universal principle of being (Chap. XV). Therefore it is not proper to Him to act only by movement or change, or to need pre-existent material to

make anything.

5. Every agent has a term of action like itself, for its acts inasmuch as it is in actuality. Given then an agent in actuality by some form inherent in it, and not to the whole extent of its substance, it will be proper to such an agent to produce its effect by causing a form in some way inherent in matter. But God is in actuality, not by anything inhering in Him, but to the whole extent of His substance (B. I, Chap. XVIII). Therefore the proper mode of divine action is to produce the whole subsistent thing, and not a mere inherent thing, as is form in matter.

10. Between actuality and potentiality such an order obtains, that, though in one and the same being, which is sometimes in potentiality sometimes in actuality, potentiality is prior in time to actuality (although actuality is prior in nature), yet, absolutely speaking, actuality must be prior to potentiality, as is clear from this, that potentiality is not reduced to actuality except by some actual being. But matter is being in potentiality. Therefore God, first and pure actuality, must be absolutely prior to matter, and consequently cause thereof.

This truth divine Scripture confirms, saying: In the beginning God created heaven and earth (Gen. i, 1). For to create is nothing else than to bring a thing into being without any pre-existent material.

Hereby is confuted the error of the ancient philosophers, who supposed no cause at all for matter, since in the actions of particular agents they always saw some matter pre-existent to every action. Hence they took up the common opinion that nothing is made out of nothing, which indeed is true of the actions of particular agents. But they had not yet arrived at a knowledge of the universal agent, the active cause of all being, whose causative action does not necessarily suppose any pre-existent material.

## CHAPTER XVII—That Creation is not a Movement nor a Change

EVERY movement or change is the actualization of something that was in potentiality, as such: but in this action of creation there is nothing pre-existent in potentiality to become the object of the action.
2. The extremes of movement or change fall under the same order, being either of the same kind, as contraries are, or sharing one common potentiality of matter. But nothing of this can be in creation, to which no previous condition of things is supposed.
3. In every change or movement there must be something coming to be otherwise than as it was before. But where the whole substance of a thing is brought into being, there cannot be any permanent residuum, now in this condition, now in that: because such a residuum would not be produced, but presupposed to production.

## CHAPTER XVIII—Solution of Arguments against Creation

HENCE appears the futility of arguments against creation drawn from the nature of movement or change, — as that creation must be in some subject, or that non-being must be transmuted into being: for creation is not a change, but is the mere dependence of created being on the principle by which it is set up, and so comes under the category of relation: hence the subject of creation may very well be said to be the thing created. Nevertheless creation is spoken of as a 'change' according to our mode of conceiving it, inasmuch as our understanding takes one and the same thing to be now non-existent and afterwards existing. If Creation (creaturedom) is a relation, it is evidently some sort of reality; and this reality is neither uncreated, nor created by a further act of creation. For since the created effect really depends on the Creator, this relation must be a certain reality. Now every reality is brought into being by God; and therefore also this reality is brought into being by God, and yet was not created by any other creation than that of the first creature, because accidents and forms do not exist by themselves, and therefore neither are they terms of separate creation, since creation is the production of substantial being; but as they are 'in another,' so are they created in the creation of other things.

CHAPTER XIX—That Creation is not Successive

SUCCESSION is proper to movement. But creation is not movement. Therefore there is in it no succession.

2. In every successive movement there is some medium between the extremes. But between being and not-being, which are the extremes in creation, there can be no medium, and therefore no succession.

3. In every making, in which there is succession, the process of being made is before the state of achieved completion. But this cannot happen in creation, because, for the process of being made to precede the achieved completion of the creature, there would be required some subject in which the process might take place. Such a subject cannot be the creature itself, of whose creation we

are speaking, because that creature is not till the state of its achieved completion is realized. Nor can it be the Maker, because to be in movement is an actuality, not of mover, but of moved. And as for the process of being made having for its subject any pre-existing material, that is against the very idea of creation. Thus succession is impossible in the act of creation.

5. Successive stages in the making of things become necessary, owing to defect of the matter, which is not sufficiently disposed from the first for the reception of the form. Hence, when the matter is already perfectly disposed for the form, it receives it in an instant. Thus because a transparent medium is always in final disposition for light, it lights up at once in the presence of any actually shining thing. Now in creation nothing is prerequisite on the part of the matter, nor is anything wanting to the agent for action. It follows that creation takes place in an instant: a thing is at once in the act of being created and is created, as light is at once being shed and is shining.

CHAPTER XXI—That it belongs to God alone to create

SINCE the order of actions is according to the order of agents, and the action is nobler of the nobler agent, the first and highest action must be proper to the first and highest agent. But creation is the first and highest action, presupposing no other, and in all others presupposed. Therefore creation is the proper action of God alone, who is the highest agent.

2. Nothing else is the universal cause of being but God (Chap. XV).

3. Effects answer proportionally to their causes. Thus actual effects we attribute to actual causes, potential effects to potential causes, particular effects to particular causes, and universal effects to universal causes. Now the first thing caused is 'being,' as we see by its presence in all things. Therefore the proper cause of 'being,' simply as such, is the first and universal agent, which is God. Other agents are not causes of 'being,' simply as such, but causes of 'being this,' as 'man' or 'white': but 'being,' simply as such, is caused by creation, which presupposes nothing, because nothing can be outside of the extension of 'being,' simply as such. Other productions result in 'being this,' or 'being of this quality': for out of pre-existent being is made 'being this,' or 'being of this quality.'

6. Every agent that acts as an instrument completes the action of the principal agent by some action proper and connatural to itself, as a saw operates to the making of a stool by cutting. If then there be any nature that operates to creation as an instrument of the prime creator, this being must operate through some action due and proper to its own nature. Now the effect answering to the proper action of an instrument is prior in the way of production to the effect answering to the principal agent; hence it is that the final end answers to the principal agent: for the cutting of the wood is prior to the form of the stool. There must then be some effect due to the proper operation of the instrument used for creation; and this effect must be prior in the way of production to 'being': for 'being' is the effect answering to the action of the prime creator. But that is impossible: for the more general is prior in the way of generation to the more particular. Hereby is destroyed the error of certain

philosophers, who said that God created the first spirit, and by it was created the second, and so in order to the last.

## CHAPTER XXII—That God is Almighty

AS creation is the work of God alone, so whatever beings are producible only by creation must be immediately produced by Him. Such are all spirits, the existence of which for the present let us suppose, and likewise all bodily matter. These several existences are immediate effects of creative power. Now power is not determined and limited to one effect, when it is productive of several effects immediately, and that not out of any pre-existent material. I say 'immediately,' because if the production were through intermediate agents, the diversity of effects might be ascribed to those intermediate causes. I say again 'not out of any preexistent material,' because the same agent by the same action causes different effects according to the difference of material. God's power then is not determined and limited to one effect.

2. Every perfect active power is co-extensive with and covers all cases of its own proper effect: thus perfect building power would extend to everything that could be called a house. But the divine power is of itself the cause of being, and being is its proper effect. Therefore that power extends to all things that are not inconsistent with the idea of being: for if the divine power were available only for one particular effect, it would not be the ordinary cause of being, as such, but cause of 'this being.' Now what is inconsistent with the idea of 'being' is the opposite of 'being,' which is 'not-being.' God then can do

all things that do not include in themselves the element of not-being, that is to say, that do not involve a contradiction.

3. Every agent acts inasmuch as it is in actuality. According then to the mode of actuality of each agent in the mode of its active power. Now God is perfect actuality, having in Himself the perfections of all beings (B. I, Chap. XXVIII): therefore His active power extends to all things that are not inconsistent with actual being.

5. There are three ways in which an effect may not be in the power of an agent. In one way, because it has no affinity or likeness to the agent, for every agent acts to the production of its own likeness somehow: hence man cannot be the parent of brute or plant, though he can be parent of man, who is more than they. In another way, on account of the excellence of the effect, transcending the compass of the active power: thus the active power of matter cannot produce spirit. In a third way, on account of the material being determined to some effect, and the agent having no power over it: thus a carpenter cannot make a saw, because his art gives him no power over iron. But in none of these ways can an effect be withdrawn from the divine power: not for the unlikeness of the effect, since every being, in so much as it has being, is like God (Chap. XV): nor again for the excellence of the effect, since God is above all in goodness and perfection (B. I, Chapp. XXVIII, XLI): nor lastly for the defect of the material, since God in His action needs no material (Chap. XVI).

This also is taught by divine Scripture as a tenet of faith. *I am God Almighty, walk before me and be perfect* (Gen. xvii, 1): *I know that thou canst do all things* (Job xlii, 2): *No word shall be impossible with God* (Luke i,

37).

Hereby is excluded the error of sundry philosophers, who have laid it down that God can do nothing except according to the course of nature. On such it is said: As though the Almighty had no power, they reckoned of him (Job xxii, 17).

CHAPTER XXIII—That God's Action in Creation is not of Physical Necessity, but of Free Choice of Will

THE power of every necessary agent is determined and limited to one effect. That is the reason why all physical effects always come out in the same way, unless there be some interference: but acts of the will not so. But the divine power is not directed to one effect only (Chap. XXII). God then does not act by physical necessity, but by will.

2. Whatever does not involve a contradiction, is within the range of the divine power. But many things that do not exist in creation would still involve no contradiction if they did exist. This is most evidently the case in regard of the number and size and distances of the stars and other bodies. They would present no contradiction, no intrinsic absurdity, if they were arranged on another plan. Many things therefore lie within the range of divine power that are not found in nature. But whoever does some and leaves out others of the things that he can do, acts by choice of will and not by physical necessity.

4. Since God's action is His substance (B. I, Chap. LXXIII), the divine action cannot come under the category of those acts that are 'transient' and not in the

agent, but must be an act 'immanent' in the agent, such as are acts of knowing and desiring, and none other. God therefore acts and operates by knowing and willing.

6. A self-determined agent is prior to an agent determined from without: for all that is determined from without is reducible to what is self-determined, or we should have process to infinity. But he who is not master of his own action is not self-determined: for he acts as led by another, not as his own leader. The prime agent then must act in such a way as to remain master of his own action. But no one is master of his own action except he be a voluntary agent.

7. Will-action is naturally prior to physical action: for that is naturally prior which is more perfect, albeit in the individual it be posterior in time. But will-action is the more perfect, as within our experience voluntary agents are more perfect than physical. Therefore will-action must be assigned to God, the prime agent.

8. Where will-action and physical action go together, will-action represents the higher power and uses the other as an instrument. But the divine power is supreme, and therefore must act by will-action, not under physical necessity.

This truth also divine Scripture teaches us. All things, whatsoever he hath willed, the Lord hath done (Ps. cxxxiv, 6): Who worked all things according to the counsel of his will (Eph. i, 11).

CHAPTER XXIV—That God acts by His Wisdom

THE will is moved by some apprehension. But God acts by willing. Since then in God there is intellectual apprehension only, and He understands nothing otherwise than by understanding Himself, whom to understand is to be wise (B. I, Chap. LIV), it follows that God works out all things according to His wisdom.

2. Every agent acts in so far as it has within it something corresponding to the effect to be produced. But in every voluntary agent, as such, what corresponds to the effect to be produced is some intellectual presentation of the same. Were there no more than a mere physical disposition to produce the effect, the agent could act only to one effect, because for one physical cause there is only one physical mode of operation (ratio naturalis unius est una tantum). Every voluntary agent therefore produces its effect according to the mode of intellectual operation proper to itself. But God acts by willing, and therefore it is by the wisdom of His intellect that he brings things into being.

3. The function of wisdom is to set things in order. Now the setting of things in order can be effected only through a knowledge of the relation and proportion of the said things to one another, and to some higher thing which is the end and purpose of them all: for the mutual order of things to one another is founded upon their order to the end which they are to serve. But it is proper to intelligence alone to know the mutual relations and proportions of things. Again, it is proper to wisdom to judge of things as they stand to their highest cause. Thus every setting of things in order by wisdom must be the work of some intelligence. But the things produced by God bear an orderly relation to one another, which cannot be attributed to chance, since it (sit not sint) obtains always or for the most part. Thus it is evident that God, in bringing things into being, intended them in a certain

order. Therefore His production of them was a work of wisdom.

All this is confirmed by divine authority, for it is said: Thou has made all things in wisdom (Ps. ciii, 24); and the Lord in wisdom founded the earth (Prov. iii, 19).

Hereby is excluded the error of some who said that all things depend on the absolute will of God, independent of any reason.

CHAPTER XXV—In what sense some things are said to be Impossible to the Almighty

IN God there is active power, but no potentiality. Now possibility is spoken of both as involving active power and as involving potentiality. Those things then are impossible to God, the possibility of which would mean in Him potentiality. Examples: God cannot be any material thing: He cannot suffer change, nor defect, nor fatigue, nor forgetfulness, nor defeat, nor violence, nor repentance, anger, or sadness.

Again, since the object and effect of active power is some produced reality, it must be said to be impossible for God to make or produce anything inconsistent with the notion of 'reality,' or 'being,' as such, or inconsistent with the notion of a reality that is 'made,' or 'produced,' inasmuch as it is 'made,' or 'produced.' Examples: God cannot make one and the same thing together to be and not to be. He cannot make opposite attributes to be in the same subject in the same respect. He cannot make a thing wanting in any of its essential constituents, while the thing itself remains: for instance, a man without a soul.

Since the principles of some sciences, as logic, geometry, and arithmetic, rest on the formal, or abstract, constituents on which the essence of a thing depends, it follows that God cannot effect anything contrary to these principles, as that genus should not be predicable of species, or that lines drawn from the center of a circle to the circumference should not be equal. God cannot make the past not to have been. Some things also God cannot make, because they would be inconsistent with the notion of a creature, as such: thus He cannot create a God, or make anything equal to Himself, or anything that shall maintain itself in being, independently of Him. He cannot do what He cannot will: He cannot make Himself cease to be, or cease to be good or happy; nor can He will anything evil, or sin. Nor can His will be changeable: He cannot therefore cause what He has once willed not to be fulfilled. There is however this difference between this last impossibility on God's part and all others that have been enumerated. The others are absolute impossibilities for God either to will or do: but the things now spoken of God might will and do if His will or power be considered absolutely, but not if it be considered under the presupposition of His will to the contrary. And therefore all such phrases as, 'God cannot act contrary to what He has arranged to do,' are to be understood in *sensu composito*; but, understood in *sensu diviso*, they are false, for in that sense they regard the power and will of God considered absolutely.

CHAPTER XXVI—That the Divine Understanding is not limited to certain fixed Effects

NOW that it has been shown (Chap. XXIII) that

the divine power does not act of physical necessity, but by understanding and will, lest anyone should think that God's understanding or knowledge extend only to certain fixed effects, and that thus God acts under stress of ignorance, though not under stress of physical constraint, it remains to show that His knowledge or understanding is bounded by no limits in its view of effects.

2. We have shown above (B. I, Chap. XLIII) the infinity of the divine essence. Now the plane of the infinite can never be reached by any piling up of finite quantities, because the infinite infinitely transcends any finite quantities however many, even though they were infinite in number. But no other being than God is infinite in essence: all others are essentially included under limited genera and species. Howsoever then and to whatsoever extent the effects of divine production are comprehended, it is ever within the compass of the divine essence to reach beyond them and to be the foundation of more. The divine understanding then, in perfectly knowing the divine essence (B. I, Chap. XLVII), transcends any infinity of actual effects of divine power and therefore is not necessarily limited to these or those effects.

4. If the causality of the divine understanding were limited, as a necessary agent, to any effects, it would be to those effects which God actually brings into being. But it has been shown above (B. I, Chap. LXVI) that God understands even things that neither are nor shall be nor have been.

5. The divine knowledge stands to the things produced by God as the knowledge of an artist to the knowledge of his art. But every art extends to all that can possibly be contained under the kind of things subject to

that art, as the art of building to all houses. But the kind of thing subject to the divine art is 'being' (genus subjectum divinae artis est ens), since God by His understanding is the universal principal of being (Chapp. XXI, XXIV). Therefore the divine understanding extends its causality to all things that are not inconsistent with the notion of 'being,' and is not limited to certain fixed effects.

Hence it is said: Great is our Lord, and great his power, and of his wisdom; there is no reckoning by number (Ps. cxlvi, 5).

Hereby is excluded the position of some philosophers who said that from God's understanding of Himself there emanates a certain arrangement of things in the universe, as though He did not deal with creatures at His discretion fixing the limits of each creature and arranging the whole universe, as the Catholic faith professes. It is to be observed however that, though the divine understanding is not limited to certain effects, God nevertheless has determined to Himself fixed effects to be produced in due order by His wisdom, as it is said: Thou hast disposed all things in measure, number and weight(Wisd. xi, 21).

CHAPTER XXVIII—That God has not brought things into being in discharge of any Debt of Justice

JUSTICE is to another, rendering him his due. But, antecedently to the universal production of all things, nothing can be presupposed to which anything is due.

2. An act of justice must be preceded by some act, whereby something is made another's own; and that act, whereby first something is made another's own, cannot be an act of justice. But by creation a created thing first

begins to have anything of its own. Creation then cannot proceed from any debt of justice.

3. No man owes anything to another, except inasmuch as he in some way depends on him, receiving something from him. Thus every man is in his neighbor's debt on God's account; from whom we have received all things. But God depends on none, and needs nothing of any.

5. Though nothing created precedes the universal production of all things, something uncreated does precede it: for the divine goodness precedes as the end and prime motive of creation, according to Augustine, who says: "Because God is good, we exist" (De Verb. Apost. Serm.13). But the divine goodness needs nothing external for its perfection. Nor is it necessary, for all that God wills His own goodness, that He should will the production of things other than Himself. God wills His own goodness necessarily, but He does not necessarily will other things. Therefore the production of creatures is not a debt of necessity to the divine goodness. But, taking justice in the wider sense of the term, there may be said to be justice in the creation of the world, inasmuch as it befits the divine goodness.

7. But if we consider the divine plan, according as God has planned it in His understanding and will to bring things into being, from that point of view the production of things does proceed from the necessity of the divine plan (B. I, Chap. LXXXIII): for it is impossible for God to have planned the doing of anything, and afterwards not to do it. Thus fulfilment is necessarily due to His every plan. But this debt is not sufficient to constitute a claim of justice, properly so called, in the action of God creating the world: for justice, properly so called, is not of self to

self.

Hence it is said: Who hath first given to Him, and recompense shall be made him? (Rom. xi, 35.) Who hath first given to me, that I may repay him? (Job xli, 2.)

Hereby is shut out the error of some who have tried to prove that God can do no otherwise than as He does, because He can do no otherwise than as He owes, or ought.

CHAPTER XXIX—How in the Production of a Creature there may be found a debt of Justice in respect of the necessary Sequence of something posterior upon something prior I

SPEAK here of what is prior, not in order of time merely, but by nature. The debt is not absolute, but conditional, of the form: 'If this is to be, this must go before.' According to this necessity a triple debt is found in the production of creatures. First, when the conditional proceeds from the whole universe of things to some particular part requisite for the perfection of the universe. Thus, if God willed the universe to be such as it is, it was due that He should make the sun and water and the like, without which the universe cannot be. Second, when the conditional proceeds from one creature to another. Thus, if God willed man to be, He was obliged to make plants and animals and such like, which man needs to his perfect being: though God has made both the one and the other out of His mere will. Third, when the conditional proceeds from the existence of the individual creature to its parts and properties and accidents, on which the creature depends for its being or perfection. Thus, supposing that God wished to make man, it was due, on this supposition, that He should unite in him soul and body, senses, and other appurtenances, intrinsic and extrinsic. In all these matters, rightly considered, God is not said to be a debtor to the creature, but a debtor to the fulfilment of His own plan.

On these explanations of the meaning of the term 'debt' and 'due,' natural justice is found in the universe both in respect of the creation of things and in respect of their propagation; and therefore God is said to have established and to govern all things justly and reasonably. Thus then is shut out a two-fold error: on the one hand of those who would limit the divine power, saying that God can do only as He does, because so He is bound to do; on the other, of those who say that all things follow on His sheer will, and that no other reason is to be sought or assigned in creation than that God wills it so.

CHAPTER XXX—How Absolute Necessity may have place in Creation

ALTHOUGH all things depend on the will of God as their first cause, and this first cause is not necessitated in its operation except on the supposition of its own purpose, not for that however is absolute necessity excluded from creation, need we aver that all things are contingent.

1. There are things in creation which simply and absolutely must be. Those things simply and absolutely must be, in which there is no possibility of their not being. Some things are so brought into being by God that there is in their nature a potentiality of not being: which happens

from this, that the matter in them is in potentiality to receive another form. Those things then in which either there is no matter, or, if there is any, it is not open to receive another form, have no potentiality of not being: such things then simply and absolutely must be. If it be said that things which are of nothing, of themselves tend to nothingness, and thus there is in all creatures a potentiality of not being, — it is manifest that such a conclusion does not follow. For things created by God are said to tend to nothingness only in the way in which they are from nothing; and that is only in respect of the power of the agent who has created them. Thus then creatures have no potentiality of not being: but there is in the Creator a power of giving them being or of stopping the influx of being to them.

4. The further a thing is distant from the self-existent, that is, from God, the nigher it is to not being; and the nigher it is to God, the further it is withdrawn from not being. Those things therefore which are nighest to God, and therefore furthest removed from not being, — in order that the hierarchy of being (ordo rerum) may be complete, — must be such as to have in themselves no potentiality of not being, or in other words, their being must be absolutely necessary.

We observe therefore that, considering the universe of creatures as they depend on the first principles of all things, we find that they depend on the will (of God), — not as necessarily arising therefrom, except by an hypothetical, or consequent necessity, as has been explained (Chap. XXVIII). But, compared with proximate and created principles, we find some things having an absolute necessity. There is no absurdity in causes being originally brought into being without any necessity, and yet, once they are posited in being, having such and such an effect necessarily following from them. That such natures were produced by God, was voluntary on His part: but that, once established, a certain effect proceeds from them, is a matter of absolute necessity. What belongs to a thing by reason of its essential principles, must obtain by absolute necessity in all things.

CHAPTER XXXI—That it is not necessary for Creatures to have existed from Eternity

IF either the entire universe or any single creature necessarily exists, this necessity must arise either from the being itself or from some other being. From the being itself it cannot arise: for every being must be from the first being; and what has not being of itself, cannot necessarily exist of itself. But if this supposed necessity arises from another being, that is, from some extrinsic cause, then, we observe, an extrinsic cause is either efficient or final. Now an effect necessarily arising from an efficient cause means that the agent acts of necessity: when the agent does not act of necessity, neither is it absolutely necessary for the effect to arise. But God does not act under any necessity in the production of creatures (Chap. XXIII). So far therefore as the efficient cause is concerned, there is not any absolute necessity for any creature to be. Neither is there any such necessity in connexion with the final cause. For means to an end receive necessity from their end only in so far as without them the end either cannot be at all, or cannot well be.

Now the end proposed to the divine will in the production of things can be no other than God's own goodness, as has been shown (B. I, Chap. LXXV): which goodness depends on creatures neither for its being nor for its wellbeing (B. I, Chapp. XIII, XXVIII). There is then no absolute necessity for the being of any creature: nor is it necessary to suppose creation always to have existed.

3. It is not necessary for God to will creation to be at all (B. I, Chap. LXXXI): therefore it is not necessary for God to will creation always to have been.

CHAPTER XXXII, XXXV—Reasons alleged for the Eternity of the World on the part of God, with Answers to the same

ARG. 1. Every agent that is not always in action, suffers some change when it comes to act. But God suffers no change, but is ever in act in the same way; and from His action created things come to be: therefore they always have been.

Reply (Chap. XXXV). There is no need of God suffering any change for fresh effects of His power coming to be. Novelty of effect can only indicate change in the agent in so far as it shows novelty of action. Any new action in the agent implies some change in the same, at least a change from rest to activity. But a fresh effect of God's power does not indicate any new action in God, since His action is His essence (B. I, Chap. XLV).

Arg. 2. The action of God is eternal: therefore the things created by God have been from eternity.

Reply. That does not follow. For, as shown above (Chap. XXIII), though God acts voluntarily in creation, yet it does not follow that there need be any action on His part intermediate between the act of His will and the effect of the same, as in us the action of our motor activities is so intermediate. With God to understand and will is to produce; and the effect produced follows upon the understanding and will according to the determination of the understanding and the command of the will. But as by the understanding there is determined the production of the thing, and its every other condition, so there is also prescribed for it the time at which it is to be; just as any art determines not only that a thing be of this or that character, but also that it be at this or that time, as the physician fixes the time for giving the medicine. Thus, assuming God's will to be of itself effectual for the production of an effect, the effect would follow fresh from the ancient will, without any fresh action coming to be put forth on the part of God.

Arg. 3. Given a sufficient cause, the effect will ensue: otherwise it would be possible, when the cause was posited, for the effect either to be or not to be. At that rate, the sequence of effect upon cause would be possible and no more. But what is possible requires something to reduce it to act: we should have therefore to suppose a cause whereby the effect was reduced to act, and thus the first cause would not be sufficient. But God is the sufficient cause of the production of creatures: otherwise He must be in potentiality, and become a cause by some addition, which is clearly absurd.

Reply. Though God is the sufficient cause of the production and bringing forth of creatures into being, yet the effect of His production need not be taken to be eternal. For, given a sufficient cause, there follows its effect, but not an effect alien from the cause. Now the proper effect of the will is that that should be which the will wants. If it were anything else than what the will wanted, not the proper effect of the cause would be secured, but a foreign effect. Now as the will wishes that this should be of this or that nature, so it also wishes that it should be at this or that time. Hence, for will to be a sufficient cause, it is requisite that the effect should be when the will wishes it to be. The case is otherwise with physical agencies: they cannot wait: physical action takes place according as nature is ready for it: there the effect must follow at once upon the complete being of the cause. But the will does not act according to the mode of its being, but according to the mode of its purpose; and therefore, as the effect of a physical agent follows the being of the agent, if it is sufficient, so the effect of a voluntary agent follows the mode of purpose.

Arg.4. A voluntary agent does not delay the execution of his purpose except in expectation of some future condition not yet realized. And this unfulfilled futurity is sometimes in the agent himself, as when maturity of active power or the removal of some hindrance is the condition expected: sometimes it is without the agent, as when there is expected the presence of someone before whom the action is to take place, or the arrival of some opportune time that is not yet come. A complete volition is at once carried into effect by the executive power, except for some defect in that power. Thus at the command of the will a limb is at once moved, unless there be some break-down in the motor apparatus. Therefore, when any one wishes to do a thing and it is not at once done, that must be either for some defect of power, the removal of which has to be waited for, or because of the incompleteness of the volition to do the thing. I call it 'completeness of volition,' when there is a will absolutely to do the thing, anyhow. The volition I say is 'incomplete,' when there is no will absolutely to do the thing, but the will is conditioned on the existence of some circumstance not yet present, or the withdrawal of some present impediment. But certainly, whatever God now wills to be, He has from eternity willed to be. No new motion of the will can come upon Him: no defect or impediment can have clogged His power: there can have been nothing outside Himself for Him to wait for in the production of the universe, since there is nothing else uncreated save Him alone (Chapp. VI, XV). It seems therefore necessary that God must have brought the creature into being from all eternity.

Reply. The object of the divine will is not the mere being of the creature, but its being at a certain time. What is thus willed, namely, the being of the creature at that time, is not delayed: because the creature began to exist then exactly when God from eternity arranged that it should begin to exist.

Arg.5. An intellectual agent does not prefer one alternative to another except for some superiority of the one over the other. But where there is no difference, there can be no superiority. But between one non-existence and another non-existence there can be no difference, nor is one non-existence preferable to another. But, looking beyond the entire universe, we find nothing but the eternity of God. Now in nothing there can be assigned no difference of instants, that a thing should be done in one instant rather than in another. In like manner neither in eternity, which is all uniform and simple (B. I, Chap. XV), can there be any difference of instants. It follows that the will of God holds itself in one unvarying attitude to the production of creatures throughout the whole of eternity. Either therefore His will is that creation never be realized at all under His eternity, or that it always be realized.

    Reply. It is impossible to mark any difference of parts of any duration antecedent to the beginning of all creation, as the fifth objection supposed that we could do. For nothingness has neither measure nor duration, and the eternity of God has no parts, no before and no after. We cannot therefore refer the beginning of all creation to any severally marked points in any pre-existing measure. There are no such points for the beginning of creation to be referred to according to any relation of agreement or divergence. Hence it is impossible to demand any reason in the mind of the agent why he should have brought the creature into being in this particular marked instant of duration rather than in that other instant preceding or following. God brought into being creation and time simultaneously. There is no account to be taken therefore why He produced the creature now, and not before, but only why the creature has not always been. There is an analogy in the case of place: for particular bodies are produced in a particular time and also in a particular place; and, because they have about them a time and a place within which they are contained, there must be a reason assignable why they are produced in this place and this time rather than in any other: but in regard of the whole stellar universe (coelum), beyond which there is no place, and along with which the universal place of all things is produced, no account is to be taken why it is situated here and not there. In like manner in the production of the whole creation, beyond which there is no time, and simultaneously with which time is produced, no question is to be raised why it is now and not before, but only why it has not always been, or why it has come to be after not being, or why it had any beginning.

Arg.6. Means to the end have their necessity from the end, especially in voluntary actions. So long then as the end is uniform, the means to the end must be uniform or uniformly produced, unless they come to stand in some new relation to the end. Now the end of creatures proceeding from the divine will is the divine goodness, which alone can be the end in view of the divine will. Since then the divine goodness is uniform for all eternity, alike in itself and in comparison with the divine will, it seems that creatures must be uniformly brought into being by the divine will for all eternity. It cannot be said that any new relation to the end supervenes upon them, so long as the position is clung to that they had no being at all before a certain fixed time, at which they are supposed to have begun to be.

Reply. Though the end of the divine will can be none other than the divine goodness, still the divine will has not to work to bring this goodness into being, in the way that the artist works to set up the product of his art, since the divine goodness is eternal and unchangeable and incapable of addition. Nor does God work for His goodness as for an end to be won for Himself, as a king works to win a city: for God is His own goodness. He works for this end, only inasmuch as He produces an effect which is to share in the end. In such a production of things for an end, the uniform attitude of end to agent is not to be considered reason enough for an everlasting work. Rather we should consider the bearing of the end on the effect produced to serve it. The one evinced necessity is that of the production of the effect in the manner better calculated to serve the end for which it is produced.

Arg. 7. Since all things, so far as they have being, share in the goodness of God; the longer they exist, the more they share of that goodness: hence also the perpetual being of the species is said to be divine. But the divine goodness is infinite. Therefore it is proper to it to communicate itself infinitely, and not for a fixed time only.

Reply. It was proper for the creature, in such likeness as became it, to represent the divine goodness. Such representation cannot be by way of equality: it can only be in such way as the higher and greater is represented by the lower and less. Now the excess of the divine goodness above the creature is best expressed by this, that creatures have not always been in existence: for thereby it appears that all other beings but God Himself have God for the author of their being; and that His power is not tied to producing effects of one particular character, as physical nature produces physical effects, but that He is a voluntary and intelligent agent.

CHAPTERS XXXIII, XXXVI—Reasons alleged for the Eternity of the World on the part Creatures, with answers to the same

ARG. 1. There are creatures in which there is no potentiality of not being (see Chap. XXX): it is impossible for them not to be, and therefore they always must be.

Reply (Chap. XXXVI). The necessity of such creatures being is only a relative necessity, as shown above (Chap. XXX): it does not involve the creature's always having been: it does not follow upon its substance:

but when the creature is already established in being, this necessity involves the impossibility of its not-being.

Arg.3. Every change must either go on everlastingly, or have some other change preceding it. But change always has been: therefore also changeable things: therefore creatures.

Reply. It has already been shown (Chapp. XII, XVII) that without any change in God, the agent, He may act to the production of a new thing, that has not always been. But if a new thing may be produced by Him, He may also originate a process of change.

Arg.5. If time is perpetual, motion must be perpetual, time being the 'record of motion.' But time must be perpetual: for time is inconceivable without a present instant, as a line is inconceivable without a point: now a present instant is always inconceivable without the ending of a past and the beginning of a future instant; and thus every given present instant has before it a time preceding and after it a time succeeding, and so there can be no first or last time. It follows that created substances in motion have been from eternity.

Reply. This argument rather supposes than proves the eternity of motion. The reason why the same instant is the beginning of the future and the end of the past is because any given phase of motion is the beginning and end of different phases. There is no showing that every instant must be of this character, unless it be assumed that every given phase of time comes between motion going before and motion following after, which is tantamount to assuming the perpetuity of motion. Assuming on the contrary that motion is not perpetual, one may say that the first instant of time is the beginning of the future, and not the end of any past instant. Even in any particular case of motion we may mark a phase which is the beginning only of movement and not the end of any: otherwise every particular case of motion would be perpetual, which is impossible.

Arg.6. If time has not always been, we may mark a non-existence of time prior to its being. In like manner, if it is not always to be, we may mark a non-existence of it subsequent to its being. But priority and subsequence in point of duration cannot be unless time is; and at that rate time must have been before it was, and shall be after it has ceased, which is absurd. Time then must be eternal. But time is an accident, and cannot be without a subject. But the subject of it is not God, who is above time and beyond motion (B. I, Chapp. XIII, XV). The only alternative left is that some created substance must be eternal.

Reply. There is nothing in this argument to evince that the very supposition of time not being supposes that time is (read, Si ponitur tempus non esse, ponatur esse). For when we speak of something prior to the being of time, we do not thereby assert any real part of time, but only an imaginary part. When we say, 'Time has being after not being', we mean that there was no instant of time before this present marked instant: as when we say that there is nothing above the stellar universe, we do not mean that there is any place beyond the stellar universe, which may be spoken of as 'above' it, but that above it there is no 'place' at all.

CHAPTER XXXIV, XXXVII—Reasons alleged for the Eternity of the World on the part of the Creative Process itself, with Answers to the same

ARG. 1. It is the common opinion of all philosophers, and therefore it must be true, that nothing is made of nothing (Aristotle, Physics, B. I, Chapp. VII, VIII). Whatever is made, then, must be made of something; and that again, if it is made at all, must be made of something else. But this process cannot go on to infinity; and therefore we must come to something that was not made. But every being that has not always been must have been made. Therefore that out of which all things are first made must be something everlasting. That cannot be God, because He cannot be the material of anything. Therefore there must be something eternal outside God, namely, primordial matter.64

Reply (Chap. XXXVII). The common position of philosophers, that nothing is made of nothing, is true of the sort of making that they considered. For all our knowledge begins in sense, which is of singular objects; and human investigation has advanced from particular to general considerations. Hence, in studying the beginning of things, men gave their attention to the making of particular things in detail. The making of one sort of being out of another sort is the making of some particular being, inasmuch as it is 'this being,' not as it is 'being' generally: for some prior being there was that now is changed into 'this being.' But entering more deeply into the origin of things, philosophers came finally to consider the issuing of all created being from one first cause (Chapp. XV, XVI). In this origin of all created being from God, it is impossible to allow any making out of pre-existent material: for such making out of pre-existent material would not be a making of the whole being of the creature. This first making of the universe was not attained to in the thought of the early physicists, whose common opinion it was that nothing was made of nothing: or if any did attain to it, they considered that such a term as 'making' did not properly apply to it, since the name 'making' implies movement or change, whereas in this origin of all being from one first being there can be no question of the transmutation of one being into another (Chap. XVII). Therefore it is not the concern of physical science to study this first origin of all things: that study belongs to the metaphysician, who deals with being in general and realities apart from motion. We may however by a figure of speech apply the name of 'making' to creation, and speak of things as 'made,' whatsoever they are, the essence or nature whereof has its origin from other being.

Arg.2. Everything that takes a new being is now otherwise than as it was before: that must come about by some movement or change: but all movement or change is in some subject: therefore before anything is made there must be some subject of motion.

Reply. The notion of motion or change is foisted in here to no purpose: for what nowise is, is not anywise, and affords no hold for the conclusion that, when it begins to be, it is otherwise than as it was before.

These then are the reasons which some hold to as demonstrative, and necessarily evincing that creatures have always existed, wherein they contradict the Catholic faith, which teaches that nothing but God has always existed, and that all else has had a beginning of being except the one eternal God. Thus then it evidently appears that there is nothing to traverse our assertion, that the world has not always existed. And this the Catholic faith teaches: In the beginning God created heaven and earth (Gen. i, 1): and, Before he made anything, from the beginning (Prov. viii, 22).

CHAPTER XXXVIII—Arguments wherewith some try to show that the World is not Eternal, and Solutions of the same

ARG. 1. God is the cause of all things (Chap. XV). But a cause must be prior in duration to the effects of its action.
Reply. That is true of things that act by motion, for the effect is not till the termination of the motion: but with causes that act instantaneously there is no such necessity.

Arg.2. Since the whole of being is created by God, it cannot be said to be made out of any being: whence the conclusion follows that it is made out of nothing, and consequently that it has existence after not existing.
Reply. To the notion of being made out of something, if that is not admitted one must supply the contradictory notion: which contradictory notion is not being made out of anything. Observe, it is not being made out of nothing, except in the former sense of not being made out of anything.

Arg.3. It is not possible to pass through infinity. But if the world always had been, infinity would have been passed through by this time, there being infinite days, or daily rounds of the sun, if the world always has been.
Reply. An infinite quantity, though not existing in simultaneous actual realization, may nevertheless be in succession, because every infinite, so taken, is really finite. Any given round of the sun could be passed, because so far the number of them was finite: but when they are all viewed together, on the supposition that the

world had always existed, it would be impossible to fix upon any first day, and so to make any transition from that to the present day, since transition always requires two extreme points.

Arg 4. It would follow that addition is made to the infinite, because to past days, or sunrounds, a new round is daily added.

Reply. There is nothing to hinder addition to the infinite on that side on which it is finite. Supposing time eternal, it must be infinite as preceding, but finite as succeeding, for the present is the limit of the past.

Arg.5. It would follow in a world always existing that we should have an infinite series of efficient causes, father being cause of child, and grandfather to father, and so to infinity.

Reply. The impossibility of an infinite series of efficient causes, according to philosophers (Aristotle, Metaph. ii, 2), holds for causes acting together: because then the effect has to depend on an infinity of co-existent actions; and the infinity of causes there is essential, the whole infinite multitude of them being requisite for the production of the effect. But in the case of causes not acting together no such impossibility holds, in the opinion of those who suppose an endless series of generations. The infinity in this case is accidental to the causes: for to Socrates's father, as such, it is quite an accident whether he be the son of another man or no: whereas to a stick, inasmuch as it moves a stone, it is not an accident whether it be moved by an hand: for it only moves inasmuch as it is moved.

Arg. 6. It would follow that an infinite multitude exists, to wit, the immortal souls of infinite men who have been in the past.

Reply. This objection is more difficult: nevertheless the argument is not of much use, because it supposes many things. Since these reasons, alleged by some to prove that the world has not always existed, are not necessarily conclusive, though they have a certain probability, it is sufficient to touch on them slightly, without insisting too much, that the Catholic faith may not seem to rest on empty reasonings, and not rather on the solid basis of the teaching of God.

CHAPTER XLI—That the Variety of Creatures does not arise from any Contrariety of Prime Agents

IF the diversity of things proceeds from diversity or contrariety of diverse agents, this would seem to hold especially of the contrariety of good and evil, so that all good things should proceed from a good principle, and evils from an evil principle. Now there is good and evil in all genera. But there cannot be one first principle of all evils: for the very essence of such a principle would be evil, and that is impossible. Everything that is, inasmuch as it is a being, must necessarily be good: for it loves and strives to preserve its own being, a sign whereof is this fact that everything fights against its own destruction: now what all things seek is good. It is impossible therefore for the diversity of things to arise from two principles, one good and one evil.

9. What in no manner of way is, is neither good nor evil: while everything that is, in so far as it is, is good. A thing can be evil therefore only inasmuch as it is not-being, that is, privative being; and the evil is precisely the privation. Now privation never comes of the ordinary

action of any cause: because every cause acts inasmuch as it is endowed with 'form'; and thus the ordinary effect of its action must also be endowed with 'form,' since every agent acts to the production of its own likeness, unless it be accidentally hindered. It follows that evil does not come of the ordinary action of any cause, but is accidentally incident among the effects of ordinary causation. There is therefore no one primary and essential principle of all evil: but the first principle of all is one primary good, among the effects of which there ensues evil incidentally.

Hence it is said: I am the Lord, and there is none other, forming light and creating darkness, making peace and creating evil: I am the Lord doing all these things (Isa. xlv, 6, 7). And, Good things and evil things, life and death, poverty and rank are from God (Ecclus xi, 14). And, Against evil is good, and against life death; so against the just man is the sinner. And so behold all the works of the Most High, two and two, and one against one (Ecclus xxxiii, 15).

God is said to make and create evil things, inasmuch as He creates things that are good in themselves and yet hurtful to others: thus the wolf, though a good thing naturally in his kind, is evil to the sheep. Hence it is said: Shall there be evil in the city that the Lord hath not done? (Amos iii, 6.)

Hereby is excluded the error of those who suppose two primitive contrary principles, good and evil. This error of the early philosophers some evil-minded men have presumed to introduce into Christian teaching, the first of whom was Marcion, and afterwards the Manicheans, who have done most to spread this error.

CHAPTER XLIV—That the Variety of Creatures has not arisen from Variety of Merits and Demerits

ORIGEN in his book περὶ ἀρχῶν says that God out of mere bounty in His first production of creatures made them all equal, all spiritual and rational, and they by free will behaved in various ways, some adhering to God more or less, and others receding from Him more or less; and thus by order of divine justice various grades ensued among spiritual substances, some appearing as angels of various orders, some as human souls also of various states and conditions, some again as demons in various states. He also said that it was through this variety of rational creatures that God instituted a variety also of material creatures, so that the nobler spiritual substances should be united to the nobler bodies, and that in divers other ways the material creation might serve to express the variety of spiritual substances. According to Origen, man, sun, and stars are composed of rational substances united with corresponding bodies. Now all this opinion can be shown to be manifestly false.

1. The better a thing is, the higher place does it hold in the intention of the agent who produces it. But the best thing in creation is the perfection of the universe, which consists in the orderly variety of things: for in all things the perfection of the whole is preferable to the perfection of parts and details. Therefore the diversity of creatures does not arise from diversity of merits, but was primarily intended by the prime agent.

2. If all rational creatures were created equal from the beginning, we should have to allow that they do not depend for their activity one on another. What arises by the concurrence of divers causes working independently

of one another is matter of chance; and thus the diversity and order of creation comes by chance, which is impossible.

12. Since a spiritual creature, or angel, does not deserve to be degraded except for sin, — and it is degraded from its high, invisible estate, by being united with a visible body, — it seems that visible bodies have been added to these spiritual creatures because of sin; which comes near to the error of the Manicheans, who laid it down that the visible creation proceeded from an evil principle.

Origen seems not to have given sufficient weight to the consideration that, when we give, not in discharge of any debt, but out of liberality, it is not contrary to justice if we give in unequal measure: but God brought things into being under no debt, but of sheer liberality (Chap. XXVIII): therefore the variety of creatures does not presuppose variety of merits.

CHAPTER XLV—The Real Prime Cause of the Variety of Creatures.

SINCE every agent intends to induce its own likeness in the effect, so far as the effect can receive it, an agent will do this more perfectly the more perfect itself is. But God is the most perfect of agents: therefore it will belong to Him to induce His likeness in creation most perfectly, so far as befits created nature. But creatures cannot attain to any perfect likeness of God so long as they are confined to one species of creature; because, since the cause exceeds the effect, what is in the cause simply and as one thing is found in the effect in a composite and manifold way, unless the effect be of the same species as the cause; which is impossible in the case before us, for no creature can be equal to God. Multiplicity therefore and variety was needful in creation, to the end that the perfect likeness of God might be found in creatures according to their measure.

2. As the things that are made of any material are contained in the potentiality of the material, so the things done by any agent must be in the active power of the agent. But the potentiality of the material would not be perfectly reduced to actuality, if out of the material were made only one of those things to which the material is in potentiality. Therefore if any agent whose power extends to various effects were to produce only one of those effects, his power would not be so completely reduced to actuality as by making many. But by the reduction of active power to actuality the effect attains to the likeness of the agent. Therefore the likeness of God would not be perfect in the universe, if there was only one grade of all beings.

3. A creature approaches more perfectly to the likeness of God by being not only good itself, but able to act for the good of others. But no creature could do anything for the good of another creature, unless there were plurality and inequality among creatures, because the agent must be other than the patient and in a position of advantage (honorabilius) over it.

5. The goodness of the species transcends the goodness of the individual. Therefore the multiplication of species is a greater addition to the good of the universe than the multiplication of individuals of one species.

7. To a work contrived by sovereign goodness there ought not to be lacking the height of perfection proper to it. But the good of order in variety is better than

the isolated good of any one of the things that enter into the order: therefore the good of order ought not to be wanting to the work of God; which good could not be, if there were no diversity and inequality of creatures. There is then diversity and inequality between creatures, not by chance, not from diversity of elements, not by the intervention of any (inferior) cause, or consideration of merit, but by the special intention of God, wishing to give the creature such perfection as it was capable of having.

Hence it is said, God saw all things that he had made, and they were very good (Gen. i, 31); and this after He had said of them singly, that they were good; because while things are goodsingly in their several natures, all taken together they are very good, because of the order of the universe, which is the final and noblest perfection of creation.

CHAPTER XLVI—That it was necessary for the Perfection of the Universe that there should be some Intellectual Natures

THIS then being the cause of the diversity among creatures, it remains now to treat of the several distinct creatures themselves as we proposed to do in the third part of this book (Chap. V). And we will show first that by the disposition of Divine Providence assigning perfection to creatures in the way best befitting them, it was consonant with reason that some intellectual creatures should be placed at the head of creation.

5. Nothing else moves God to the production of creatures but His own goodness, which He has wished to communicate to other beings according to the manner of their assimilation to Himself (B. I, Chap. LXXXVII).

Now the likeness of one thing may be found in another in two ways: in one way in point of natural being, as the likeness of heat is found in the body heated; in another way in point of knowledge, as the likeness of fire (perceived) is in sight or touch. In order then that the likeness of God might be in creatures in such modes as were possible, it was necessary that the divine goodness should be communicated to creatures, not only by likeness in being, but also by likeness in knowing. But mind alone can know the divine goodness. Therefore there needed to be intelligent creatures.

6. In all comely arrangements of things, the attitude of the secondary to the last imitates the attitude of the first to all, as well secondary as last, though the imitation is not always perfect. Now God comprehends in Himself all creatures (B. I, Chapp. XXV, LI, LIV); and this is represented in material creatures, although in another way: for the higher body comprehends and contains the lower, according to quantitative extension; whereas God contains all creatures in simple mode, and not by quantitative extension. In order then that an imitation of God might not be wanting to creatures even in this mode of containing, there were made intellectual creatures to contain material creatures, not by any extension of quantity, but simply by mode of intelligence: for what is understood is in the mind that understands it, and is comprehended in its intellectual activity.

CHAPTER XLVII—That Subsistent Intelligences are Voluntary Agents

GOOD is what all things yearn after, and in all beings there is a craving (appetitus) for good. In beings unendowed with any sort of cognition, this craving is called 'physical appetite' (appetitus naturalis). In beings that have sensitive cognition it is called 'animal appetite,' and is divided into 'concupiscible' and 'irascible.' In intelligent beings it is called the 'intellectual' or 'rational appetite,' otherwise the 'will.'

## CHAPTER XLVIII—That Subsistent Intelligences have Free Will

THEY must be free, if they have dominion over their own acts.

2. A free agent is an agent that is cause of its own action (sui causa, sibi causa agendi). Agents that are determined (moventur) and act only inasmuch as they are determined by others, are not causes of their own acts. Only self-determining agents (moventia seipsa) have liberty of action; and these alone are guided in their action by judgement. A self-determining agent is made up of two elements, one determining and another determined. The element determined is the appetite; and that is determined either by intellect, or by phantasy, or by sense: for to these powers it belongs to judge. Of such self-determining agents, those alone judge freely which determine their own judgement. But no faculty of judging determines its own judgement unless it reflects upon its own act. If then it is to determine itself to judge, it must know its own judgement; and that knowledge belongs to intellect alone. Irrational animals then have a sort of free determination, or action, but not a free judgement (sunt quodammodo liberi quidem motus, sive actionis, non autem liberi judicii): while inanimate things, being dependent for their every determination on things other than themselves, have

not so much as free action, or determination. On the contrary, intelligent beings have not only free action, but also free judgement, which is having free will.

3. An apprehension becomes a motive according as the thing apprehended takes the form of something good or suitable. In agents that determine their own movements, the outward action goes upon some judgement pronouncing a thing good or suitable according as it is apprehended. If the agent pronouncing the judgement is to determine himself to judge, he must be guided to that judgement by some higher form or idea in his apprehension. This idea can be no other than the universal idea (ipsa ratio) of goodness or fitness, by aid whereof a judgement is formed of any given definite good, fit, or suitable thing. Therefore those agents alone determine themselves to judge, which have this general concept of goodness or fitness, — that is to say, only intelligent agents. Therefore intelligent agents alone determine themselves, not only to act, but also to judge. They therefore alone are free in judging, which is having free will.

4. No movement or action follows from a general concept except by the medium of some particular apprehension, as all movement and action deals with particulars. Now the understanding naturally apprehends the universal. In order then that movement or any manner of action may follow upon the intellectual apprehension, the universal concept of the understanding must be applied to particular objects. But the universal contains in potentiality many particular objects. Therefore the application of the intellectual concept may be made to many divers objects; and consequently the judgement of the understanding about things to be done is not

determined to one thing only.

5. Some agents are without liberty of judgement, either because they have no judgement at all, as is the case with things that have no knowledge, as stones and plants, or because they have a judgement naturally determined to one effect, as irrational animals. For by natural reckoning the sheep judges that the wolf is hurtful to it, and on this judgement flies from the wolf. But whatever agents have their judgement of things to be done not determined by nature to one effect, they must have free will. Such are all intelligent agents; for the understanding apprehends, not only this or that good, but good itself in general. Hence, since it is through the idea in apprehension that the understanding moves the will; and in all things the motive, or moving power, and the object moved must be proportioned to one another; it follows that the will of an intelligent subsistent being is not determined by nature except to good in general. Whatever therefore is presented to the will under the specific notion of good (sub ratione boni), the will may incline to it, without let or hindrance from any natural determination to the contrary. Therefore all intelligent agents have free will, arising out of the judgement of the understanding; and free will is defined 'a free judgement on the matter of a specific notion, or general concept.'

## CHAPTER XLIX—That Subsistent Intelligence is not Corporeal

IF the understanding were a corporeal substance, intelligible ideas of things would be received in it only as representing individual things. At that rate, the understanding would have no conception of the universal, but only of the particular, which is manifestly false.

4. If the understanding were a corporeal substance, its action would not transcend the order of corporeal things, and therefore it would understand nothing but corporeal things, which is manifestly false, for we do understand many things that are not corporeal.

5. There can be no infinite power in any finite body: but the power of the understanding is in a manner infinite in the exercise of intelligence: for it knows the universal, which is virtually infinite in its logical extension.

7 and 8. Of no bodily substance is the action turned back upon the agent. But the understanding in its action does reflect and turn round upon itself: for as it understands an object, so also it understands that it does understand, and so endlessly.

Hence Holy Scripture calls intelligent subsistent beings by the name of 'spirits,' using of them the style which it is wont to use for the incorporeal Deity, according to the text, God is a Spirit (John iv, 24).

Hereby is excluded the error of the ancient natural philosophers, who admitted no substance but corporeal substance: which opinion some have endeavored to foist into the Christian faith, saying that the soul is an effigy of the body, a sort of outline contour of the human body.

CHAPTER LII—That in Created Subsistent Intelligences there is a Difference between Existence and Essence

THOUGH subsistent intelligences are not corporeal, nor compounded of matter and form, nor existent as material forms in matter, still it must not be thought that they come up to the simplicity of the being of God: for there is found in them a certain composition, inasmuch as existence (esse) and essence (quod est) is not in them the same.

4. Whatsoever reality subsists of and by itself, nothing attaches to that reality except what is proper to being as being. For what is said of any reality not as such, does not belong to that reality otherwise than accidentally by reason of the subject: hence, considered apart from the subject in a particular case, the attribute does not belong to that reality at all. Now to be 'caused by another' does not belong to being, as being: otherwise every being would be caused by another, which is impossible (B. I, Chap. XIII) Therefore that existence which is being of itself and by itself, must be uncaused. No caused being therefore is its own existence.

5. The substance of every reality is a being of itself and not through another. Hence actual illumination is not of the substance of air, because it accrues to it through another. But to every created reality existence accrues through another, otherwise it would not be a creature. Therefore of no created substance is it true to say that its existence is its substance.

Hence in Exodus iii, 14, existence is assigned as the proper name of God, He who is: because it is proper to God alone that His substance is none other than His existence.

## CHAPTER LIII—That in Created Subsistent Intelligences there is Actuality and Potentiality

IN whatever being there are found two elements, the one complementary to the other, the proportion of the one element to the other is as the proportion of potential to actual: for nothing is completed except by its own actuality. But in a created intelligent subsistent being there are two elements, the substance itself and the existence thereof which is not the same thing as the substance. Now that existence is the complement of the existing substance: for everything actually exists by having existence. It follows that in every one of the aforesaid substances there is a composition of actuality and potentiality.

2. What is in any being, and comes of the agent that produced it, must be the actuality of that being: for it is an agent's function to make a thing be in actuality. But, as shown above (Chap. XV), all other substances have their existence of the prime agent: indeed their being created substances consists precisely in this, that they have their existence of another. Existence itself therefore is in these created substances as a sort of actualization of the same. But that in which actuality is received is potentiality: for actuality is such in relation to potentiality. In every created subsistent being therefore there is potentiality and actuality.

CHAPTER LV—That Subsistent Intelligences are Imperishable

WHAT ordinarily and of itself attaches to a thing, inheres in it necessarily and invariably and inseparably, as roundness ordinarily and of itself inheres in a circle, but in a bit of brass metal only incidentally. It is possible for a bit of brass metal to be other than round: it is impossible for a circle to be other than round. Now existence ordinarily follows upon the form: for we call that 'ordinary,' which the thing is inasmuch as it is itself; and everything has existence inasmuch as it has form. Substances therefore that are not pure forms may be deprived of existence inasmuch as they lose their form, as brass is deprived of roundness inasmuch as it ceases to be circular. But substances that are pure forms are never deprived of existence: thus if the ideal circle had substantial existence, that substance could never be made other than round. But subsistent intelligences are pure subsistent forms: therefore it is impossible for them ever to cease to exist.

8. Everything that perishes, perishes by suffering something. Destruction is a sort of suffering. But no subsistent intelligence can suffer any impression such as to lead to its destruction. For to suffer is to receive something; and whatever is received in a subsistent intelligence must be received according to the manner of the same: that is to say, it must be received as an intelligible impression. But whatever is so received in a subsistent intelligence, goes to perfect that intelligence, not to destroy it: for the intelligible is the perfection of the intelligent. A subsistent intelligence therefore is indestructible.

10. The intelligible is the proper perfection of the intellect: hence the understanding in the act of understanding, and its term, or object in the act of being understood, are one. What therefore belongs to the object as intelligible, must belong also to the mind as cognizant of that object; because perfection and perfectible are of the same genus. Now the intelligible object, as such, is necessary and imperishable: for things necessary, or things that must be, are perfectly cognizable to the understanding; while things contingent, that are but might

not be, as such, are cognizable only imperfectly: they are not matter of science, but of opinion. Hence the understanding attains to science of perishable things, only in so far as they are imperishable, — that is to say, in so far as they become to the mind universals. Intellect therefore, as such, must be indestructible.

13. It is impossible for a natural desire to be void of object, for nature does nothing in vain. But every intelligence naturally desires perpetuity of being, not only perpetuity of being in the species, but in the individual: which is thus shown. The natural desire which some creatures have arises from conscious apprehension: thus the wolf naturally desires the killing of the animals on which he feeds, and man naturally desires happiness. Other creatures, without any conscious apprehension, are led by the inclination of primitive physical tendencies, which is called in some 'physical appetite.' The natural desire of being is contained under both modes: the proof of which is that creatures devoid of any sort of cognitive faculty resist destructive agencies to the full strength of their natural constitution, while creatures possessed of any manner of cognitive faculty resist the same according to the mode of their cognition. Those creatures therefore, devoid of cognition, who have in their natural constitution strength enough to preserve perpetual being, so as to remain always the same numerically, have a natural appetite for perpetuity of being even in respect of sameness of number: while those whose natural constitution has not strength for this, but only for preservation of perpetuity of being in respect of sameness of species, also have a natural appetite for perpetuity. This difference then must be noted in those creatures whose desire of being is attended with cognition, that they who

do not know being except in the present time, desire it for the present time, but not for ever, because they have no apprehension of everlasting existence: still they desire the perpetual being of their species, a desire unattended with cognition, because the generative power, which serves that end, is preliminary to and does not come under cognition. Those then that do know and apprehend perpetual being as such, desire the same with a natural desire. But this is the case with all subsistent intelligences. All such subsistent intelligences therefore have a natural desire of everlasting being. Therefore they cannot possibly cease to be.

13. All things that begin to be, and afterwards cease to be, have both their beginning and their ceasing from the same power: for the same is the power to make to be and to make not to be. But subsistent intelligences could not begin to be except through the power of the prime agent. Therefore neither is there any power to make them cease to be except in the prime agent, inasmuch as that agent may cease to pour being into them. But in respect of this power alone nothing can be called perishable; as well because things are called necessary or contingent in respect of the power that is in them, not in respect of the power of God (Chap. XXX), as also because God, the author of nature, does not withdraw from things that which is proper to their nature; and it has been shown that it is proper to intellectual natures to be perpetual.

CHAPTER LVI, LXIX—How a Subsistent Intelligence may be united with a Body, with a Solution of the Arguments alleged to prove that a Subsistent Intelligence cannot be united with a Body as its Form

A SUBSISTENT intelligence cannot be united with a body by any manner of combination: for combined elements, when the combination is complete, do not remain actually, but virtually only: for if they remained actually, it would not be a combination, but a mere mechanical mixture. But this combination and consequent cessation of actual existence cannot befall subsistent intelligences; for they are imperishable.

It is likewise evident that a subsistent intelligence cannot be united with a body by any manner of contact, properly so called. For contact is only of bodies: those things are in contact, the extremities of which are together, as points, or lines, or circumferences, which are the extremities of bodies.

Still there is one mode of contact whereby a subsistent intelligence may be mingled with a body. For natural bodies in touching one another involve a change, and thus are united together, not only in their quantitative extremities, but also by likeness of one same quality or form, the one in pressing its form on the other. And though, if we regard only quantitative extremities, the contact must be mutual in all cases, yet, if we consider action and passion, there will be found some cases of touching without being touched, and some cases of being touched without touching. Any cases that may be found of contact without contact in quantitative extremities must still be called instances of contact, inasmuch as they are instances of action: thus we say that he who saddens another 'touches' him. According to this mode of touch it is possible for a subsistent intelligence to be united to a body by contact: for subsistent intelligences act upon bodies and move them, being more highly actualized than bodies are.

This contact is not quantitative but virtual, and differs from bodily contact in three respects. First, because in this contact the indivisible can touch the divisible, which cannot happen in bodily contact: for only that which is indivisible can be touched by a point, whereas a subsistent intelligence, indivisible though it be, can touch a divisible quantity by acting upon it. The point and the subsistent intelligence are not indivisible in the same way. The point is indivisible as a term of quantity, and has a definite situation in a continuous surface, beyond which it cannot be thrown: whereas a subsistent intelligence is indivisible by being outside of the category of quantity altogether: hence no indivisible element of quantity is marked out for contact with it. Secondly, because quantitative contact is only with extremities, but virtual contact is with the whole subject touched: for the subject is touched inasmuch as it is acted upon and moved; but that is inasmuch as it is in potentiality; and potentiality extends to the whole, not merely to the extremities of the whole: hence the whole is touched. From this appears a third difference: because in quantitative touch, which is of extremities, the touching body must be outside of the touched, and cannot pervade it, but is stopped by it; whereas the virtual contact, which is proper to subsistent intelligences, reaching to the inmost recesses of things, makes the touching substance be within the touched and pervade it without let or hindrance. Thus then a subsistent intelligence may be united with a body by virtual contact.

Elements united by such contact are not absolutely one: they are one in action and in being acted upon, which does not involve absolute oneness of being. Such absolute oneness may be in three ways: in the way of indivisibility, in the way of continuity, and in the way of natural unity. Now out of a subsistent intelligence and a body there cannot be made an indivisible unity: it must be a compound of two things. Nor again a continuous unity, because the parts of a continuum are quantitative. It remains to be enquired whether out of a subsistent intelligence and a body there can result such a unity as means oneness of nature. But out of two permanent elements there results no being one by nature except that which results of the union of substantial form with matter: for out of substance and accident there results no being one by nature, for the nature or essence of 'man' and 'whiteness' is not the same. This question then remains to be studied, whether a subsistent intelligence can be the substantial form of any body. Looking at the matter argumentatively, it might seem that the thing is impossible.

Arg.1. Of two actually existent substances no one being can be made: for the actuality of every being is that whereby it is distinguished from another being. But a subsistent intelligence is an actually existing substance: so likewise is a body. Apparently therefore no one being can be made of a subsistent intelligence and a body.

Arg. 2. Form and matter are contained under the same genus: for every genus is divided into actual and potential. But a subsistent intelligence and a body are of different genera.

Arg. 3. All that is in matter must be material. But if subsistent intelligence is the form of a body, the being of such intelligence must be in matter: for there is no being of the form beyond the being of the matter. It follows that a subsistent intelligence could not be immaterial, as supposed.

Arg. 4. It is impossible for anything having its being in a body to be apart from the body. But intelligence is shown to be apart from the body, as it is neither the body itself nor a bodily faculty.

Arg. 5. Whatever has being in common with the body, must also have activity in common with the body: for the active power of a thing cannot be more exalted than its essence. But if a subsistent intelligence is the form of a body, one being must be common to it and the body: for out of form and matter there results absolute unity, which is unity in being. At that rate the activity of a subsistent intelligence, united as a form to the body, will be exerted in common with the body, and its faculty will be a bodily (or organic) faculty: positions which we regard as impossible.

(Chap. LXIX). It is not difficult to solve the objections alleged against the aforesaid union.

Reply1. The first objection contains a false supposition: for body and soul are not two actually existing substances, but out of the two of them is made one substance actually existing: for a man's body is not the same in actuality when the soul is present as when it is absent: it is the soul that gives actual being.

Reply2. As for the second objection, that form and matter are contained under the same genus, it is not true in the sense that both are species of one genus, but inasmuch as both are elements of the same species. Thus then a subsistent intelligence and a body, which as separate existences would be species of different genera, in their union belong to one genus as elements of the same.

Reply3. Nor need a subsistent intelligence be a material form, notwithstanding that its existence is in matter: for though in matter, it is not immersed in matter, or wholly comprised in matter.

Reply4. Nor yet does the union of a subsistent intelligence with a body by its being that body's form stand in the way of intelligence being separable from body. In a soul we have to observe as well its essence as also its power. In point of essence it gives being to such and such a body, while in point of power it executes its own proper acts. In any activity of the soul therefore which is completed by a bodily organ, the power of the soul which is the principle of that activity must bring to act that part of the body whereby its activity is completed, as sight brings the eye to act. But in any activity of the soul that we may suppose not to be completed by any bodily organ, the corresponding power will not bring anything in the body to act; and this is the sense in which the intellect is said to be 'separate,' — not but that the substance of the soul, whereof intellect is a power, or the intellectual soul, brings the body to act, inasmuch as it is the form which gives being to such body.

Reply 5. Nor is it necessary, as was argued in the fifth place, that if the soul in its substance is the form of the body, its every operation should be through the body, and thus its every faculty should be the actuation of some part of the body: for the human soul is not one of those forms which are entirely immersed in matter, but of all forms it is the most exalted above matter: hence it is capable of a certain activity without the body, being not dependent on the body in its action, as neither in its being is it dependent on the body.

CHAPTER LVII—Plato's Theory of the Union of the Intellectual Soul with the Body

MOVED by these and the like objections, some have said that no subsistent intelligence can possibly be the form of a body. But because the nature of man of itself seemed to give the lie to this statement, inasmuch as man is seen to be composed of an intellectual soul and a body, they have thought out various ways to save the nature of man and adjust their theory to fact. Plato therefore and his followers laid it down that the intellectual soul is not united with the body as form with matter, but only as the mover is with the moved, saying that the soul is in the body as a sailor in his boat: thus the union of soul and body would be virtual contact only, of which above (Chap. LVI). But as such contact does not produce absolute oneness, this statement leads to the awkward consequence that man is not absolutely one, nor absolutely a being at all, but is a being only accidentally. To escape this conclusion, Plato laid it down that man is not a compound of soul and body, but that the soul using the body is man. This position is shown to be impossible: for things different in being cannot have one and the same activity. I call an activity one and the same, not in respect to the effect to which the activity is terminated, but as it comes forth from the agent. It is true that many men towing a boat make one action in respect of the thing done, which is one; but still on the part of the men towing there are many actions, as there are many different strains and exertions to haul the boat along: for as action is consequent upon form and power, it follows that where there are different forms and powers there must also be different actions. Now though the soul has a certain proper motion of its own, which it performs independently of the body, namely, the act of understanding, there are however other activities common to soul and body, namely, those of fear, anger, sensation, and the like; for these only come about by some change wrought in some definite part of the body; hence evidently they are conjoint activities of soul and body. Therefore out of soul and body there must result one being, and the two cannot be distinct in being.

But this reasoning may be met by the following reply on behalf of Plato's view. — There is no difficulty, it will be said, in mover and moved having the same act, notwithstanding their difference in being: for motion is at once the act of the moving force, from which it is, and the act of the thing moved, in which it is. Thus then, on Plato's theory, the aforesaid activities may be common to soul and body, belonging to the soul as the moving force, and to the body as the thing moved. But this explanation cannot hold for the following reasons.

1. As the Philosopher proves (De Anima, II), sensation results by the sentient subject being moved or impressed by external sensible things: hence a man cannot have a sensation without some external sensible thing, as nothing can be moved without a mover. The sensory organ therefore is moved and impressed in sensation, but that is by the external sensible object. What receives the impression is the sense, as is evident from this, that senseless things do not receive any such manner of impression from sensible objects. The sense therefore is the passive power of the sensory organ. The sentient soul therefore in sensation does not play the part of mover and agent, but is that principle in the subject impressed, in virtue of which the said subject lies open to the impression. But such a principle cannot be different in being from the subject impressed. Therefore the sentient

soul is not different in being from the animated body.

2. Though motion is the common act of moving force and object moved, still it is one activity to impart motion and another to receive motion: hence the two several categories of action and passion. If then in sensation the sentient soul stands for the agent, and the body for the patient, there will be one activity of the soul and another of the body. The sentient soul therefore will have an activity and proper motion of its own: it will have therefore its own subsistence: therefore, when the body perishes, it will not cease to be. Thus sentient souls, even of irrational animals, will be immortal; which seems improbable, although it is not out of keeping with Plato's opinion. But this will be matter of enquiry further on (Chap. LXXXII).

3. A body moved does not take its species according to the power that moves it. If therefore the soul is only united to the body as mover to moved, the body and its parts do not take their species from the soul: therefore, when the soul departs, the body and the parts thereof will remain of the same species. But this is manifestly false: for flesh and bone and hands and such parts, after the departure of the soul, do not retain their own names except by a façon de parler; since none of these parts retains its proper activity, and activity follows species. Therefore the union of soul and body is not that of mover with moved, or of a man with his dress.

6. If the soul is united with the body only as mover with moved, it will be in the power of the soul to go out of the body when it wishes, and, when it wishes, to reunite itself with the body.

That the soul is united with the body as the proper form of the same, is thus proved. That whereby a thing emerges from potential to actual being, is its form and actuality. But by the soul the body emerges from potentiality to actuality: for the being of a living thing is its life: moreover the seed before animation is only potentially alive, and by the soul it is made actually alive: the soul therefore is the form of the animated body.

Again: as part is to part, so is the whole sentient soul to the whole body. But sight is the form and actuality of the eye: therefore the soul is the form and actuality of the body.

## CHAPTER LVIII—That Vegetative, Sentient, and Intelligent are not in man Three Souls

PLATO lays it down that not one and the same soul is in us at once intelligent, sentient, and vegetative. In this view, granted that the sentient soul is the form of the body, it does not follow that any subsistent intelligence can be the form of a body. The untenableness of this position is thus to be shown.

1. Attributes of the same subject representing different forms are predicated of one another accidentally: thus 'white' is said to be 'musical' accidentally, inasmuch as whiteness and music happen both to be in Socrates. If then the intelligent, sentient, and vegetative soul are different powers or forms in us, then the attributes that we have according to these forms will be predicated of one another accidentally. But according to the intelligent soul we are called 'men,' according to the sentient 'animals,' according to the vegetative 'living.' This then will be an accidental predication, 'man is an animal,' or 'an animal is a living creature.' But on the contrary these are cases of essential predication: for man, as man, is an animal; and

an animal, as an animal, is a living creature. Therefore it is from the same principle that one is man, animal, and alive.

2. A thing has unity from the same principle whence it has being, for unity is consequent upon being. Since then everything has being from its form, it will have unity also from its form. If therefore there are posited in man several souls, as so many forms, man will not be one being but several. Nor will the order of the forms to one another, one ensuing upon the other, suffice for the unity of man: for unity in point of orderly succession is not absolute unity: such unity of order in fact is the loosest of unities.

4. If man, as Plato held, is not a compound of soul and body, but is a soul using a body; either this is understood of the intelligent soul, or of the three souls, if there are three, or of two of them. If of three, or two, it follows that man is not one, but two, or three: for he is three souls, or at least two. But if this is understood of the intelligent soul alone, so that the sentient soul is to be taken for the form of the body, and the intelligent soul, using the animate and sentient body, is to be man, there will still ensue awkward consequences, to wit, that man is not an animal, but uses an animal; and that man does not feel, but uses a thing that does feel.

5. Of two or three there cannot be made one without anything to unite them, unless one of them stands to the other as actuality to potentiality: for so of matter and form there is made one without any external bond to bind them together. But if in man there are several souls, they do not stand to one another as matter and form, but they are all supposed to be actualities and principles of action. If then they are to be united to make one man, or

one animal, there must be something to unite them. This cannot be the body, since rather the body is made one by the soul: the proof of which fact is that, when the soul departs, the body breaks up. It must be some more formal principle that makes of those several entities one; and this will be rather the soul than those several entities which are united by it. If this again has several parts, and is not one in itself, there must further be something to unite those parts. As we cannot proceed to infinity, we must come to something which is in itself one; and this of all things is the soul. There must therefore in one man, or one animal, be one only soul.

CHAPTER LIX—That the Potential Intellect of Man is not a Spirit subsisting apart from Matter

THERE were others who used another invention in maintaining the point, that a subsistent intelligence cannot be united with a body as its form. They say that the intellect which Aristotle calls 'potential,' is a spiritual being, subsisting apart by itself, and not united with us as a form. And this they endeavor to prove from the words of Aristotle, who says, speaking of this intellect, that it is "separate, unmixed with body, simple and impassible," terms which could not be applied to it, they say, if it were the form of a body. Also from the argument by which Aristotle proves that because the potential intellect receives all impressions of sensible things, and is in potentiality to them all, it must be devoid of all to begin with, as the pupil of the eye, which receives all impressions of colors, is devoid of all color; because if it had of itself any color, that color would prevent other colors from being seen; nay, nothing would be seen except under that color; and the like would be the case of the potential intellect, if it had of itself any form or nature of sensible things, as it would have were it the form of anybody; because, since form and matter make one, the form must participate to some extent in the nature of that whereof it is the form.

These passages moved Averroes to suppose the potential intellect, whereby the soul understands, to be separate in being from the body, and not to be the form of the body. But because this intellect would have no connexion with us, nor should we be able to understand by it unless it were somehow united with us, Averroes fixes upon a mode in which it is united with us, as he thinks, sufficiently. He says that an impression actually made in the understanding is a 'form' of the potential intellect, in the same way that an actually visible appearance, as such, is a 'form' of the visual faculty; hence out of the potential intellect, and this form or impression actually made in the same, there results one being. With whatever being therefore this 'form' of the understanding is conjoined, the potential intellect is also conjoined with that being. But this 'form 'is conjoined with us by means of the 'phantasm,' or image in the phantasy, which image is a Sort of subject receiving in itself that 'form' of understanding.

1. It is easy to see how frivolous and impossible all this construction is. For what has understanding is intelligent; and that of which an intelligible impression is united with the understanding, is understood. The fact that an intelligible impression, united with a (foreign) understanding, comes somehow to be in man, will not render man intelligent; it will merely make him understood by that separately subsisting intelligence.

2. Besides, the impression actually in understanding is the form of the potential intellect, in the same way that the actual visible appearance is the form of the visual power, or eye. But the impression actually in understanding is to the phantasms as the actual visible appearance is to the colored surface, which is outside the soul. This similitude is used by Averroes, as also by Aristotle. Therefore the supposed union of the potential intellect (by means of the intelligible form) with the phantasm that is in us will resemble the union of the visual power with the color that is in the stone. But this union does not make the stone see, but be seen. Therefore the aforesaid union does not make us understand, but be understood. But, plainly, it is properly and truly said that man understands: for we should not be investigating the nature of understanding were it not for the fact that we have understanding. The above mode of union then is insufficient.

5. The intellect in the act of understanding and the object as represented in understanding are one, as also the sense in the act of sensation and the object as represented in sense. But the understanding as apt to understand and its object as open to representation in understanding are not one, as neither is sense, so far as it is apt to have sensation, one with its object, so far as that is open to be represented in sensation. The impression made by the object, so far as it lies in images of the phantasy, is not any representation in the understanding. Only by undergoing a process of abstraction from such images does the impression became one with the intellect in the act of understanding. In like manner the impression of color is actually felt in sense, not as it is in the stone, but as it is in the eye. Now, on the theory of Averroes, the

intelligible form, or impression in the understanding, only comes to be conjoined with us by finding place in the images of our phantasy. Therefore it is not conjoined with us inasmuch as it is one with the potential intellect, being its form. Therefore it cannot be the medium whereby the potential intellect is conjoined with us: because, in so far as it is conjoined with the potential intellect, it is not conjoined with us; and in so far as it is conjoined with us, it is not conjoined with the potential intellect.

CHAPTER LX—That Man is not a Member the Human Species by possession of Passive Intellect, but by possession of Potential Intellect

AVERROES endeavors to meet these arguments and to maintain the position aforesaid. He says accordingly that man differs from dumb animals by what Aristotle calls the 'passive intellect,' which is that 'cogitative power' (vis cogitativa) proper to man, in place whereof other animals have a certain 'estimative power' (aestimativa). The function of this 'cogitative power' is to distinguish individual ideas and compare them with one another, as the intellect, which is separate and unmixed, compares and distinguishes between universal ideas. And because by this cogitative power, along with imagination and memory, phantasms, or impressions of phantasy, are prepared to receive the action of the 'active intellect,' whereby they are made actual terms of understanding, therefore the aforesaid cogitative power is called by the names of 'intellect' and 'reason.' Doctors say that it has its seat in the middle cell of the brain. According to the disposition of this power one man differs from another in genius, and in other points of intelligence; and by the use and exercise of this power man acquires the habit of knowledge. Hence the passive intellect is the subject of the various habits of knowledge. And this passive intellect is in a child from the beginning; and by virtue of it he is a member of the human species before he actually understands anything. So far Averroes. The falsity and perverseness of his statements evidently appears.

1. Vital activities stand to the soul as second actualities to the first. Now the first actuality is prior in time to the second in the same subject, as knowledge is prior in time to learned speculation. In whatever being therefore there is found any vital activity, there must be some portion of soul standing to that activity as the first actuality to the second. But man has one activity proper to him above all other animals, namely that of understanding and reasoning. Therefore we must posit in man some proper specific principle, which shall be to the act of understanding as the first actuality to the second. This principle cannot be the aforesaid 'passive intellect': for the principle of the aforesaid activity must be "impassible and nowise implicated with the body," as the Philosopher proves, whereas evidently quite the contrary is the case with the passive intellect. Therefore that cognitive faculty called the 'passive intellect' cannot possibly be the speciality that differentiates the human species from other animals.

2. An incident of the sensitive part cannot constitute a being in a higher kind of life than that of the sensitive part, as an incident of the vegetative soul does not place a being in a higher kind of life than the vegetative life. But it is certain that phantasy and the faculties consequent thereon, as memory and the like, are

incidents of the sensitive part. Therefore by the aforesaid faculties, or by any one of them, an animal cannot be placed in any higher rank of life than that which goes with the sentient soul. But man is in a higher rank of life than that. Therefore the man does not live the life that is proper to him by virtue of the aforesaid 'cogitative faculty,' or 'passive intellect.'

4. The 'potential intellect' is proved not to be the actualization of any corporeal organ from this consideration, that the said intellect takes cognizance of all sensible forms under a universal aspect. Therefore no faculty, the activity of which can reach to the universal aspects of all corporeal forms, can be the actualization of any corporeal organ. But such a faculty is the will: for of all of the things that we understand we can have a will, at least of knowing them. And we also find acts of the will in the general: thus, as Aristotle says (Rhet. II, 4), we hate in general the whole race of robbers. The will then cannot be the actualization of any bodily organ. But every portion of the soul is the actualization of some bodily organ, except only the intellect properly so called. The will therefore belongs to the intellectual part, as Aristotle says. Now the will of man is not extrinsic to man, planted as it were in some separately subsisting intelligence, but is in the man himself: otherwise he would not be master of his own acts, but would be worked by the will of a spirit other than himself: those appetitive, or conative, faculties alone would remain in him, the activity whereof is conjoined with passion, to wit the irascible and concupiscible in the sentient part of his being, as in other animals, which are rather acted upon than act. But this is impossible: it would be the undoing of all moral philosophy and all social and political science. Therefore

there must be in us a potential intellect to differentiate us from dumb animals: the passive intellect is not enough.

6. A habit and the act proper to that habit both reside in the same faculty. But to view a thing intellectually, which is the act proper to the habit of knowledge, cannot be an exercise of the faculty called 'passive intellect,' but must properly belong to the potential intellect: for the condition of any faculty exercising intelligence is that it should not be an actualization of any corporeal organ. Therefore the habit of knowledge is not in the passive intellect, but in the potential intellect.

8. Habitual understanding, as our opponent acknowledges, is an effect of the 'active intellect.' But the effects of the active intellect are actual representations in understanding, the proper recipient of which is the potential intellect, to which the active intellect stands related, as Aristotle says, "as art to material." Therefore the habitual understanding, which is the habit of knowledge, must be in the potential intellect, not in the passive.

CHAPTER LXI—That the aforesaid Tenet is contrary to the Mind of Aristotle

ARISTOTLE defines soul, "the first actuality of a natural, organic body, potentially alive"; and adds, "this definition applies universally to every soul." Nor does he, as the aforesaid Averroes pretends, put forth this latter remark in a tentative way, as may be seen from the Greek copies and the translation of Boethius. Afterwards in the same chapter he adds that there are "certain parts of the soul separable," and these are none other than the intellectual parts. The conclusion remains that the said parts are actualizations of the body.

2. Nor is this explanation inconsistent with Aristotle's words subjoined: "About the intellect and the speculative faculty the case is not yet clear: but it seems to be another kind of soul." He does not hereby mean to separate the intellect from the common definition of 'soul,' but from the peculiar natures of the other parts of soul: as one who says that fowls are a different sort of animal from land animals, does not take away from the fowl the common definition of 'animal.' Hence, to show in what respect he called it "another kind," he adds: "And of this alone is there possibility of separation, as of the everlasting from the perishable." Nor is it the intention of Aristotle, as the Commentator aforesaid pretends, to say that it is not yet clear whether intellect be soul at all, as it is clear of other and lower vital principles. For the old text has not, "Nothing has been declared," or "Nothing has been said," but "Nothing is clear," which is to be understood as referring to the peculiar properties of intellect, not to the general definition (of soul). But if, as the Commentator says, the word 'soul' is used not in the same sense of intellect and other varieties, Aristotle would have first distinguished the ambiguity and then made his definition, as his manner is: otherwise his argument would rest on an ambiguity, an intolerable procedure in demonstrative sciences.

3. Aristotle reckons 'intellect' among the 'faculties' of the soul. Also, in the passage last quoted, he names 'the speculative faculty.' Intellect therefore is not outside the human soul, but is a faculty thereof.

4. Also, when beginning to speak of the potential intellect, he calls it a part of the soul, saying: "Concerning

the part of the soul whereby the soul has knowledge and intellectual consciousness."

5. And still more clearly by what follows, declaring the nature of the potential intellect: "I call intellect that whereby the soul thinks and under stands": in which it is manifestly shown that the intellect is something belonging to the human soul.

The above tenet (of Averroes) therefore is contrary to the mind of Aristotle and contrary to the truth: hence it should be rejected as chimerical.

CHAPTER LXII—Against the Opinion of Alexander concerning the Potential Intellect

UPON consideration of these words of Aristotle, Alexander determined the potential intellect to be some power in us, that so the general definition of soul assigned by Aristotle might apply to it. But because he could not understand how any subsistent intelligence could be the form of a body, he supposed the aforesaid faculty of potential intellect not to be planted in any subsistent intelligence, but to be the result of some combination of elements in the human body. Thus a definite mode of combination of the components of the human body puts a man in potentiality to receive the influence of the active intellect, which is ever in act, and according to him, is a spiritual being subsisting apart, under which influence man becomes actually intelligent. But that in man whereby he is potentially intelligent is the potential intellect: hence it seemed to Alexander to follow that the potential intellect in us arises from a definite combination of elements. But this statement appears on first inspection to be contrary to the words and argument of Aristotle. For

Aristotle shows (De anima, III, iv, 2-4) that the potential intellect is unmingled with the body: but that could not be said of a faculty that was the result of a combination of bodily elements. To meet this difficulty Alexander says that the potential intellect is precisely the 'predisposition' (praeparatio, ἐπιτηδεώτης) which exists in human nature to receive the influence of the active intellect; and that this 'predisposition' is not any definite sensible nature, nor is it mingled with the body, for it is a relation and order between one thing and another. But this is in manifest disagreement with the mind of Aristotle, as the following reasons show:

3. Aristotle assigns these characteristics to the potential intellect: to be impressed by the intelligible presentation, to receive intelligible impressions, to be in potentiality towards them (De anima, III, iv, 11, 12): all which things cannot be said of any 'disposition,' but only of the subject predisposed. It is therefore contrary to the mind of Aristotle, that the mere 'predisposition' should be the potential intellect.

4. An effect cannot stand higher above the material order than its cause. But every cognitive faculty, as such, belongs to the immaterial order. Therefore it is impossible for any cognitive faculty to be caused by a combination of elements. But the potential intellect is the supreme cognitive faculty in us: therefore it is not caused by a combination of elements.

6. No bodily organ can possibly have a share in the act of understanding. But that act is attributed to the soul, or to the man: for we say that the soul understands, or the man through the soul. Therefore there must be in man some principle independent of the body, to be the principle of such an act. But any predisposition, which is

the result of a combination of elements, manifestly depends on the body. Therefore no such predisposition can be a principle like the potential intellect, whereby the soul judges and understands.

But if it is said that the principle of the aforesaid operation in us is the intellectual impression actually made by the active intellect, this does not seem to suffice: because when man comes to have actual intellectual cognition from having had such cognition potentially, he needs to understand not merely by some intelligible impression actualizing his understanding, but likewise by some intellectual faculty as the principle of such activity. Besides, an impression is not in actual understanding except so far as it is purified from particular and material being. But this cannot happen so long as it remains in any material faculty, that is to say, in any faculty either caused by material principles or actualizing a material organ. Therefore there must be posited in us some immaterial intellectual faculty, and that is the potential intellect.

CHAPTER LXIV—That the Soul is not a Harmony

THE maintainers of this view did not mean that the soul is a harmony of sounds, but a harmony of contrary elements, whereof they saw living bodies to be composed. The view is rejected for the following reasons:

1. You may find such a harmony in any body, even a mere chemical compound (corpus mixtum). A harmony cannot move the body, or govern it, or resist the passions, as neither can a temperament. Also a harmony, and a temperament also, admits of degrees. All which considerations go to show that the soul is neither harmony

nor temperament.

2. The notion of harmony rather befits qualities of the body than the soul: thus health is a harmony of humors; strength, of muscles and bones; beauty, of limb and color. But it is impossible to assign any components, the harmony of which would make sense, or intellect, or other appurtenances of the soul.

3. Harmony may mean either the composition itself or the principle of composition. Now the soul is not a composition, because then every part of the soul would be composed of certain parts of the body, an arrangement which cannot be made out. In like manner the soul is not the principle of composition, because to different parts of the body there are different principles of composition, or proportions of elements, which would require the several parts of the body to have so many several souls, — one soul for bone, one for flesh, one for sinew; which is evidently not the case.

CHAPTER LXV—That the Soul is not a Body

LIVING beings are composed of matter and form, — of a body, and of a soul which makes them actually alive. One of these components must be the form, and the other the matter. But a body cannot be a form, because a body is not in another as in its matter and subject. Therefore the soul must be the form: therefore it is not a body.

5. The act of understanding cannot be the act of anything corporeal. But it is an act of the soul. Therefore the intellectual soul at least is not a body. It is easy to solve the arguments whereby some have endeavored to prove that the soul is a body. They point such facts as

these, — that the son resembles the father even in the accidents of his soul, being generated from the father by severance of bodily substance; and that the soul suffers with the body; and is separated from the body, separation supposing previous bodily contact. Against these instances we observe that bodily temperament is a sort of predisposing cause of affections of the soul: that the soul suffers with the body only accidentally, as being the form of the body: also that the soul is separated from the body, not as touching from touched, but as form from matter; although there is a certain contact possible between an incorporeal being and the body, as has been shown above (Chap. LVI). Many have been moved to this position by their belief that what is not a material body has no existence, being unable to transcend the imagination, which deals only with material bodies. Hence this opinion is proposed in the person of the unwise: *The breath of our nostrils is smoke, and reason a spark in the beating of the heart* (Wisdom ii, 2).

CHAPTER LXVI—*Against those who suppose Intellect and Sense to be the same*

SENSE is found in all animals, but animals other than man have no intellect: which is proved by this, that they do not work, like intellectual agents, in diverse and opposite ways, but just as nature moves them fixed and uniform specific activities, as every swallow builds its nest in the same way.

2. Sense is cognizant only of singulars, but intellect is cognizant of universals.

3. Sensory knowledge extends only to bodily things, but intellect takes cognizance of things

incorporeal, as wisdom, truth, and the relations between objects.

4. No sense has reflex knowledge of itself and its own activity: the sight does not see itself, nor see that it sees. But intellect is cognizant of itself, and knows that it understands.

## CHAPTER LXVII—Against those who maintain that the Potential Intellect is the Phantasy

PHANTASY is found in other animals besides man, the proof of which is that, as objects of sense recede from sense, these animals still shun or pursue them. But intellect is not in them, as no work of intelligence appears in their conduct.

2. Phantasy is only of things corporeal and singular; but intellect, of things universal and incorporeal.

4. Intelligence is not the actualization of any bodily organ. But phantasy has a fixed bodily organ.

Hence it is said: Who teaches us above the beasts of the earth, and above the fowls of the air instructed us(Job xxxv, 11): whereby we are given to understand that there is in man a certain cognitive power, above the sense and fancy that are in other animals.

## CHAPTER LXVIII—How a Subsistent Intelligence may be the Form of a Body

If a subsistent intelligence is not united with a body merely as its mover, as Plato thought (Chap. LVII);

nor is the intellect, whereby man understands, a predisposition in human nature, as Alexander said (Chap. LXII; nor a temperament, as Galen (Chap. LXIII); nor a harmony, as Empedocles (Chap. LXIV); nor a body, nor a sense, nor a phantasy (Chapp. LXV, LXVI, LXVII); it remains that the human soul is a subsistent intelligence, united with the body as its form: which may be thus made manifest.

There are two requisites for one thing to be the substantial form of another. One requisite is that the form be the principle of substantial being to that whereof it is the form: I do not mean the effective, but the formal principle, whereby a thing is and is denominated 'being.' The second requisite is that the form and matter should unite in one 'being'; namely, in that being wherein the substance so composed subsists. There is no such union of the effective principle with that to which it gives being. A subsistent intelligence, as shown in Chap. LVI, is not hindered by the fact that it is subsistent from communicating its being to matter, and becoming the formal principle of the said matter. There is no difficulty in the identification of the being, in virtue of which the compound subsists, with the form itself of the said compound, since the compound is only through the form, and neither subsist apart.

It may be objected that a subsistent intelligence cannot communicate its being to a material body in such a way that there shall be one being of the subsistent intelligence and the material body: for things of different kinds have different modes of being, and nobler is the being of the nobler substance. This objection would be in point, if that being were said to belong to that material thing in the same way in which it belongs to that subsistent intelligence. But it is not so: for that being belongs to that material body as to a recipient subject raised to a higher state; while it belongs to that subsistent intelligence as to its principle and by congruence of its own nature.

In this way a wonderful chain of beings is revealed to our study. The lowest member of the higher genus is always found to border close upon the highest member of the lower genus. Thus some of the lowest members of the genus of animals attain to little beyond the life of plants, certain shellfish for instance, which are motionless, have only the sense of touch, and are attached to the ground like plants. Hence Dionysius says: "Divine wisdom has joined the ends of the higher to the beginnings of the lower." Thus in the genus of bodies we find the human body, composed of elements equally tempered, attaining to the lowest member of the class above it, that is, to the human soul, which holds the lowest rank in the class of subsistent intelligences. Hence the human soul is said to be on the horizon and boundary line between things corporeal and incorporeal, inasmuch as it is an incorporeal substance and at the same time the form of a body.

Above other forms there is found a form, likened to the supramundane substances in point of understanding, and competent to an activity which is accomplished without any bodily organ at all; and this is the intellectual soul: for the act of understanding is not done through any bodily organ. Hence the intellectual soul cannot be totally encompassed by matter, or immersed in it, as other material forms are: this is shown by its intellectual activity, wherein bodily matter has no share. The fact however that the very act of understanding in the human soul needs certain powers that work through bodily organs, namely, phantasy and sense, is a clear proof that the said soul is naturally united to the body to make up the human species.

CHAPTER LXIX—Solution of the Arguments alleged to show that a Subsistent Intelligence cannot be united with a Body as the Form of that Body

The arguments wherewith Averroes endeavors to establish his opinion do not prove that the subsistent intelligence is not united with the body as the form of the same.

1. The words of Aristotle about the potential intellect, that it is "impassible, unmixed, and separate," do not necessitate the admission that the intellectual substance is not united with the body as its form, giving it being. They are sufficiently verified by saying that the intellectual faculty, which Aristotle calls the 'speculative faculty,' is not the actualization of any organ, as exercising its activity through that organ.

2. Supposing the substance of the soul to be united in being with the body as the form of the body, while still the intellect is not the actualization of any organ, it does not follow that intellect falls under the law of physical determination, as do sensible and material things: for we do not suppose intellect to be a harmony, or function (ratio, γόλος) of any organ, as Aristotle says that sense is.

3. That Aristotle is saying that the intellect is

'unmingled,' or 'separate,' does not intend to exclude it from being a part, or faculty, of the soul, which soul is the form of the whole body, is evident from this passage, where he is arguing against those who said that there were different parts of the soul in different parts of the body: — "If the whole soul keeps together the body as a whole, it is fitting that each part of the soul should keep together some part of the body: but this looks like an impossibility: for it is difficult even to imagine what part of the body the intellect shall keep together, or how."

### CHAPTER LXXIII—That the Potential Intellect is not One and the Same in all Men

HENCE it is plainly shown that there is not one and the same potential intellect, belonging to all men who are and who shall be and who have been, as Averroes pretends.

A. 1. It has been shown that the substance of the intellect is united with the human body and is its form (Chap. LVII). But it is impossible for there to be one form otherwise than of one matter. Therefore there is not one intellect for all men.

A. 2 and 3. It is not possible for a dog's soul to enter a wolf's body, or a man's soul any other body than the body of a man. But the same proportion that holds between a man's soul and a man's body, holds between the soul of this man and the body of this man. It is impossible therefore for the soul of this man to enter any other body than the body of this man. But it is by the soul of this man that this man understands. Therefore there is not one and the same intellect of this man and of that.

A. 4. A thing has being from that source from

whence it has unity: for one and being are inseparable. But everything has being by its own form. Therefore the unity of the thing follows the unity of the form. It is impossible therefore for there to be one form of different individual men. But the form of any individual man is his intellectual soul. It is impossible therefore for there to be one intellect of all men.

But if it is said that the sentient soul of this man is other than the sentient soul of that, and so far forth the two are not one man, though there be one intellect of both, such explanation cannot stand. For the proper activity of every being follows upon and is indicative of its species. But as the proper activity of an animal is to feel, so the proper activity of a man is to understand. As any given individual is an animal in that he has feeling, so is he a man by virtue of the faculty whereby he understands. But the faculty whereby the soul understands, or the man through the soul, is the potential intellect. This individual then is a man by the potential intellect. If then this man has another sentient soul than another man, but not another potential intellect, but one and the same, it follows that they are two animals, but not two men.

B. To these arguments the Commentator replies by saying that the potential intellect is conjoined with us through its own form, namely, through an intelligible impression, one subject of which [is the said potential intellect, and one subject again] is the phantasm existing in us, which differs in different men; and thus the potential intellect is multiplied in different men, not by reason of its substance, but by reason of its form.

The nullity of this reply appears by what has been shown above (Chap. LIX), that it would be impossible for any man to have understanding, if this were the only way in which the potential intellect were conjoined with us. But suppose that the aforesaid conjunction (continuatio) were sufficient to render man intelligent, still the said answer does not solve the arguments already alleged.

B. 1. According to the above exposition, nothing belonging to intellect will remain multiplied as men are multiplied except only the phantasm, or impression in phantasy; and this very phantasm will not be multiplied as it is actually understood, because, as so understood, it is in the potential intellect, and has undergone abstraction of material conditions under the operation of the active intellect; whereas the phantasm, as a potential term of intelligence, does not transcend the grade of the sentient soul.

B. 2. Still the objection holds, that this man will not be differentiated from that except by the sentient soul; and the awkward consequence follows that this man and that together do not make a plurality of men.

B. 3. Nothing attains its species by what it is potentially, but by what it is actually. But the impression in phantasy, as multiplied in this man and that, has only a potentially intelligible being. Therefore that impression, as so multiplied, does not put any given individual in the species of 'intelligent animal,' which is the definition of 'man.' Thus it remains true that the specific ratio of 'man' is not multiplied in individual men.

B. 4. It is the first and not the second perfection that gives the species to every living thing. But the impression in phantasy is a second perfection; and therefore not from that multiplied impression has man his species.

B. 6. That which puts a man in the species of man

must be something abiding in the same individual as long as he remains: otherwise the individual would not be always of one and the same species, but now of one species and now of another. But the impressions of phantasy do not remain always the same in the same man; but new impressions come, and previous impressions perish. Therefore the individual man does not attain his species by any such impression: nor is it anything in the phantasy that conjoins him with the formal principle of his species, which is the potential intellect.

C. But if it is said that the individual does not receive his species by the phantasms themselves, but by the faculties in which the phantasms are, namely, the phantasy, the memory, and the vis cogitativa which is proper to man, and which in the De anima, III, v, Aristotle calls the 'passive intellect,' the same awkward consequences still follow.

C. 1. Since the vis cogitativa operates only upon particulars, the impressions of which it puts apart and puts together; and further, since it has a bodily organ through which it acts, it does not transcend the rank of the sentient soul. But in virtue of his sentient soul, as such, man is not a man, but an animal. It still therefore remains true that the element, supposed to be multiplied in us, belongs to man only in his animal capacity.

C. 2. The cogitative faculty, since it acts through an organ, is not the faculty whereby we understand. But the principle whereby we understand is the principle whereby man is man. Therefore no individual is man by virtue of the cogitative faculty: nor does man by that faculty essentially differ from dumb animals, as the Commentator pretends.

C. 3. The cogitative faculty is united to the

potential intellect, the principle of human intelligence, only by its action of preparing phantasms for the active intellect to render them actual terms of intelligence and perfections of the potential intellect. But this preliminary activity of the cogitative faculty does not always remain the same in us. Therefore it cannot be the means whereby man is conjoined with the specific principle of the human species, or made a member of that species.

C. 4. If the potential intellect of this and that man were numerically one and the same, the act of understanding would be one and the same in both which is an impossibility.

D. But if it is said that the act of understanding is multiplied according to the diversity of impressions in phantasy, that supposition cannot stand.

D. 3. For the potential intellect understands a man, not as this individual man, but as man simply, according to the specific essence of the race. But this specific essence remains one, however much impressions in phantasy are multiplied, whether in the same man or in different men. Therefore no multiplication of phantasms can be the cause of multiplication of the act of understanding in the potential intellect, considering the same species; and thus we shall still have numerically one action in different men.

D. 4. The proper subject in which the habit of knowledge resides is the potential intellect. But an accident, so long as it remains specifically one, is multiplied only by coming to reside in different subjects. If then the potential intellect is one in all men, any habit of knowledge specifically the same, say, the habit of grammar, must be numerically the same in all men, which is unthinkable.

E. But to this they say that the subject of the habit of knowledge is not the potential intellect, but the passive intellect and the cogitative faculty (Chap. LX): which it cannot be.

E. 1. For, as Aristotle shows in the Ethics (II, i), like acts engender like habits; and like habits reproduce like acts. Now by the acts of the potential intellect there comes to be the habit of knowledge in us; and we are competent for the same acts by possession of the habit of knowledge. Therefore the habit of knowledge is in the potential intellect, not in the passive.

E. 2. Scientific knowledge is of demonstrated conclusions; and demonstrated conclusions, like their premises, are universal truths. Science therefore is in that faculty which takes cognizance of universals. But the passive intellect is not cognizant of universals, but of particular notions.

F. The error of placing the habit of scientific knowledge in the passive intellect seems to have arisen from the observation that men are found more or less apt for the study of science according to the several dispositions of the cogitative faculty and the phantasy.

F. 1. But this aptitude depends on those faculties only as remote conditions: so it also depends on the complexion of the body, as Aristotle says that men of delicate touch and soft flesh are clever. But the proximate principle of the act of speculative understanding is the habit of scientific knowledge: for this habit must perfect the power of understanding to act readily at will, as other habits perfect the powers in which they are.

F. 2. The dispositions of the cogitative faculty and the phantasy regard the object: they regard the phantasm, which is prepared by the efficiency of these faculties readily to become a term of actual understanding under the action of the active intellect. But habits do not condition objects: they condition faculties. Thus conditions that take the edge off terrors are not the habit of fortitude: fortitude is a disposition of the conative part of the soul to meet terrors. Hence it appears that the habit of knowledge is not in the passive but in the potential intellect.

F. 3. If the potential intellect of all men is one, we must suppose that the potential intellect has always existed, if men have always existed, as Averroists suppose; and much more the active intellect, because agent is more honorable than patient, as Aristotle says (De anima, III, v). But if the agent is eternal, and the recipient eternal, the contents received must be eternal also. Therefore the intellectual impressions have been from eternity in the potential intellect: therefore it will be impossible for it to receive afresh any new intellectual impressions. But the only use of sense and phantasy in the process of understanding is that intellectual impressions may be gathered from them. At this rate then neither sense nor phantasy will be needed for understanding; and we come back to the opinion of Plato, that we do not acquire knowledge by the senses, but are merely roused by them to remember what we knew before.

G. But to this the Commentator replies that intellectual presentations reside in a twofold subject: in one subject, from which they have everlasting being, namely, the potential intellect; in another subject, from which they have a recurring new existence, namely, the phantasm, or impression in phantasy. He illustrates this by the comparison of a sight-presentation, which has also a twofold subject, the one subject being the thing outside the soul, the other the visual faculty. But this answer cannot stand.

G. 1. For it is impossible that the action and perfection of the eternal should depend on anything temporal. But phantasms are temporal things, continually springing up afresh in us from the experience of the senses. Therefore the intellectual impressions, whereby the potential intellect is actuated and brought to activity, cannot possibly depend on phantasms in the way that visual impressions depend on things outside the soul.

G. 2. Nothing receives what it has already got. But before any sensory experience of mine or yours there were intellectual impressions in the potential intellect: for the generations before us could not have understood had not the potential intellect been reduced to act by intellectual impressions. Nor can it be said that those impressions, formerly received in the potential intellect, have ceased to be: because the potential intellect not only receives, but keeps what it receives: hence it is called the "place of ideas." Therefore, on this showing, no impressions from our phantasms are received in the potential intellect.

G. 6 and 7. If the potential intellect receives no intellectual impressions from the phantasms that are in us, because it has already received them from the phantasms of those who were before us, then for the like reason we must say that it receives impressions from the phantasms of no generation of men, whom another generation has preceded. But every generation has been preceded by some previous generation, if the world and human society is eternal, as Averroists suppose. Therefore the potential intellect never receives any impressions from phantasms; and from this it seems to follow that the potential intellect has no need of phantasms to understand. But we (nos) understand by the potential intellect. Therefore neither shall we need sense and phantasm for our understanding: which is manifestly false and contrary to the opinion of Aristotle.

For the potential intellect, like every other substance, operates according to the mode of its nature. Now according to its nature it is the form of the body. Hence it understands immaterial things, but views them in some material medium; as is shown by the fact that in teaching universal truths particular examples are alleged, in which what is said may be seen. Therefore the need which the potential intellect has of the phantasm before receiving the intellectual impression is different from that which it has after the impression has been received. Before reception, it needs the phantasm to gather from it the intellectual impression, so that the phantasm then stands to the potential intellect as an object which moves it. But after receiving the impression, of which the phantasm is the vehicle, it needs the phantasm as an instrument or basis of the impression received. Thus by command of the intellect there is formed in the phantasy a phantasm answering to such and such an intellectual impression; and in this phantasm the intellectual impression shines forth as an exemplar in the thing exemplified, or as in an image.

G. 8. If the potential intellect is one for all men and eternal, by this time there must have been received in it the intellectual impressions of all things that have been known by any men whatsoever. Then, as every one of us understands by the potential intellect, — nay, as the act of understanding in each is the act of that potential intellect understanding, — every one of us must understand all that has been understood by any other men whatsoever.

H. To this the Commentator replies that we do not understand by the potential intellect except in so far as it is conjoined with us through the impressions in our phantasy, and that these phantasms are not the same nor similar amongst all men. And this answer seems to be in accordance with the doctrine that has gone before: for, apart from any affirmation of the unity of the potential intellect, it is true that we do not understand those things, the impressions whereof are in the potential intellect, unless the appropriate phantasms are at hand. But that this answer does not altogether escape the difficulty, may be thus shown.

When the potential intellect has been actualized by the reception of an intellectual impression, it is competent to act of itself: hence we see that, once we have got the knowledge of a thing, it is in our power to consider it again when we wish: nor are we at a loss for lack of phantasms, because it is in our power to form phantasms suitable to the consideration which we wish, unless there happens to be some impediment on the part of the organ, as in persons out of their mind or in a comatose state. But if in the potential intellect there are intellectual impressions of all branches of knowledge, — as we must say, if that intellect is one and eternal, — then the necessity of phantasms for the potential intellect will be the same as in his case who already has knowledge, and wishes to study and consider some point of that knowledge, for that also he could not do without phantasms. Since then every man understands by the potential intellect so far as it is reduced to act by intellectual impressions, so every man should be able on this theory to regard, whenever he would, all the known points of all sciences: which is manifestly false, for at that rate no one would need a teacher. Therefore the potential intellect is not one and eternal.

CHAPTER LXXIV—Of the Opinion of Avicenna, who supposed Intellectual Forms not to be preserved in the Potential Intellect

THE above arguments (against Averroes) seem to be obviated by the theory of Avicenna. He says that intellectual impressions do not remain in the potential intellect except just so long as they are being actually understood. And this he endeavors to prove from the fact that forms are actually apprehended so long as they remain in the faculty that apprehends them: thus in the act of perception both sense and intellect become identified with their objects: hence it seems that whenever sense or intellect is united with its object, as having taken its form, actual apprehension, sensible or intellectual, occurs. But the faculties which preserve forms which not actually apprehended, he says, are not the faculties that apprehend those forms, but storehouses (thesauros) attached to the said apprehensive faculties. Thus phantasy is the storehouse of forms apprehended by sense; and memory, according to him, is the storehouse of notions apprehended independently of sensation, as when the sheep apprehends the hostility of the wolf. The capacity of these faculties for storing up forms not actually apprehended comes from their having certain bodily organs in which the forms are received, such reception following close upon the (first) apprehension; and thereby the apprehensive faculty, turning to these storehouses, apprehends in act. But it is acknowledged that the potential intellect is an apprehensive faculty, and has no bodily organ: hence Avicenna concludes that it is impossible for intellectual impressions to be preserved in the potential intellect except so long as it is actually understanding. Therefore, one of three things: either (1) these intellectual impressions must be preserved in some bodily organ, or faculty having a bodily organ: or (2) they must be self-existent intelligible forms, to which our potential intellect stands in the relation of a mirror to the objects mirrored: or (3) whenever the potential intellect understands, these intellectual impressions must flow into it afresh from some separate agent. The first of these three suppositions is impossible: because forms existing in faculties that use bodily organs are only potentially intelligible. The second supposition is the opinion of Plato, which Aristotle rejects. Hence Avicenna concludes that, whenever we actually understand, there flow into our potential intellect intellectual impressions from the active intellect, which he assumes to be an intelligence subsisting apart. If anyone objects against him that then there is no difference between a man when he first learns, and when he wishes to review and study again something which he has learnt before, he replies that to learn and con over again what we know is nothing else than to acquire a perfect habit of uniting ourselves with the (extrinsic) active intelligence, so as to receive therefrom the intellectual form; and therefore, before we come to reflect on and use our knowledge, there is in man a bare potentiality of such reception, but reflection on our knowledge is like potentiality reduced to act. And this view seems consonant with what Aristotle teaches, that memory is not in the intellectual but in the sensitive part of the soul. So it seems that the preservation of intellectual impressions does not belong to the intellectual part of the soul. But on careful consideration this theory will be found ultimately to differ little or nothing from the theory of Plato. Plato supposed forms of intellect to be separately existing substances, whence knowledge flowed in upon our souls: Avicenna supposes one separate substance, the active intellect, to be the source when knowledge flows in upon our souls. Now it makes no matter for the acquirement of knowledge whether our knowledge is caused by one separate substance or by several. Either way it will follow that our knowledge is not caused by sensible things: the contrary of which conclusion appears from the fact that anyone wanting in any one sense is wanting in acquaintance with the sensible objects of which that sense takes cognizance.

1. It is a novelty to say that the potential intellect, viewing the impressions made by singular things in the phantasy, is lit up by the light of the active intellect to know the universal; and that the action of the lower faculties, phantasy, memory, and cogitative faculty, fit and prepare the soul to receive the emanation of the active intellect. This, I say, is novel and strange doctrine: for we see that our soul is better disposed to receive impressions from intelligences subsisting apart, the further it is removed from bodily and sensible things: the higher is attained by receding from the lower. It is not therefore likely that any regarding of bodily phantasms should dispose our soul to receive the influence of an intelligence subsisting apart. Plato made a better study of the basis of his position: for he supposed that sensible appearances do not dispose the soul to receive the influence of separately subsisting forms, but merely rouse the intellect to consider knowledge that has been already caused in it by

an external principle: for he supposed that from the beginning knowledge of all things intellectually knowable was caused in our souls by separately existing forms, or ideas: hence learning, he said, was nothing else than recollecting.

3. Intellectual knowledge is more perfect than sensory. If therefore in sensory knowledge there is some power of preserving apprehensions, much more will this be the case in intellectual knowledge.

6. This opinion is contrary to the mind of Aristotle, who says that the potential intellect is "the place of ideas": which is tantamount to saying that it is a "storehouse" of intellectual impressions, to use Avicenna's own phrase.

The arguments to the contrary are easily solved. For the potential intellect is perfectly actuated about intellectual impressions when it is actually considering them: when it is not actually considering them, it is not perfectly actuated about them, but is in a condition intermediate between potentiality and actuality. As for memory, that is located in the sentient part of the soul, because the objects of memory fall under a definite time for there is no memory but of the past; and therefore, since there is no abstraction of its object from individualizing conditions, memory does not belong to the intellectual side of our nature, which deals with universals This however does not bar the potential intellect's preservation of intellectual impressions, which are abstracted from all particular conditions.

CHAPTER LXXV—Confutation of the Arguments which seem to prove the Unity of the Potential Intellect

ARG. 1. Apparently, every form that is specifically one and numerically multiplied, is individualized by its matter: for things specifically one and numerically many agree in form, and are distinguished according to matter. If then the potential intellect is multiplied according to number in different men, while it remains one in species, it must be multiplied in this and that man by matter, — by the matter which is that man's body the form of which it is supposed to be. But every form, individualized by matter which it actuates, is a material form: for the being of everything must depend on that on which its individuation depends: for as general constituents are of the essence of the species, so individualizing constituents are of the essence of this individual. It follows therefore that the potential intellect is a material form, and consequently that it does not receive any thing, nor do anything, except through a bodily organ: which is contrary to the nature of the potential intellect.

Reply. We confess that the potential intellect is specifically one in different men, and many according to number, — waiving the point that the constituents of man are not put into genus and species for what they are in themselves, but for what they are as constituents of the whole. Still it does not follow that the potential intellect is a material form, dependent for its being on the body. For as it is specifically proper to the human soul to be united to a certain species of body, so any individual soul differs from any other individual soul, in number only, inasmuch as it is referable to numerically another body. Thus then human souls, — and consequently the potential intellect, which is a faculty of the human soul, — are individualized according to bodies, not that the individuation is caused by the bodies.

Arg.2. If the potential intellect were different in this man and that, the impression understood would have to be numerically different in this man, while remaining one in species: for since the proper subject of impressions actually understood is the potential intellect, when that intellect is multiplied there must be a corresponding multiplication of intellectual impressions according to the number of different individuals. But the only impressions or forms which are the same in species and different in number, are individual forms, which cannot be intellectual forms, because objects of intellect are universal, not particular. It is impossible therefore for the potential intellect to be multiplied in different individual men.

Reply. This second argument fails from neglecting to distinguish between that whereby (quo) we understand, and that which (quod) we understand. The impression received in the potential intellect is not to be taken for that which is understood. For as all arts and sciences have for their object-matter things which are understood, it would follow that the subject matter of all sciences was impressions on the potential intellect: which is manifestly false, for no science has anything to say to such mental impressions except psychology and metaphysics: though it is true that through those mental impressions there is known the whole content of all the sciences. Therefore, in the process of understanding, the intellectual impression received in the potential intellect is that whereby we understand, as the impression of color in the eye is not that which is seen, but that whereby we see. On the other hand, that which is understood is the nature (ratio) of things existing outside the soul, as also it is things existing outside the soul that are seen with the bodily sight: for to this end were arts and sciences invented, that things might be known in their natures (naturis).

Still it does not follow that, if sciences are of universal truths, universals should subsist by themselves outside the soul, as Plato supposed. For though for the truth of knowledge it is necessary that the knowledge should answer to the thing, still it is not necessary that the mode of the knowledge and the mode of the thing should be the same: for properties that are united in the thing are sometimes known separately. Thus one and the same thing is white and sweet: still sight takes cognizance only of the whiteness, and taste only of the sweetness. Thus again intellect understands a line drawn in sensible matter apart from that sensible matter, though it might understand it also along with the sensible matter. This difference arises according to the diversity of intellectual impressions received in the intellect, which sometimes are the likeness of quantity only, sometimes of a sensible quantitative substance. In like manner also, though the nature of genus and species never exists except in concrete individuals, still the intellect understands the nature of genus and species without understanding the individualizing elements; and this is the meaning of understanding universals. And so these two positions are reconciled, that universals have no subsistence outside the soul; and yet that the intellect, understanding universals, understands things which are outside the soul.

The fact of the intellect understanding the nature of genus and species stripped of its individualizing elements, arises from the condition of the intellectual impression received in understanding, which impression is rendered immaterial by the active intellect, inasmuch as it is abstracted from matter and materializing conditions whereby a thing is individualized. And therefore the sentient faculties can take no cognizance of universals, since they cannot receive an immaterial form, seeing that they receive always in a bodily organ.

It is not therefore necessary that the intellectual impression of this and that intelligence should be numerically one: for it would follow thereupon that the act of understanding in them both was also numerically one, since activity follows form, which is the principle of species: but it is necessary, to the end that one object should be understood by both minds, that there should be a like impression of one and the same object in them both. And this is possible enough, although the intellectual impressions differ in number: for there is no difficulty in having different images of one thing; hence the contingency of one than being seen by several persons. There is nothing inconsistent then with the universalizing knowledge of the understanding in their being different intellectual impressions in different minds. Nor need it ensue, because these intellectual impressions are many in number and the same in species, that they are not actual but only potential terms of understanding, as is the case with other individual things. Mere individuality is not inconsistent with intelligibility: for we must admit the potential and active intellects themselves, if we may suppose the two to subsist apart, united to no body, but subsistent by themselves, to be individual beings and still intelligible. What is inconsistent with intelligibility is materiality: as is shown by this consideration, that for the forms of material things to become actually intelligible, abstraction has to be made from the particular matter in which they are lodged; and therefore in cases in which individuation is due to particular matter involving particular dimensions, the things so individualized are not actually intelligible. But where individuation is not due to matter, such individual things may without difficulty be actually intelligible. Now intellectual impressions, like all other forms, are individualized by their subject, which is the potential intellect; and since the potential intellect is not material, it does not stand in the way of the actual intelligibility of the impressions individualized by it.

But though we have said that the intellectual impression, received in the potential intellect, is not that which is understood, but that whereby we understand, still it remains true that by reflection the intellect understands itself and its own intellectual act and the impression whereby it understands. Its own intellectual act it understands in two ways, — in one way, in particular, for it understands that it is now understanding; in another way, in general, inasmuch as it reasons about the said act. And likewise it understands intellect and the impression in intellect in two ways, — by remarking that itself is and has an intellectual impression, which is particular knowledge; and by studying its own nature and the nature of the intellectual impression, which is knowledge of the universal. According to this latter way we treat of intellect and of the intelligible in science.

Arg.3. The master transfuses the knowledge which he has into the scholar. Either then the knowledge transfused is the same in number, or different in number, though the same in species. The latter alternative seems impossible: because it supposes the master to cause his own knowledge in the scholar in the same way that an agent causes its own form in another being, by generating a nature specifically like its own; which seems proper to material agents. It must be then that numerically the same knowledge is caused in the scholar that was in the master; which would be impossible, were there not one potential intellect of them both.

Reply. The saying that the knowledge in master and scholar is numerically one, is partly true and partly not: it is numerically one in point of the thing known, but not in point of the intellectual impressions whereby the thing is known, nor in point of the habit of knowledge itself. It is to be observed however that, as Aristotle (Metaph.VII, ix) teaches, there are arts in whose subject matter there is not any principle active in producing the effect of the art, as is clear in the building art: for in wood and stones there is no active power moving to the erection of a house, but only a passive aptitude. But there is an art in whose subject matter there is an active principle moving in the direction of the effect of the art, as is clear in the healing art: for in the sick subject there is an active principle tending to health. And therefore the effect of the former kind of art is never produced by nature, but always by art, as every house is a work of art: but the effect of the latter kind is produced as well by art as by nature without art: for many are healed by the operation of nature without the art of medicine. In these things that can be done both by art and nature, art imitates nature: thus if one is sick of a chill, nature heals him by warming him: hence the physician also, if he is to cure him, heals him by warming. Similar is the case with the art of teaching: for in the pupil there is an active principle making for knowledge, namely, the understanding, and those primary axioms which are naturally understood; and therefore knowledge is acquired in two ways, — without teaching, by a man's own finding out, and again by teaching. The teacher therefore begins to teach in the same way that the discoverer begins to find out, by offering for the consideration of the scholar elements of knowledge already possessed by him: because all education and all knowledge starts from pre-existing knowledge, drawing conclusions from elements already in the mind, and proposing sensible examples whereby there may be formed in the scholar's soul those impressions of phantasy which are necessary or intelligence. And because the working of the teacher from without would affect nothing, unless borne out by an internal principle of knowledge, which is within us by the gift of God, so it is said among theologians that man teaches by rendering the service of ministry, but God by working within: so too the physician is called nature's minister in healing.

A final remark. Since the Commentator makes the passive intellect the residence of habits of knowledge (Chap. LX), the unity of the potential intellect helps not at all to the numerical unity of knowledge in master and scholar: for certainly the passive intellect is not the same in different men, since it is an organic faculty. Hence, on his own showing, this argument does not serve his purpose.

CHAPTER LXXVI—That the Active Intellect is not a separately Subsisting Intelligence, but a Faculty of the Soul

WE may further conclude that neither is the active intellect one in all men, as Alexander and Avicenna suppose, though they do not suppose the potential intellect to be one in all men.

4. Plato supposed knowledge in us to be caused by Ideas, which he took to subsist apart by themselves. But clearly the first principle on which our knowledge depends is the active intellect. If therefore the active intellect is something subsisting apart by itself, the difference will be none, or but slight, between this opinion and that of Plato, which the Philosopher rejects.

5. If the active intellect is an intelligence subsisting apart, its action upon us will either be continual and uninterrupted, or at least we must say that it is not continued or broken off at our pleasure. Now its action is to make the impressions on our phantasy actual terms of intelligence. Either therefore it will do this always or not always. If not always, still it will not do it at our discretion. Either therefore we must be always in the act of understanding, or it will not be in our power actually to understand when we wish.

But it may be said that the active intellect, so far as with it lies, is always in action, but that the impressions in our phantasy are not always becoming actual terms of intelligence, but only when they are disposed thereto; and they are disposed thereto by the act of the cogitative faculty, the use of which is in our power; and therefore actually to understand is in our power; and this is why not all men understand the things whereof they have the impressions in their phantasy, because not all have at command a suitable act of the cogitative faculty, but only those who are accustomed and trained thereto. But this answer does not appear to be altogether sufficient. That the impressions in phantasy are marshalled by the cogitative faculty to the end that they may become actual terms of understanding and move the potential intellect, does not seem a sufficient account, if it be coupled with the supposition of the potential intellect being a separately subsistent intelligence. This seems to go with the theory of those who say that inferior agents supply only predispositions to final perfection, but that final perfection is the work of an extrinsic agency: which is contrary to the mind of Aristotle: for the human soul does not appear to be worse off for understanding than inferior natures are for their own severally proper activities.

9. In the nature of every cause there is contained a principle sufficient for the natural operation of that cause. If the operation consists in action, there is at hand an active principle, as we see in the powers of the vegetative soul in plants. If the operation consists in receiving impressions, there is at hand a passive principle, as we see in the sentient powers of animals. But man is the most perfect of all inferior causes; and his proper and natural operation is to understand, an operation which is not accomplished without a certain receiving of impressions, inasmuch as every understanding is determined by its object; nor again without action, inasmuch as the intellect makes potential into actual terms of understanding. There must therefore be in the nature of man a proper principle of both operations, to wit, both an active and a potential intellect, and neither of them must be separate in being (or physically distinct), from the soul of man.

10. If the active intellect is an intelligence subsisting apart, it is clearly above the nature of man. But any activity which a man exercises by mere virtue of a supernatural cause is a supernatural activity, as the working of miracles, prophecy, and the like effects, which are wrought by men in virtue of a divine endowment. Since then man cannot understand except by means of the

active intellect, it follows, supposing that intellect a separately subsistent being, that to understand is not an operation proper and natural to man; and thus man cannot be defined as intellectual or rational.

11. No agent works except by some power which is formally in the agent as a constituent of its being. But the working both of potential and of active intellect is proper to man: for man produces ideas by abstraction from phantasms, and receives in his mind those ideas; operations which it would never occur to us to think of, did we not experience them in ourselves. The principles therefore to which these operations are attributable, namely, the potential and the active intellect, must be faculties formally existing in us.

12. A being that cannot proceed to its own proper business without being moved thereto by an external principle, is rather driven to act than acts of itself. This is the case with irrational creatures. Sense, moved by an exterior sensible object, makes an impression on the phantasy; and so in order the impression proceeds through all the faculties till it reaches those which move the rest. Now the proper business of man is to understand; and the prime mover in understanding is the active intellect, which makes intellectual impressions whereby the potential intellect is impressed; which potential intellect, when actualized, moves the will. If then the active intellect has a separate subsistence outside man, the whole of man's activity depends on an extrinsic principle. Man then will not be his own leader, but will be led by another; and thus will not be master of his own acts, nor deserve praise nor blame; and the whole of moral science and political society will perish: an awkward conclusion. Therefore the active intellect has no subsistence apart

from man.

CHAPTER LXXVII—That it is not impossible for the Potential and the Active Intellect to be united in the one Substance of the Soul

SOME one perhaps may think it impossible for one and the same substance, that of our soul, to be in potentiality to receive all intellectual impressions (which is the function of the potential intellect), and to actualize those impressions (which is the function of the active intellect); since nothing acts as it is in potentiality to receive, but only as it is in actual readiness to act. But, looking at the matter rightly, no inconvenience or difficulty will be found in this view of the union of the active and potential intellect in the one substance of the soul. For a thing may well be in potentiality in one respect and in actuality in another; and this we find to be the condition of the intellectual soul in its relation to phantasms, or impressions in phantasy. For the intellectual soul has something in actuality, to which the phantasm is in potentiality; and on the other hand the intellectual soul potentiality that which is actually found in the phantasms. For the substance of the human soul has the attribute of immateriality: but it is not thereby assimilated to this or that definite thing; and yet such assimilation is requisite for our soul to know this or that thing definitely, since all cognition takes place by some likeness of the object known being stamped on the knowing mind. Thus then the intellectual soul remains in potentiality, open to the reception of definite impressions in the likeness of things that come within our observation and knowledge, which are the natures of sensible things.

These definite natures of sensible things are represented to us by phantasms, which however have not yet reached the stage of being objects of intellect, seeing that they are likenesses of sensible things under material conditions, which are individualizing properties, — and besides they are in bodily organs. They are therefore not actual objects of understanding; and yet since in the case of this man [or other sensible object], whose likeness is represented by phantasms, it is possible to fix upon a universal nature stripped of all individualizing conditions, these phantasms are potentially intelligible. Thus then they have a potentially intelligible being, but an actually definite likeness to things, whereas in the intellectual soul, as we saw, the situation was the other way about. There is then in the intellectual soul a power exercising its activity upon phantasms, making them actual objects of understanding; and this power of the soul is called the active intellect. There is also in the soul a power that is potentially open to definite impressions of sensible things; and this power is the potential intellect.

But the intellectual soul does not lie open to receive impressions of the likenesses of things that are in phantasms in the way that the likeness exists in the phantasm, but according as those likenesses are raised to a higher stage, by being abstracted from individualizing material conditions and rendered actual objects, or terms, of understanding. And therefore the action of the active intellect upon the phantasms precedes their being received into the potential intellect; and thus the prime agency is not attributable to the phantasms, but to the active intellect.

There are some animals that see better by night than by day, because they have weak eyes, which are stimulated by a little light, but dazzled by much. And the case is similar with our understanding, which is "to the clearest truths as the bat's eye to the sun" (Aristotle, Metaph.I, Appendix): hence the little intellectual light that is connatural to us is sufficient for us to understand with. But that the intellectual light connatural to our soul is sufficient to produce the action of the active intellect, will be clear to anyone who considers the necessity for positing such an intellect. Our soul is found to be in potentiality to intelligible objects as sense to sensible objects: for as we are not always having sensations, so we are not always understanding. These intelligible objects Plato assumed to exist by themselves, calling them 'Ideas': hence it was not necessary for him to posit any 'active intellect' rendering objects intelligible. But if this Platonic position were true, the absolutely better objects of intelligence should be better also relatively to us, and be better understood by us, which is manifestly not the case: for things are more intelligible to us which are nigher to sense, though in themselves they are less excellent objects of understanding. Hence Aristotle was moved to lay down the doctrine, that the things which are intelligible to us are not any self-existent objects of understanding, but are gathered from objects of sense. Hence he had to posit some faculty to do this work of making terms of understanding: that faculty is the active intellect. The active intellect therefore is posited to make terms of understanding proportionate to our capacity. Such work does not transcend the measure of intellectual light connatural to us. Hence there is no difficulty in attributing the action of the active intellect to the native light of our soul, especially as Aristotle compares the active intellect to light (De anima, III, v, 2).

CHAPTER LXXVIII—That it was not the opinion of Aristotle that the Active Intellect is a separately Subsistent Intelligence, but rather that it is a part of the Soul

This chapter is a running commentary on De anima, III, v, and may be more profitably presented by a description of its contents than by a translation.1. On ἀνάγκη καὶ ἐν τῇ ψυχῇ ὑπάρχειν ταύτας τὰς διαφοράς (these differences must also be in the soul), St Thomas points out that the differences in question, to wit, the potential and the active intellect, are both said to be "in the soul," which excludes either of them from being a faculty extrinsic to the soul.2. On ἐν ἀπάσῃ τῇ φύσει, which in his translation appears as in omni natura, and which he takes to mean, not as the Greek means, "in all nature," but in every natural substance," he argues that both the ὕλη, or potential intellect, and the αἴτιον καὶ ποιητικόν, or active intellect, must be in the natural substanceof the soul.3. Upon the words, used of the active intellect, that it is ὡς ἕξις τις, οἷον τὸ φῶς(as a habit, like light), he says that as a habit does not exist by itself, so neither can, on this showing, the active intellect. He adds that 'habit' here does not mean 'habitual knowledge,' as when we speak of 'a habit (i.e., habitual knowledge) of first principles,' but a positive endowment, actual and formal, as opposed to privation and potentiality.4. Of the four epithets bestowed on the active intellect, χωριστός, ἀμιγής, ἀπαθής, τῇ οὐσίᾳ ὢν ἐνεργείᾳ(separate, unmingled, impassible, by essence being in act), he observes that the first and second have already been applied to the potential intellect: see Chap. IV, n. 6, ὁ δὲ χωριστός: IV, 3, ἀμιγῆ εἶναι .... οὐδὲ μεμῖχθαι τῳ σώματι. The third, he says, has been applied to the potential intellect with a distinction (he refers to iv, 5, 6): the potential intellect is impassible, as not being acted on by matter, having no bodily organ to receive direct impressions from material things: but it receives impressions from the active intellect. The fourth, he says, has been flatly denied of the potential intellect, which is said, iv, 12, to be δυνάμει πως τὰ νοητά, ἀλλ᾽ ἐντελεχείᾳ οὐδὲν πρίν ἂν νοῇ(potentially identified with the intelligible forms, but actually nothing before it understands). He concludes that the word χωριστός is only applied to the active intellect in the same sense in which it has already been referred to the potential intellect, iv, 9, τὸ μὲν γὰρ αἰσθητικὸν οὐκ ἄνευ σώματος, ὁ δὲ χωριστός(the faculty of sense is not without body, but this is separate). He identifies χωριστός with ἄνευ σώματος, as meaning 'operative without bodily organ.' 5. On τὸ δ᾽ αὐτό ἐστιν ἡ κατ᾽ ἐνέργειαν ἐπιστήμη τῷ πράγματι(actual knowledge is identical with its object), — which means that, inasmuch as objects of knowledge become present by representation in the mind, the mind in knowing anything knows itself, — St Thomas blames Averroes for taking this to be true only of the active intellect: he cites iv, 13, τὸ αὐτό ἐστι τὸ νοοῦν καὶ τὸ νοούμενον, ἡ γὰρ θεωρητικὴ ἐπιστήμη καὶ τὸ οὕτως ἐπιστητὸν τὸ αὐτό ἐστιν(knower and known are identical, for speculative science and its object are one), where he says that Aristotle speaks, not of the active, but of the potential intellect. In the words ἡ κατ᾽ ἐνέργειαν ἐπιστήμη(scientia in acta) St Thomas discovers a tertium quid, which is neither potential nor active intellect, but a combination of the two: he calls it intellectus in actu, 'the intellect as actually understanding,' the concrete mind at work. 6. On ἡ δὲ κατὰ δύναμιν χρόνῳ προτέρα ἐν τῷ ἑνί, ὅλως οὐδὲ χρόνῳ (potential knowledge is prior in time to actual knowledge in the individual, but all the world over it is not prior even in time), he is misled by his Latin translation, qui vero secundum potentiam, as though the Greek had been ὁ δὲ κατὰ δύναμιν νοῦς. He takes it for a question of priority in time between the potential intellect and the concrete, actually thinking mind (intellectus in actu). The error is not serious. 7. Coming to οὐχ ὁτὲ μὲν νοεῖ, ὁτὲ δὲ οὐ νοεῖ (it does not at one time think, and at another time not think), he says that this is spoken of the actually thinking mind, to mark it off from the potential intellect. His conclusion is: "The mind comes to be actually thinking by being identified with the objects of thought: hence it is not open to it at times to think and at times not to think." This may mean — as undoubtedly it is Aristotle's meaning: 'There must be thinking so long as there are things: but there are always things: therefore there is always thinking.' Then the question comes: 'Yes, but whose thinking?' — to which St Thomas gives no answer. To interpret with Silvester Maurus, 'so long as the mind is actually thinking, it thinks unceasingly,' is to father no very profound truth upon the Philosopher. 8. Upon χωρισθεὶς δέ ἐστι μόνον τοῦθ' ὅπερ ἐστί (when separated, it is only that which it is) St. Thomas is altogether thrown out by his Latin, separatum hoc solum quod vere est (that alone is separate which truly is), as though χωρισθεὶς (separatum) were the predicate. He takes the meaning to be that the actually thinking mind in man, inclusive at once of potential and active intellect, is 'separate' in the sense of not operating through a bodily organ. On τοῦτο μόνον ἀθάνατον καὶ ἀΐδιον (this alone is mortal and everlasting), all his comment is "as being independent of the body, since it is separate." On the last sentence, οὐ μνημονεύομεν δὲ κ.τ.λ., he makes no comment whatever in this place, but see Chap. LXXX, arg. 5. No one can seriously contend that, working under such disadvantages, St Thomas has succeeded in adequately interpreting this, one of the most difficult chapters in Aristotle. I recommend the reader to study it in G. Rodier's masterly work, Aristote, Traité de l'âme, 2 vols., text, translation, and notes (Leroux, Paris, 1900). I offer these few final remarks.(a) From ἀεὶ γὰρto οὐδὲ χρόνῳ, is a parenthesis; as Philoponus says, τοῦτο ἐν μέσῳ ἔρριψεν. The meaning is, as St Thomas well indicates, that though in the individual mind knowledge is first potential, then actual, yet somewhere in the range of being there is an actual knowledge prior to all potential. This is only carrying out the Aristotelian principle that ultimately the actual always precedes the potential: ἐστὶ γὰρ ἐξ ἐνελεχείᾳ ὄντος πάντα τὰ γιγνόμενα (De anima, III, vii, 1), a principle well put forward by Rodier, vol. II, p. 490. What actually thinking mind precedes all potentiality of thought, Aristotle does not tell us in this chapter.(b) The words, ἀλλ' οὐχ ὁτὲ μὲν νοεῖ, ὅτε δὲ οὐ νοεῖ, are to be taken in close connexion with τῇ οὐσίᾳ ὢν ἐνεργείᾳ, the whole meaning: 'this mind, ever essentially active, thinks continually, and not merely at intervals.' Whether this refers to the mind of the race, Aristotle agreeing with Averroes that mankind have existed from eternity, or whether it points to some superhuman intelligence, is a question which will be debated as long as Aristotle continues to be read.(c) χωρισθεὶς δ'ἐστὶ μόνον τοῦθ' ὅπερ ἐστί, "when separated from the body [in death, as Rodier rightly explains], it is its proper self, and nothing else," — pure νοῦς, apart from phantasy and sensation and bodily organism; and this pure νοῦςis, in some undefined way, "immortal and everlasting." In ἐστὶ τοῦθ' ὅπερ ἐστίI think we may further recognise some slight influence of a familiar idiom, by which a Greek says that a thing 'is what it is,' when he is either unable or reluctant to enter into further detail.(d) The concluding words mean: 'We have no memory [after death, of the transactions of our earthly existence], because though the νοῦςis unaffected by death (ἀπαθές), yet the passive intellect [ὁ παθητικὸς νοῦς, the cogitative faculty with the phantasy, see St Thomas, Chap. LX], is perishable [and perishes with the body], and without this there is no understanding [of things learnt in life with its concurrence, — cf. De anima, III, viii, 5, ὅταν θεωρῇ ἀνάγκη ἅμα φάντασμά τι θεωρεῖν].' This sense seems definitely fixed as the mind of Aristotle by a previous passage, De anima, I, iv, 12-15: — "The νοῦςwithin us seems to be a subsistent being (οὐσία) and imperishable. If it could be impaired, it would be impaired most in the feebleness of old age: whereas, we may say, the case is the same with intellect as with sense: for if the old man got a young man's eye, he would see as the young man does. So old age is not an affection of the soul, but an affection of what contains the soul, as in drunken bouts and illnesses. Thus the intellectual and speculative faculty decays when something else in the man decays, but of itself it is imperishable (ἀπαθές). But the exercise of the cogitative faculty (τὸ διανοεῖσθαι), and the passions of love and hate, are not functions of νοῦς, but of this individual organism that contains νοῦς, as containing it. Therefore when this organism perishes in death, the soul neither remembers nor loves: for memory and [the passion of] love were not affections of the intelligent soul, but of the compound organism wherein soul and matter met, which has not perished: but νοῦςperhaps is something more divine and imperishable (ὁ δὲ νοῦς ἴσως θειότερόν τι καὶ ἀπαθές ἐστιν).

CHAPTER LXXIX—That the Human Soul does not Perish with the Body

EVERY intelligent subsisting being is imperishable (Chap. LV): but the human soul is an intelligent subsisting being.

2. Nothing is destroyed by that which makes its perfection. But the perfection of the human soul consists in a certain withdrawal from the body: for the soul is perfected by knowledge and virtue: now in knowledge there is greater perfection, the more the view is fixed on high generalizations, or immaterial things; while the perfection of virtue consists in a man's not following his bodily passions, but tempering and restraining them by reason. — Nor is it of any avail to reply that the perfection of the soul consists in its separation from the body in point of activity, but to be separated from the body in point of being is its destruction. For the activity of a thing shows its substance and being, and follows upon its nature: thus the activity of a thing can only be perfected inasmuch as its substance is perfected. If then the soul is perfected in activity by relinquishing the body and bodily things, its substance cannot fail in being by

separation from the body.

4. A natural craving cannot be in vain. But man naturally craves after permanent continuance: as is shown by this, that while existence is desired by all, man by his understanding apprehends existence, not in the present moment only, as dumb animals do, but existence absolutely. Therefore man attains to permanence on the part of his soul, whereby he apprehends existence absolute and for all time.

6. Intelligible being is more permanent than sensible being. But the substratum of material bodies (materia prima) is indestructible, much more the potential intellect, the recipient of intelligible forms. Therefore the human soul, of which the potential intellect is a part, is indestructible.

8. No form is destroyed except either by the action of the contrary, or by the destruction of the subject wherein it resides, or by the failure of its cause. Thus heat is destroyed by the action of cold: by the destruction of the eye the power of sight is destroyed; and the light of the atmosphere fails by the failure of the sun's presence, which was its cause. But the human soul cannot be destroyed by the action of its contrary, for it has no contrary, since by the potential intellect the soul is cognitive and receptive of all contraries. Nor again by the destruction of the subject in which it resides, for it has been shown above that the human soul is a form not dependent on the body for its being. Nor lastly by the failure of its cause, for it can have no cause but one which is eternal, as will be shown (Chap. LXXXVII). In no way therefore can the human soul be destroyed.

9. If the human soul is destroyed by the destruction of the body, it must be weakened by the

weakening of the body. But the fact is that if any faculty of the soul is weakened by the body being weakened, that is only incidentally, inasmuch as that faculty of the soul stands in need of a bodily organ, as the sight is weakened by the weakening of the organ of sight, but only incidentally, as may be shown by this consideration: if any weakness fell essentially upon the faculty, the faculty would not be restored by the restoration of the organ; but now we see that however much the faculty of sight seems weakened, it is restored, if only the organ is restored. Since then the soul's faculty of understanding needs no bodily organ, the understanding itself is not weakened, neither essentially nor incidentally, either by old age or by any other weakness of body. But if in the working of the understanding there happens fatigue or hindrance through bodily weakness, this is not due to weakness of the understanding itself, but to weakness of other faculties that the understanding has need of, to wit, the phantasy, the memory, and the cogitative faculty.

10. The same is evidenced by the very words of Aristotle: "Moving causes pre-exist, but formal causes are along with the things whereof they are causes: for when a man is well, then there is health. But whether anything remains afterwards, is a point to consider: in some cases there may well be something remaining: the soul is an instance, not the whole soul, but the intelligence: as for the whole soul remaining, that is perhaps an impossibility." Clearly then, in speaking of forms, he wishes to speak of the intellect, which is the form of man, as remaining after its matter, that is, after the body. It is clear also that though Aristotle makes the soul a form, yet he does not represent it as non- subsistent and consequently perishable, as Gregory of Nyssa imputes to

him: for he excludes the intellectual soul from the general category of other forms, saying that it remains after the body and is a subsistent being (substantiam quandam). Hereby is banished the error of the impious in whose person it is said: *We were born out of nothingness, and hereafter we shall be as though we had never been* (Wisd. ii, 2); in whose person again Solomon says: *One is the perishing of man and beast, and even is the lot of both: as man dies, so do beasts die: all breathe alike, and man hath no advantage over beasts* (Eccles iii, 19): that he does not say this in his own person, but in the person of the ungodly, is clear from what he says at the end, as it were drawing a conclusion: *Till the dust return to the earth, from whence it came; and the spirit go back to the God who gave it*(Eccles xii, 7).

CHAPTER LXXX, LXXXI—*Arguments of those who wish to prove that the Human Soul perishes with the Body, with Replies to the same*

ARG. 1. If human souls are multiplied according to the multiplication of bodies, as shown above (Chap. LXXV), then when the bodies perish, the souls cannot remain in their multitude. Hence one of two conclusions must follow: either the human soul must wholly cease to be; or there must remain one soul only, which seems to suit the view of those who make that alone incorruptible which is one in all men, whether that be the active intellect alone, as Alexander says, or with the active also the potential intellect, as Averroes says.

Reply. Whatever things are necessarily in conjunction and proportion with one another, are made many or one together, each by its own cause. If the being of the one depends on the other, its unity or multiplication also will depend on the same: otherwise it will depend on some extrinsic cause. Form then and matter must always be in proportion with one another, and conjoined by a certain natural tie. Hence matter and form must vary together in point of multiplicity and unity. If then the form depends on the matter for its being, the multiplication of the form will depend on the matter, and so will its unity. But if the form is in no such dependence on the matter, then, — though it will still be necessary for the form to be multiplied with the multiplication of the matter, — the unity or multiplicity of the form will not depend on the matter. But it has been shown (Chap. LXVIII, and note, p. 154, that the human soul is a form not dependent on matter for its being. Hence it follows that, though souls are multiplied as the bodies which they inform are multiplied, still the fact of bodies being many cannot be the cause of souls being many. And therefore there is no need for the plurality of souls to cease with the destruction of their bodies.

Arg. 2. The formal nature (ratio formalis, pp. 111, 116) of things is the cause of their differing in species. But if souls remain many after the perishing of their bodies, they must differ in species, since in souls so remaining the only diversity possible is one of formal nature. But souls do not change their species by the destruction of the body, otherwise they would be destroyed too, for all that changes from species to species is destroyed in the transition. Then they must have been different in species even before they parted from their bodies. But compounds take their species according to their form. So then individual men must differ in species, an awkward conclusion consequent upon the position that

souls remain a multitude after their bodies are gone.
Reply. It is not any and every diversity of form that makes a difference of species. The fact of souls separated from their bodies making a multitude follows from their forms being different in substance, inasmuch as the substance of this soul is different from the substance of that. But this diversity does not arise from the souls differing in their several essential constitutions, but from their being differently commensurate with different bodies: for one soul is commensurate with one body and not with another. These commensurations remain in souls even when their bodies perish, as the substances of the souls also remain, not being dependent on their bodies for their being. For it is by their substances that souls are forms of bodies: otherwise they would be united with their bodies only accidentally, and soul and body would not make up an essential but only an accidental unity. But inasmuch as they are forms, they must be commensurate with their bodies. Hence it is clear that their several different commensuratenesses remain in the departed souls, and consequently plurality.

Arg.3. It seems quite impossible, on the theory of those who suppose the eternity of the world, for human souls to remain in their multitude after the death of the body. For if the world is from eternity, infinite men have died before our time. If then the souls of the dead remain after death in their multitude, we must say that there is now an actual infinity of souls of men previously dead. But actual infinity is impossible in nature.

Reply. Of supporters of the eternity of the world, some have simply allowed the impossibility, saying that human souls perish altogether with their bodies. Others have said that of all souls there remains one spiritual existence which is common to all, — the active intellect according to some, or with the active also the potential intellect according to others. Others have supposed souls to remain in their multitude after their bodies; but, not to be obliged to suppose an infinity of souls, they have said that the same souls are united to different bodies after a fixed period; and this was the opinion of the Platonists, of which hereafter (Chap. LXXXIII). Others, avoiding all the aforesaid answers, have maintained that there was no difficulty in the existence of an actual infinity of departed souls: for an actual infinity of things, not related to one another, was only an accidental infinity, in which they saw no difficulty; and this is the position of Avicenna and Algazel. Which of these was the opinion of Aristotle is not expressly set down in his writings, although he does expressly hold the eternity of the world. But the last mentioned opinion is not inconsistent with his principles: for in the Physics, III, v, his argument against an actual infinity is confined to natural bodies, and is not extended to immaterial substances. Clearly however the professors of the Catholic faith can feel no difficulty on this point, as they do not allow the eternity of the world.

Arg.5. It is impossible for any substance to exist destitute of all activity. But all activity of the soul ends with the body, as may be shown by simple enumeration. For the faculties of the vegetative soul work through bodily qualities and a bodily instrument; and the term of their activity is the body itself, which is perfected by the soul, is thereby nourished and developed, and comes to furnish the generative products. Also all the activities of the faculties of the sensitive soul are accomplished through bodily organs; and some of them are accompanied by (sensible) bodily change, as in the case of the passions. As for the act of understanding, although it is not an activity exercised through any bodily organ, nevertheless its objects are phantasms, which stand to it as colors to sight: hence as sight cannot see without colors, so the intellectual soul cannot understand without phantasms. The soul also needs, for purposes of understanding, the faculties which prepare the phantasms to become actual terms of intellect, namely, the cogitative faculty and the memory, of which it is certain that they cannot endure without the body, seeing that they work through organs of the body. Hence Aristotle says that "the soul by no means understands without a phantasm," and that "nothing understands without the passive intellect," by which name he designates the cogitative faculty, "which is perishable"; and that "we remember nothing" after death of the things that we knew in life. Thus then it is clear that no activity of the soul can continue after death, and therefore neither can its substance continue.

Reply. The assertion that no activity can remain in the soul after its separation from the body, we say, is incorrect: for those activities remain which are not exercised through organs, and such are understanding and will. As for activities exercised through bodily organs, as are the activities of the vegetative and sentient soul, they do not remain. But we must observe that the soul separated from the body does not understand in the same way as when united with the body: for everything acts according as it is. Now though the being of the human soul, while united with the body, is perfect (absolutum), not depending on the body, still the body is a sort of housing (stramentum) to it and subject receptive of it. Hence the proper activity of the soul, which is understanding, while independent of the body in this that it is not exercised through any bodily organ, nevertheless finds in the body its object, which is the phantasm. Hence, so long as the soul is in the body, it cannot understand without a phantasm, nor remember except by the cogitative and reminiscent faculty whereby phantasms are shaped and made available (Chap. LXXIII); and therefore this method of understanding and remembering has to be laid aside when the body is laid aside. But the being of the departed soul belongs to it alone without the body: hence its intellectual activity will not be accomplished by regard to such objects as phantasms existing in bodily organs, but it will understand by itself after the manner of those intelligences that subsist totally apart from bodies (Chapp. XCI-CI), from which superior beings it will be able to receive more abundant influence in order to more perfect understanding.

We may see some indication of this even in living men. When the soul is hampered by preoccupations about its body, it is less disposed to understand higher things. Hence the virtue of temperance, withdrawing the soul from bodily delights, helps especially to make men apt to understand. In sleep again, when men are not using their bodily senses, they have some perception of things to come, impressed upon them by superior beings, and attain to facts that transcend the measure of human reasonings. This is much more the case in states of syncope and ecstasy, as the withdrawal from the bodily senses is there greater. And that is what one might expect, because, as has been pointed out above (Chap. LXVIII), the human soul being on the boundary line between corporeal and incorporeal substances, and dwelling as it were on the horizon of eternity and time, it approaches the highest by receding from the lowest. Therefore, when it shall be totally severed from the body, it will be perfectly assimilated to the intelligences that subsist apart, and will receive their influence in more copious streams. Thus then, though the mode of our understanding according to the conditions of the present life is wrecked with the wreck of the body, it will be replaced by another and higher mode of understanding.

But memory, being an act exercised through a bodily organ, as Aristotle shows, cannot remain in the soul after the body is gone; unless memory be taken in another sense for the intellectual hold upon things known before: this intellectual memory of things known in life must remain in the departed soul, since the intellectual impressions are indelibly received in the potential intellect (Chap. LXXIV). As regards other activities of the soul, such as love, joy, and the like, we must beware of a double meaning of the terms: sometimes they mean passions, or emotions, which are activities of the sensitive appetite, concupiscible or irascible, and as such they cannot remain in the soul after death, as Aristotle shows: sometimes they mean a simple act of will without passion, as Aristotle says that "The joy of God is one, everlasting, and absolute," and that "In the contemplation of wisdom there is admirable delight"; and again he distinguishes the love of friendship from the love of passion. But as the will is a power that uses no bodily organ, as neither does the understanding, it is evident that such acts, inasmuch as they are acts of will, may remain in the departed soul.

CHAPTER LXXXII—That the Souls of Dumb Animals are not Immortal

NO activity of the sentient part can have place

without a body. But in the souls of dumb animals we find no activity higher than the activities of the sentient part. That animals neither understand nor reason is apparent from this, that all animals of the same species behave alike, as being moved by nature, and not acting on any principle of art: for every swallow makes its nest alike, and every spider its web alike. Therefore there is no activity in the soul of dumb animals that can possibly go on without a body.

2. Every form separated from matter is actually understood. Thus the active intellect makes impressions actually understood, inasmuch as it abstracts them. But if the soul of a dumb animal remains after the body is gone, it will be a form separated from matter. Therefore it will be form actually understood. But "in things separated from matter understanding and understood are the same" (De Anima, III, iv, 13). Therefore the soul of a dumb animal will have understanding, which is impossible.

3. In everything that is apt to arrive at any perfection, there is found a natural craving after that perfection: for good is what all crave after, everything its own good. But in dumb animals there is no craving after perpetuity of being except in the form of perpetuity of the species, inasmuch as they have an instinct of generation, whereby the species is perpetuated, — and the same is found in plants. But they have not that craving consequent upon apprehension: for since the sentient soul apprehends only what is here and now, it cannot possibly apprehend perpetuity of being, and therefore has no physical craving after such perpetuity. Therefore the soul of a dumb animal is incapable of perpetuity of being.

CHAPTER LXXXIII, LXXXIV—Apparent Arguments to show that the Human Soul does not begin with the Body, but has been from Eternity, with Replies to the same

ARG. 1. (A.) What will never cease to be, has a power of being always. But of that which has a power of being always it is never true to say that it is not: for a thing continues in being so far as its power of being extends. What therefore will never cease to be, will never either begin to be.

Reply. The power of a thing does not extend to the past, but to the present or future: hence with regard to past events possibility has no place. Therefore from the fact of the soul having a power of being always it does not follow that the soul always has been, but that it always will be. — Besides, that to which power extends does not follow until the power is presupposed. It cannot therefore be concluded that the soul is always except for the time that comes after it has received the power.

Arg. 2. Truth of the intellectual order is imperishable, eternal, necessary. Now from the imperishableness of intellectual truth the being of the soul is shown to be imperishable. In like manner from the eternity of that truth there may be proved the eternity of the soul.

Reply. The eternity of understood truth may be regarded in two ways, — in point of the object which is understood, and in point of the mind whereby it is understood. From the eternity of understood truth in point of the object, there will follow the eternity of the thing, but not the eternity of the thinker. From the eternity of understood truth in point of the understanding mind, the eternity of that thinking soul will follow. But understood truth is eternal, not in the latter but in the former way. As we have seen, the intellectual impressions, whereby our soul understands truth, come to us fresh from the phantasms through the medium of the active intellect. Hence the conclusion is, not that our soul is eternal, but that those understood truths are founded upon something which is eternal. In fact they are founded upon the First Truth, the universal Cause comprehensive of all truth. To this truth our soul stands related, not as the recipient subject to the form which it receives, but as a thing to its proper end: for truth is the good of the understanding and the end thereof. Now we can gather an argument of the duration of a thing from its end, as we can argue the beginning of a thing from its efficient cause: for what is ordained to an everlasting end must be capable of perpetual duration. Hence the immortality of the soul may be argued from the eternity of intellectual truth, but not the eternity of the soul.

Arg.3. That is not perfect, to which many of its principal parts are wanting. If therefore there daily begin to be as many human souls as there are men born, it is clear that many of its principal parts are daily being added to the universe, and consequently that very many are still wanting to it. It follows that the universe is imperfect, which is impossible.

Reply. The perfection of the universe goes by species, not by individuals; and human souls do not differ in species, but only in number (Chap. LXXV).

(B.) Some professing the Catholic faith, but imbued with Platonic doctrines, have taken a middle course [between Platonists, who held that individual souls were from eternity, now united with bodies, now released by turns; and Alexander, Averroes, — and possibly Aristotle himself, — deniers of personal immortality]. These men, seeing that according to the Catholic faith nothing is eternal but God, have supposed human souls not to be eternal, but to have been created with the world, or rather before the visible world, and to be united with bodies recurrently as required. Origen was the first professor of the Christian faith to take up this position, and he has since had many followers. The position seems assailable on these grounds.

1. The soul is united with the body as the form and actualizing principle thereof. Now though actuality is naturally prior to potentiality, yet, in the same subject, it is posterior to it in time: for a thing moves from potentiality to actuality. Therefore the seed, which is potentially alive, was before the soul, which is the actuality of life.

2. It is natural to every form to be united to its own proper matter: otherwise the compound of matter and form would be something unnatural. Now that which belongs to a thing according to its nature is assigned to it before that which belongs to it against its nature: for what belongs to a thing against its nature attaches to it incidentally, but what belongs to it according to its nature attaches to it ordinarily; and the incidental is always posterior to the ordinary. It belongs to the soul therefore to be united to the body before being apart from the body.

3. Every part, separated from its whole, is imperfect. But the soul, being the form (Chap. XLVII), is a part of the human species. Therefore, existing by itself, apart from the body, it is imperfect. But the perfect is before the imperfect in the order of natural things.

(C.) If souls were created without bodies, the

question arises how they came to be united with bodies. It must have been either violently or naturally. If violently, the union of the soul with the body is unnatural, and man is an unnatural compound of soul and body, which cannot be true. But if souls are naturally united with bodies, then they were created with a physical tendency (appetitus naturalis) to such union. Now a physical tendency works itself out at once, unless something comes in the way. Souls then should have been united with bodies from the instant of their creation except for some intervening obstacle. But any obstacle intervening to arrest a physical tendency, or natural craving, does violence to the same. Therefore it would have been by violence that souls were for a period separated from their bodies, which is an awkward conclusion.

(D.) But if it be said that both states alike are natural to the soul, as well the state of union with the body as the state of separation, according to difference of times, this appears to be impossible, — because points of natural variation are accidents to the subject in which they occur, as age and youth: if then union with body and separation from a body are natural variations to the soul, the union of the soul with the body will be an accident; and man, the result of that union, will not be an ordinary, regular entity (ens per se), but a casual, incidental being (ens per accidens).

(E.) But if it is said that souls are united with bodies neither violently nor naturally, but of their own spontaneous will, that cannot be. For none is willing to come to a worse state except under deception. But the soul is in a higher state away from the body, especially according to the Platonists, who say that by union with the body the soul suffers forgetfulness of what it knew before, and is hindered from the contemplation of pure truth. At that rate it has no willingness to be united with a body except for some deceit practiced upon it. Threfore, supposing it to have pre-existed before the body, it would not be united therewith of its own accord.

(F.) But if as an alternative it is said that the soul is united with the body neither by nature, nor by its own will, but by a divine ordinance, this again does not appear a suitable arrangement, on the supposition that souls were created before bodies. For God has established everything according to the proper mode of its nature: hence it is said: God saw all things that he had made, and they were very good (Gen. i, 31). If then He created souls apart from bodies, we must say that this mode of being is better suited to their nature. But it is not proper for an ordinance of divine goodness to reduce things to a lower state, but rather to rise them to a higher. At that rate the union of soul with body could not be the result of a divine ordinance.

(G.) This consideration moved Origen to suppose that when souls, created from the beginning of time, came by divine ordinance to be united with bodies, it was for their punishment. He supposed that they had sinned before they came into bodies, and that according to the amount of their guilt they were united with bodies of various degrees of nobility, shut up in them as in prisons. But this supposition cannot stand for reasons alleged above (Chap. XLIV).

CHAPTER LXXXV—That the Soul is not of the substance of God

The divine substance is eternal, and nothing

appertaining to it begins anew to be (B. I, Chap. XV). But the souls of men were not before their bodies (Chap. LXXXIII).

3. Everything out of which anything is made is in potentiality to that which is made out of it. But the substance of God, being pure actuality, is not in potentiality to anything (B. I, Chap. XVI).

4 and 5. That out of which anything is made is in some way changed. Moreover the soul of man is manifestly variable in point of knowledge, virtue, and their opposites. But God is absolutely unchangeable (B. I, Chap. XII): therefore nothing can be made out of Him, nor can the soul be of His substance.

7. Since the divine substance is absolutely indivisible, the soul cannot be of that substance unless it be the whole substance. But the divine substance cannot but be one (B. I, Chap. XLII). It would follow that all men have but one intellectual soul, a conclusion already rejected (Chap. LXXV).

This opinion seems to have had three sources. Some assumed that there was no incorporeal being, and made the chiefest of corporeal substances God. Hence sprang the theory of the Manichean, that God is a sort of corporeal light, pervading all the infinities of space, and that the human soul is a small glimmer of this light. Others have posited the intellect of all men to be one, either active intellect alone, or active and potential combined. And because the ancients called every self-subsistent intelligence a deity, it followed that our soul, or the intellect whereby we understand, had a divine nature. Hence sundry professors of the Christian faith in our time, who assert the separate existence of the active intellect, have said expressly that the active intellect is God. This opinion might also have arisen from the likeness of our soul to God: for intelligence, which is taken to be the chief characteristic of Deity, is found to belong to no substance in the sublunary world except to man alone, on account of his soul.

CHAPTER LXXXVI—That the Human Soul is not transmitted by Generation

Where the activities of active principles suppose the concurrence of a body, the origination also of such principles supposed bodily concurrence: for a thing has existence according as it has activity: everything is active according to its being. But when active principles have their activities independent of bodily concurrence, the reverse is the case: the genesis of such principles is not by any bodily generation. Now the activity of the vegetative and sentient soul cannot be without bodily concurrence (Chapp. LVII, LXVIII): but the activity of the intellectual soul has place through no bodily organ (Chap. LXIX). Therefore the vegetative and sentient souls are generated by the generation of the body, and date their existence from the transmission of the male semen, but not the intellectual soul.

2. If the human soul owed its origin to the transmission of the male semen, that could be only in one of two ways. Either we must suppose that the soul is actually in the male semen, being as it were accidentally separated from the soul of the generator as the semen is separated from the body: — we see something of this sort in Annelid animals, that live when cut in pieces: these creatures have one soul actually and many potentially; and when the body is divided, a soul comes to be actually

in every living part: — or in another way it may be supposed that there is in the male semen a power productive of an intellectual soul, so that the intellectual soul may be taken to be in the said semen virtually, not actually. The first of these suppositions is impossible for two reasons. First, because the intelligent soul being the most perfect of souls and the most potent, the proper subject for it to perfect is a body having a great diversity of organs apt to respond to its manifold activities: hence the intellectual soul cannot be in the male semen cut off from the body (in semine deciso), because neither are the souls of the lower animals of the more perfect sort multiplied by cutting them in pieces (per decisionem), as is the case with Annelid animals. Secondly, because the proper and principal faculty of the intelligent soul, the intellect, not being the actualization of any part of the body, cannot be accidentally divided with the division of the body: therefore neither can the intelligent soul. The second supposition (that the intelligent soul is virtually contained in the male semen) is also impossible. For the active power in the semen is effectual to the generation of an animal by effecting a bodily transmutation: there is no other way for a material power to take effect. But every form, which owes its being to a transmutation of matter, has being in dependence on matter: for (n. 3) every form, educed into existence by a transmutation of matter, is a form educed out of the potentiality of matter: for this is the meaning of a transmutation of matter, that something is educed into actuality out of potentiality. But an intelligent soul cannot be educed out of the potentiality of matter: for it has been shown above (Chap. LXVIII) that the intelligent soul transcends the whole power of matter, as it has an immaterial activity (Chap. LXIX). Therefore the intelligent soul is not induced into being by any transmutation of matter, and therefore not by the action of any power that is in the male semen.

5. It is ridiculous to say that any subsistent intelligence is either divided by division of the body or produced by any corporeal power. But the soul is a subsistent intelligence (Chap. LXVIII). Therefore it can neither be divided by the separation of the semen from the body, nor produced by any active power in the same.

6. If the generation of this is the cause of that coming to be, the destruction of this will be the cause of that ceasing to be. But the destruction of the body is not the cause of the human soul ceasing to be (Chap. LXXIX). Neither then is the generation of the body the cause of the soul commencing to be.

CHAPTER LXXXVII—That the Human Soul is brought into Being by a Creative Act of God

Everything that is brought into being is either generated or created. But the human soul is not generated, either by way of composition of parts or by the generation of the body (Chap. LXXXVI); and yet it comes new into existence, being neither eternal nor pre-existent (Chapp. LXXXIII, LXXXIV): therefore it comes into being by creation. Now, as has been shown above, God alone can create (Chap. XXI).

2. Whatever has existence as subsistent being, is also made in the way that a subsistent being is made: while whatever has no existence as a subsistent being, but is attached to something else, is not made separately, but only under condition of that having been made to which it is attached. But the soul has this peculiarity to distinguish

it from other forms, that it is a subsistent being; and the existence which is proper to it communicates to the body. The soul then is made as a subsistent being is made: it is the subject of a making process all its own, unlike other forms, which are made incidentally in the making of the compounds to which they belong. But as the soul has no material part, it cannot be made out of any subject-matter: consequently it must be made out of nothing, and so created.

5. The end of a thing answers to its beginning. Now the end of the human soul and its final perfection is, by knowledge and love to transcend the whole order of created things, and attain to its first principle and beginning, which is God. Therefore from God it has properly its first origin.

Holy Scripture seems to insinuate this conclusion: for whereas, speaking of the origin of other animals, it scribes their souls to other causes, as when it says: Let the waters produce the creeping thing of living soul (Gen. i, 20): coming to man, it shows that his soul is created by God, saying: God formed man from the slime of the earth, and breathed into his face the breath of life (Gen. ii, 7).

CHAPTER LXXXVIII, LXXXIX—Arguments against the Truth of the Conclusion last drawn, with their Solution

For the better understanding of the solutions given, we must prefix some exposition of the order and process of human generation, and of animal generation generally. First then we must know that that is a false opinion of certain persons who say that the vital acts which appear in the embryo before its final development (ante ultimum complementum), come not from any soul or power of soul existing in it, but from the soul of the mother. If that were true, we could no longer call the embryo an animal, as every animal consists of soul and body. The activities of life do not proceed from an active principle from without, but from a power within; a fact which seems to mark the distinction between inanimate and living things, it being proper to the latter to move themselves. Whatever is nourished, assimilates nourishment to itself: hence there must be in the creature that is nourished an active power of nutrition, since an agent acts to the likeness of itself. This is still more manifest in the operations of sense: for sight and hearing are attributable to a power existing in the sentient subject, not in another. Hence, as the embryo is evidently nourished before its final development, and even feels, this cannot be attributed to the soul of another.

It has been alleged that the soul in its complete essence is in the male semen from the first, its activities not appearing merely for want of organs. But that cannot be. For since the soul is united with the body as a form, it is only united with that body of which it is properly the actualization. Now the soul is the actualization of an organized body. Therefore before the organization of the body the soul is in the male semen, not actually, but virtually. Hence Aristotle says that seed and fruit have life potentially in such a way that they "cast away," i.e. are destitute of soul; whereas that (body) whereof the soul is the actualization has life potentially, and does not "cast away" soul.

It would follow, if the soul were in the male semen from the first, that the generation of an animal was only by fissure (per decisionem), as is the case with

Annelid animals, that are made two out of one. For if the male semen has a soul the instant it was cut off from the body, it would then have a substantial form. But every substantial generation precedes and does not follow the substantial form. Any transmutations that follow the substantial form are not directed to the being of the thing generated, but to its well-being. At that rate the generation of the animal would be complete in the mere cutting off of the male semen from the body of the parent; and all subsequent transmutations would be irrelevant to generation. The supposition is still more ridiculous when applied to the rational soul, as well because it is impossible for that to be divided according to the division of the body, so as even to be in the semen cut off therefrom; as also because it would follow that in all cases of the semen being wasted, without conception ensuing, souls were still multiplied.

Nor again can it be said, as some say, that though there is not in the male semen at its first cutting off any soul actually, but only virtually, for want of organs, nevertheless, as the said semen is a bodily substance, organisable although not organized, so the active power of that semen is itself a soul, potential but not actual, proportional to the condition of the semen. The theory goes on to say that, as the life of a plant requires fewer organs than the life of an animal, the aforesaid active power turns into a vegetative soul as soon as the semen is sufficiently organized for the life of a plant; and further that, when the organs are more perfected and multiplied, the same power is advanced to be a sentient soul; and further still that, when the form of the organs is perfect, the same becomes a rational soul, not indeed by the action of the power of the semen itself, but only by the influence of some exterior agent: and this the advocates of this theory take to be the reason why Aristotle said (De gen. animal., II, iii) that the intellect is from without.

Upon this view it would follow that numerically the same active power was now a vegetative soul only, and afterwards a sentient soul; and so the substantial form itself was continually more and more perfected: it would further follow that a substantial form was educed from potentiality to actuality, not instantaneously, but successively; and further than generation was a continuous change, as is alteration, — all so many physical impossibilities. There would ensue even a still more awkward consequence, that the rational soul was mortal. For no formal constituent added to a perishable thing makes it naturally imperishable: otherwise the perishable would be changed into the imperishable, which is impossible, as the two differ in kind. But the substance of the sentient soul, which is supposed to be incidentally generated when the body is generated in the process above described, is necessarily perishable with the perishing of the body. If therefore this soul becomes rational by the bringing in of some manner of light from without to be a formal constituent of the soul, it necessarily follows that the rational soul perishes when the body perishes, contrary to which has been shown (Chap. LXXIX) and to the teaching of Catholic faith.

Therefore the active power which is cut off, or emitted, with the male semen from the body, and is called 'formative,' is not itself the soul, nor ever becomes the soul in the process of generation. But the frothy substance of the male semen contains gas (spiritus), and this gas is the subject on which the formative power rests, and in which it is inherent. So the formative power works out the formation of the body, acting in virtue of the soul of the father, the prime author of generation, not in virtue of the soul of the offspring, even after the offspring comes to have a soul: for the offspring does not generate itself, but is generated by the father. This is clear by enumeration of the several powers of the soul. The formation is not attributable to the soul of the embryo itself on the score of that soul's generative power: for that power puts forth no activity till the work of nutrition and growth is complete; and besides, its work is not directed to the perfection of the individual, but to the preservation of the species. Nor can it be assigned to the embryo's nutritive power, the work of which is to assimilate nourishment to the body nourished; for in this case there is no room for such a work; since nourishment taken while the body is in formation is not applied to assume the likeness of a pre-existent body, but goes to the production of a more perfect form and a nearer approach to the likeness of the father. Nor is the development of the embro attributable to its own power of growth: for to power of growth there does not belong change of form, but only change in bulk. And as for the sensitive and intellectual powers, it is clear that theirs is no office bearing on such a development. It follows that the formation of the body, particularly of its earliest and principal parts, does not proceed from the engendered soul, nor from any formative power acting in virtue thereof, but from a formative power acting in virtue of the generative soul of the father, the work of which is to make another like in species to the progenitor. This formative power therefore remains the same in the subject aforesaid from the beginning of the formation even to the end. But the appearance of the being under formation does not remain the same: for first it has the appearance of semen, afterwards of blood, and so on until it arrives at its final completeness.

Nor need we be uneasy in admitting the generation of an intermediate product, the existence of which is presently after broken off, because such transitional links are not complete in their species, but are on the way to a perfect species; and therefore they are not engendered to endure, but as stages of being, leading up to finality in the order of generation. The higher a form is in the scale of being, and the further it is removed from a mere material form, the more intermediate forms and intermediate generation must be passed through before the finally perfect form is reached. Therefore in the generation of animal and man, — these having the most perfect form, — there occur many intermediate forms and generations, and consequently destructions, because the generation of one being is the destruction of another. The vegetative soul therefore, which is first in the embryo, while it lives the life of a plant, is destroyed, and there succeeds a more perfect soul, which is at one nutrient and sentient, and for that time the embryo lives the life of an animal: upon the destruction of this, there succeeds the rational soul, infused from without, whereas the preceding two owed their existence to the virtue of the male semen.

With these principles recognized, it is easy to answer the objections.

Arg. 1. Man being an animal by the possession of a sentient soul, and the notion of 'animal' befitting man in the same sense as it befits other animals, it appears that the sentient soul of man is of the same kind as the souls of other animals. But things of the same kind have the same manner of coming to be. Therefore the sentient soul of man, as of other animals, comes to be by the active power that is in the male semen. But the sentient and the intelligent soul in man is one in substance (Chap. LVIII). It appears then that even the intelligent soul is produced by the active power of the semen.

Reply. Though sensitive soul in man and brute agree generically, yet they differ specifically. As the animal, man, differs specifically from other animals by being rational, so the sentient soul of a man differs specifically from the sentient soul of a brute by being also intelligent. The soul therefore of a brute has sentient attributes only, and consequently neither its being nor its activity rises above the order of the body: hence it must be generated with the generation of the body, and perish with its destruction. But the sentient soul in man, over and above its sentient nature, has intellectual power: hence the very substance of this soul must be raised above the bodily order both in being and in activity; and therefore it is neither generated by the generation of the body, nor perishes by its destruction.

Arg.2. As Aristotle teaches, in point of time the fetus is an animal before it is a man. But while it is an animal and not yet a man, it has a sentient and not an intelligent soul, which sentient soul beyond doubt is produced by the active power of the male semen. Now that self-same sentient soul is potentially intelligent, even as that animal is potentially a rational animal: unless one chooses to say that the intelligent soul which supervenes is another substance altogether, a conclusion rejected above (Chap. LVIII). It appears then that the substance of the intelligent soul comes of the active power that is in the semen.

Reply. The sentient soul, whereby the human fetus was an animal, does not last, but its place is taken by a soul that is at once sentient and intelligent.

Arg.3. The soul, as it is the form of the body, is one being with the body. But unity of thing produced, unity of productive action, and unity of producing agent, all go together. Therefore the one being of soul and body must be the result of one productive action of one productive agent. But confessedly the body is produced by the productive action of the power that is in the male semen. Therefore the soul also, as it is the form of the body, is produced by the same productive action, and not by any separate agency.

Reply. The principle of corresponding unity of produced, production, and producer, holds good to the exclusion of a plurality of productive agents not acting in co-ordination with one another. Where they are co-ordinate, several agents have but one effect. Thus the prime efficient cause acts to the production of the effect of the secondary efficient cause even more vigorously than the secondary cause itself; and we see that the effect produced by a principal agent through the agency of an instrument is more properly attributed to the principal agent than to the instrument. Sometimes too the action of the principal agent reaches to some part of the thing done, to which the action of the instrument does not reach. Since then the whole active power of nature stands to God as an instrument to the prime and principal agent, we find no difficulty in the productive action of nature being terminated to a part only of that one term of generation, man, and not to the whole of what is produced by the action of God. The body then of man is formed at once by the power of God, the principal and prime agent, and by the power of the semen, the secondary agent. But the action of God produces the human soul, which the power of the male semen cannot produce, but only dispose thereto.

Arg.4. Man generates his own specific likeness by the power that is in the detached semen, which generation means causing the specific form of the generated. The human soul therefore, the specific form of man, is caused by the power in the semen.

Reply. Man generates his specific likeness, inasmuch as the power of his semen operates to prepare for the coming of the final form which gives the species to man.

Arg.5. If souls are created by God, He puts the last hand to the engendering of children born sometimes of adultery.

Reply. There is no difficulty in that. Not the nature of adulterers is evil, but their will: now the effect which their semen produces is natural, not voluntary: hence there is no difficulty in God's co-operating to that effect and giving it completeness.

In a book ascribed to Gregory of Nyssa there are found further arguments, as follows:

Arg.6. Soul and body make one whole, that is, one man. If then the soul is made before the body, or the body before the soul, the same thing will be prior and posterior to itself. Therefore body and soul are made together. But the body begins in the cutting off, or emission, of the semen. Therefore the soul also is brought into being by the same.

Reply. Allowing that the human body is formed before the soul is created, or conversely, still it does not follow that the same man is prior to himself: for man is not his body or his soul. It only follows that one part of him is prior to another part; and in that there is no difficulty: for matter is prior in time to form, — matter, I mean, inasmuch as it is in potentiality to form, not inasmuch as it is actually perfected by form, for so it is together with form. The human body then, inasmuch as it is in potentiality to soul, as not yet having the soul, is prior in time to the soul: but, for that time, it is not actually human, only potentially so: but when it is actually human, as being perfected by a human soul, it is neither prior nor posterior to the soul, but together with it.

Arg.7. An agent's activity seems to be imperfect, when he does not produce and bring the whole thing into being, but only half makes it. If then God brought the soul into being, while the body was formed by the power of the male semen, body and soul being the two parts of man, the activities of God and of the seminal power would be both imperfect. Therefore the body and soul of man are both produced by the same cause. But certainly the body of man is produced by the power of the semen: therefore also the soul.

Reply. Body and soul are both produced by the power of God, though the formation of the body is of God through the intermediate instrumentality of the power of the natural semen, while the soul He produces immediately. Neither does it follow that the action of the power of the semen is imperfect, since it fulfils the purpose of its existence.

Arg.8. In all things that are engendered of seed, the parts of the thing engendered are all contained together in the seed, though they do not actually appear: as we see that in wheat or in any other send the green blade and stalk and knots and grains and ears are virtually contained in the original seed; and afterwards the seed gathers bulk and expansion by a process of natural consequence leading to its perfection, without taking up any new feature from without. But the soul is part of man. Therefore in the male semen of man the human soul is virtually contained, and it does not take its origin from any exterior cause.

Reply. In seed are virtually contained all things that do not transcend corporeal power, as grass, stalk, knots, and the like: from which there is no concluding that the special element in man which transcends the whole range of corporeal power is virtually contained in the seed.

Arg.9. Things that have the same development and the same consummation must have the same first origin. But in the generation of man we find the same development and the same consummation: for as the configuration and growth of the limbs advances, the activities of the soul show themselves more and more: for first appears the activity of the sentient soul, and last of all, when the body is complete, the activity of the intelligent soul. Therefore body and soul have the same origin. But the first origin of the body is in the emission of the male semen: such therefore also is the origin of the soul. Reply. All that this shows is that a certain arrangement of the parts of the body is necessary for the activity of the soul.

Arg.10. What is conformed to a thing, is set up according to the plan of that to which it is conformed, as wax takes the impress of a seal. But the body of man and of every animal is conformed to its own soul, having such disposition of organs as suits the activities of the power to be exercised through those organs. The body then is formed by the action of the soul: hence also Aristotle says that the soul is the efficient cause of the body. This could not be, if the soul were not in the male semen: for the body is formed by the power that is in that semen: therefore the soul has its origin in that emission of it.

Reply. That the body is conformed and fashioned according to the soul, and that therefore the soul prepares a body like unto itself, is a statement partly true and partly false. Understood of the soul of the generator, it is true: understood of the soul of the generated, it is false. The formation of the body in its prime and principal parts is not due to the soul of the generated, but to the soul of the generator, as has been shown.

Arg.11. Nothing lives except by a soul. But the male semen is alive, of which fact there are three indications. In the first place, the semen is cut off and detached from a living being: secondly, there appears in it vital heat and activity: thirdly, the seeds of plants, committed to earth, could never warm to life from the lifeless earth, had they not life in themselves.

Reply. The semen is not alive actually, but potentially, and has a soul, not actually, but virtually. In the process of generation the embryo comes to have a vegetative and a sentient soul by the virtue of the semen, which souls do not endure, but pass away and are succeeded by a rational soul.

Arg.12. If the soul is not before the body (Chap. LXXXIII), nor begins with the liberation of the semen, it follows that the body is first formed, and afterwards there is infused into it a soul newly created. But if this is true, it follows further that the soul is for the body: for what is for another appears after it, as clothes are for men and are made after them. But that is false: rather the body is for the soul, as the end is ever the more noble. We must say then that the origin of the soul is simultaneous with the emission of the semen.

Reply. There are two ways of one thing being 'for another.' A thing may be to serve the activity, or secure the preservation, or otherwise promote the good of another, presupposing its being; and such things are posterior to that for which they are, as clothes for the person, or tools for the mechanic. Or a thing may be 'for another' in view of that other's being: what is thus 'for another' is prior to it in time and posterior to it in nature. In this latter way the body is for the soul, as all matter is for its form. The case would be otherwise, if soul and body did not make one being, as they say who take the soul not to be the form of the body.

CHAPTER XCI—That there are Subsistent Intelligences not united with Bodies

WHEN human bodies perish in death, the substance of the intelligence remains in perpetuity (Chap. LXXIX). Now if the substance of the intelligence that remains is one for all, as some say, it follows necessarily that it has being apart from body; and thus our thesis is proved, that some subsistent intelligence exists apart from a body. But if a multitude of intelligent souls remain after the destruction of their bodies, then some subsistent intelligences will have the property of subsisting without bodies, all the more inasmuch as it has been shown that souls do not pass from one body to another (Chap LXXXIII). But the property of subsisting apart from bodies is an incidental property in souls, since naturally they are the forms of bodies. But what is ordinary must be prior to what is incidental. There must then be some subsistent intelligences naturally prior to souls; and to these intelligences the ordinary property must attach of subsisting without bodies.

3. The higher nature in its lowest manifestation touches the next lower nature in its highest. But intelligent nature is higher than corporeal, and at the same time touches it in some part, which is the intelligent soul. As then the body perfected by the intelligent soul is highest in the genus of bodies, so the intelligent soul united to the body must be lowest in the genus of subsistent intelligences. There are then subsistent intelligences not united with bodies, superior in the order of nature to the soul.

7. The substance of a thing must be proportionate to its activity, because activity is the actualization and perfection of an active substance. But understanding is the proper activity of an intelligent substance. Therefore an intelligent substance must be competent for such activity. But understanding is an activity not exercised through any bodily organ, and not needing the body except in so far as objects of understanding are borrowed from objects of sense. But that is an imperfect mode of understanding: the perfect mode of understanding is the understanding of those objects which are in themselves intelligible: whereas it is an imperfect mode of understanding when those things only are understood, which are not of themselves intelligible, but are rendered intelligible by intellect. If then before everything imperfect there must be something perfect in that kind, there must be antecedently to human souls, which understand what they gather from phantasms, sundry subsistent intelligences which understand things in themselves intelligible, not gathering their knowledge from sensible objects, and therefore in their nature separate from anything corporeal.

CHAPTER XCIII—That Intelligences subsisting apart are not more than one in the same Species

INTELLIGENCES subsisting apart are subsistent essences. Now the definition of a thing being the mark of its essence, is the mark of its species. Subsistent essences therefore are subsistent species.

2. Difference in point of form begets difference of species, while difference in point of matter begets difference in number. But intelligences subsisting apart have nothing whatever of matter about them. Therefore it is impossible for them to be several in one species.

4. The multiplication of species adds more nobility and perfection to the universe than the multiplication of individuals in the same species. But the perfection of the universe consists principally in intelligences subsisting apart. Therefore it makes more for the perfection of the universe that there should be many intelligences different in species than many different in number in the same species.

CHAPTER XCIV—That an Intelligence subsisting apart and a Soul are not of one Species

A DIFFERENT type of being makes a different species. But the being of the human soul and of an intelligence subsisting apart is not of one type: the body can have no share in the being of a separately subsisting intelligence, as it can have in the being of the human soul, united with the body as form with matter.

3. What makes a species by itself cannot be of the same species with that which does not make a species by

itself, but is part of a species. Now a separately subsisting intelligence makes a species by itself, but a soul not, it is part of the human species.

4. The species of a thing may be gathered from the activity proper to it: for activity shows power, and that is an indication of essence. Now the proper activity of a separately subsisting intelligence and of an intelligent soul is understanding. But the mode of understanding of a separately subsisting intelligence is quite different from that of the soul. The soul understands by taking from phantasms: not so the separately subsisting intelligence that has no bodily organs in which phantasms should be.

CHAPTER XCVI—That Intelligences subsisting apart do not gather their Knowledge from Objects of Sense

A HIGHER power must have a higher object. But the intellectual power of a separately subsisting intelligence is higher than the intellectual power of the human soul, the latter being lowest in the order of intelligences (Chap. LXXVII). Now the object of the intelligence of the human soul is a phantasm (Chap. LX), which is higher in the order of objects than the sensible thing existing outside and apart from the soul. The object therefore of a separately subsisting intelligence cannot be an objective reality (res) existing outside the soul, as though it could get knowledge immediately from that; nor can it be a phantasm: it must then be something higher than a phantasm. But nothing is higher than a phantasm in the order of knowable objects except that which is an actual term of intelligence. Intelligences subsisting apart therefore do not gather their intellectual knowledge from objects of sense, but understand objects which are of themselves terms of intelligence.

3. According to the order of intelligences is the order of terms of intelligence. But objects that are of themselves terms of intelligence are higher in order than objects that are terms of intelligence only because we make them so. Of this latter sort are all terms of intelligence borrowed from sensible things: for sensible things are not of themselves intelligible: yet these sensible things are the sort of intelligible things that our intellect understands. A separately subsisting intelligence therefore, being superior to our intelligence, does not understand the intellectual aspects of things by gathering them from objects of sense: it seizes upon those aspects as they are in themselves.

4. The manner of activity proper to a thing corresponds to the manner and nature of its substance. But an intelligence subsisting apart is by itself, away from anybody. Therefore its intellectual activity will be conversant with objects not based upon anything corporeal.

From these considerations it appears that in intelligences subsisting apart there is no such thing as active and potential intellect, except perchance by an improper use of those terms. The reason why potential and active intellect are found in our intelligent soul is because it has to gather intellectual knowledge from sensible things: for the active intellect it is that turns the impressions, gathered from sensible things, into terms of intellect: while the potential intellect is in potentiality to the knowledge of all forms of sensible things. Since then separately subsisting intellects do not gather their knowledge from sensible things, there is in them no active and potential intellect.

Nor again can distance in place hinder the knowledge of a disembodied soul (animae separatae). Distance in place ordinarily affects sense, not intellect, except incidentally, where intellect has to gather its data from sense. For while there is a definite law of distance according to which sensible objects affect sense, terms of intellect, as they impress the intellect, are not in place, but are separate from bodily matter. Since then separately subsistent intelligences do not gather their intellectual knowledge from sensible things, distance in place has no effect upon their knowledge.

Plainly too neither is time mingled with the intellectual activity of such beings. Terms of intellect are as independent of time as they are of place. Time follows upon local motion, and measures such things only as are in some manner placed in space; and therefore the understanding of a separately subsisting intelligence is above time. On the other hand, time is a condition of our intellectual activity, since we receive knowledge from phantasms that regard a fixed time. Hence to its judgements affirmative and negative our intelligence always appends a fixed time, except when it understands the essence of a thing. It understands essence by abstracting terms of understanding from the conditions of sensible things: hence in that operation it understands irrespectively of time and other conditions of sensible things. But it judges affirmatively and negatively by applying forms of understanding, the results of previous abstraction, to things, and in this application time is necessarily understood as entering into the combination.

CHAPTER XCVII—That the Mind of an Intelligence subsisting apart is ever in the act of understanding

What is sometimes in actuality, sometimes in potentiality, is measured by time. But the mind of an intelligence subsisting apart is above time (Chap. XCVI). Therefore it is not at times in the act of understanding and at times not.

2. Every living substance has by its nature some actual vital activity always going on in it, although other activities are potential: thus animals are always repairing waste by assimilation of nourishment, though they do not always feel. But separately subsisting intelligences are living substances, and have no other vital activity but that of understanding. Therefore by their nature they must be always actually understanding.

CHAPTER XCVIII—How one separately subsisting Intelligence knows another

AS separately subsisting intelligences understand proper terms of intellect; and the said intelligences are themselves such terms, — for it is independence of matter that makes a thing be a proper term of intellect; it follows that separately subsisting intelligences understand other such intelligences, finding in them their proper objects. Every such intelligence therefore will know both itself and its fellows. It will know itself, but in a different way from that in which the human potential intellect knows itself. For the potential intellect is only potentially intelligible, and becomes actually such by being impressed with an intellectual impression. Only by such an impression does it become cognizant of itself. But separately subsisting intelligences by their nature are actually intelligible: hence every one of them knows himself by his own essence, not by any impression representative of another thing.

A difficulty: Since all knowledge, as it is the knowing mind, is a likeness of the thing known, and one separately subsistent intelligence is like another generically, but differs from it in species (Chap. XCIII), it appears that one does not know another in species, but only so far as the two meet in one common ratio, that of the genus.

Reply. With subsistent beings of a higher order than we are, the knowledge contained in higher generalities is not incomplete, as it is with us. The likeness in the mind of 'animal,' whereby we know a thing generically only, yields us a less complete knowledge than the likeness of 'man,' whereby we know an entire species. To know a thing by its genus is to know it imperfectly and, as it were, potentially; to know it by its species is to know it perfectly and actually. Holding as it does the lowest rank among subsistent intelligences, our intellect stands in such pressing need of particular detailed likenesses, that for every distinct object of its knowledge it requires a distinct likeness in itself: hence the likeness of 'animal' does not enable it to know 'rational,' consequently not 'man' either, except imperfectly. But the intellectual presentation in an intelligence subsisting apart is of a higher power, apt to represent more, and leads to a knowledge, not less perfect, but more perfect. By one presentation such an intelligence knows both 'animal' and the several specific differentias which make the several species of animals: this knowledge is more or less comprehensive according to the hierarchical rank of the intelligence. We may illustrate this truth by contrasting the two extremes, the divine and human intellect. God knows all things by the one medium of His essence; man requires so many several likenesses, images or presentations in the mind, to know so many several things. Yet even in man the higher understanding gathers more from fewer presentations: slow minds on the other hand need many particular examples to lead them to knowledge. Since a separately subsistent intelligence, considered in its nature, is potentially open to the presentations whereby 'being' in its entirety (totum ens) is known, we cannot suppose that such an intelligence is denuded of all such presentations, as is the case with the potential intellect in use ere it comes to understand. Nor again can we suppose that this separately subsistent intelligence has some of these presentations actually, and others, potentially only. For separate intelligences do not change (Chap. XCVII); but every potentiality in them must be actualized. Thus then the intellect of the separately subsistent intelligence is perfected to the full extent of its capacity by intelligible forms, so far as natural knowledge goes.

CHAPTER XCIX—That Intelligences subsisting apart know Material Things, that is to say, the Species of Things Corporeal

SINCE the mind of these intelligences is perfect with all natural endowments, as being wholly actualized, it must comprehend its object, which is intelligible being, under all its aspects. Now under intelligible being are included the species also of things corporeal.

2. Since the species of things are distinguished like the species of numbers, whatever is in the lower species must be contained somehow in the higher, as the larger number contains the smaller. Since then separately subsistent intelligences rank higher than corporeal substances, all properties that in a material way are in corporeal substances must be in these separately subsistent intelligences in an intelligible and spiritual way: for what is in a thing is in it according to the mode of the thing in which it is.

CHAPTER C—That Intelligences subsisting apart know Individual Things

INASMUCH as the likenesses representative of things in the mind of a separately subsistent intelligence are more universal than in our mind, and more effectual means of knowledge, such intelligences are instructed by such likenesses of material things not only to the knowledge of material things generically or specifically, as would be the case with our mind, but also to the knowledge of individual existences.
1. The likeness or presentation of a thing in the mind of a separately subsistent intelligence is of far-reaching and universal power, so that, one as that presentation is and immaterial, it can lead to the knowledge of specific principles, and further to the knowledge of individualizing or material principles. Thereby the intelligence can become cognizant, not only of the matter of genus and species, but also of that of the individual.
2. What a lower power can do, a higher power can

do, but in a more excellent way. Hence where the lower power operates through many agencies, the higher power operates through one only: for the higher a power is, the more it is gathered together and unified, whereas the lower is scattered and multiplied. But the human soul, being of lower rank than the separately subsistent intelligence, takes cognizance of the universal and of the singular by two principles, sense and intellect. The higher and self-subsistent intelligence therefore is cognizant of both in a higher way by one principle, the intellect.

3. Intelligible impressions of things come to our understanding in the opposite order to that in which they come to the understanding of the separately subsisting intelligence. To our understanding they come by way of analysis (resolutio), that is, by abstraction from material and individualizing conditions: hence we cannot know individual things by aid of such intelligible or universal presentations. But to the understanding of the separately subsisting intelligence intelligible impressions arrive by way of synthesis (compositio). Such an intelligence has its intelligible impressions by virtue of its assimilation to the original intelligible presentation of the divine understanding, which is not abstracted from things but productive of things, — productive not only of the form, but also of the matter, which is the principle of individuation. Therefore the impressions in the understanding of a separately subsisting intelligence regard the whole object, not only the specific but also the individualizing principles. The knowledge of singular and individual things therefore is not to be withheld from separately subsistent intelligences, for all that our intellect cannot take cognizance of the singular and individual.

CHAPTER CI—whether to Separately Subsisting Intelligences all Points of their Natural Knowledge are Simultaneously Present

Not everything is actually understood, of which there is an intellectual impression actually in the understanding. For since a subsistent intelligence has also a will, and is thereby master of his own acts, it is in his power, when he has got an intellectual impression, to use it by actually understanding it; or, if he has several, to use one of them. Hence also we do not actually consider all things whereof we have knowledge. A subsistent intelligence therefore, knowing by a plurality of impressions, uses the one impression which he wishes, and thereby actually knows at once all things which by one impression he does know. For all things make one intelligible object inasmuch as they are known by one presentation, — as also our understanding knows many things together, when they are as one by composition or relation with one another. But things that an intelligence knows by different impressions, it does not take cognizance of together. Thus, for one understanding, there is one thing at a time actually understood. There is therefore in the mind of a separately subsisting intelligence a certain succession of acts of understanding; not however movement, properly so called: since it is not a case of actuality succeeding potentiality, but of actuality following upon actuality. But the Divine Mind, knowing all things by the one medium of its essence, and having its act for its essence, understands all things simultaneously: hence in its understanding there is incident no succession, but its act of understanding is entire, simultaneous, perfect, abiding, world without end. Amen.

## BOOK III GOD THE END OF CREATURES

CHAPTER I.—Preface to the Book that Follows
The Lord is a great God, and a great king above all gods. For the Lord will not reject his people, because in his hands are all the ends of the earth, and the heights of the mountains he beholdeth. For the sea is his, and he made it, and his hands have formed the dry land. (Ps. xciv). IT has been shown above (B. I, Chap. XIII) that there is one first of beings, possessing the full perfection of all being, whom we call God. Out of the abundance of His perfection He bestows being on all things that exist; and thus He proves to be not only the first of beings, but also the first principle of all. He bestows being on other things, not out of any necessity of his nature, but by the free choice of His will, as has been shown (B. II, Chap. XXIII). Consequently He is master of the things that He has made: for we have dominion over the things that are subject to our will. This His dominion over the things that He has brought into being is a perfect dominion, since in producing them He needs the aid of no exterior agent, nor any subject matter to work upon, seeing that He is the universal efficient cause of all being. Of the things produced by the will of an agent everyone is directed by that agent to some end: for some good and some end is the proper object of the will: hence the things that proceed from will must be directed to some end. Everything attains its last end by its own action, which is directed by

Him who has given to things the principles whereby they act. It needs must be then that God, who is by nature perfect in Himself and by His power bestows being on all things that are, should be the ruler of all beings, Himself ruled by none: nor is there anything exempt from His government, as there is nothing that does not derive being from Him. He is then perfect in government, as He is perfect in being and causation.

The effect of this government appears variously in various natures according to the difference between them. Some creatures are brought into being by God to possess understanding, to bear his likeness and present His image. They not only are directed, but also direct themselves by proper actions of their own to their due end. If in the direction of themselves they remain subject to the divine guidance, they are admitted in course of that guidance to the attainment of their last end. Other beings, devoid of understanding, do not direct themselves to their own end, but are directed by another. Some of those are imperishable; and as they can suffer no defect in their natural being, so in their proper actions they never deflect one whit from the path that leads to the end prefixed to them, but are indefectibly subject to the rule of the prime ruler.1Other creatures are perishable, and liable to the failure of their natural being, which however is compensated by the gain of another: for the perishing of one is the engendering of another. In like manner in their proper actions they swerve from the natural order from which swerving however there accrues some compensatory good. Hence it appears that even apparent irregularities and departures from the order of the first rule escape not the power of the first ruler. These perishable bodies, created as they are by God, are perfectly subject to His power.

The Psalmist, filled with God's spirit, considering this truth, and wishing to point out to us the divine government of things, first describes to us the perfection of the first ruler, — of His nature, when he says God; of His power, when he says, is a great Lord, needing no cooperation to work the effect of His power; of His authority, when he says a great king above all gods, because, though there be many rulers, all are subject to His rule. Secondly he describes to us the manner of government, — as well in respect of intelligent beings, which follow His rule and gain from Him their last end, which is Himself, and therefore he says, for the Lord will not reject his people, — as also in respect of perishable beings, which, however they sometimes depart from their proper modes of action, still are never let go beyond the control of the prime ruler: hence it is said, in his hands are all the ends of the earth, — likewise in respect of the heavenly bodies, which exceed all the height of the earth and of perishable bodies, and always observe the right order of divine rule: hence he says, and the heights of the mountains he beholdeth. Thirdly he assigns the reason of this universal control, which is, because things created by God needs must be ruled by Him: hence he says, For the sea is his, etc. Since then in the first Book we have treated of the perfection of the divine nature, and in the second of the perfection of God's power, it remains for us in this third Book to treat of His perfect authority, or dignity, in as much as He is the last end and ruler of all things. This therefore will be our order of procedure, to treat first of God, as the final end of all things; secondly of His universal control, whereby He governs every creature; thirdly of the special control which He exercises in the government of creatures endowed with understanding.

CHAPTER II.—That every Agent acts to some End

IN the case of agents that manifestly act to some end, we call that the end to which the effort of the agent tends. Gaining that, he is said to gain his end; and missing that, he is said to miss his intended end. Nor on this point does it make any difference whether the end be tended to with knowledge or not: for as the target is the end of the archer, so is it also the end of the path of the arrow.3The effort of every agent tends to some certain end. Not any and every action can proceed from any and every power. Action is sometimes terminated to some product, sometimes not. When action is terminated to some product, the effort of the agent tends to the same. When action is not terminated to any product, the effort of the agent tends to the action itself. Every agent therefore must intend some end in his action, sometimes the action itself, sometimes something produced by the action.

3. It is impossible for the chain of actions to extend to infinity: there must then be something, in the getting of which the effort of the agent comes to rest. Therefore every agent acts to some end.

6. Actions are open to criticism only so far as they are taken to be done as means to some end. It is not imputed as a fault to any one, if he fails in effecting that for which his work is not intended. A physician is found fault with if he fails in healing, but not a builder or a grammarian. We find fault in points of art, as when a

grammarian does not speak correctly; and also in points of nature, as in monstrous births. Therefore both the natural agent, and the agent who acts according to art and with a conscious purpose, acts for an end.

7. To an agent that did not tend to any definite effect, all effects would be indifferent. But what is indifferent to many things, does not do one of them rather than another: hence from an agent open to both sides of an alternative (a contingente ad utrumque) there does not follow any effect, unless by some means it comes to be determined to one above the rest: otherwise it could not act at all. Every agent therefore tends to some definite effect, and that is called its end.

Still there are actions that do not seem to be for any end, as things done for sport, and acts of contemplation, and things done without advertence, as the stroking of the beard and the like: from which instances one may suppose that there is such a thing as an agent acting not for any end. But we must observe that though acts of contemplation are not for any other end, they are an end in themselves: as for things done in sport, sometimes they are their own end, as when one plays solely for the amusement that he finds in play; sometimes they are for an end, as when we play that afterwards we may resume work more vigorously: while things done without advertence may proceed not from the understanding, but from some phantasy or physical principle; yet even these acts tend to certain ends, though beyond the scope of the intellect of the agent.

Hereby is banished the error of certain ancient natural philosophers (Empedocles and Democritus, mentioned in Aristotle, Physics II, ii, 6) who supposed all things to happen by necessity of matter, and eliminated final causes from the universe.

## CHAPTER III—That every Agent acts to some Good

THAT to which an agent definitely tends must be suited to it: for it would not tend to the thing except for some suitability to itself. But what is suitable to a thing is good for it. Therefore every agent acts to some good.

6. An intellectual agent acts for an end by determining its own end. A physical agent, though acting for an end, does not determine its own end, having no idea of an end, but moves in the direction of an end determined for it by another. Now an intellectual agent does not fix for itself an end except under some aspect of good: for a term of intellect is a motive only under an aspect of good, which is the object of will. Therefore a physical agent also does not move or act to any end except inasmuch as it is good. Such an agent has its end determined by some natural appetite or tendency.

7. It is part of the same plan of action to shun evil and to seek good. But all things are found to shun evil. Intellectual agents shun a thing for this reason, that they apprehend its evil: while all physical agents, to the full extent of the power that is in them, resist destruction, because that is the evil of everything. All things therefore act to some good.

## CHAPTER IV—That Evil in things is beside the Intention of the Agent

WHAT follows from an action different from what was intended by the agent, manifestly happens beside his intention. But evil is different from good, which every agent intends. Therefore evil happens beside the intention.

2. Failure in effect and action follows upon some defect in the principles of action, as a halting gait follows upon crookedness of legs. Now an agent acts by whatever of active power he has, not by what defect of active power he suffers; and according as he acts, so does he intend his end. He intends therefore an end answering to his power. Anything therefore that ensues answering to defect of power will be beside the intention of the agent. But such is evil.

4. In agents that act by intellect, or by any sort of judgement, intention follows apprehension: for intention tends to that which is apprehended as an end. If then experience lights upon something not of the species apprehended, the event will be beside the intention: thus if one intends to eat honey, and eats gall, taking it for honey, that will be beside the intention. But every intellectual agent intends a thing according as he takes it for something good: if then it turns out not to be good but evil, that will be beside the intention.

CHAPTERS V, VI—Arguments against the Truth of the Conclusion last drawn, with Solutions of the Same Chapter VI

FOR the clearer solution of the arguments alleged we must observe that evil may be considered either in a substance or in some action of a substance. Evil in a substance consists in its lack of something which it is naturally apt to have and ought to have. It is no evil to a man not to have wings, because he is not by nature apt to have them; nor not to have yellow hair, because, though his nature is apt to have such hair, still that color of hair is not due to his nature. But it is an evil to him not to have hands, because he is apt by nature to have them, and ought to have them, if he is to be perfect; and yet the same is no evil to a bird. Every privation, properly and strictly speaking, is of something which one is naturally apt to have and ought to have. The essence of evil consists in privation, thus understood. Primordial matter, being in potentiality to all forms, is naturally in actuality without any one particular form that you like to mention.6But some particular form is due to each of the things that are constituted out of such matter. The privation therefore of such a form, in regard of primordial matter, is no evil to the nature of primordial matter; but in regard of the compound whereof it is the form, it is an evil to that compound thing: thus it is evil to incandescent gas (ignis) to be deprived of the form of incandescent gas. And since privations are not said to 'be' except so far as they are in a subject, a privation will be 'simply evil,' when it is evil in regard of the subject in which it is: otherwise, it will be 'evil relatively to something' (malum alicujus), but not 'simply evil.'

Arg.1 (Chap. V). What happens beside the intention of the agent is said to be 'matter of luck and chance and rare occurrence.' But evil is not said to be matter of luck and chance, or rare occurrence, but to happen continually, or for the most part: thus in the physical order the unmaking of one thing is always attached to the making of another; and in the moral order sin is of usual occurrence. This does not look like evil arising contrary to intention.

Reply (Chap. VI). Not everything that is beside the intention of the doer need be the result of luck or chance. For if what is beside the intention follows upon what is intended either always or frequently, it cannot be said to happen by luck or chance. Thus in him who intends to enjoy the pleasantness of wine, if from his drinking wind drunkenness follows always or frequently, it will be no matter of bad luck or chance: but it would be by chance, if it were quite the exception. Although then the evil of one thing perishing in course of nature follows beside the intention of him who brings the other thing into being, such evil nevertheless follows invariably: for invariably to the positing of one form there is annexed the privation of another: hence this perishing does not happen by chance, nor as the exception, though the privation is sometimes not evil simply, but only a relative evil, as has been said. But if it be such a privation as to deprive the new being produced of what is due to it, it will be matter of chance and simply evil, as is the case of monstrous births: for such a mishap does not follow of necessity upon what is intended, but is contrary to it, since the agent intends the perfection of the being that he engenders. — Evil affecting action happens in physical agents for want of active power: hence, if the agent's power is defective, this evil happens contrary to intention, yet not by chance, because it necessarily follows upon such an agent, when such agent suffers this failure of power either always or frequently: but it will be by chance, if the failure rarely accompanies such an agent. — Coming to voluntary agents, intention in them must be of some particular good, if action is to follow: for universal considerations of themselves do not move the will, unless there be added the consideration of the particular circumstances under which the action is to take place. If then the good that is intended has conjoined with it the privation of rational good either always or frequently, there follows moral evil, and that not by chance, as is clear in his case who wishes to cohabit with a woman for pleasure, while the inordination of adultery is annexed to that pleasure: in that case the evil of adultery does not ensue by chance: but it would be an evil happening by chance, if upon the thing intended there followed some exceptional misadventure, as when one aiming at a bird kills a man. That goods of this sort, upon which privations of rational good follow, are so generally intended, arises from the practice of most men living according to sense, which they do because sensible things are more manifest to us, and make more effectual motives in the particular circumstances in which our action is cast; and many such goods are attended with privation of rational good.

Arg. 2. Aristotle (Eth. Nic., III, vii) expressly says that wickedness is voluntary, and proves it from the fact that men do unjust acts voluntarily: but, he adds, it is irrational to pretend that a man voluntarily acting unjustly does not wish to be unjust, or voluntarily committing rape does not wish to be incontinent; and that is why legislators punish wicked men as voluntary evil-doers. It seems then that evil is not irrespective of will or intention.

Reply. Though evil be beside the intention, it is still voluntary, not as it is in itself, but incidentally. The object of intention is the final end, willed for its own sake: but the object of volition is also that which is willed for the sake of something else, though absolutely it would not be willed, — as one throws cargo into the sea to save the ship, not intending the casting away of the cargo, but the safety of the vessel; and yet willing the casting away of the cargo, not simply and absolutely, but for the sake of safety. In like manner, for the gaining of some sensible good, one wills to do an inordinate action, not intending the inordinateness, nor willing it simply, but for that purpose. And therefore in this way wickedness and sin are said to be voluntary, like the casting away of cargo at sea.

Arg.3. Every process of nature serves as an end intended by nature. But destruction is as much a natural change as production: therefore its end, which is a privation and counts as evil, is intended by nature as much as form and goodness, which are the end of production.

Reply. From what has been said it appears that what is simply evil is altogether contrary to intention in the works of nature, as are monstrous births: but what is not simply evil, but only evil in a particular relation, is not intended by nature in itself, but incidentally.

## CHAPTER VII—That Evil is not a Nature or Essence

EVIL is nothing else than a privation of that which a thing is naturally apt to have and ought to have. But a privation is not an essence, but a negation in a substance.

5. Every essence is natural to something. If the essence ranks as a substance, it is the very nature of the thing. If it ranks as an accident, it must be caused by the principles of some substance, and thus will be natural to that substance, though perhaps not natural to some other substance. But what is in itself evil cannot be natural to anything: for the essence of evil is privation of that which

is naturally apt to be in a thing and is due to it. Evil then, being a privation of what is natural, cannot be natural to anything. Hence whatever is naturally in a thing is good, and the want of it an evil. No essence then is in itself evil.

6. Whatever has any essence is either itself a form or has a form, for by form everything is assorted in some genus or species. But form, as such, has a character of goodness, being the principle of action and the end which every maker intends, and the actuality whereby every subject of form is perfected. Whatever therefore has any essence, as such, is good.

7. Being is divided into actuality and potentiality. Actuality, as such, is good, because everything is perfected by that whereby it actually is. Potentiality too is something good: for potentiality tends to actuality, and is proportionate to actuality, not contrary to it; and is of the same genus with actuality; and privation does not attach to it except accidentally. Everything therefore that is, in whatsoever way it is, in so far as it is a being, is good.

8. All being, howsoever it be, is from God (B. II, Chap. VI). But God is perfect goodness (B. I, Chap. XLI). Since then evil cannot be the effect of goodness, it is impossible for any being, as being, to be evil.

Hence it is said: God saw all things that he had made, and they were very good (Gen. i, 31): He made all things good in his own time (Eccles. iii, 11): Every creature of God is good (1 Tim. iv, 4).

CHAPTERS VIII, IX—Arguments against the aforsesaid Conclusion, with Answers to the same

ARG. 1. Evil is a specific difference in certain kinds of things, namely, in moral habits and acts: for as every virtue in its species is a good habit, so the contrary vice in its species is an evil habit; and similarly of acts. Evil therefore is something that gives species to certain things: it is therefore an essence, and natural to some things.

Reply. The reason why good and evil are reckoned specific differences in moral matters, is because moral matters depend on the will: for a thing enters into the sphere of morality inasmuch as it is voluntary. But the object of the will is the end in view and good: hence moral actions are specified by the end for which they are done, as physical actions are from the form of their active principle. Since then good and evil are designated according to due bearing on the end, or the lack of such due bearing, good and evil must be the first differentias marking species in moral matters. But the measure of morality is reason. Therefore things must be called morally good or evil according as they bear on the end which reason determines. Whatever therefore in moral matters derives its species from an end, which is according to reason, is said to be good in its species: while what derives its species from an end contrary to reason, is said to be evil in its species. But that end, though inconsistent with the end which reason assigns, is nevertheless some sort of good, as being pleasurable according to sense, or the like: hence such ends are good in some animals, and even in man when they are moderated by reason; and what is evil for one may very well be good for another. And therefore evil, inasmuch as it is a specific differentia in the genus of moral matters, does not involve anything that is essentially evil, but something that is in itself good, but evil to man inasmuch as it sets aside the order of reason, which is man's good.

Arg.4. All that acts is something. But evil acts inasmuch as it is evil: for it understands good and spoils it. Evil therefore, inasmuch as it is evil, is something.

Reply. A privation, as such, is no principle of action. Hence it is well said that evil does not fight against good except in the power of good: but in itself it is impotent and weak and originative of no action. Evil is said however to spoil good also formally in itself, as blindness is said to spoil sight, or whiteness to color a wall.

Arg.5. Where there is found more and less, there must be an order of things, for negations and privations are not susceptible of more and less. But we find among evils one worse than another. Therefore evil must be something.

Reply. Conditions that imply privation are intensified or relaxed as are inequality and unlikeness: for a thing is more unequal according as it is further removed from inequality, and more unlike according as it is more removed from likeness: hence a thing is more evil according as it is a greater privation of good, or at a greater distance from good.

Arg.6. Thing and being are convertible terms. But evil is in the world. Therefore it is something and nature.

Reply. Evil is said 'to be' in the world, not as having any essence, or existing as a thing, but in the way in which a thing 'is' evil precisely by evil, as blindness, an in the way in which any privation is said 'to be,' inasmuch as an animal 'is' blind by blindness. For there are two senses of 'being': in one sense it means the essence of a thing, and is divided into the ten predicaments; and in this sense no privation can be called a being: in another sense, it signifies the truth of an affirmative proposition (veritatem compositionis); and thus evil and privation is said to be a being, inasmuch as a thing is said to 'be' thereby under a privation.

CHAPTER X—That the Cause of Evil is good

WHAT is not, is cause of nothing: every cause must be some being. But evil is not any being (Chapp. VII, IX): therefore evil cannot be the cause of anything. If then evil is caused by anything, what causes it must be good.

4. Every cause is either material, formal, efficient, or final. But evil can be neither matter nor form: for it has been shown (Chapp. VII, IX) that both actual being and potential being is good. In like manner evil cannot be an efficient cause, since everything acts according as it is actually and has a form. Nor can it be a final cause, since it is beside the intention (Chap. IV). Evil therefore cannot be the cause of anything; and therefore, if there be any cause of evil, it must be caused by good.

But since good and evil are opposites, and one opposite cannot be cause of another except accidentally, it follows that good cannot be the active cause of evil except accidentally. In physics, this accident may happen either on the part of the agent or on the part of the effect. On the part of the agent, when the agent suffers from a lack of power, whence it follows that the action is defective and the effect deficient. But to an agent, as such, it is quite an accident to suffer from a lack of power: for an agent does not act inasmuch as power is lacking to him, but according as he has anything of power. Thus then evil is caused accidentally on the part of the agent, inasmuch as the agent runs short of power: therefore it is said that evil has not got an efficient cause, but a deficient cause, because evil does not follow from an efficient cause except in so far as it is deficient in power, and in this respect is not efficient. It comes to the same thing if the defect of the action and effect arises from some defect of the instrument, or of any other thing requisite for the agent's action, as when motive power produces halting through crookedness of the shin-bone: for the agent acts by both the power and the instrument. On the part of the effect evil is caused accidentally as well in respect of the matter of the effect as also in respect of its form. For if the matter is indisposed to receive the impression of the agent, some defect must follow in the effect. Nor is it imputable to any defect of the agent, that it does not transmute an indisposed matter to a perfect act: for the power of every natural agent is determined according to the limit of its nature; and its failure to transcend that cannot be brought in against it as a defect in power: such defect can then only be argued when it falls short of the measure of power due to it by nature. On the part of the form of the effect evil is accidentally incident, inasmuch as one form necessarily involves the privation of another form, and with the production of one thing there must needs ensue the destruction of another. But this evil does not belong to the effect intended by the agent, but attaches to something else. In the processes of nature therefore evil is caused by good only accidentally. The same is the case also in the processes of art: for art in its operation imitates nature, and is at fault in the same way as nature.

But in moral matters the case seems to be different. For a flaw in morals does not follow from any lack of power, seeing that weakness either entirely removes, or at least diminishes, moral reprehensibleness:

for weakness does not deserve the punishment which is due to fault, but rather compassion and indulgence: to be blameworthy, a point of conduct must be a voluntary act, not an inevitable necessity. On careful consideration we find that the case of morals is in some respects like, in some respects unlike the case of physics. The unlikeness consists in this, that a moral fault is viewed as consisting in the action alone, not in any effect produced: for moral virtues are not effective, but active, while arts are effective; and therefore it has been said that art is at fault in the same way as nature. Moral evil therefore is not estimated according to the matter and form of the effect, but follows simply from the agent. Now in moral actions there are found in orderly enumeration four active principles. One principle is the executive power, namely, the motor power which moves the limbs to execute the command of the will. This power is moved by the will, and so the will is another principle. The will is moved by the judgement of the apprehensive faculty, which judges the particular thing proposed to be good or bad. — good and bad being the (formal) objects of the will, the one object of seeking, the other of avoidance. Lastly, the apprehensive faculty is moved by the thing apprehended. The first active principle then in moral actions is the thing apprehended; the second is the apprehensive faculty; the third is the will; the fourth is motor power which executes the command of reason. But the act of the executive power already presupposes moral good or evil; for these exterior acts bear a moral character only in so far as they are voluntary. Hence if the act of the will is good, the exterior act will also be called good; and evil, if the volition is evil. It would be no point of moral badness for the exterior act to fail by some defect unconnected with the will: thus lameness is not a moral but a natural blemish. Such a lack of executive power diminishes, if it does not totally excuse from, moral blemish. Again, the act whereby the object moves the apprehensive faculty is exempt from moral blemish: for it is according to the order of nature that what is visible affects the sight, and every object affects the corresponding passive potentiality. Even the act of the apprehensive faculty, considered in itself, is nowise morally blameworthy, as we see that any defect in it excuses from or diminishes moral blame, like the lack of executive power: for infirmity and ignorance alike excuse from sin, or diminish it. It remains then that moral blameworthiness is found first and foremost in the act of the will alone; and reasonably so, since an act is called 'moral' from being voluntary. In the act of the will then is to be sought the root and origin of what in the moral order is sin.

But this investigation leads us into an apparent difficulty. On the understanding that defect in an act arises from some defect in the principle of action, some defect in the will must be presupposed before there can be any moral fault. If this defect is natural, it is ever inherent in the will; and the consequence is that the will must always do wrong in action, a consequence proved false by the fact of there being such things as acts of virtue. On the other hand, if the defect is voluntary, that is already a moral fault, the cause of which must stand over for further enquiry; and so we shall have a running account to infinity. We must therefore say that the defect pre-existing in the will is no natural necessity, otherwise it would follow that the will sinned in every act: nor again is a thing of chance and ill luck, for at that rate there could be in us no moral fault, since events of chance are unpremeditated and beyond the control of reason. The defect therefore is voluntary, but not a moral fault: so we must supposed to save the account running to infinity.

Now we must consider how that can be. In every active principle the perfection of its power depends on some superior active principle: for a secondary agent acts by virtue of the power of the prime agent. So long then as the secondary agent remains under the power of the prime agent, it will act unfailingly: but it will fail in its action whenever it happens to swerve from the order of the prime agent, as appears in an instrument when it ceases to respond to the movement of the agent who uses it. Now it has been said above that in the order of moral actions principles go before volition, the apprehensive faculty and the object apprehended, which is the end in view. But since to everything movable there corresponds a proper motive power, not any and every apprehensive faculty is the due motive power of any and every appetite, but one apprehension is the proper motive of one appetite, another of another. As then the sensible apprehensive faculty is the proper motive power of the sensible appetite, so the proper motive power of the will is reason itself. Further, as reason can apprehend many sorts of good things and many ends of action; as moreover every power has its own proper end; the will also must have some object and end of action and prime motive, and that must be not any and every sort of good, but some definite good. Whenever then the will tends to act under the motive of an apprehension of reason representing to it its own proper good, a due action ensues. But when the will bursts out into action upon the apprehension of the sensible apprehensive faculty, or even upon the apprehension of reason itself, representing some other good than the proper good of the will, there ensues in the action of the will a moral fault. Therefore any faulty action in the will is preceded by a lack of due regard to reason and to the proper end of willing. I say 'a lack of due regard to reason,' in such cases as when, upon some sudden aprehension of sense, the will tends to some good that is pleasant according to sense. I say 'a lack of due regard to the proper end of willing,' in cases when the reason arrives by reasoning at some good, which is not either now or in this way good, and still the will tends to it as though it were its proper good. Now this lack of due regard is voluntary: for it is in the power of the will to will and not to will: it is likewise in its power to direct reason actually to consider or to cease from considering, or to consider this or that. Still this failure of due consideration is not a moral evil: for, consideration or no consideration, or whatever the consideration be on reason's part, there is not sin until the will comes to tend to some undue end, which then is an act of will. — Thus it remains true that in moral as well as in physical actions, evil is not caused by good except accidentally.

## CHAPTER XI—That Evil is founded in some Good

EVIL cannot exist by itself, having no essence (Chap. VII): it must therefore be in some subject: but every subject, being a substance, is some good.
3. A thing is called evil because it does harm: that can only be because it does harm to good: for to do harm to evil is a good thing, since the undoing of evil is good. But it would not do harm to good, formally speaking, unless it were in good: thus blindness does harm to a man

inasmuch as it is within him.

But since good and evil are opposites, and one opposite cannot be the subject of another, but expels it, it seems at first sight strange if good is said to be the subject of evil. But if the truth is sought out, we shall find nothing strange or awkward in this conclusion. Good is commonly predicated as being is predicated, since every being, as such, is good. It is not strange that not-being should be in being as its subject: for every privation is some not-being, and still its subject is a substance, which is a being. Still not-being has not for its subject the being that is its opposite: thus sight is not the subject in which blindness is, but the animal. So the subject in which evil is, is not the good opposed to it, for that is taken away by the evil, but some other good. Thus the subject of moral evil is natural good: while natural evil, which is a privation of form, is in matter, and matter is good, as also is potential being.

CHAPTER XII—That Evil does not entirely swallow up Good

THE subject of evil must always remain, if evil is to remain. But the subject of evil is good: therefore good always remains.

But on the contingency of evil being infinitely intensified, and good being continually diminished by that intensification of evil, it appears that good may be diminished by evil even to infinity. And the good so diminished must be finite, for infinite good is not capable of evil. It seems then that in time good may be entirely taken away by evil.

This then is the reply. Evil, as we have seen, entirely takes away the good to which it is opposed, as blindness takes away sight: but there must remain that good which is the subject of evil, which subject, as such, bears a character of goodness, inasmuch as it is in potentiality to the actuality of good, whereof it is deprived by evil. The less then it is in potentiality to that good, the less good it will be. But a subject comes to be less in potentiality, or openness to a form, not only by the subtraction of some part of its potentiality, which is tantamount to subtraction of part of the subject itself, but also by the said potentiality being impeded by some contrary act from issuing in the actuality of the form. Good therefore is diminished by evil rather by the planting of evil, its contrary, than by the taking off of any portion of good. And this agrees with what has been already said about evil: for we said that evil happens beside the intention of the doer, who always intends some good, and upon the good intended there follows the exclusion of some other good opposite to that good. The greater then the multiplication of that good, upon which, contrary to the intention of the agent, evil follows, the greater the diminution of potentiality in respect of the opposite good; and so all the more may good be said to be diminished by evil. This diminution however of good by evil in the physical world cannot go on indefinitely: for all the physical forms and powers are limited, and come to some term beyond which they cannot go. But in moral matters this diminution of good by evil may proceed to infinity: for the understanding and the will have no limits to their acts: thus he who wills to commit a theft may will it again and commit another, and so to infinity. The further then the will tends towards undue ends, the more difficult it becomes for it to return to its proper and due end, as may be seen in persons in whom the habit of vice has been induced by a custom of sinning. Thus then by moral evil the good of natural aptitude may be diminished without limit: yet it can never be totally taken away, but always waits on nature while that remains.

CHAPTER XIV—That Evil is an Accidental Cause

RUNNING through all the species of causes, we find that evil is a cause accidentally. In the species of efficient cause, since through the deficiency of power in the active cause there follows defect in the effect and action. In the species of material cause, since through the indisposition of the matter there follows a defect in the product. In the species of formal cause, since to one form there is always annexed the privation of another form. In the species of final cause, since the evil annexed to an undue end means the hindering of the end that is due.

CHAPTER XV—That there is not any Sovereign Evil, acting as the Principle of All Evils

A SOVEREIGN evil should be without participation in any good, as that is the sovereign good which is wholly removed from evil. But there cannot be any evil wholly removed from good, since evil is founded on good (Chap. XI).
2. If anything is sovereignly evil, it must be evil by its very essence, as that is sovereignly good which is good by its essence. But evil has no essence (Chap. VII).
3. That which is a first principle is not caused by

anything. But all evil is caused by good (Chap. X). There is therefore no evil first principle.

5. The incidental must be posterior to the ordinary. But evil happens only incidentally and beside the intention (Chap. IV). Therefore it is impossible for evil to be a first principle. Hereby is excluded the error of the Manicheans.

CHAPTER XVI—That the End in View of everything is some Good

THAT to which a thing tends when in absence from it, and in which it rests when in possession of it, is the scope and aim and end in view. But everything, so long as it lacks the perfection proper to it, moves towards gaining that perfection, so far as it depends upon itself so to do; and when it has gained that perfection, therein it rests. The end then of everything is its perfection. But the perfection of everything is its own good. Everything therefore is ordained to good as to its end.

4. Things that are aware of an end and things that are unaware of an end are alike ordained to an end, with this difference, that things that are aware of an end tend to an end of themselves, while things that are unaware of an end tend to an end under the direction of another, as appears in the case of archer and arrow. But things that are aware of an end are always ordained to good for their end: for the will, which is the appetite of a fore-known end, never tends to anything except under the aspect of good, which is its object. Therefore things also which are unaware of an end are ordained to good for their end, and so good is the end of all things.

## CHAPTER XVII—That all Things are ordained to one End, which is God

THE sovereign good, which is God, is the cause of goodness in all good things. He is therefore also the cause of every end being an end, since whatever is an end is such inasmuch as it is good. But that whereby another thing has an attribute, has more of that attribute itself. Therefore God above all things is the end of all.

4. In every series of ends the last end must be the end of all the ends preceding. But we find all things arranged in various grades of goodness under our sovereign good, which is the cause of all goodness; and thereby, since good bears the character of an end, all things are ordered under God as ends preceding under their last end.

5. Private good is subordinated to the end of the common good: for the being of a part is for the sake of the being of the whole: hence the good of the race is more godlike than the good of the individual man. But the sovereign good, which is God, is the common good, since the good of the whole community depends on Him: while the goodness which marks any given thing is its own private good, and also the good of other things which depend upon it. All things therefore are subordinate to the end of one good, which is God.

7. The last end of every producer, in so far as he is a producer, is himself: for the things produced by us we use for ourselves; and if ever a man makes anything for another man that is referred to his own good, — his utility, his pleasure, or his honor. But God is the productive cause of all things, either immediately or mediately. And therefore He is the end of all.

Hence it is said: God hath wrought all things for himself (Prov. xvi, 4): and, I am alpha and omega, the first and the last (Apoc. xxii, 13).

CHAPTER XVIII—How God is the End of all Things

GOD is at once the last end of all things, and is nevertheless before all things in being. There is an end which, while holding the first place in causation according as it is in intention, is nevertheless posterior in being; and this is the case with every end that an agent establishes by his action, as the physician establishes health by his action in the sick man, which health nevertheless is his end. There is again an end which is prior in causation, and also is prior in being: such an end one aims at winning by one's actions or movement, as a king hopes to win a city by fighting. God then is the end of things, as being something which everything has to gain in its own way.

2. God is the last end of things and the prime agent of all (Chap. XVII). But an end established by the action of an agent cannot be the prime agent: rather it is the effect produced by the agent. God therefore cannot be the end of things as though He were anything established in being thereby, but only as some pre-existent object for them to attain.

4. An effect tends to an end in the same way that the producer of the effect acts for that end. But God, the first producer of all things, does not act in view of acquiring anything by His action, but in view of bestowing something by His action: for He is not in potentiality to acquire anything, but only in perfect

actuality, whereby He can give and bestow. Things then are not directed to God as though God were an end unto which any accretion or acquisition were to be made: they are directed to Him so that in their own way they may gain from God God Himself, since He Himself is their end.

CHAPTER XIX—That all Things aim at Likeness to God

ALL things evidently have a natural appetite for being, and resist destructive agencies wherever they are threatened with them. But all things have being inasmuch as they are likened to God, who is the essential subsistent Being, all other things having being only by participation. All things therefore have an appetite for likeness to God, making that their last end.

4. All created things are some sort of image of the prime agent, God: for every agent acts to the production of its own likeness: now the perfection of an image consists in representing its original by likeness thereto: the image in fact is made on purpose. All things then exist for the attainment of the divine likeness; and that is their last end.

CHAPTER XX—How Things copy the Divine Goodness

NOT all creatures are established in one and the same degree of goodness. The substance of some is form and actuality, — that is to say, something which, in point of essence, has the attribute of actual being and goodness. The substance of other beings is composed of matter and form: this substance has the attribute of actual being and goodness, but only in respect of part of itself, namely, the form. While then the divine substance is its own goodness, a simple substance (or pure spirit) partakes of this goodness to the extent of its essence, but a composite substance to the extent of some part of its essence. In this third grade of substance again there is found a difference in being. For, composed as they are of matter and form, the form of some of them fills the whole potentiality of the matter, so that there remains not in the matter any potentiality to any other form, and consequently not in any other matter any potentiality to this form: such are the heavenly bodies, into the essential constitution of which their whole matter enters. In other bodies the form does not fill the whole potentiality of the matter: hence there still remains in the matter a potentiality to another form, and in some portion of matter there remains a potentiality to this form, as appears in the (four) elements and bodies composed thereof. Now because a privation is a negation in a substance of that which may well be in the substance, it is clear that with this form, which does not fill the whole potentiality of the matter, there is compatible the privation of some form due to that substance. No such privation can attach to a substance, the form of which fills the whole potentiality of its matter; nor to a substance which is essentially a form; still less to that Substance, whose very being is His essence. Further it is clear that, since evil is the privation of good, there is in this lowest order of substances changeable good with admixture of evil, a changeableness to which the higher orders are not liable. The substance therefore that ranks lowest in being is lowest also in rank of goodness.

We likewise find an order of goodness among the

parts of a substance composed of matter and form. For since matter, considered in itself, is potential being, while form is the actualization of that being, and the substance composed of the two is actually existent through the form, the form will be good in itself; the composed substance will be good as it actually has the form; and the matter will be good inasmuch as it is in potentiality to the form. But though everything is good in so far as it is being, it need not be supposed that matter, as it is only potential being, is only potentially good. For 'being' is an absolute term, while there is goodness even in relation: for not only is a thing called 'good' because it is an end, or is in possession of an end, but also, though it has not yet arrived at any end, provided only it be ordained to some end, a thing is called 'good' even on that account. Though then matter cannot absolutely be called 'being' on the title of its potentiality involving some relation to being, yet it may absolutely be called 'good' on account of this very relation. Herein it appears that 'good' is a term of wider extension than 'being.'

Yet in another way does the goodness of the creature fall short of the divine goodness. As has been said, God possesses the highest perfection of goodness in his mere being: but a created thing does not possess its perfection in point of one attribute only, but in point of many: for what is united in the highest is multiple and manifold in the lowest. Hence God is said to be fraught with virtue and wisdom and activity in one and the same respect, but a creature in different respects. The greater the distance at which a creature stands removed from the first and highest goodness, the greater the multiplication of points requisite for it to be perfectly good. But if it cannot attain to perfect goodness, it will hold on to an imperfect goodness in a few points. Hence it is that, though the first and highest goodness is absolutely simple, and the substances nearest to it approach it alike in goodness and in simplicity, still the lowest substances are found to be more simple than other substances higher than they are, as the elements are more simple than animals and men, because they cannot attain to the perfection of knowledge and understanding to which animals and men attain. It appears therefore from what has been said that, though God has His goodness perfect and entire in the simplicity of His being, creatures nevertheless do not attain to the perfection of their goodness by their mere being, but only by many details of being. Hence, though every one of these creatures is good in so far as it has being, still it cannot absolutely be called good if it is destitute of other qualities requisite for its goodness; as a man devoid of virtues and subject to vices is good in a certain way, inasmuch as he is a being and inasmuch as he is a man, but on the whole he is not good, but rather evil. For no creature then is it the same thing to bean to be good, absolutely speaking, although every creature is good in so far as it has being: but for God it is quite the same thing to bean to be good, absolutely speaking. Now, as it has been shown, everything tends finally to some likeness of the divine goodness; and a thing is likened to the divine goodness in respect of all the points which appertain to its own proper goodness; and the goodness of a thing consists not only in its being but in all other qualities requisite for its perfection: from which considerations the consequence is clear, that a thing is finally ordained to God, not only in its substantial being, but likewise in those accidental qualities that appertain to its perfection, and also in respect of its proper activity, which likewise belongs to the perfection of a thing.

CHAPTER XXI—That Things aim at Likeness to God in being Causes of other Things

A THING must be first perfect in itself before it can cause another thing. The last perfection to supervene upon a thing is its becoming the cause of other things. While then a creature tends by many ways to the likeness of God, the last way left open to it is to seek the divine likeness by being the cause of other things, according to what the Apostle says, We are God's coadjutors(1 Cor. iii, 9).

CHAPTER XXIV—That all Things seek good, even Things devoid of Consciousness

AS the heavenly sphere is moved by a subsistent intelligence (Chap. XXIII), and the movement of the heavenly sphere is directed to generation in sublunary creatures, the generations and movements of these sublunary creatures must originate in the thought of that subsistent intelligence. Now the intention of the prime agent and of the instrument is bent upon the same end. The heavenly spheres then (coelum) are the cause of sublunary motions by virtue of their own motion, which is impressed upon them by a spirit. It follows that the heavenly spheres are the instrument of spirit. Spirit then is the prime agent, causing and intending the forms and motions of sublunary bodies; while the heavenly spheres are the instruments of the same. But the intellectual outlines of all that is caused and intended by an intelligent agent must pre-exist in his mind, as the forms of works of art pre-exist in the mind of the artificer, and from that mind (et ex eo) those forms must pass into the things made. All the forms then that are in sublunary creatures, and all their motions, are determined by the forms that are in the mind of some subsistent intelligence, or intelligences. Therefore Boethius says that the forms which are in matter have come from forms apart from matter. In this respect the saying of Plato is verified, that forms existing apart are the originating principles of the forms that are in matter: only, Plato supposed these forms to subsist by themselves, and to be immediate causes of the forms of sensible things; we suppose them to exist in a mind, and to cause sublunary forms through the instrumentality of the motion of the heavenly spheres. Thus it is not difficult to see how natural bodies, devoid of intelligence, move and act for an end. For they tend to their end, being directed thereto by a subsistent intelligence, in the way that an arrow tends to its end, directed by the archer: as the arrow from the impulse of the archer, so do natural bodies receive their inclination to their natural ends from natural moving causes, whence they derive their forms and virtues and motions. Hence it is plain that every work of nature is the work of a subsistent intelligence. The credit of an effect rests by preference with the prime mover, who guides instruments to their purpose, rather than with the instruments which he guides. Thus we find the operations of nature proceeding in due course and order to an end, like the operations of a wise man. It is evident therefore that even agents devoid of consciousness can work for an end, and strive after good with a natural appetite, and seek the divine likeness and their own perfection. It is further evident that, the more perfect the power and the more eminent the degree of goodness, the more general is the appetite for good, and the more distant from self are the objects for which good is sought and unto which good is done. For imperfect beings tend solely to the good of the individual; perfect beings to the good of the species; more perfect beings to the good of the genus; and God, who is the most perfect in goodness, to the good of all being. Hence some say, not without reason, that goodness as such is diffusive of itself.

CHAPTER XXV—That the End of every Subsistent Intelligence is to understand God

THE proper act of everything is its end, as being its second perfection: hence what is well disposed to its own proper act is said to be virtuous and good. But to understand is the proper act of a subsistent intelligence: that then is its end. And the most perfect instance of this act is its final end and perfection: this is particularly true of acts which are not directed to production, acts such as understanding and feeling. But since such acts take their species from their objects, and are known through their objects, any given one of these acts will be the more perfect, the more perfect its object is. Consequently, to understand the most perfect intelligible object, which is God, will be the most perfect instance of the activity of understanding. To know God then by understanding is the final end of every subsistent intelligence.

But one may say: 'It is true that the last end of a subsistent intelligence consists in understanding the best intelligible object, still the best intelligible object, absolutely speaking, is not the best object for this or that subsistent intelligence; but the higher any subsistent intelligence is, the higher is its best intelligible object; and therefore the highest subsistent intelligence created has for its best intelligible object that which is best absolutely; hence its happiness will be in understanding God; but the happiness of a lower subsistent intelligence will be to understand some lower intelligible object, which is at the same time the highest of the objects that can be understood by it. And particularly it seems to be the lot of the human understanding, on account of its weakness, not to understand the absolutely best intelligible object: for in respect of the knowledge of that truth of which there is most to be known the human intellect is as the bat's eye to the sun.

 Nevertheless it may be manifestly shown that the end of every subsistent intelligence, even the lowest, is to understand God. For (a) the final end of all beings, to which they tend, is God (Chap. XVIII. But the human understanding, however it be lowest in the order of subsistent intelligences, is nevertheless superior to all beings devoid of understanding. Since then the nobler substance has not the ignobler end, God Himself will be the end also of the human understanding. But every intelligent being gains its last end by understanding it. Therefore it is by understanding that the human intellect attains God as its end.

 (c). Everything most of all desires its own last end. But the human mind is moved to more desire and love and delight over the knowledge of divine things, little as it can discern about them, than over the perfect knowledge that it has of the lowest things.

 (e). All sciences and arts and practical faculties are

attractive only for the sake of something else: for in them the end is not knowledge but production of a work. But speculative sciences are attractive for their own sake, for their end is sheer knowledge. Nor is there found any action in human life, with the exception of speculative study, which is not directed to some other and further end. Even actions done in sport, which seem to be done in view of no end, have a due end, which is refreshment of mind, to enable us thereby to return stronger to serious occupations: otherwise we should play always, if play was sought for its own sake, which would be unbefitting. Therefore the practical arts are ordained to the speculative, and all human activity has intellectual speculation for its end. In all due ordination of sciences and arts, the character of final end attaches to that science or art which issues precepts as master-builder to the rest: thus the art of navigation, to which belongs the management of a ship, lays down precepts for ship-building. In this relation Metaphysics (philosophia prima) stand to all speculative sciences. On metaphysics they all depend, and from that science they receive their principles and directions how to proceed against deniers of principles. This first philosophy is wholly directed to the final end of the knowledge of God: hence it is called a divine science. The knowledge of God therefore is the final end of all human study and activity.

(f). In all series of agents and causes of change the end of the prime agent and mover must be the ultimate end of all, as the end of a general is the end of all the soldiers who serve under him. But among all the component parts of man we find the intellect to be the superior moving power: for the intellect moves the appetite, putting its object before it; and the intellectual appetite, or will, moves the sensible appetites, the irascible and concupiscible: hence we do not obey concupiscence except under the command of the will. The sensitive appetite, crowned by the consent of the will, proceeds to move the body. The end therefore of the intellect is the end of all human actions. But the end and good of the intellect is truth; and consequently its last end is the first truth. The last end then of the whole man and of all his activities and desires is to know the first truth, which is God.

(g). There is a natural desire in all men of knowing the causes of the things that they see. It was through wonder at seeing things, the causes of which were unseen, that men first began to philosophize. Nor does enquiry cease until we arrive at the first cause: then we consider our knowledge perfect, when we know the first cause. Man then naturally desires so to know the first cause as his last end. But the first cause is God; and the last end of man and of every subsistent intelligence, is called blessedness or happiness. To know God then is the blessedness and happiness of every subsistent intelligence.

Hence it is said: *This is eternal life, that they know thee, the only true God* (John xvii, 3).

CHAPTER XXVI—That Happiness does not consist in any Act of the Will

SINCE a subsistent intelligence in its activity arrives at God, not by understanding alone, but also by an act of the will desiring and loving Him and taking delight in Him, someone may think that the last end and final felicity of man is not in knowing God, but rather in loving

Him, or exercising some other act of the will upon Him; especially seeing that the object of the will is good, which bears the character of an end, whereas truth, which is the object of the intellect, does not bear the character of an end except in so far as it (ipsum) too is good. Hence it seems that man does not attain his last end by an act of intellect, but rather by an act of will. But this position is manifestly proved to be untenable.

1. Happiness, being the peculiar good of an intelligent nature, must attach to the intelligent nature on the side of something that is peculiar to it. But appetite is not peculiar to intelligent nature, but is found in all things, though diversely in diverse beings: which diversity however arises from the different ways in which they stand to consciousness. Things wholly devoid of consciousness have only natural appetite, or physical tendency. Things that have sensitive consciousness have sensible appetite, under which the irascible and concupiscible are included. Things that have intellectual consciousness have an appetite proportionate to that consciousness, namely, the will. The will therefore, as being an appetite, is not a peculiar appurtenance of an intelligent nature, except so far as it is dependent on the intelligence: but intelligence in itself is peculiar to an intelligent nature. Happiness therefore consists in an act of the intellect substantially and principally rather than in an act of the will.

2. In all powers that are moved by their objects the objects are naturally prior to the acts of those powers. But such a power is the will, for the desirable object moves desire. The object therefore of the will is naturally prior to the act. The prime object of will then precedes every act of will. No act of will therefore can be the prime object of

volition. But the prime object of will is the last end, which is happiness. Happiness therefore cannot possibly be itself an act of will.

3. In all powers that can reflect on their own acts, the act of that power must first fix on some object, and then fix on its own act. For if the intellect understands that it understands, we must suppose that it first understands something, and afterwards understands its own understanding of that thing: for the act of understanding, which the intellect understands, means the understanding of some object. Hence we must either proceed to infinity; or, coming to some first object of understanding, this object, we must say, will not be a sheer act of understanding, but some intelligible thing. Similarly the first object of will cannot be any sheer act of willing, but some other good. But the first object of will to an intelligent nature is happiness: for it is for the sake of happiness that we will whatever we do will. Happiness therefore cannot possibly consist essentially in any act of will.

4. Everything has the truth of its nature by having the constituents of its substance: for a real man differs from a painted one by the constituents of the substance of man. But true happiness does not differ from false happiness in respect of the act of will: for the will is in the same attitude of desire, or love, or delight, whatever the object proposed to it for its sovereign good, true or false: but whether the object so proposed be the true sovereign good or a counterfeit, that difference is decided by intellect. Happiness therefore consists essentially in intellect rather than in any act of will.

5. If any act of will were happiness itself, that act would be either desire or love or delight. Now it is

impossible for desire to be the last end: for desire obtains inasmuch as the will tends to something which it has not yet got: but such straining after the absent is inconsistent with the idea of an achieved last end. Love again cannot be the last end: for good is loved not only in its presence but also in its absence: for it is from love that good not possessed is sought for by desire. And though the love of good already attained is more perfect, that access of perfection is to be ascribed to the attainment and established possession of the good loved. The attainment of good then, which is the end, is a different thing from the love of good, which love is imperfect before attainment, and perfect after attainment. In like manner neither is delight the last end: for the very possession of good is the cause of delight, while we either feel the good now possessed, or remember the good possessed before, or hope for the good to be possessed in future: delight therefore is not the last end. No act of will therefore can be the substance of happiness.

6. If delight were the last end, it would be desirable of itself. But that is false: for it makes a difference what delight is desired, considering the object from which delight ensues: for the delight which follows upon good and desirable activities is good and desirable: but that which follows upon evil activities is evil and to be shunned. Delight therefore has its goodness and desirability from something beyond itself. Therefore it is not itself the final end, happiness.

7. The right order of things coincides with the order of nature, for natural things are ordained to their end without mistakes. But in natural things delight is for activity, and not the other way about: for we see that nature has attached delight to those activities of animals

which are manifestly ordained to necessary ends, as in the use of food, which is ordained to the preservation of the individual, and in the intercourse of the sexes, which is ordained to the preservation of the species: for if delight were not in attendance, animals would abstain from the aforesaid necessary acts. It is impossible therefore for delight to be the final end.

8. Delight seems to be nothing else than a rest of the will in some befitting good, as desire is an inclination of the will to the gaining of some good. Now it is ridiculous to say that the end of movement is not the coming to be in one's proper place, but the satisfaction of the inclination whereby one tended to go there. If the principle aim of nature were the satisfaction of the inclination, it would never give the inclination. It gives the inclination that thereby one may tend to one's proper place: when that end is gained, there follows the satisfaction of the inclination: thus the satisfaction of the inclination is not the end, but a concomitant of the end.

9. If any exterior thing is to be any one's end, we must assign the title of last end to that activity whereby the thing is first gained: thus to people who make money their end, the getting of the money is the end, not the love or desire of it. But the last end of a subsistent intelligence is God. That activity then in man makes the substance of his happiness, whereby he first attains to God. But that is the activity of understanding: for we cannot will what we do not understand. The final happiness of man then substantially consists in knowing God by the understanding, and not in any act of the will.

From what has been said we may solve the objections to the contrary. The fact of the sovereign good being the object of the will does not necessitate sovereign good being substantially the act of the will itself, as was the tenor of the argument first proposed: nay, from the fact of its being the first object, it follows that it is not the act.

Arg. 2. The last perfection of activity is delight, which perfects activity as beauty does youth. If then any perfect activity is the last end, it seems that the last end is rather in the activity of the will than of the intellect.

Reply. There are two ways of being a perfection to a thing. In one way there is a perfection to a thing already complete in its species: in another way there is a perfection going to make up the species. Thus the perfection of a house, considered as complete in its species, is that use for which the house is intended, namely, being inhabited: hence this should be put in the definition of a house, if the definition is to be adequate. A perfection going to make up the species of a house may be one of the constituents and substantial principles of the species: or it may be something that goes to the preservation of the species, as the buttresses made to prop the house up: lastly, under this head we must count whatever makes the house more comely for use, as its beauty. That therefore which is the perfection of a thing, considered as already complete in its species, is the end of a thing, as being inhabited is the end of a house. And in like manner the proper activity of each thing, which is a sort of use of it, is the end of the thing. But the perfections which go to make up the species are not the end of the thing: rather the thing is their end. Thus matter and form are for the species. In like manner the perfections that preserve a thing in its species, as health and nutrition, though they perfect the animal, are not the end of its existence, but rather the other way about. Those perfections also whereby a thing is fitted to discharge the proper activities of its species and gain its due end more becomingly, are not the end of the thing, but rather the other way about, e.g., a man's beauty and bodily strength, and other accomplishments, of which the philosopher says that they minister to happiness instrumentally. Now when we say that delight is the perfection of activity, we do not mean that activity specifically considered is directed to the purpose of delight, — the fact is, it is ordained to other ends, as eating is ordained to the preservation of the individual, — we mean that delight ranks among the perfections which go to make up the species of a thing: for through the delight that we take in any action we apply ourselves to it more attentively and becomingly.

Arg. 3. Delight seems to be so desired for its own sake as never to be desired for the sake of anything else: for it is foolish to ask of any one why [he] wishes to be delighted. But this is the condition of the last end, to be desired for its own sake. Therefore the last end is rather in an act of the will than of the understanding, so it seems.

Reply. Delight, though it is not the last end, is still a concomitant of the last end, since from the attainment of the last end delight supervenes.

Arg. 4. In the desire of the last end there is the greatest agreement amongst all men, because it is natural. But more seek delight than knowledge. Therefore it seems that delight is the end rather than knowledge.

Reply. There are not more seekers of the delight that there is in knowing than there are seekers of knowledge: but there are more seekers after sensible delights than there are seekers of intellectual knowledge and the delight thence ensuing; and the reason is because external things are more known to the majority of men, as human knowledge starts from objects of sense.

Arg. 5. The will seems to be a higher power than the understanding: for the will moves the understanding to its end: for when there is the will so to do, then it is that the understanding actually considers the knowledge which it habitually possesses. The action therefore of the will seems to be nobler than the action of the understanding; and therefore the final end of happiness seems in the act of will rather than in the act of understanding.

Reply. It is manifestly false to say that the will is higher than the understanding as moving it; for primarily and ordinarily the understanding moves the will. The will, as such, is moved by its object, which is the good apprehended: but the will moves the understanding, we may say, incidentally, inasmuch as the act of understanding itself is apprehended as good and so is desired by the will. Hence it follows that the understanding actually understands, and in this has the start of the will; for never would the will desire to understand, unless first the understanding apprehended the act of understanding itself as good. And again the will moves the understanding to actual activity in the way in which an efficient cause is said to move: but the understanding moves the will in the way in which a final cause moves, for good understood is the end of the will. Now the efficient cause is posterior in motion to the final cause, for the efficient cause moves only for the sake of the final cause. Hence it appears that, absolutely speaking, the understanding is higher than the will, but the will is higher than the understanding accidentally and in a qualified sense.

## CHAPTER XXVII—That the Happiness of Man does not consist in Bodily Pleasures

ACCORDING to the order of nature, pleasure is for the sake of activity, and not the other way about. If therefore certain activities are not the final end, the pleasures ensuing upon these activities are neither the final end nor accessories of the final end. But certainly the activities on which bodily pleasures follow are not the final end: for they are directed to other obvious ends, the preservation of the body and the begetting of offspring. Therefore the aforesaid pleasures are not the final end, nor accessories of the final end, and happiness is not to be placed in them.

3. Happiness is a good proper to man: dumb animals cannot be called happy except by an abuse of language. But bodily pleasures are common to man and brute: happiness therefore cannot consist in them.

4. The final end of a thing is noblest and best of all that appertains to the thing. But bodily delights do not appertain to a man in respect of what is noblest in him.

5. The highest perfection of man cannot consist in his being conjoined with things lower than himself, but in his conjunction with something above him.

7. In all things that are said to be 'ordinarily' (per se), 'more' follows upon 'more,' if 'absolutely' goes with 'absolutely.' If then bodily pleasures were good in themselves, to take them to the utmost would be the best way of taking them. But this is manifestly false: for excessive use of such things is accounted a vice, injures the body, and bars further enjoyments of the same sort.

8. If human happiness consisted in bodily pleasures, it would be a more praiseworthy act of virtue to

take such pleasures than to abstain from them. But this is manifestly false, for it is the special praise of the act of temperance to abstain from such pleasures.

9. The last end of everything is God (Chap. XVIII). That then must be laid down to be the last end of man, whereby he most closely approaches to God. But bodily pleasures injure a man from any close approach to God: for God is approached by contemplation, and the aforesaid pleasures are a hindrance to contemplation.

Hereby is excluded the error of the Epicureans, who placed the happiness of man in these pleasures: in whose person Solomon says: This seemed to me good, that man should eat and drink and make merry on the fruit of his toil (Eccles. V, 17). Everywhere let us leave behind us signs of mirth, for this is our portion and this our lot (Wisd. ii, 9). Also the error of the followers of Cerinthus is excluded, who spread the fable of a thousand years of the pleasures of the belly as an element in the kingdom of Christ after the resurrection, hence they are called Chiliasts, or Millennarians. Also the fables of the Saracens, who place the rewards of the just in the aforesaid pleasures.

CHAPTER XXVIII, XXIX—That Happiness does not consist in Honors nor in Human Glory

THE last end and happiness of man is his most perfect activity (Chap. XXVI). But the honor paid to a man does not consist in any act of his own, but in the act of another towards him.

2. That is not the last end, which is good and desirable on account of something else. But such is honor:

for a man is not rightly honored except for some other good thing existing in him.

4. Even bad men may be honored. It is better then to become worthy of honor than to be honored. Therefore honor is not the highest good of man.

Hence it appears that neither does man's chief good consist in glory, or celebrity of fame. For glory, according to Cicero, is "a frequent mention of a man with praise"; or according to St Augustine, "brilliant notoriety with praise" (clara notitia cum laude). So then men wish for notoriety, attended with praise and a certain brilliance, that they may be honored by those to whom they become known. Glory then is sought for the sake of honor. If then honor is not the highest good, much less is glory.

CHAPTER XXX—That Man's Happiness does not consist in Riches

RICHES are not desired except for the sake of something else: for of themselves they do no good, but only as we use them. But the highest good is desired for its own sake, and not for the sake of something else.

2. The possession or preservation of those things cannot be the highest good, which benefit man most in being parted with. But such is the use of riches, to spend.

3. The act of liberality and munificence, the virtues that deal with money, is more praiseworthy, in that money is parted with, than that money is got. Man's happiness therefore does not consist in the possession of riches.

4. That in the gaining of which man's chief good lies must be something better than man. But man is better than his riches, which are things ordained to his use.

5. The highest good of man is not subject to fortune: for fortuitous events happen without effort of reason, whereas man must gain his proper end by reason. But fortune has great place in the gaining of riches.

CHAPTER XXXI—That Happiness does not consist in Worldly Power

A MAN is called good inasmuch as he attains to the sovereign good. But inasmuch as he has power he is not called either good or evil: for he is not good who can do good things, nor is a man evil of being able to do evil things. Therefore the highest good does not consist in being powerful.
3. All power is over another (ad alterum). But the highest good is not over another.

CHAPTER XXXII—That Happiness does not consist in the Goods of the Body

THE soul is better than the body. Therefore the good of the soul, as understanding and the like, is better than the good of the body. The good of the body therefore is not the highest good of man.
3. These goods are common to man and other animals: but happiness is the proper good of man alone.
4. For goods of the body, many animals are better off than man: some are swifter, some are stronger, and so of the rest. If in these things the highest good consisted, man would not be the most excellent of animals.

CHAPTER XXXIV—That the Final Happiness Man does not consist in Acts of the Moral Virtues

HUMAN happiness, if it is final, is not referable to any further end. But all moral acts are referable to something further: thus acts of fortitude in war are directed to securing victory and peace: acts of justice to the preservation of peace amongst men by every one remaining in quiet possession of his own.

2. Moral virtues aim at the observance of the golden mean in passions and in the disposal of external things. But the moderation of the passions or of external things cannot possibly be the final end of human life, since these very passions and external things are referable to something else.

3. Man is man by the possession of reason; and therefore happiness, his proper good, must regard what is proper to reason. But that is more proper to reason which reason has in itself than what it does in another. Since then the good of moral virtue is something which reason establishes in things other than itself, moral virtue cannot be the best thing in man, which is happiness.

CHAPTER XXXVII—That the Final Happiness of Man consists in the Contemplation of God

IF then the final happiness of man does not consist in those exterior advantages which are called goods of fortune, nor in goods of the body, nor in goods of the soul in its sentient part, nor in the intellectual part in respect of the moral virtues, nor in the virtues of the practical intellect, called art and prudence, it remains that the final happiness of man consists in the contemplation of truth. This act alone in man is proper to him, and is in no way shared by any other being in this world. This is sought for its own sake, and is directed to no other end beyond itself. By this act man is united in likeness with pure spirits, and even comes to know them in a certain way. For this act also man is more self-sufficient, having less need of external things. Likewise to this act all other human activities seem to be directed as to their end. For to the perfection of contemplation there is requisite health of body; and all artificial necessaries of life are means to health. Another requisite is rest from the disturbing forces of passion: that is attained by means of the moral virtues and prudence. Likewise rest from exterior troubles, which is the whole aim of civil life and government. Thus, if we look at things rightly, we may see that all human occupations seem to be ministerial to the service of the contemplators of truth.

Now it is impossible for human happiness to consist in that contemplation which is by intuition of first principles, — a very imperfect study of things, as being the most general, and not amounting to more than a potential knowledge: it is in fact not the end but the beginning of human study: it is supplied to us by nature, and not by any close investigation of truth. Nor can happiness consist in the sciences, the object-matter of which is the meanest things, whereas happiness should be an activity of intellect dealing with the noblest objects of intelligence. Therefore the conclusion remains that the final happiness of man consists in contemplation guided by wisdom to the study of the things of God. Thus we have reached by way of induction the same conclusion that was formerly established by deductive reasoning, that the final happiness of man does not consist in anything short of the contemplation of God.


CHAPTER XXXVIII—That Human Happiness does not consist in such Knowledge of God as is common to the majority of Mankind

THERE is a certain general and vague knowledge of God in the minds of practically, all men, whether it be by the fact of God's existence being a self-evident truth, as some think (B. I, Chap. X); or, as seems more likely, because natural reasoning leads a man promptly to some sort of knowledge of God: for men seeing that natural things follow a certain course and order, and further considering that order cannot be without an ordainer, they perceive generally that there is some ordainer of the things which we see. But who or what manner of being the ordainer of nature is, and whether He be one or many, cannot be gathered offhand from this slight study. Thus, seeing a man move and do other acts, we perceive that there is in him a cause of these activities, which is not in other things; and this cause we call the soul; and still we do not yet know what the soul is, whether it is anything corporeal or not, or how it performs the aforesaid acts. Now such knowledge as this cannot possibly suffice for happiness.

1. For happiness must be an activity without defect. But this knowledge is susceptible of admixture of many errors: thus some have believed that the ordainer of mundane events is no other than the heavenly bodies: hence they have affirmed the heavenly bodies to be gods.

Others have said the same of the elements, thinking that their natural movements and activities come not from any controlling power outside them, but that they control other things. Others, believing that human acts are not subject to any other than human control, have called those men who control other men gods. Such knowledge of God is not sufficient for happiness.

3. No one is blameworthy for not possessing happiness: nay, men who have it not, and go on tending to it, are praised. But lack of the aforesaid knowledge of God renders a man particularly blameworthy. It is a great indication of dullness of perception in a man, when he perceives not such manifest signs of God; just as anyone would be counted lacking in perception, who, seeing a man, did not understand that he had a soul. Hence it is said in the Psalms (xiii and lii): *The fool said in his heart: There is no God.*

4. Knowledge of a thing in general, not descending into any details, is a very imperfect knowledge, as would be the knowledge of man merely as something that moves. By such knowledge a thing is known potentially only, for details are potentially contained in generalities. But happiness, being a perfect activity and the supreme good of man, must turn upon what is actual and not merely potential.

CHAPTER XXXIX—That Happiness does not consist in the Knowledge of God which is to be had by Demonstration

AGAIN there is another knowledge of God, higher than the last mentioned: this knowledge is acquired by demonstration, by means of which we come nearer to a proper knowledge of Him, since demonstration removes from Him many attributes, by removal of which the mind discerns God standing apart from other beings. Thus demonstration shows God to be unchangeable, eternal, incorporeal, absolutely simple, one. A proper knowledge of an object is arrived at, not only by affirmations, but also by negations. Thus as it is proper to man to be a rational animal, so it is proper to him also not to be inanimate or irrational. But between these two modes of proper knowledge there is this difference, that when a proper knowledge of a thing is got by affirmations, we know both what the thing is and how it is distinct from others: but when a proper knowledge of a thing is got by negations, we know that the thing is distinct from other things, but what it is remains unknown. Such is the proper knowledge of God that we have by demonstrations. But that is not sufficient for the final happiness of man.

1. The individuals of a species arrive at the end and perfection of that species for the most part; and natural developments have place always or for the most part, though they fail in a minority of instances through something coming in to mar them. But happiness is the end and perfection of the human species, since all men naturally desire it. Happiness then is a common good, possible to accrue to all men, except in cases where an obstacle arises to deprive some of it. But few they are who arrive at this knowledge of God by way of demonstration, on account of the difficulties mentioned above (B. I, Chap. IV). Such scientific knowledge then is not the essence of human happiness.

3. Happiness excludes all misery. But deception and error is a great part of misery. Now in the knowledge of God by demonstration manifold error may be mingled,

as is clear in the case of many who have found out some truths about God in that way, and further following their own ideas, in the failure of demonstration, have fallen into many sorts of error. And if any have found truth in the things of God so perfectly by the way of demonstration as that no error has entered their minds, such men certainly have been very few: a rarity of attainment which does not befit happiness, happiness being the common end of all.

4. Happiness consists in perfect activity. Now for the perfection of the activity of knowledge certainty is required: but the aforesaid knowledge has much of uncertainty.

CHAPTER XL—That Happiness does not consist in the Knowledge of God by Faith

HAPPINESS is the perfect activity of the human intellect (Chap. XXVI). But in the knowledge that is of faith, though there is high perfection on the part of the object so apprehended, there is great imperfection on the side of intellect, for intellect does not understand that to which it assents in believing.

2. Final happiness does not consist principally in any act of will (Chap. XXVI). But in the knowledge of faith the will has a leading part: for the understanding assents by faith to the things proposed to it, because it wills to do so, without being necessarily drawn by the direct evidence of truth.

3. He who believes, yields assent to things proposed to him by another, which himself he does not see: hence the knowledge of faith is more like hearing than seeing. Since then happiness consists in the highest

knowledge of God, it cannot consist in the knowledge of faith.

4. Happiness being the last end, all natural desire is thereby appeased. But the knowledge of faith, far from appeasing desire, rather excites it, since every one desires to see that which he believes.

## CHAPTERS XLI–XLV

"A separately subsistent intelligence," writes St Thomas (Chap. XLI), "by knowing its own essence, knows both what is above it and what is below it, particularly if what is above it is also its cause, since the likeness of the cause must be found in the effect. Hence, since God is the cause of all created subsistent intelligences, they, by knowing their own essences, know by some sort of vision (per modum visionis cujusdam) even God Himself: for a thing is known by intellect in a manner of vision, when its likeness exists in intellect: whatever intellect then apprehends a separately subsistent intelligence, and knows the same in its essential nature, sees God in a higher way than is possible by any of the modes of cognition already mentioned." Know an angel, then, or pure spirit, in his essence, and you will thereby have a higher knowledge of God than any that you could attain by any other speculation of science or philosophy. Consequently, if the knowledge of God be happiness, happiness, it seems, will best open to us men, if we can find some method of reading the innermost natures of angels. Alexander of Aphrodisias (fl A.D. 200), Avempace (Ibn-Badja, d. 1138), and Averroes (Ibn-Roschd, d. 1198), each was quoted in St Thomas's day as the author of a method enabling men to do this, methods which St Thomas elaborately confutes in these chapters. Avempace's plan was to study the speculative sciences, and thence forming abstract generalizations, one higher than the other, — or perhaps he meant (what is by no means the same thing) one fuller of 'content' than the other, — to ascend to the cognition of pure intelligence. St Thomas describes the process in scholastic terms, thus; "to extract the quiddity of everything which is not its own quiddity; and if that quiddity has a quiddity, again to abstract the quiddity of that quiddity, till we come to a stand somewhere, arriving by the method of analysis at the knowledge of the quiddity of a being, subsisting apart, which has not another quiddity" (Chap. XLI): which words perhaps need some explanation. "The quiddity of a thing which is not its own quiddity" means then an essence, or essential quality, which is shared by many subjects, and is not all embodied in one subject, constituting that subject entirely. Thus prudence is in Cato, and in many others besides. Cato is not all prudence: he is not the embodiment of sheer prudence and nothing else. Prudence then in Cato is a quiddity which is not its own quiddity. St Thomas well observes that Avempace's method is Platonic Idealism revived. He adds that, starting as our abstractions must, from sensible objects, we can never attain to a view of the essential nature of a pure spirit. "If by understanding of the natures and quiddities of sensible things, we arrive at an understanding of separately subsistent intelligences, that understanding of such intelligences must be reached through some one of the speculative sciences. But we do not see how this is to be done: for there is no speculative science which teaches concerning any one of the separately subsistent intelligences what it is in essence, but only the fact of its existence" (Chap. XLI). — Averroes, as might have been expected, proceeds upon his favorite notion of the continuatio, or conjunction of the individual mind with the one vast intelligence, active and potential, that is without (B. II, Chap. LX). St Thomas's summary of the Commentator's views ends thus — (it is a very free paraphrase of Averroes's words as they appear in the Latin of the Venice edition of 1574, pp. 186, 187): "This perfect progress towards conjunction with the supreme intelligence comes of zealous study of the speculative sciences, whereby true intellectual notions are acquired, and false opinions are excluded, such opinions lying beyond the line of this progress, like monstrous births outside of the line of the operation of nature. To this advance men help one another by helping one another in the speculative sciences. When then all things now potentially intelligible come to be in us actually understood, then the active intellect: will be perfectly conjoined with us as a form, and we shall understand by it perfectly. Hence, since it belongs to the active intellect to understand substances existing apart, we shall then understand those separately subsistent beings as we now understand the notions of speculative science; and this will be man's final happiness, in which man shall be as a god" (Chap. XLIII).If any one used such language in our time, we should understand him to mean by continuatio, or union with the supreme intelligence, as regards the individual, his instruction up to the level of the science of his age; and as regards the age itself, the maintenance of the level of science reached by the previous generation, and the further raising of that level. But it is not safe to make out an ancient author to have meant exactly what his words would mean, if spoken now. St Thomas gives a reference to the commentary of Averroes on Aristotle, De anima, III, a reference which I have duly followed up. I find that Averroes quotes Alexander and Avempace, disagreeing with them both. St Thomas, I believe, is indebted to Averroes for his knowledge of Alexander and Avempace. Now nowhere in Averroes, nor in either of the two authors whom he quotes, do I find any reference whatever to separate substances personified as thinking intelligences, or angels, — nor, for that matter, in Aristotle either. The discussion had its origin in an unfulfilled promise of Aristotle (De Anima III, vii, 10) to enquire, ἆρα ἐνδέχεται τῶν κεχωρισμένων τι νοεῖν ὄντα αὐτὸν μὴ κεχωρισμένον μεγέθους; (is it possible for the mind, without being itself separate from extended body, to understand any of the things that are so separated?) To interpret τὰ κεχωρισμένα to mean 'pure spirits' seems going a long way beyond Aristotle, who probably meant no more than 'products of high abstraction': nor did Averroes, commenting on the third book of the De anima, or Alexander, or Avempace, as quoted in that commentary, mean anything more. The transformation of these high abstractions (κεχωρισμένα) into thinking beings, pure spirits, or angels, was, I conjecture, the work of the Neo-Averroists, whom St Thomas encountered at the University of Paris. It is with these Averroists, not with Averroes himself that St Thomas mainly contends in these chapters. The argument is intricate, the theory which it impugns obsolete, nor is it worthwhile further to detain the modern reader with the discussion. No man now living expects to 'pick the brains' of angels, and so find happiness in this life by sharing an angel's natural knowledge of God. Nor did Averroes, so far as his comments on the De anima show, dream of anything so absurd. Lest anyone should think the expression 'to pick the brains of angels' a travesty, I quote the Latin of St Thomas: Si igitur per cognitionem intellectivam, quae est ex phantasmatibus, possit pervenire aliquis nostrum ad intelligendas substantias separatas, possibile erit quod aliquis in hac vita intelligat ipsas substantias separatas, et per consequens videndo ipsas substantias separatas participabis modum illius cognitionis quo substantia separata intelligens se intelligit Deum (Chap. XLI). This is the translation: "If then by intellectual knowledge, got out of impressions on the phantasy, any one of us could arrive to understand subsistent beings existing apart [i.e., pure spirits], it would be possible for one in this life to understand those same pure spirits, and consequently by seeing [in his mind's eye] those pure spirits he would share in the mode of that knowledge whereby a pure spirit, understanding itself, understands God." I need hardly remind the reader that St Thomas himself rejects this notion, and is, I think, mistaken in attributing it to Averroes.

CHAPTER XLVI—That the Soul in this life does not understand itself by itself

AN apparent difficulty may be alleged against what has been said from some words of Augustine, which require careful treatment. He says (De Trinitate, IX, iii): "As the mind gathers knowledge of corporeal things by the senses of the body, so of incorporeal things by itself: therefore it knows itself by itself, because itself is incorporeal." By these words it appears that our mind understands itself by itself, and, understanding itself, understands separately subsistent intelligences, or pure spirits, which would militate against what has been shown above. But it is clear that such is not the mind of Augustine. For he says (De Trinitate, X, ix, 12) of the soul seeking knowledge of itself: "Let it not then seek to find (cernere) itself as though it were absent, but let its care be to discern (discernere) itself as it is present: let it not observe itself as though it did not know itself but let it distinguish itself from that other thing which it has mistaken for itself." Whence he gives us to understand that the soul of itself knows itself as present, but not as distinct from other things; and therefore he says (De Trin.X, x) that some have erred in not distinguishing the soul from things that are different from it. But by the knowledge of a thing in its essence the thing is known as distinct from other things: hence definition, which marks the essence of a thing, distinguishes the thing defined from all other things. Augustine then did not mean that the soul of itself knows its own essence. So then, according to the thought of Augustine, our mind of itself knows itself, inasmuch as it knows concerning itself that it exists: for by the very perceiving of itself to act it perceives itself to be. But it acts of itself. Therefore of itself it knows concerning itself that it exists.

1. But it cannot be said that the soul of itself knows concerning itself what it essentially is. For a cognitive faculty comes to be actually cognizant by there being in it the object which is known. If the object is in it potentially, it knows potentially: if the object is in it actually, it is actually cognizant: if in an intermediate way, it is habitually cognizant. But the soul is always present to itself actually, and never potentially or habitually only. If then the soul of itself knows itself by its essence, it must ever have an intellectual view of itself,

what it essentially is, which clearly is not the case.

2 and 3. If the soul of itself knows itself in its essence, every man, having a soul, knows the essence of the soul: which clearly is not the case, for many men have thought the soul to be this or that body, and some have taken it for a number or harmony.

So then, by knowing itself, the soul is led to know concerning separately subsistent intelligences the fact of their existence, but not what they are essentially, which would mean understanding their substances. For whereas we know, either by demonstration or by faith, concerning these pure spirits that they are intelligent subsistent beings, in neither way could we gather this knowledge but for the fact that our soul knows from itself the meaning of intelligent being. Hence we must use our knowledge of the intelligence of our own soul as a starting-point for all that we can know of separately subsistent intelligences. But even granting that by speculative sciences we could arrive at a knowledge of the essence of our own soul, it does not follow that we could thereby arrive at a knowledge of all that is knowable about pure spirits; for our intelligence falls far short of the intelligence of a pure spirit. A knowledge of the essence of our own soul might lead to a knowledge of some remote higher genus of pure spirits: but that would not be an understanding of their substances.

CHAPTER XLVII—That we cannot in this life see God as He essentially is

If the connatural dependence of our understanding on phantasms prevents us in this life from understanding other pure spirits, much less can we in this life see the divine essence, which transcends all angels. Of this fact the following may also be taken as an indication: the higher our mind is raised to the contemplation of spiritual things, the more it is abstracted from sensible things: but the final terminus to which contemplation can possibly arrive is the divine substance: therefore the mind that sees the divine substance must be totally divorced from bodily senses, either by death or by some rapture. Hence it is said in the person of God: No man shall see me and live (Exod. xxxiii, 20). Whereas in Holy Scripture some are said to have seen God, that must be understood to have been inasmuch as by some vision of the phantasy or corporeal appearance the presence of divine power was shown.

Certain words of Augustine raise a difficulty in this matter. Thus he says (De Trinitate, IX, vii): "In the eternal truth, whence all corporeal creatures are, we see with our mind's eye the form according to which we are, and according to which we execute anything truly and rightly either in ourselves or in corporeal things." Also he says (Confess.I, xxv): "If both of us see that what you say is true, and we both see that what I say is true, where, I pray, do we see it? Neither I in you, nor you in me, but both of us in that unchangeable truth which is above our minds." And to the like effect (De Trin.XII, ii): "It belongs to the higher reason to judge of these bodily things according to aspects (rationes) eternal and everlasting, which certainly would not be unchangeable, were they not above the human mind." But aspects unchangeable and everlasting cannot be elsewhere than in God, since, according to Catholic faith, God alone is eternal. It seems to follow that we can see God in this life, and that by seeing Him, and aspects of things in Him, we judge of the rest of things.

On the other hand it is incredible that in the above words Augustine should mean to assert that in this life we can understand God as He essentially is, seeing that in his book De videndo Deumhe says the contrary. It remains to enquire how in this life we can see that unchangeable truth or those everlasting aspects. That truth is in the soul, Augustine himself confesses: hence he proves the immortality of the soul from the eternity of truth. But truth is not in the soul alone as God is said to be 'essentially' (per essentiam) in all things; nor as He is by His likeness in all things, inasmuch as everything is called 'true' so far as it approaches to the likeness of God: for from those points of view the soul stands in no better position than other beings: truth then is in the soul in a special manner, inasmuch as the soul knows truth. As then the soul and other beings are called 'true' in their natures, as bearing some likeness to the supreme nature of God, — which is truth itself, as being its own fullness of actual understanding (suum intellectum esse), — so what is known by the soul is manifestly known, inasmuch as there exists in the soul a likeness of that divine truth which God knows. Hence on the text (Ps. xi, 2) truths are diminished from the sons of men, the Gloss [Augustine, Enarrationesin h.l.] says: "The truth is one, whereby holy souls are illumined: but since there are many souls, there may be said to be in them many truths, as from one face many images appear in as many mirrors." Though different things are known and believed to be true by different minds, yet there are some truths in which all men agree, for instance, the primary intuitions of intellect as well speculative as practical, because, so far as these go, an image of divine truth comes out universally in the minds of all. As then whatever any mind knows for certain, it knows it by virtue of these intuitions, which are the canons of all judgements, and into which all judgements may be resolved, the mind is said to see all things in the divine truth, or in everlasting aspects, and to judge of all things according to those aspects. This explanation is confirmed by the words of Augustine (Soliloq. I, viii, 15): "Even the truths taught in the schools, which everyone, who understands them, unhesitatingly allows to be true, we must believe, could not possibly be understood, were they not lit up by the light of another, what I may call a sun proper to them (nisi ab alio quasi sole suo illustrantur)." He says then that the theories of science are seen in the divine truth as visible objects are seen in the light of the sun: but certainly such objects are not seen in the very body of the sun, but by the light which is a likeness of the solar brightness, remaining in the air and similar bodies. From these words then of Augustine it cannot be gathered that God is seen in His substance in this life, but only as in a mirror, which the Apostle also confesses of the knowledge of this life, saying (1 Cor. xiii, 12): We see now as in a glass darkly.

Though the human mind represents the likeness of God more closely than lower creatures, still such knowledge of God as can be gathered from the human mind does not transcend that kind of knowledge which is borrowed from sensible objects, since the soul knows her own essential nature by understanding the nature of things of sense (Chap. XLVI). Hence neither by this method can God be known in any higher way than as the cause is known by the effect.

CHAPTER XLVIII—That the Final Happiness of

## Man is not in this Life

IF then human happiness does not consist in the knowledge of God whereby He is commonly known by all or most men according to some vague estimate, nor again in the knowledge of God whereby He is known demonstratively in speculative science, nor in the knowledge of God whereby He is known by faith, as has been shown above (Chapp. XXXVIIIXL); if again it is impossible in this life to arrive at a higher knowledge of God so as to know Him in His essence, or to understand other pure spirits, and thereby attain to a nearer knowledge of God (Chapp. XLI-XLVI); and still final happiness must be placed in some knowledge of God (Ch. XXXVII); it follows that it is impossible for the final happiness of man to be in this life.

2. The last end of man bounds his natural desire, so that, when that is reached, nothing further is sought: for if there is still a tendency to something else, the end of rest is not yet gained. But that cannot be in this life: for the more one understands, the more is the desire of understanding. natural to all men, increased.

3. When one gains happiness, he gains also stability and rest. All have this idea of happiness, that it involves stability as a necessary condition: hence the philosopher says that we do not take man for a chameleon. But in this life there is no stability: for however happy a man be called, sicknesses and misfortunes may always happen to debar him from that activity, whatever it is, wherein happiness consists.

4. It seems unfitting and irrational that the period of development should be great and the period of duration small: for it would follow that nature for the greater part

of its time went without its final perfection. Hence we see that animals that live for a short time take a short time in arriving at maturity. But if human happiness consists in perfect activity according to perfect virtue, whether intellectual or moral, such happiness cannot accrue to man till after a long lapse of time; and this is especially apparent in speculative activity, in which the happiness of man is ultimately placed. For scarcely in extreme age can a man arrive [at] a perfect view of scientific truth; and then for the most part there is little of human life left.

5. That is the perfect good of happiness, which is absolutely free from admixture of evil, as that is perfect whiteness, which is absolutely unmingled with black. But it is impossible for man in the state of this life to be altogether free from evils, — not to say bodily evils, as hunger, thirst, cold and heat, but even from evils of the soul. There is no man living who is not at times disturbed by inordinate passions, who does not at times overstep the mean in which virtue consists, or fall short of it, who is not in some things deceived, or ignorant of what he wishes to know, or driven to weak surmises on points where he would like absolute certainty.

6. Man naturally shrinks from death, and is sad at the thought of it. Yet man must die, and therefore cannot be perfectly happy while here he lives.

7. Happiness consists, not in habit, but in activity: for habits are for the sake of acts. But it is impossible in this life to do any act continually.

8. The more a thing is desired and loved, the greater grief and sadness does its loss bring. But if final happiness be in this world, it will certainly be lost, at least by death; and it is uncertain whether it will last till death, since to any man there may possibly happen in this life

diseases totally debarring him from any virtuous activity, such as insanity. Such happiness therefore must always have a natural pendent of sadness.

But it may be replied that whereas happiness is the good of an intelligent nature, true and perfect happiness belongs to those in whom intelligent nature is found in its perfection, that is, in pure spirits; but in man it is found imperfectly by way of a limited participation. And this seems to have been the mind of Aristotle: hence, enquiring whether misfortunes take away happiness, after showing that happiness lies in virtuous activities, which are the most permanent things in this life, he concludes that they who enjoy such perfection in this life are "happy for men," meaning that they do not absolutely attain happiness, but only in a human way.

Now it is demonstrable that the aforesaid answer is not to the undoing of the arguments above alleged. For (a) though man is inferior in the order of nature to pure spirits, yet he is superior to irrational creatures; and therefore he must gain his final end in a more perfect way than they. But they gain their final end so perfectly as to seek nothing further. Thus the natural desire of dumb animals is at rest in the enjoyment of sensual delights. Much more must the natural desire of man be put to rest by his arrival at his last end. But that is impossible in this life: therefore it must be attained after this life.

(b) It is impossible for a natural desire to be empty and vain: for nature does nothing in vain. But the desire of nature (for happiness) would be empty and vain, if it never possibly could be fulfilled. Therefore this natural desire of man is fulfillable. But not in this life. Therefore it must be fulfilled after this life.

Alexander and Averroes laid it down that the final

happiness of man is not in such knowledge as is possible to man through the speculative sciences, but in a knowledge gained by conjunction with a separately subsistent intelligence, which conjunction they conceived to be possible to man in this life. But because Aristotle saw that there was no other knowledge for man in this life than that which is through the speculative sciences, he supposed man not to gain perfect happiness, but a limited measure of happiness suited to his state. In all which investigation it sufficiently appears how hard pressed on this side and on that these fine geniuses (praeclara ingenia) were. From this stress of difficulty we shall find escape in positing, according to the proofs already given, that man can arrive at true happiness after this life, the soul of man being immortal. In this disembodied state the soul will understand in the way in which pure spirits understand (B. II, Chapp. XCVI, sq.) The final happiness of man then will be in the knowledge of God, which the human soul has after this life according to the manner in which pure spirits know Him.

Therefore the Lord promises us reward in heaven (Matt. v, 12), and says that the saints shall be as the angels (Matt. xxii, 30), who see the face of God in heaven (Matt. xviii, 10).

CHAPTER XLIX—*That the Knowledge which Pure Spirits have of God through knowing their own Essence does not carry with it a Vision of the Essence of God*

WE must further enquire whether this very

knowledge, whereby separately subsistent intelligences and souls after death know God through knowing their own essences, suffices for their own happiness. For the investigation of this truth we must first show that the divine essence is not known by any such mode of knowledge. In no way can the essence of a cause be known in its effect, unless the effect be the adequate expression of the whole power of the cause. But pure spirits know God through their own substances, as a cause is known through its effect inasmuch as each sees God as mirrored in another, and each sees God as expressed in himself. But none of these pure spirits is an effect adequate to the power of God (B. II, Chapp. XXVI, XXVII). It is impossible therefore for them to see the divine essence by this method of knowledge.

2. An intelligible likeness, whereby a thing is understood in its substance must be of the same species as that thing, or rather it must be its species, — thus the form of a house in the architect's mind is the same species as the form of the house which is in matter, or rather it is its species, — for by the species of man you do not understand the essence of ass or horse. But the nature of an angel is not the same as the divine nature in species, nay not even in genus (B. I, Chap. XXV).

3. Everything created is bounded within the limits of some genus or species. But the divine essence is infinite, comprising within itself every perfection of entire being (B. I, Chapp. XXVIII, XLIII). It is impossible therefore for the divine substance to be seen through any created medium.

Nevertheless a pure spirit by knowing its own substance knows the existence of God, and that God is the cause of all, and eminent above all, and removed (remotus) from all, not only from all things that are, but from all that the created mind can conceive. To this knowledge of God we also may attain in some sort: for from the effects of His creation we know of God that He is, and that He is the cause (sustaining principle) of other beings, supereminent above other beings, and removed from all. And this is the highest perfection of our knowledge in this life: hence Dionysius says (De mystica theologiac. 2) that "we are united with God as with the unknown"; which comes about in this way, that we know of God what He is not, but what He is remains absolutely unknown. And to show the ignorance of this most sublime knowledge it is said of Moses that he drew nigh to the darkness in which God was (Exod. xx, 21).

But because an inferior nature at its height attains only to the lowest grade of the nature superior to it, this knowledge must be more excellent in pure spirits than in us. For (a) the nearer and more express the effect, the more evidently apparent the existence of the cause. But pure spirits, that know God through themselves, are nearer and more express likenesses of God than the effects through which we know God.

(c) High dignity better appears, when we know to what other high dignities it stands preferred. Thus a clown, knowing the king to be the chief man in the kingdom, but for the rest knowing only some of the lowest officials of the kingdom, with whom he has to do, does not know the king's pre-eminence so well as another, who knows the dignity of all the princes of the realm. But we men know only some of the lowest of things that are. Though then we know that God is high above all beings, still we do not know the height of the Divine Majesty as the angels know it, who know the highest order of beings and God's elevation above them all.

CHAPTER L—That the desire of Pure Intelligences does not rest satisfied in the Natural Knowledge which they have of God

EVERYTHING that is imperfect in any species desires to gain the perfection of that species. He who has an opinion about a thing, opinion being an imperfect knowledge of the thing, is thereby egged on to desire a scientific knowledge of the thing. But the aforesaid knowledge, which pure spirits have of God without knowing His substance fully, is an imperfect kind of knowledge. The main point in the knowledge of anything is to know precisely what it essentially is. Therefore this knowledge which pure spirits have of God does not set their natural desire to rest, but rather urges it on to see the divine substance.

2. The knowledge of effects kindles the desire of knowing the cause: this search after causes set men upon philosophizing. Therefore the desire of knowing, naturally implanted in all intelligent beings, does not rest unless, after finding out the substances of things made, they come also [etiam, not etiamsi] to know the cause on which those substances depend. By the fact then of pure spirits knowing that God is the cause of all the substances which they see, the natural desire in them does not rest unless they come also to see the substance of God Himself.

4. Nothing finite can set to rest the desire of intelligence. Given any finite thing, intelligence always

sets to work to apprehend something beyond it. But the height and power of every created substance is finite. Therefore the intelligence of a created spirit rests not in the knowledge of any created substances, however excellent, but tends still further in a natural desire to understand that substance which is of infinite height and excellence, namely, the divine substance (Chap. XLIII).

6. The nearer a thing is to the goal, the greater is its desire. But the intelligences of pure spirits are nearer to the knowledge of God than is our intelligence: therefore they desire that knowledge more intensely than we do. But even we, however much we know that God exists and has the attributes above mentioned, have not our desire assuaged, but still further desire to know God in His essence: much more then do pure spirits. The conclusion is, that the final happiness of pure spirits is not in that knowledge of God whereby they know Him through knowing their own substances, but their desire leads them further to the substance of God.

Hereby it sufficiently appears that final happiness is to be sought in no other source than in activity of intellect, since no desire carries so high as the desire of understanding truth. All our other desires, be they of pleasure or of anything else desirable by man, may rest in other objects; but the aforesaid desire rests not until it arrives at God, on whom all creation hinges and who made it all. Hence Wisdom aptly says: *I dwell in the heights of heaven, and my throne is in the pillar of a cloud* (Ecclus xxiv, 7); and it is said, *Wisdom calls her handmaids to the citadel* (Prov. ix, 3). Let them blush therefore who seek in basest things the happiness of man so highly placed.

## CHAPTER LI—How God is seen as He essentially is

AS shown above (Chap. XLIX), the divine substance cannot be seen by the intellect in any created presentation. Hence, if God's essence is to be seen, the intelligence must see it in the divine essence itself, so that in such vision the divine essence shall be at once the object which is seen and that whereby it is seen.

This is the immediate vision of God that is promised us in Scripture: We see now in a glass darkly, but then face to face(i Cor. xiii, 2): a text absurd to take in a corporeal sense, as though we could imagine a bodily face in Deity itself, whereas it has been shown that God is incorporeal (B. I, Chap. XX). Nor again is it possible for us with our bodily face to see God, since the bodily sense of sight, implanted in our face, can be only of bodily things. Thus then shalt we see God face to face, in that we shall have an immediate vision of Him, as of a man whom we see face to face. By this vision we are singularly assimilated to God, and are partakers in His happiness: for this is His happiness, that He essentially understands His own substance. Hence it is said: When He shall appear, we shall be like Him, for we shall see Him as He is (1 John iii, 2). And the Lord said: I prepare for you as my Father hath prepared for me a kingdom, that ye may eat and drink at my table in my kingdom (Luke xxii, 29). This cannot be understood of bodily meat and drink, but of that food which is taken at the table of Wisdom, whereof it is said by Wisdom: Eat ye my bread and drink the wine that I have mingled for you (Prov. ix, 5). They therefore eat and drink at the table of God, who enjoy the same happiness wherewith God is happy, seeing Him in the way which He sees Himself.

CHAPTER LII—That no Created Substance can of its natural power arrive to see God as He essentially is

THE property of a higher nature cannot be attained by a lower nature except by the action of that higher nature to which it properly belongs. But to see God by the divine essence is the property of the divine nature: for it is proper to every agent to act by its own proper form. Therefore no subsistent intelligence can see God by the divine essence except through the action of God bringing it about.

5. To see the substance of God transcends the limits of every created nature: for it is proper to every intelligent created nature to understand according to the mode of its substance: but the divine substance is not intelligible according to the mode of any created substance (Chap. XLIX).

Hence it is said: The grace of God is life everlasting (Rom. vi, 23). For we have shown that the happiness of man consists in the vision of God, which is called life everlasting, whereunto we are led solely by the grace of God, because such vision exceeds the faculty of every creature, and it is impossible to attain it except by an endowment from God. And the Lord says: I will manifest myself to him (John xiv, 21).

CHAPTER LIII—That a Created Intelligence needs some influx of Divine Light to see God in His

Essence

IT is impossible for that which is the proper form of one thing to become the form of another thing, unless that latter thing comes to partake of some likeness to the former. But the divine essence is the proper intelligible form of the divine intelligence, and is proportioned to it: for in God these three are one, that which understands, that whereby it understands, and that which is understood. It is impossible therefore for the very essence of God to become an intelligible form to any created intellect otherwise than by the said intellect coming to be partaker in some likeness to God.

3. If two things, not previously united, come afterwards to be united, this must be either by a change in both or by a change in one of them. If therefore any created intellect begins anew to see the essence of God, the divine essence must be conjoined anew with that intellect by way of intelligible presentation. But it is impossible for the divine essence to change; and therefore such union must begin by some change in the created intellect, that is to say, by its making some new acquisition.

But because we arrive at the knowledge of things intelligible through things sensible, we also transfer the names of sensible cognition to intelligible cognition, and particularly the properties of sight, which among senses is the nobler and more spiritual and more akin to intellect: hence intellectual knowledge itself is called sight, or vision. And because bodily vision is not accomplished except through light, the means whereby intellectual vision is fulfilled borrow the name of light. That disposition therefore whereby a created intelligence is raised to the intellectual vision of the divine substance is called the 'light of glory.'

This is the light of which it is said: In thy light we shall see light(Ps. xxxv, 10), to wit, of the divine substance; and, The city needed not sun nor moon, for the brightness of God illuminated it (Apoc. xxi, 23); and, No more shall there be sun to shine on thee by day, nor brightness of moon to enlighten thee, but the Lord shall be to thee an everlasting light, and thy God shall be thy glory Isaias lx, 19). And because in God being and understanding are the same and He is to all the cause of understanding, He is on that account called 'light': He was the true light, that enlightened every man coming into this world John i, 8): God is light (1 John i, 5): Clad in light as in a garment (Ps. ciii, 2). And therefore also as well God as the angels in Holy Scripture are described in figures of fire, because of the brightness of fire.

CHAPTER LIV—Arguments against the aforesaid statements, and their Solutions

ARG. 1. No access of light to the eye can elevate the sight to see things that transcend the natural faculty of bodily vision. But the divine substance transcends the entire capacity of created intelligence, even more than intellect transcends the capacity of sense. Therefore no light can supervene upon any created intelligence, to elevate it to the capacity of seeing the divine substance.

Reply. The divine substance is not beyond the capacity of created intelligence as though it were something altogether alien from it, as sound is alien from sight, or an immaterial substance from sense, — for the divine substance is the prime object of intelligence, and the beginning of all intellectual knowledge, — but it is beyond the capacity of created intelligence as exceeding its power, as the more excellent sensible objects are beyond the capacity of sense.

Arg. 2. That light which is received in the created intelligence is itself created, and therefore falling infinitely short of God. Therefore no such light can raise the creature to the vision of the divine substance.

Reply. This light raises the creature to the vision of God, not that there is no interval between it and the divine substance, but it does so in virtue of the power which it receives from God to such effect, although in its own being it falls infinitely short of God. For this created light does not conjoin the intelligence with God in point of being, but only in point of understanding.

Arg. 4. What is created, may very well be connatural with some created thing. If then that light is created, there may be some created intelligence, which by its own connatural light will see the divine substance, contrary to what has been shown (Chap. XLII).

Reply. The vision of the divine substance exceeds all natural faculty: hence the light whereby a created intelligence is perfected to the vision of the divine substance must be supernatural.

Arg. 6. There must be proportion between the intelligence and the thing understood. But there is no proportion between a created intelligence, perfected in the aforesaid light, and the divine substance, since the distance between them still remains infinite.

Reply. So there is a proportion between a created intelligence and God as an object of understanding, not a proportion implying any commensurateness of being, but a proportion implying a reference of one to the other, as matter is referred to form, or cause to effect. Thus there may well be a proportion between the creature and God, as the understanding is referred to the understood, or the effect to the cause.

Some have been moved by these and the like arguments to lay down the statement that God is never to be seen by any created intelligence. But this position, besides taking away the true happiness of the rational creature, which cannot be except in the vision of the divine substance, as has been shown (Chap. LI), is also in contradiction with the authority of Holy Scripture, and is to be rejected as false and heretical.

CHAPTER LV—That the Created Intelligence does not comprehend the Divine Substance

THE aforesaid light is a principle of divine knowledge, since by it the created intelligence is elevated to see the divine substance. Therefore the mode of divine vision must be commensurate with the intensity of the aforesaid light. But the aforesaid light falls far short in intensity of the brightness of the divine understanding. It is impossible therefore for the divine substance to be seen by such light so perfectly as the divine understanding sees it. The divine understanding sees that substance as perfectly as it is perfectly visible: for the truth of the divine substance and the clearness of the divine understanding are equal, nay are one. It is impossible therefore for created intelligence through the aforesaid light to see the divine substance as perfectly as it is perfectly visible. But everything that is comprehended by any knowing mind is known by it as perfectly as it is knowable. Thus he who knows that a triangle has three angles equal to two right angles, taking it as a matter of opinion on probable grounds because wise men say so, does not yet comprehend that truth: he alone comprehends it, who knows it as matter of science, through the medium of a demonstration showing cause. It is impossible therefore for any created intelligence to comprehend the divine substance.

2. Finite power cannot compass in its activity an infinite object. But the divine substance is infinite in comparison with every created intellect, since every created intellect is bounded within the limits of a certain species.

When it is said that the divine substance is seen but not comprehended by created intelligence, the meaning is not that something of it is seen and something not seen, since the divine substance is absolutely simple: what is meant is that it is not seen perfectly so far as it is visible. In the same way he who holds a demonstrable conclusion as a matter of opinion, is said to know it but not to comprehend it, because he does not know it perfectly, that is, scientifically, though there is no part of it that he does not know.

CHAPTER LVI—That no Created Intelligence in seeing God sees all things that can be seen in Him

THEN only does the knowledge of a principle necessitate the knowledge of all its effects, when the principle is thoroughly comprehended by the understanding: for so a principle is known to the whole extent of its power, all its effects being known as caused by it. But through the divine essence other things are known as effects from their cause. Since then created intelligence cannot know the divine substance so as to comprehend it, there is no necessity for it in seeing the divine substance to see all things that can be known thereby.

3. The extent of any power is measured by the objects to which it reaches. To know then all the objects to which any power reaches is to comprehend the power itself. But the divine power, being infinite, can be comprehended by no created intelligence, as neither can the divine essence (Chap. LV). Neither then can any created intelligence know all the objects to which the divine power extends.

5. No cognitive faculty knows anything except under the aspect of its proper object: thus by sight we know things only as colored. Now the proper object of intelligence is whatever is in the substance of a thing. Therefore whatever the intelligence knows of a thing, it knows by a knowledge of the substance of the thing. If ever we know the substance of a thing by its accidents, that happens accidentally, inasmuch as our intellectual knowledge arises from sense, and thus we need to arrive at an intellectual view of substance through a knowledge of accidents: wherefore this does not take place in mathematics, but in the natural sciences only. Whatever therefore in a thing cannot be known by a knowledge of its substance, must remain unknown to the knowing mind. But what a voluntary agent wishes cannot be known by a knowledge of his substance: for the will does not tend to its objects altogether by natural necessity: hence 'will' and 'nature' are counted two distinct active principles. What therefore a voluntary agent wills is not knowable except haply through certain effects, as, when we see one acting voluntarily, we know what he has willed: or it may

be known in its cause, as God knows our wills, as He knows other effects of His production, by the fact of His being to us the cause of willing (B. I, Chap. LXVIII ad fin.): or it may be known by one intimating his will to another, as when one expresses his desire by speech. Since then many things depend on the absolute will of God, as has been partly shown already, and will hereafter appear, a created intelligence, even though seeing the substance of God, does not for all that see all that God sees by his substance.

It may be objected that God's substance is something greater than all that He can make, or understand, or will beyond Himself; and that therefore, if a created intelligence can see the substance of God, much more can it know all that God through Himself either understands or wills or can do. But on careful study we see that it is not one and the same thing for an object to be known in itself and known in its cause. There are things easy enough to know in themselves, but not easily known in their causes. Though it is true that it is a grander thing to have understanding of the divine substance than to understand anything else, knowable in itself, away from that substance, still it is more perfect knowledge to know the divine substance, and in it to see its effects, than to know the divine substance without seeing its effects. Now the seeing of the divine substance may be without comprehension of it: but to have all things rendered intelligible through that substance and actually known, that cannot come about without comprehension.

CHAPTER LVII—That every Intelligence of every grade can be partaker of the vision of God

SINCE it is by supernatural light that a created intelligence is raised to the vision of the divine substance, there is no created intelligence so low in its nature as to be incapable of being raised to this vision. For that light cannot be connatural to any creature (Chap. LIV), but transcends the faculty of every created nature. But what is done by supernatural power is not hindered by diversity of nature, since divine power is infinite. Hence in the miraculous healing of the sick it makes no difference whether one be very ill or slightly indisposed. Therefore diversity of grade in intelligent nature is no hindrance to the lowest subject of such a nature being raised by that light to that vision.

2. The distance from God of the intelligence highest in order of nature is infinite in respect of perfection and goodness: whereas the distance of that intelligence from the very lowest intelligence is finite, for between finite and finite there cannot be infinite distance. The distance therefore between the lowest created intelligence and the highest is as nothing in comparison with the distance between the highest created intelligence and God. But what is as nothing can make no sensible variation, as the distance between the center of the earth and our point of vision is as nothing in comparison with the distance between our point of vision and the eighth sphere, compared with which the whole earth counts as a point; and therefore no sensible error follows from our astronomers in their calculations taking their point of observation for the center of the earth. Whatever intellect then is raised to the vision of God by the above mentioned light, — be it highest, or lowest, or middlemost, — it makes no difference.

3. Every intelligence naturally desires the vision of the divine substance (Chapp. XXV, L). But a natural desire cannot be in vain. Any and every created intelligence then can arrive at the vision of the divine substance; and inferiority of nature is no impediment.

Hence the Lord promises to man the glory of the angels: They shall be as the angels of God in Heaven (Matt. xxii, 30); and in the Apocalypse the same measure is said to be of man and angel: the measure of a man, that is, of an angel (Apoc. xxi, 17). Therefore often in Holy Scripture the angels are described in the form of men, either entirely so, as with the angels who appeared to Abraham (Gen. xviii), or partially, as with the living creatures of whom it is said that the hand of a man was under their wings (Ezech. i, 8).

CHAPTER LVIII—That one may see God more perfectly than another

THE light of glory raises to the vision of God in this, that it is a certain likeness to the divine understanding (Chap. LIII). But a thing may be likened to God with more or less of closeness. Therefore one may see the divine substance with more or less of perfection.

4. The end must correspond to the means taken to gain it. But not all subsistent intelligences are equally prepared for their end, which is the vision of the divine substance: for some are of greater virtue, some of less, virtue being the way to happiness. Therefore there must be a diversity in their vision of God.

Hence it is said: in my Father's House there are many mansions (John xiv, 2). In the mode of vision then there appear diverse grades of glory among the Blessed, but in respect of the object of vision their glory is the same. Hence to all the laborers in the vineyard, though they have not labored equally, the Lord tells us that the same reward, or penny, is to be given, because the same object is given to all to see and enjoy, namely, God.

CHAPTER LIX—How they who see the Divine Substance see all things

SINCE the vision of the divine substance is the final end of every subsistent intelligence, and the natural desire of every being is at rest when it has attained to its final end, the natural desire of every intelligence that sees the divine substance must be perfectly set at rest. But it is the mind's natural desire to know the genera and species and capabilities of all things and the whole order of the universe, as is shown by the zeal of mankind in trying to find out all these things. Every one therefore of those who see the divine substance will know all the above-mentioned objects.

2. In this is the difference between sense and intellect, as shown in De anima, III, iv, that sense is spoilt or impaired by brilliant or intense sensible objects, so that afterwards it is unable to appreciate similar objects of lower degree: but intellect, not being spoilt or checked by its object, but simply perfected, after understanding an object in which there is more to understand, is not less but better able to understand other objects which afford less scope for understanding. But the highest in the category of intelligible beings is the divine substance. When then an understanding is raised by divine light to see the substance of God, much more is it perfected by the same light to understand all other objects in nature.

4. Though of those who see God one sees Him more perfectly than another, every one nevertheless sees Him with such perfection as to fill all his natural capacity, nay, the vision transcends all natural capacity (Chap. LII). Every one therefore, seeing the divine substance, must know in that substance all things to which his natural capacity extends. But the natural capacity of every intelligence extends to the knowledge of all genera and species and the order of creation. These things therefore every one of those who see God will know in the divine substance.

Hence to Moses asking for a sight of the divine substance the Lord replied: *I will show thee all good* (Exod. xxxiii, 19); and Gregory says (Dialoguesiv, 33): "What is it that they do not know, who know Him who knows all things?"

But on careful reflection upon what has been said it appears that they who see the divine substance in one way know all things, and in one way they do not. If by 'all things' is meant whatever belongs to the perfection of the universe, the arguments alleged prove that they do see all things. To the perfection of natural being belong specific natures, with their properties and powers: for the intention of nature fixes on specific natures: as for individuals, they are for the species. It belongs then to the perfection of a subsistent intelligence, that it should know the natures and capabilities and proper accidents of all species. And by the knowledge of natural species individuals also existing under these species are known by the intelligence that sees God.

But if by 'all things' is meant all things that God knows by seeing His essence, no created intelligence sees all things in the substance of God, as has been shown above (Chap. LVI). This may be verified in various respects. First, as regards things that God can do, but neither does nor ever means to do. All such things cannot be known without a thorough comprehension of His power, which is not possible to any created intelligence (Chap. LV). Hence it is said: Perchance thou wilt seize upon the footprints of God and perfectly discover the Almighty. He is higher than heaven, and what wilt thou do? He is deeper than hell, and whence shalt thou know? Longer than the earth is his measure, and broader than the sea (Job xi, 7-9). Secondly, as regards the plans of things made, no intelligence can know them all without comprehending the divine goodness. For the plan of everything made is taken from the end which the maker intends; and the end of all things made by God is the divine goodness: the plan therefore of things made is the diffusion of the divine goodness in creation. To know then all the plans of things made, one would have to know all the good things that can come about in creation according to the order of the divine wisdom: which would mean comprehending the divine goodness and wisdom, a thing that no created intelligence can do. Hence it is said: I understood that of all the works of God man cannot find out the plan (Eccles. viii, 17). Thirdly, as regards things that depend on the mere will of God, as predestination, election, justification, and the like, which belong to the sanctification of the creature, it is said: The things that are in man none knoweth but the spirit of man that is in him: in like manner the things that are of God none knoweth but the Spirit of God (1 Cor. ii, 11).

CHAPTER LX—That they who see God see all things in Him at once

SINCE it has been shown that a created intelligence in seeing the divine substance understands therein all the species of things; since moreover all things that are seen by one presentation must be seen together by one vision; it necessarily follows that the intelligence which sees the divine substance views all things, not successively, but simultaneously. Hence Augustine says (De Trinitate XV, xvi): "Our thoughts will not then be unstable, coming and going from one thing to another, but we shall see all our knowledge together at one glance."

CHAPTER LXI—That by the Sight of God one is Partaker of Life Everlasting

ETERNITY differs from time in this, that time has being in succession, but the being of eternity is all present together. But in the sight of God there is no succession: all things that are seen in that vision are seen at one glance. That vision therefore is accomplished in a certain participation of eternity. That vision also is a certain life: for activity of intellect is a life. Therefore by that sight the created intelligence is partaker of life everlasting.

4. The intellectual soul is created on the confines of eternity and time: because it is last in order of intelligences, and yet its substance is raised above corporeal matter, being independent of the same. But its action, inasmuch as it touches inferior things that are in time, is temporal. Therefore, inasmuch as it touches superior things that are above time, its action partakes of eternity. Such is especially the vision whereby it sees the divine substance. Therefore by such vision it enters into participation of eternity, and sees God in the same way as

any other created intelligence.

Hence the Lord says: This is life everlasting, to know thee the only true God (John xvii, 3).

### CHAPTER LXII—That they who see God will see Him forever

WHATEVER now is, and now is not, is measured by time. But the vision that makes the happiness of intellectual creatures is not in time, but in eternity (Chap. LXI). It is impossible therefore that from the moment one becomes partaker of it he should ever lose it.

2. An intelligent creature does not arrive at its last end except when its natural desire is set at rest. But as it naturally desires happiness, so it naturally desires perpetuity of happiness: for, being perpetual in its substance, whatever thing it desires for the thing's own sake, and not for the sake of something else, it desires as a thing to be had for ever. Happiness therefore would not be the last end, if it did not endure perpetually.

3. Everything that is loved in the having of it brings sadness, if we know that at some time we must part with it. But the beatific vision, being of all things most delightful and most desired, is of all things most loved by them who have it. They could not therefore be otherwise than saddened, if they knew that at some time they were to lose it. But if it were not meant to last forever, they would be aware of the fact: for in seeing the divine substance, they also see other things that naturally are (Chap. LIX).

6. It is impossible for one to wish to resign a good thing that he enjoys, except for some evil that he discerns

in the enjoyment of that good, or because he reckons it a hindrance to greater good. But in the enjoyment of the beatific vision there can be no evil, since it is the best thing to which an intelligent creature can attain: nor can he who enjoys that vision possibly think that there is any evil in it, or anything better than it, since the vision of that sovereign truth excludes all false judgement.

5. Nothing that is viewed with wonder can grow tedious: as long as it is an object of wonder, the desire of seeing it remains. But the divine substance is always viewed with wonder by any created intelligence, since no created intelligence can comprehend it. Therefore such intelligence can never find that vision tedious.

9. The nearer a thing comes to God, who is wholly unchangeable, the less changeable it is and the more enduring. But no creature can draw nearer to God than that which beholds His substance. The intelligent creature then gains in the vision of God a certain immutability, and cannot fall from that vision.

Hence it is said: Blessed are they who dwell in thy house, O Lord: they shall praise thee for ever and ever (Ps. lxxxiii, 5): He shall never be moved from his place, that dwelled in Jerusalem (Ps. cxxiv, 1): Whoever shall overcome, I will make him a pillar in the temple of my God, and he shall not go out any more (Apoc. iii, 12).

CHAPTER LXIII—How in that Final Happiness every Desire of Man is fulfilled

FROM what has been said it evidently appears that in that final happiness which comes of the vision of God every human desire is fulfilled, according to the text: Who filleth thy desire with good things (Ps. cii, 5). And every human endeavor there finds its final good: as may be seen by discussing the several heads. — I. As man is an intelligent being, there is in him a desire of investigating truth, which desire men follow out in the pursuit of a contemplative life. And this will manifestly be fulfilled in that vision, since by the sight of the first and highest truth all things that man naturally desires to know will become known to him (Chap. L).

2. There is also a desire which a man has in keeping with his rational faculty of managing and disposing of inferior things: which desire men prosecute in the pursuit of an active and civil life. And the chief scope and purpose of this desire is the laying out of man's whole life according to reason, which means living virtuously. This desire will then be altogether fulfilled when reason shall be in the height of its vigor, being enlightened by divine light that it may not fall away from what is right.

3. Upon civil life there follow certain goods which a man needs for his social and political activities. Thus there is honor and high estate, the inordinate desire of which makes men intriguing and ambitious. But that vision elevates men to the supreme height of honor, uniting them with God; and therefore, as God is the king of ages (1 Tim. i, 17), so the Blessed united with Him are said to reign: They shall reign with Christ (Apoc. xx, 6).

4. Another object of desire following upon civil life is celebrity of fame, by inordinate desire of which men are said to be covetous of vain glory. By that divine vision the blessed become celebrated, not before men, who may deceive and be deceived, but in the truest knowledge of God and of all their companions in bliss. And therefore that happiness is very frequently termed

'glory' in Holy Scripture, as in Ps. cxliv, 5: *The saints shall exult in glory.*

5. There is also another thing desirable in civil society, namely, riches, by inordinate craving and love for which men become illiberal and unjust. But in that blissful state there is sufficiency of all good things, inasmuch as the Blessed enjoy Him who comprises the perfection of them: wherefore it is said: *All good things came to me with her*(Wisdom vii, 11); and, *Glory and wealth is in this house*(Ps. cxi, 3).

6. There is also a third desire in man, common to him with other animals, the desire of pleasurable enjoyments, which men pursue in the life of pleasure, and thereby become intemperate and incontinent. But in the happiness of the sight of God there is perfect delight, all the more perfect than the pleasure of sense, which brute animals also can enjoy, as intellect is higher than sense; all the more perfect as (quanto) the good in which we shall take delight is greater than any sensible good, and comes more home to us, and is more continually delightful; all the more perfect again as the delight is more pure and free from all admixture of sadness or harassing solicitude; and of this it is said: *They shall be inebriated by the plenty of thy house, and thou wilt make them drink of the torrent of thy pleasure*(Ps. xxxv, 9).

7. There is also a natural desire common to all things, in that they all desire self-preservation, so far as possible; by the immoderation of which desire men are rendered timid and spare themselves too much from labors. This desire also shall be perfectly fulfilled when the Blessed attain to perfect everlasting duration, secure from all hurt, according to the text: *They shall not hunger nor thirst any more, neither shall the sun fall upon them,*

nor any heat (Isa. xlix, 10; Apoc. vii, 16).

Thus it appears that by the vision of God subsistent intelligences gain true happiness, in which every desire is wholly laid to rest, and in which there is abundant sufficiency of all good things, which Aristotle considers a requisite of happiness. Nothing in this life is so like this final and perfect happiness as the life of them who contemplate truth so far as possible. For the contemplation of truth begins in this life, but will be consummated in the life to come, whereas the life of action and the political life do not transcend the bounds of this present.

CHAPTER LXIV—That God governs things by His Providence

THE foregoing conclusions sufficiently show that God is the end of all things. Hence it may be further gathered that by His providence He governs and rules all things. For whatever things are referred to an end, are all subject to His management to whom principally that end belongs, as appears in an army: for all the components of the army and all their works are referred to one last end, the good of the general, which is victory, and therefore it belongs to the general to govern the whole army. In like manner the art which is concerned with the end gives commands and laws to the art which is concerned with the means, as politics to the art of war, the art of war to the management of cavalry, navigation to shipbuilding. Since therefore all things are referred to an end, which is the divine goodness (Chapp. XVII, XVIII), God, to whom that goodness principally belongs, — as being His own substance, possessed, understood, and loved, — must have the chief control of all things.

5. Things that are distinct in their natures do not combine into one system, unless they be bound up in one by one directing control (ab uno ordinante). But in the universe there are things, having distinct and contrary natures, which nevertheless all combine in one system, some things taking up the activities of other things, some things being aided or even wrought by others. There must then be one ordainer and governor of the universe.

8. Every agent that intends an end cares more for that which is nearer to the last end. But the last end of the divine will is the divine goodness, and the nearest thing to that in creation is the goodness of the order of the entire universe, that being the end to which every particular good of this or that thing is referred, as the less perfect is referred to the more perfect, and every part is for its whole. What therefore God most cares for in creation is the order of the universe: He is therefore its controller.

Hence Holy Scripture ascribes the course of events to the divine command: Who giveth command to the sun, and it rises not, and enclosed the stars as under a seal (Job ix, 7): He hath given a command, and it shall not pass away (Ps. cxlviii, 6).

## CHAPTER LXV—That God preserves things in being

FROM God's governing all things by His providence it follows that He preserves them in being. For everything whereby things gain their end is part of the governing of them. But to the last end which God intends, namely, the divine goodness, things are directed not only by their activities, but also by the fact of their existence, because by that mere fact they bear some likeness to the divine goodness. Therefore it is proper to divine providence to keep things in being.

5. As a work of art presupposes a work of nature, so a work of nature presupposes a work of God creating: for the material of artificial things is from nature, and the material of natural things is through creation of God. But artificial things are preserved in being by virtue of natural things, as a house by the solidity of its stones. Therefore natural things are not preserved in being otherwise than through the power of God.

6. The impression made by an agent does not remain in the effect when the action of the agent ceases, unless that impression turns into and becomes part of the nature of the effect. Thus the forms and properties of things generated remain in them to the end, after the generation is done, because they are made natural to the things: in like manner habits are difficult to change, because they turn into nature. But dispositions, bodily impressions, and emotions, though they remain for some little while after the action of the agent, do not remain permanently: they find place in the subject as being on the way to become part of its nature. But what belongs to the nature of a superior genus in no way remains after the action of the agent is over, as light does not remain in a transparent medium after the source of light is taken away. But being is not the nature or essence of anything created, but of God alone (B. I, Chapp. XXI, XXII). Nothing then can remain in being when the divine activity ceases.

7. Concerning the origin of things there are two theories, one of faith, that things had a first commencement, and were then brought into being by

God; the other the theory of sundry philosophers, that things have emanated (fluxerint) from God from all eternity. On either theory we must say that things are preserved in being by God. For if things are brought into being by God after not being, the being of things must be consequent upon the divine will; and similarly their not being, because He has permitted things not to be when He willed and made things to be when He willed. Things therefore are, so long as He wills them to be. His will then is the upholder of creation. On the other hand, if things have emanated from God from all eternity, it is impossible to assign any time or instant in which first they emanated from God. Either then they were never produced by God at all, or their being is continually coming forth from God so long as they exist.

Hence it is said: Bearing up all things by the word of his power(Heb. i, 3). And Augustine says (De Gen. ad lit.iv, 12): "The power of the Creator, and the might of the Almighty and All-containing, is the cause of the permanence of every creature. If this power ever ceased from governing creation, all the brave show of creatures would at once cease, and all nature would fall to nothing. It is not like the case of one who has built a house, and goes away, and still the structure remains, when his work has ceased and his presence is withdrawn. The world could not endure for the twinkling of an eye, if God retired from the government of it."

Hereby is excluded the theory of some Doctors of the Law of the Moors, who, by way of sustaining the position that the world needs the preserving hand of God, have supposed all forms to be accidents, and that no accident lasts for two successive instants, the consequence being that the formation of things is always in the making,

— as though a thing needed no efficient cause except while it is in the making. Some of them are further said to hold that the indivisible atoms, out of which they say that all substances are composed, — which atoms, according to them, alone are indestructible, — could last for some short time, even though God were to withdraw His guidance from the world. Some of them further say that things would not cease to be but for God causing in them an accident of 'ceasing.' All which positions are manifestly absurd.

CHAPTER LXVI—That nothing gives Being except in as much as it acts in the Power of God

NOTHING gives being except in so much as it is an actual being. But God preserves things in actuality.
5. The order of effects is according to the order of causes. But among all effects the first is being: all other things, as they proceed from their cause, are determinations of being. Therefore being is the proper effect of the prime agent, and all other things act inasmuch as they act in the power of the prime agent. Secondary agents, which are in a manner particular determinants of the action of the prime agent, have for the proper effects of their action other perfections determinant of being.
6. What is essentially of a certain nature, is properly the cause of that which comes to have that nature only by participation. But God alone is being by essence, all others are beings by participation. Therefore the being of everything that exists is an effect properly due to God; so that anything that brings anything else into being does so insomuch as it acts in the power of God. Hence it is

said: God created all things to be (Wisd. i, 14).

CHAPTER LXVII—That God is the Cause of Activity in all Active Agents

AS God not only gave being to things when they first began to be, but also causes being in them so long as they exist (Chap. LXV); so He did not once for all furnish them with active powers, but continually causes those powers in them, so that, if the divine influx were to cease, all activity would cease.

Hence it is said: Thou hast wrought all our works in us, O Lord (Isa. xxvi, 12). And for this reason frequently in the Scriptures the effects of nature are put down to the working of God, because He it is that works in every agent, physical or voluntary: e.g., Hast thou not drawn me out like milk, and curdled me like cheese? with skin and flesh thou hast clothed me, with bones and sinews thou hast put me together (Job x, 10, 11).

CHAPTER LVIII—That God is everywhere and in all things

AN incorporeal thing is said to be in a thing by contact of power. Therefore if there be anything incorporeal fraught with infinite power, that must be everywhere. But it has been shown (B. I Chap. XLIII) that God has infinite power. He is therefore everywhere.

4. Since God is the universal cause of all being, in whatever region being can be found there must be the

divine presence.

6. An efficient cause must be together with its proximate and immediate effect. But in everything there is some effect which must be set down for the proximate and immediate effect of God's power: for God alone can create (B. II, Chap. XXI); and in everything there is something caused by creation, — in corporeal things, primordial matter; in incorporeal beings, their simple essences (B. II, Chapp. XV, sq). God then must be in all things, especially since the things which He has once produced from not-being to being He continually and always preserves in being (Chap. LXV).

Hence it is said: I fill heaven and earth (Jer. xxiii, 24): If I ascend into heaven, thou art there: if I descend into hell, thou art there (Ps. cxxxviii, 8).

God is indivisible, and wholly out of the category of the continuous: hence He is not determined to one place, great or small, by the necessity of His essence, seeing that He is from eternity before all place: but by the immensity of His power He reaches all things that are in place, since He is the universal cause of being. Thus then He is whole everywhere, reaching all things by His undivided power.

CHAPTER LVIX—Of the Opinion of those who withdraw from Natural Things their Proper Actions

SOME have taken an occasion of going wrong by thinking that no creature has any action in the production of natural effects, — thus that fire does not warm, but God causes heat where fire is present. So Avicebron in his book, The Fountain of Life, lays it down that nobody is active, but the power of a subsistent spirit permeating bodies does the actions which seem to be done by bodies. But on such theories many awkward consequences follow.

1. If no inferior cause, and especially no corporeal cause, does any work, but God works alone in all agencies, and God does not change by working in different agencies; no difference of effect will follow from the difference of agencies in which God works: but that is false by the testimony of sense.

2. It is contrary to the notion of wisdom for anything to be to no purpose in the works of the wise. But if created things in no way work to the production of effects, but God alone works all effects immediately, to no purpose are other things employed by Him.

3. To grant the main thing is to grant the accessories. But actually to do follows upon actually to be: thus God is at once pure actuality and the first cause. If then God has communicated to other beings His likeness in respect of being, it follows that He has communicated to them His likeness in respect of action.

4. To detract from the perfection of creatures is to detract from the perfection of the divine power. But if no creature has any action in the production of any effect, much is detracted from the perfection of the creature: for it marks abundance of perfection to be able to communicate to another the perfection which one has oneself.

5. God is the sovereign good (B. I, Chap. XLI). Therefore it belongs to Him to do the best. But it is better for good conferred on one to be common to many than for it to be confined to that one: for common good always proves to be more godlike than the good of the individual. But the good of one comes to be common to many when

it is derived from one to many, which cannot be except in so far as the agent diffuses it to others by a proper action of its own. God then has communicated His goodness in such a way that one creature can transmit to others the good which it has received.

6. To take away order from creation is to take away the best thing that there is in creation: for while individual things in themselves are good, the conjunction of them all is best by reason of the order in the universe: for the whole is ever better than the parts and is the end of the parts. But if actions are denied to things, the order of things to one another is taken away: for things differing in their natures are not tied up in the unity of one system otherwise than by this, that some act and some are acted upon.

7. If effects are not produced by the action of creatures, but only by the action of God, it is impossible for the power of any creature to be manifested by its effect: for an effect shows the power of the cause only by reason of the action, which proceeds from the power and is terminated to the effect. But the nature of a cause is not known through its effect except in so far as through its effect its power is known which follows upon its nature. If then created things have no actions of their own productive of effects, it follows that the nature of a created thing can never be known by its effect; and thus there is withdrawn from us all investigation of natural science, in which demonstrations are given principally through the effect.

Some Doctors of the Moorish Law are said to bring an argument to show that accidents are not traceable to the action of bodies, the ground of the argument being this, that an accident does not pass from subject to subject: hence they count it an impossibility for heat to pass from a hot body to another body heated by it, but they say that all such accidents are created by God. Now this is a ridiculous proof to assign of a body not acting, to point to the fact that no accident passes from subject to subject. When it is said that one hot body heats another, it is not meant that numerically the same heat, which is in the heating body, passes to the body heated; but that by virtue of the heat, which is in the heating body, numerically another heat comes to be in the heated body actually, which was in it before potentially. For a natural agent does not transfer its own form to another subject, but reduces the subject upon which it acts from potentiality to actuality.

CHAPTER LXX—How the Same Effect is from God and from a Natural Agent

SOME find it difficult to understand how natural effects are attributable At once to God and to a natural agent. For (Arg. 1) one action, it seems, cannot proceed from two agents. If then the action, by which a natural effect is produced, proceeds from a natural body, it does not proceed from God.

Arg. 2. When an action can be sufficiently done by one, it is superfluous to have it done by more: we see that nature does not do through two instruments what she can do through one. Since then the divine power is sufficient to produce natural effects, it is superfluous to employ also natural powers for the production of those same effects. Or if the natural power sufficiently produces its own effect, it is superfluous for the divine power to act to the same effect.

Arg. 3. If God produces the whole natural effect, nothing of the effect is left for the natural agent to produce.

Upon consideration, these arguments are not difficult. Reply 1. The power of the inferior agent depends upon the power of the superior agent, inasmuch as the superior agent gives to the inferior the power whereby it acts, or preserves that power, or applies it to action; as a workman applies a tool to its proper effect, frequently however without giving the tool the form whereby it acts, nor preserving it, but merely giving it motion. The action therefore of the inferior agent must proceed from that agent not merely through its own power, but through the power of all superior agents, for it acts in virtue of them all. And as the ultimate and lowest agent acts immediately, so is the power of the prime agent immediate in the production of the effect. For the power of the lowest agent is not competent to produce the effect of itself, but in power of the agent next above it; and the power of that agent is competent in virtue of the agent above it; and thus the power of the highest agent proves to be of itself productive of the effect, as the immediate cause, as we see in the principles of mathematical demonstrations, of which the first principle is inimediate. As then it is not absurd for the same action to be produced by an agent and the power of that agent, so neither is it absurd for the same effect to be produced by an inferior agent and by God, by both immediately, although in different manners.

Reply 2. Though a natural thing produces its own effect, it is not superfluous for God to produce it, because the natural thing does not produce it except in the power of God. Nor is it superfluous, while God can of Himself produce all natural effects, for them to be produced by other causes: this is not from the insufficiency of God's power, but from the immensity of His goodness, whereby He has wished to communicate His likeness to creatures, not only in point of their being, but likewise in point of their being causes of other things (Chap. XXI). Reply 3. When the same effect is attributed to a natural cause and to the divine power, it is not as though the effect were produced partly by God and partly by the natural agent: but the whole effect is produced by both, though in different ways, as the same effect is attributed wholly to the instrument, and wholly also to the principal agent.

CHAPTER LXXI—That the Divine Providence is not wholly inconsistent with the presence of Evil in Creation

PERFECT goodness could not be in creation if there were not found an order of goodness among creatures, some being better than others: or else all possible grades of goodness would not be filled up; nor would any creature be like God in having pre-eminence over another. Thus a great beauty would be lost to creation in the removal of the order of distinct and dissimilar beings, one better than the other. A dead level of goodness would be a manifest derogation to the perfection of creation. A higher grade of goodness consists in there being something which cannot fall away from goodness; a lower grade, in there being that which can fall away. The perfection of the universe requires both grades of goodness. But it is the care of a ruler to uphold perfection in the subjects of his government, not to make it less. Therefore it is no part of divine providence wholly to exclude from creation the capability of falling away from good. But upon this capability evil ensues: for what is capable of falling away, sometimes does fall away; and the mere lack of good is evil (Chap. VII).

3. The best rule in any government is to provide for everything under government according to the mode of its nature: just administration consists in this. As then it would be contrary to any rational plan of human administration for the civil government to debar its subjects from acting according to their offices and conditions of life, except perhaps in an occasional hour of emergency, so it would be contrary to the plan of divine government not to allow creatures to act according to the mode of their several natures. But by the very fact of creatures so acting there follows destruction and evil in the world, since by reason of mutual contrariety and inconsistency one thing is destructive of another.

5. There are many good things in creation which would find no place there, unless evils were there also. Thus there would be no patience of the just, if there were not the malice of persecutors: no room for vindictive justice, if there were no offences: and in the physical order one thing cannot come to be unless something else is destroyed. If then evil were wholly excluded from the universe by divine providence, the number of good things would be proportionally diminished: which ought not to be, because good is more vigorous in goodness than evil in badness (virtuosius est bonum in bonitate quam in malitia malum), as above shown (Chap. XII).

6. The good of the whole takes precedence of the good of the part. It belongs then to a prudent ruler to neglect some defect of goodness in the part for the increase of goodness in the whole, as an architect buries

the foundation under the earth for the strengthening of the whole house. But if evil were removed from certain portions of the universe, much perfection would be lost to the universe, the beauty of which consists in the orderly blending of things good and evil (pulcritudo ex ordinata bonorum et malorum adunatione consurgit), while evil things have their origin in the breaking down of good things, and still from them good things again take their rise by the providence of the ruler, as an interval of silence makes music sweet.

7. Other things, and particularly inferior things, are ordained to the end of the good of man. But if there were no evils in the world, much good would be lost to man, as well in respect of knowledge, as also in respect of desire and love of good: for good is better known in contrast with evil; and while evil results come about, we more ardently desire good results: as sick men best know what a blessing health is.

Therefore it is said: Making peace and creating evil (Isai. xlv, 7): Shall there be evil in the city that the Lord has not done? (Amos iii, 6.)

Boethius (De consolatione, Lib. I, prosa 4) introduces a philosopher asking the question: 'If there is a God, how comes evil?'. The argument should be turned the other way: 'If there is evil, there is a God.' For there would be no evil, if the order of goodness were taken away, the privation of which is evil; and this order would not be, if God were not.

Hereby is taken away the occasion of the error of the Manicheans, who supposed two primary agents, good and evil, as though evil could not have place under the providence of a good God.

We have also the solution of a doubt raised by

some, whether evil actions are of God. Since it has been shown (Chap. LXVI) that every agent produces its action inasmuch as it acts by divine power, and that thereby God is the cause of all effects and of all actions (Chap. LXVII); and since it has been further shown (Chap. X) that in things subject to divine providence evil and deficiency happens from some condition of secondary causes, in which there may be defect; it is clear that evil actions, inasmuch as they are defective, are not of God, but of defective proximate causes; but so far as the action and entity contained in them goes, they must be of God, — as lameness is of motive power, so far as it has anything of motion, but so far as it has anything of defect, it comes of curvature of the leg.

CHAPTER LXXII—That Divine Providence is not inconsistent with an element of Contingency in Creation

AS divine providence does not exclude all evil from creation, neither does it exclude contingency, or impose necessity upon all things. The operation of providence does not exclude secondary causes, but is fulfilled by them, inasmuch as they act in the power of God. Now effects are called 'necessary' or 'contingent' according to their proximate causes, not according to their remote causes. Since then among proximate causes there are many that may fail, not all effects subject to providence will be necessary, but many will be contingent.

6. On the part of divine providence no hindrance will be put to the failure of the power of created things, or to an obstacle arising through the resistance of something

coming in the way. But from such failure and such resistance the contingency occurs of a natural cause not always acting in the same way, but sometimes failing to do what it is naturally competent to do; and so natural effects do not come about of necessity.

CHAPTER LXXIII—That Divine Providence is not inconsistent with Freedom of the Will

THE government of every prudent governor is ordained to the perfection of the things governed, to the gaining, or increasing, of maintenance of that perfection. An element of perfection then is more worthy of being preserved by providence than an element of imperfection and defect. But in inanimate things the contingency of causes comes of imperfection and defect: for by their nature they are determined to one effect, which they always gain, unless there be some let or hindrance arising either from limitation of power, or the interference of some external agent, or indisposition of subject-matter; and on this account natural causes in their action are not indifferent to either side of an alternative, but for the most part produce their effects uniformly, while they fail in a minority of instances. But that the will is a contingent cause comes of its very perfection, because its power is not tied to one effect, but it rests with it to produce this effect or that, wherefore it is contingent either way. Therefore providence is more concerned to preserve the liberty of the will than to preserve contingency in natural causes.

2. It belongs to divine providence to use things according to their several modes. But a thing's mode of action depends upon its form, which is the principle of

action. But the form whereby a voluntary agent acts is not determinate: for the will acts through a form apprehended by the intellect; and the intellect has not one determined form of effect under its consideration, but essentially embraces a multitude of forms; and therefore the will can produce multiform effects.

3. The last end of every creature is to attain to a likeness to God (Chap. XVII): therefore it would be contrary to providence to withdraw from a creature that whereby it attains the divine likeness. But a voluntary agent attains the divine likeness by acting freely, as it has been shown that there is free will in God (B. I, Chap. LXXXVIII).

4. Providence tends to multiply good things in the subjects of its government. But if free will were taken away, many good things would be withdrawn. The praise of human virtue would be taken away, which is nullified where good is not done freely: the justice of rewards and punishments would be taken away, if man did not do good and evil freely: wariness and circumspection in counsel would be taken away, as there would be no need of taking counsel about things done under necessity. It would be therefore contrary to the plan of providence to withdraw the liberty of the will.

Hence it is said: God made man from the beginning, and left him in the hand of his own counsel: before man is life and death, whatever he shall please shall be given him (Ecclus xv, 14-17).

Hereby is excluded the error of the Stoics, who said that all things arose of necessity, according to an indefeasible order, which the Greeks called ymarmene(εἱμαρμένη).

## CHAPTER LXXIV—That Divine Providence is not inconsistent with Fortune and Chance

THE multitude and diversity of causes proceeds from the order of divine providence and arrangement. Supposing an arrangement of many causes, one must sometimes combine with another, so as either to hinder or help it in producing its effect. A chance event arises from a coincidence of two or more causes, in that an end not intended is gained by the coming in of some collateral cause, as the finding of a debtor by him who went to market to make a purchase, when his debtor also came to market.

Hence it is said: *I saw that the race was not to the swift . . . . but that occasion and chance are in all things* (Eccles ix, 11) to wit, in all sublunary things (in inferioribus).

## CHAPTER LXXV—That the Providence of God is exercised over Individual and Contingent Things

IF God has no care of these individual things, that is either because He does not know them, or because He has no power over them, or because He has no will to take care of them. But it has been shown above (B. I, Chap. LXV) that God has knowledge of individual things. Nor can it be said that He has no power to take care of them, seeing that His power is infinite (B. II, Chap. XXII). Nor again that God has no wilt to govern them, seeing that the object of His will is universally all good (B. I, Chap. LXXVIII).

3. This common attribute is found in productive causes, that they have a care of the things that they

produce, as animals naturally nourish their young. God thereof has care of the things of which He is the cause. But He is the cause even of these particular things (B. II, Chap. XV), and therefore He has care of them.

5. It would be a foolish providence not to take care of those things without which the objects of one's care could not exist. But certainly, if all particulars were to fail, universals could not remain. If then God has care of the universal only, and neglects the individual altogether, His providence must be foolish and imperfect. But if it is said that God has care of individuals so far as to see that they are maintained in being, but no further, that answer cannot stand. For all that befalls individuals has some bearing on their preservation or destruction. If therefore God has care of individuals so far as to see to their preservation, He must have care of all that befalls them.

7. This is the difference between speculative and practical knowledge, that speculative knowledge and all that concerns such knowledge is wrought out in generalities, whereas the sphere of practical knowledge is the particular. For the end of practical knowledge is truth, which consists primarily and ordinarily in the immaterial and universal, while the end of practical knowledge is action, which deals with particular facts. Hence the physician does not attend man in general, but this man; and to the care of the individual man the whole science of medicine is directed. But providence, being directive of things to their end, must be a department of practical knowledge. Thus the providence of God would be very imperfect, if it stopped short at the universal, and did not reach individual cases.

247

8. The perfection of speculative knowledge lies in the universal rather than in the particular: universals are better known than particulars; and therefore the knowledge of the most general principles is common to all. Still, even in speculative science, he is more perfect who has not a mere general but a concrete (propriam) knowledge of things. For he who knows in the general only, knows a thing only potentially. Thus the scholar is reduced from a general knowledge of principles to a concrete knowledge of conclusions by his master, who has both knowledges, — as a being is reduced from potentiality to actuality by another being, already in actuality. Much more in practical science is he more perfect, who disposes things for actuality not merely in the universal but in the particular. God's most perfect providence therefore extends even to individuals.

9. Since God is the cause of being, as such (B. II, Chap. XV), He must also be the provider of being, as such. Whatever then in any way is, falls under His providence. But singular things are beings, and indeed more so than universals, because universals do not subsist by themselves, but are only in singulars. Divine providence therefore has care also of singulars.

Hence it is said: Two sparrows are sold for a farthing; and not one of them falls to the ground without your Father (Matt. x, 29); and, [Wisdom] reaches from end to end strongly (Wisd. viii, 1), that is, from the highest creatures to the lowest. Also their opinion is condemned who said: The Lord hath abandoned the earth, the Lord doth not see (Ezech. ix, 9): He walketh about the poles of heaven, and doth not consider our things (Job xxii, 14).

CHAPTER LXXVI—That the Providence of God watches immediately over all Individual Things

IN matters of human administration, the higher administrator confines his care to the arrangement of general main issues, and leaves details to his subordinates, and that on account of his personal limitations, because, as for the state and condition of lesser things, he is either ignorant of them, or he cannot afford the labor and length of time that would be necessary to arrange for them. But such limitations are far from God: it is no labor for Him to understand, and it takes Him no time, since in understanding Himself He understands all things else (B. I, Chap. XLIX).

4. In human administrations, the industry and care of the lower officials arranges matters left to their charge by their chief. Their chief does not bestow upon them their faculty of industry and care, but merely allows it free play. If the industry and care came from their superior, the arrangement would be the superior's arrangement; and they would not be authors of the arrangement, but carriers of it into execution. But we have seen (B. I, Chap. LI: B. III, Chap. LXVII) that all wisdom and intelligence comes from God above; nor can any intellect understand anything except in the power of God, nor any agent do anything except in the same power. God Himself therefore by His providence immediately disposes all things; and whoever are called providers under Him, are executors of His providence.

7. If God does not by Himself take immediate care of lower individualities, that must be either because He despises them, or because He fears to sully His dignity, as some say. But that is irrational, for there is greater dignity

in devising an arrangement than in working one out. If then God works in all things, as has been shown (Chap. LXVII), and that is not derogatory to His dignity, nay rather befits His universal and sovereign power, an immediate providence over individual things is no contemptible occupation for Him either, and throws no slur upon His dignity. Hence it is said: *Thou hast done the things of old and hast devised one thing after another* (Judith ix, 4).

CHAPTER LXXVII—*That the arrangements of Divine Providence are carried into execution by means of Secondary Causes*

IT belongs to the dignity of a ruler to have many ministers and diversity of servants to carry his command into execution, the height and greatness of his lordship appearing by the multitude of persons of various ranks who are subject to him: but no dignity of any ruler is comparable with the dignity of the divine government: it is suitable therefore that the arrangements of divine providence be carried into execution by divers grades of agents.

6. As the cause is superior to the effect, the order of causes is nobler than that of effects: in that order therefore the perfection of divine providence is better shown. But if there were not intermediate causes carrying divine providence into execution, there would be in creation no order of causes, but only of effects. The perfection therefore of divine providence requires that there should be intermediate causes carrying it into execution.

Hence it is said: *Bless the Lord, all his powers, ye*

ministers that do his word(Ps. cii, 21): Fire, hail, snow, stormy winds that do his word(Ps. cxlviii, 8).

CHAPTER LXXVIII—That Intelligent Creatures are the Medium through which other Creatures are governed by God

SINCE the preservation of order in creation is a concern of divine providence, and it is a congruous order to descend by steps of due proportion from highest to lowest, divine providence must reach by a certain rule of proportion to the lowest things. The rule of proportion in this, that as the highest creatures are under God and are governed by Him, so lower creatures should be under the higher and be governed by them. But of all creatures intelligent creatures are the highest (Chap. XLIX). Therefore the plan of divine providence requires that other creatures should be governed by rational creatures.

CHAPTER LXXXI—Of the Subordination of Men one to another

SINCE man is endowed with understanding and sense and bodily power, these faculties are arranged in order in him by the disposition of divine providence according to the plan of the order that obtains in the universe, bodily power being put under that of sense and intellect as carrying out their command, and the sentient faculty itself under the faculty of intellect. And similar is the order between man and man. Men pre-eminent in understanding naturally take the command; while men poor in understanding, but of great bodily strength, seem by nature designate for servants, as Aristotle says in his Politics, with whom Solomon is of one mind, saying: *The fool shall serve the wise*(Prov. xi, 29). But as in the works of one man disorder is born of intellect following sense, so in the commonwealth the like disorder ensues where the ruler holds his place, not by pre-eminence of understanding, but by usurpation of bodily strength, or is brought into power by some burst of passion. Nor is Solomon silent upon this disorder: *There is an evil that I have seen under the sun, a fool set in high estate* (Eccles x, 5, 6). But even such an anomaly does not carry with it the entire perversion of the natural order: for the dominion of fools is weak, unless strengthened by the counsel of the wise. Hence it is said: *A wise man is strong, and a knowing man stout and valiant: because war is managed by due ordering, and there shall be safety where there are many counsels* (Prov. xxiv, 5, 6). And because he who gives counsel rules him who takes it, and becomes in a manner his master, it is said: *A wise servant shall be master over foolish sons* (Prov. xvii, 2).

CHAPTER LXXXVIII—*That other Subsistent Intelligences cannot be direct Causes of our Elections and Volitions*

NOR is it to be thought that the souls of the heavens, if any such souls there be, or any other separately subsisting created intelligences, can directly thrust a volition in upon us, or be the cause of our choice. For the actions of all creatures are contained in the order of divine providence, and cannot act contrary to the conditions of action which providence has laid down.

Now it is a law of providence that everything be immediately induced to action by its own proximate cause. But the proximate cause of volition is good apprehended by the understanding: that is the proper object of the will, and the will is moved by it as sight by color. No subsistent creature therefore can move the will except through the medium of good grasped by the understanding. That is done by showing it that something is good to do, which is called persuasion. No subsistent creature therefore can act upon our will, or be the cause of our choice, otherwise than by means of persuasion.

4. "The violent is that the origin whereof is from without, without the subject of violence in any way contributing thereto." Were then the will to be moved by any exterior principle, that motion would be violent. I call that an exterior principle of motion, which moves as an efficient cause, and not as a final cause. But violence is inconsistent with voluntariness. It is impossible therefore for the will to be moved to voluntary action by an exterior principle acting as an efficient cause, but every motion of the will must proceed from within. Now no subsistent creature is in touch with the interior of an intelligent soul: God alone is in such close connexion with the soul, as He alone is cause of its being and maintains it in existence. Therefore by God alone can a motion of the will be efficiently caused.

Hence it is said: The king's heart is in the hand of the Lord: he shall turn it whithersoever he will(Prov. xxi, 1); and, God it is worked in us both to will and to accomplish according to his good pleasure(Phil. ii, 13).

CHAPTER LXXXIX—That the Motion of the Will is caused by God, and not merely by the Power of the Will

SOME, not understanding how God can cause the movement of the will in us without prejudice to the freedom of the will, have endeavored to pervert the meaning of these texts, saying that God causes in us to will and to accomplish, inasmuch as He gives us the power of willing, but not as making us will this or that. Hence some have said that providence is not concerned with the subject-matter of free will, that is, with choices, but with extrinsic issues: for he who makes choice of something to gain or something to accomplish, for instance, building or the amassing of wealth, will not always be able to attain his end, and thus the issues of our actions are not subject to free will, but are disposed by providence.

1. But this theory runs manifestly counter to texts of Holy Scripture. For it is said: All our works thou hast wrought in us, O Lord (Isai. xxvi, 12): hence we have of God not merely the power of willing, but also the act. And the above quoted saying of Solomon, he shall turn it whithersoever he will, shows that the divine causality extends at once to will-power and to actual volition.

2. Nothing can act in its own strength unless it act also in the power of God (Chap. LXVI): therefore man cannot use the will-power given to him except in so far as he acts in the power of God.

4. God is the cause of all action, and works in every agent (Chap. LXX): therefore He is cause of the motives of the will.

CHAPTER XC—That Human Choices and Volitions are subject to Divine Providence

THE government of providence proceeds from the divine love where with God loves His creatures. Love consists chiefly in the lover wishing good to the loved one. The more God loves things, then, the more they fall under His providence. This Holy Writ teaches, saying: *God guards all that love him* (Ps. cxliv, 20); and the Philosopher also teaches that God has especial care of those who love understanding, and considers them His friends. Hence He loves especially subsistent intelligences, and their volitions and choices fall under His providence.

6. The inward good endowments of man, which depend on his will and choice, are more proper to man than external endowments, as the gaining of riches: hence it is according to the former that man is said to be good, not according to the latter. If then human choices and motions of the will do not fall under divine providence, but only external advantages, it will be more true to say that human affairs are beyond providence than that they are under providence.

CHAPTER XCI—*How Human Things are reduced to Higher Causes*

FROM what has been shown above we are able to gather how human things are reducible to higher causes, and do not proceed by chance. For choices and motives of wills are arranged immediately by God: human intellectual knowledge is directed by God through the intermediate agency of angels: corporeal events, whether interior (to the human body) or exterior, that serve the need of man, are adjusted by God through the intermediate agency of angels and of the heavenly bodies.

All this arrangement proceeds upon one general axiom, which is this: 'Everything manifold and mutable and liable to fail may be reduced to some principle uniform and immutable and unfailing.' But everything about ourselves proves to be manifold, variable, and defectible. Our choices are evidently manifold, since different things are chosen by different persons in different circumstances. They are likewise mutable, as well on account of the fickleness of our mind, which is not confirmed in its last end, as also on account of changes of circumstance and environment. That they are defectible, the sins of men clearly witness. On the other hand, the will of God is uniform, because in willing one thing He wills all other things: it is also immutable and indefectible (B. I, Chapp. XXIII, LXXV). Therefore all motions of volition and choice must be reduced to the divine will, and not to any other cause, because God alone is the cause of our volitions and elections.

In like manner our intelligence is liable to multiplicity, inasmuch as we gather intelligible truth from many sensible objects. It is also mutable, inasmuch as it proceeds by reasoning from one point to another, passing from known to unknown. It is also defectible from the admixture of phantasy and sense, as the errors of mankind show. But the cognitions of the angels are uniform, as they receive the knowledge of truth from the one fountain of truth, God (B. II, Chapp. XCVIII, C, with notes). It is also immutable, because not by any argument from effects to causes, nor from causes to effects, but by simple intuition do they gaze upon the pure truth of things. It is also indefectible, since they discern the very natures of things, or their quiddities in themselves, about which quiddities intelligence cannot err, as neither can sense err about the primary objects of the several senses. But we learn the quiddities (essences) of things from their accidents and effects. Our intellectual knowledge then must be regulated by the knowledge of the angels.

Again, about human bodies and the exterior things which men use, it is manifest that there is in them the multiplicity of mixture and contrariety; and that they do not always move in the same way, because their motions cannot be continuous; and that they are defectible by alteration and corruption. But the heavenly bodies are uniform, as being simple and made up without any contrariety of elements. Their motions also are uniform, continuous, and always executed in the same way: nor can there be in them corruption or alteration. Hence our bodies, and other things that come under our use, must necessarily be regulated by the motion of the heavenly bodies.

CHAPTER XCII—In what sense one is said to be Fortunate, and how Man is aided by Higher Causes

GOOD fortune is said to befall a man, when something good happens to him beyond his intention, as when one digging a field finds a treasure that he was not looking for. Now an agent may do something beyond his own intention, and yet not beyond the intention of some agent whom he is under: as if a master were to bid a servant to go to some place, to which he had sent another servant without the first servant knowing of it, the meeting with his fellow-servant would be beyond the intention of the servant sent, and yet not beyond the intention of the master sending: in reference to the servant it will be luck and chance, but not in reference to the master, — to him it is an arrangement. Since then man is subordinate in body to the forces of physical nature (corporibus coelestibus), subordinate in intellect to the angels, and subordinate in will to God, a thing may happen beside the intention of man, which is nevertheless according to the order of physical nature (corporum coelestium), or according to the arrangement of angels, or again of God. But though God alone works directly upon man's choice, yet the action of an angel does something for that choice by way of persuasion, while the action of the heavenly body (of the forces of physical nature) does something by way of predisposition, inasmuch as the bodily impressions of the heavenly bodies (physical forces) upon our bodies predispose us to certain choices. When then under the impression of the physical forces of nature (coelestium corporum) one is swayed to certain choices that prove useful to him, though his own reason does not discern their utility; and simultaneously under the light shed on him by separately subsistent intelligences, his understanding is enlightened to do those acts, and his will is swayed by a divine act to choose that useful course, the utility whereof goes unperceived by him, — then he is said to be a 'fortunate man.'

But here a difference is to be noted. For the action of the angel and of the physical force (corporis coelestis) merely predisposes the man to choose, but the action of God accomplishes the choice. And since the predisposition that comes of the bodily affection, or of the persuasion of the understanding, does not induce necessity of choice, man does not always choose that which his guardian angel intends, nor that to which physical nature (corpus coeleste) inclines, but man always chooses that which God works in his will. Hence the guardianship of the angels sometimes comes to naught, according to the text: We have tended Babylon, but she is not healed (Jerem. li, 9). And much more may physical inclination (inclinatio coelestium corporum) come to naught: but divine providence always holds firm.

It is further to be observed that good or ill fortune may befall a man as a matter of luck, so far as his intention goes, and so far as the working of the prime forces of nature (corpora coelestia) goes, and so far as the mind of the angels goes, but not in regard of God: for in reference to God nothing is by chance, nothing unforeseen, either in human life or anywhere else in creation.

CHAPTER XCIII—Of Fate, whether there be such a thing, and if so, what it is

SOME when they say that all things are done by fate, mean by fate the destiny that is in things by disposition of divine providence. Hence Boethius says: "Fate is a disposition inherent in changeable things, whereby providence assigns them each to their several orders." In this description of fate 'disposition' is put for 'destiny.' It is said to be 'inherent in things,' to distinguish fate from providence: for destiny as it is in the divine mind, not yet impressed on creation, is providence; but inasmuch as it is already unfolded in creatures, it is called 'fate.' He says 'in changeable things' to show that the order of providence does not take away from things their contingency and changeableness. In this understanding, to deny fate is to deny divine providence. But because with unbelievers we ought not even to have names in common, lest from agreement in terminology there be taken an occasion of error, the faithful should not use the name of 'fate,' not to appear to fall in with those who construe fate wrongly, subjecting all things to the necessity imposed by the stars. Hence Augustine says: "If any man calls by the name of fate the might or power of God, let him keep his opinion, but mend his speech" (De civit. Dei, V, 1). And Gregory: "Far be it from the minds of the faithful to say that there is such a thing as fate" (Hom. 10 in Epiphan.)

CHAPTER XCIV—Of the Certainty of Divine Providence

IT will be necessary now to repeat some of the things that have been said before, to make it evident that (a) nothing escapes divine providence, and the order of divine providence can nowise be changed; and yet (b) it does not follow that the events which happen under divine providence all happen of necessity.

(a) Our first point of study is this, that as God is the cause of all existing things, conferring being on them all, the order of His providence must embrace all things: for He must grant preservation to those to whom He has granted existence, and bestow on them perfection in the attainment of their last end. In the case of every one who has to provide for others there are two things to observe, the pre-arranging of the order intended and the setting of the pre-arranged order on foot. The former is an exercise of intellectual ability, the latter of practical. The difference between the two is this, that in the pre-arrangement of order the providence is more perfect, the further the arrangement can be extended even to the least details: there would be not many parts of prudence in him who was competent only to arrange generalities: but in the carrying of the order out into effect the providence of the ruler is marked by greater dignity and completeness the more general it is, and the more numerous the subordinate functionaries through whom he fulfils his design, for the very marshalling of those functionaries makes a great part of the foreseen arrangement. Divine providence, therefore, being absolutely perfect (B. I, Chap. XXVIII), arranges all things by the eternal forethought of its wisdom, down to the smallest details, no matter how trifling they appear. And all agents that do any work act as instruments in His hands, and minister in obedience to Him, to the unfolding of that order of providence in creation which He has from eternity devised. But if all things that act must necessarily minister to Him in their action, it is impossible for any agent to hinder the execution of divine providence by acting contrary to it. Nor is it possible for divine providence to be hindered by the defect of any agent or patient, since all active or passive power in creation is caused according to the divine arrangement. Again it is impossible for the execution of divine providence to be hindered by any change of providence, since God is wholly unchangeable (B. I, Chap. XV). The conclusion remains, that the divine provision cannot be annulled.

(b) Now to our second point of study. Every agent intends good, and better so far as it can (Chap. III). But good and better do not have place in the same way in a whole and in its parts. In the whole the good is the entire effect arising out of the order and composition of the parts: hence it is better for the whole that there should be inequality among the parts, without which inequality the order and perfection of the whole cannot be, than that all the parts should be equal, every one of them attaining to the rank of the noblest part. And yet, considered by itself, every part of lower rank would be better if it were in the rank of some superior part. Thus in the human body the foot would be a more dignified part of man if it had the beauty and power of the eye; but the whole body would be worse off for lacking the office of the foot. The scope and aim therefore of the particular agent is not the same as that of the universal agent. The particular agent tends to the good of the part absolutely, and makes the best of it that it can; but the universal agent tends to the good of the whole: hence a defect may be beside the intention of the particular agent, but according to the intention of the universal agent. It is the intention of the particular agent that its effect should be perfect to the utmost possible in its kind: but it is the intention of the universal agent that this effect be carried to a certain degree of perfection and no further. Now between the parts of the universe the first apparent difference is that of contingent and necessary. Beings of a higher order are necessary and indestructible and unchangeable: from which condition beings fall away, the lower the rank in which they are placed; so that the lowest beings suffer destruction in their being and change in their constitution, and produce their effects, not necessarily, but contingently. Every agent therefore that is part of the universe endeavors, so far as it can, to abide in its being and natural constitution, and to establish its effect: but God, the governor of the universe, intends that of the effects which take place in it one be established as of necessity, another as of contingency; and with this view He applies different causes to them, necessary causes to these effects, contingent causes to those. It falls under divine providence therefore, not only that this effect be, but also that this effect be necessarily, that other contingently. Thus, of things subject to divine providence, some are necessary, and others contingent, not all necessary.

Hence it is clear that this conditional proposition is true: 'If God has foreseen this thing in the future, it will be.' But it will be as God has provided that it shall be; and supposing that He has provided that it shall be contingently, it follows infallibly that it will be contingently, and not necessarily.

Cicero (De divinatione ii, 8) has this argument: 'If all things are foreseen by God, the order of causes is certain; but if so, all things happen by fate, nothing is left in our power, and there is no such thing as free will.' A frivolous argument, for since not only effects are subject to divine providence, but also causes, and modes of being, it follows that though all things happen by divine providence, some things are so foreseen by God as that they are done freely by us.

Nor can the defectibility of secondary causes, by means of which the effects of providence are produced, take away the certainty of divine providence: for since God works in all things, it belongs to His providence sometimes to allow defectible causes to fail, and sometimes to keep them from failing.

The Philosopher shows that if every effect has a proper cause (causam per se), every future event may be reduced to some present or past cause. Thus if the question is put concerning any one, whether he is to be slain by robbers, that effect proceeds from a cause, his meeting with robbers; and that effect again is preceded by another cause, his going out of his house; and that again by another, his wanting to find water; the preceding cause to which is thirst, and this is caused by eating salt meat, which he either is doing or has done. If then, positing the cause, the effect must be posited of necessity, he must necessarily be thirsty, if he eats salt meat; and he must necessarily will to seek water, if he is thirsty; and be must necessarily go out of the house, if he wills to seek water; and the robbers must necessarily come across him, if he goes out of the house; and if they come across him, he must be killed. Therefore from first to last it is necessary for this man eating salt meat to be killed by robbers. The philosopher concludes that it is not true that, positing the cause, the effect must be posited, because there are some causes that may fail. Nor again is it true that every effect has a proper cause: for any accidental effect, e.g., of this man wishing to look for water and falling in with robbers, has no cause.

CHAPTERS XCV, XCVI—That the Immutability of Divine Providence does not bar the Utility of Prayer

AS the immutability of divine providence does not impose necessity on things foreseen, so neither does it bar the utility of prayer. For prayer is not poured out to God that the eternal arrangement of providence may be changed, — that is impossible, — but that man may gain what he desires of God. It is fitting for God to assent to the pious desires of His rational creatures, not that our desires move the immutability of God, but it is an outcome of His goodness suitably to carry out what we desire.
4. It is proper for friends to will the same thing. Now God loves His creature (B. I, Chap. XCI) and every

creature all the more that the said creature has a share in His goodness, which is the prime and principal object of God's love. But, of all creatures, the rational creature most perfectly partakes in the divine goodness. God therefore wills the fulfilment of the desires of the rational creature. And His will is effective of things.

5. The goodness of the creature is derived in point of likeness from the goodness of God. But it is a point of special commendation in men, not to deny assent to just requests: thereupon they are called 'liberal,' 'clement,' 'merciful and kind.' This therefore is a very great function of divine goodness, to hear pious prayers.

Hence it is said: He will do the will of them that fear him, and hear their prayers and save them (Ps. cxliv, 9): Every one that asks receives, and he that seeks finds, and the door shall be opened to him that knocks (Matt. vii, 8).

From what has been said it appears that prayers and pious desires are causes of some things that are done by God. It has been shown above (Chap. LXXVII) that divine providence does not bar the working of other causes, nay, rather it directs them in the work of imposing upon creation the order which providence in its own counsels has determined upon. Thus secondary causes are not inconsistent with providence, but rather carry providence into effect. Thus then prayers are efficacious with God, not however as breaking through the order of divine providence, because this very arrangement, that such a concession be made to such a petitioner, falls under the order of divine providence. Therefore to say that we should not pray to gain anything of God, because the order of His providence is unchangeable, is like saying that we should not walk to get to a place, nor eat to support life.

Thus a twofold error concerning prayer is excluded. Some have said that there is no fruit of prayer. This was said as well on the part of those who denied divine providence, as the Epicureans did; as also on the part of those who withdrew human affairs from divine providence, as some of the Peripatetics did; as also on the part of those who thought that all things happen of necessity, as the Stoics did. From all these tenets it would follow that prayer is fruitless, and consequently all divine worship in vain: which error is referred to in Malachy iii, 14: Ye have said: he labored in vain who served God, and what profit is it that we have kept his ordinances, and that we have walked sad before the Lord of Hosts?

There were others on the contrary who said that the divine arrangement was reversible by prayer. And the prima facierendering of certain texts of scripture seems to favor this view. Thus, after Isaias by divine command had said to King Ezechias: Put thine house in order, for thou shalt die and not live; yet upon Ezechias's prayer the word of the Lord came to Isaias, saying: Go and tell Ezechias: I have heard thy prayer, lo I will add to thy days fifteen years(Isa. xxxviii, 1-5). Again it is said in the person of the Lord: I will suddenly speak against a nation and against a kingdom, to root out and pull down and destroy it. If that nation against which I have spoken shall repent of their evil, I also will repent of the evil that I have thought to do to them (Jer. xviii, 7, 8); Turn to the Lord your God, for he is gracious and merciful: who knoweth but he will turn and forgive? (Joel ii, 13, 14.) But against construing these texts to mean that the will of God is changeable, or that anything happens to God in time, or that temporal events in creation are the cause of anything coming to exist in God, there are other authorities of Holy Writ, containing infallible and express truth. Thus it is said: God is not as man, that he should die, nor as the son of man, that he should change. Has he said then and shall not do? Has he spoken and shall not fulfil? (Num. xxiii, 19): The victorious one in Israel will not spare, and will not be moved to repentance: for he is not a man that he should repent (1 Kings xv, 29): I am the Lord and change not (Malach. iii, 6).

On careful consideration it will appear that all mistakes in this matter arise from failing to note the difference between the system of the universe and any particular system (universalem ordinem et particularem). There is nothing to hinder any particular system being changed, whether by prayer or by any other means; for there is that existing beyond the bounds of the system which is capable of changing it. But beyond the system that embraces all things nothing can be posited whereby such system could possibly be changed, depending as it does on the universal cause. Therefore the Stoics laid it down that the system established by God could nowise be changed. But they failed in a right appreciation of this general system in supposing that prayers were useless, which was taking for granted that the wills of men, and their desires whence their prayers proceed, are not comprehended in that general system. For when they say that the same effect follows whether prayers are put up or not, — follows, that is, as part of the universal system of things, — they manifestly reserve and except prayers as not entering into that general system. Supposing prayers included in the system, then effects will follow from them by divine appointment as from other causes. One might as well exclude the effects of other every-day causes as exclude the effect of prayer. And if the immutability of the divine plan does not withdraw the effects of other causes, neither does it take away the efficacy of prayer.

Prayers then avail, not as changing a system arranged from eternity, but as being themselves part of that system. And there is no difficulty in the efficacy of prayer changing the particular system of some inferior cause, by the doing of God, who overpasses all causes, and who consequently is not bound by the necessity of any system depending on any cause; but on the contrary every necessity of system dependent on any inferior cause is checked by Him, as having been instituted by Him.188Inasmuch then as pious prayers avail to alter some points of the system of inferior causes that was established by God, God is said to 'turn,' or 'repent.' Hence Gregory says that God does not change His counsel, though He sometimes changes His sentence, not the sentence which declares His eternal arrangements, but the sentence which declares the order of inferior causes, according to which Ezechias was to die, or some nation to be punished for its sins. Such change of sentence is called in metaphorical language 'repentance,' inasmuch as God behaves like one repentant, to whom it belongs to change what He has done. In the same way God is said metaphorically to be 'angry,' inasmuch as by punishing He produces the effect of anger. (B. I, Chap. XCI ad fin.)

CHAPTER XCVI—That God does not hear all Prayers

THERE is no anomaly in the prayers of petitioners being sometimes not granted by God. For God fulfils the desires of His rational creature inasmuch as that creature desires good: but sometimes it happens that what is asked is not true but seeming good, which is simply evil: such a prayer is not within the hearing of God. Hence it is said: Ye ask and receive not, because ye ask amiss (James iv, 3).

2. It is suitable that God should fulfil our desires in so far as He moves us to desire. If therefore the movement of desire on our part is not kept up by earnestness in prayer, there is nothing to be surprised at if the prayer does not gain its due effect. Hence the Lord [St Luke] says: We ought always to pray and not to faint (Luke xviii, 1); and the Apostle, Pray without ceasing (1 Thess. v, 17).

3. It befits God to hear the prayer of the rational creature inasmuch as that creature draws nigh to Him. But one draws nigh to God by contemplation and devout affection and humble and firm intention. That prayer therefore which does not so draw nigh to God is not within God's hearing. Hence it is said: He hath regarded the prayer of the humble (Ps. ci, 18); and, Let him ask in faith, debating not within himself (James i, 6).

4. God hears the prayers of the pious on the ground of friendship. He then who turns away from the friendship of God is not worthy to have his prayer heard. Hence it is said: Whosoever turns away his ear from hearing the law, his prayer shall be abominable (Prov. xxviii, 9): Though ye multiply prayers, I will not hear: for your hands are full of blood (Isai. i, 15). This is why sometimes a friend of God is not heard, when he prays for those who are not God's friends, as it was said: Do not thou pray for this people, nor take unto thee praise and supplication for them, and do not withstand me: for I will not hear thee (Jerem. vii, 16).

It happens sometimes that for very friendship one denies his friend's petition, knowing it to be hurtful to him, or the contrary to be better for him, as a physician refuses what his patient asks for. No wonder then if God, who fulfils the desires put before Him by His rational creature for the love that He bears to that creature, fails sometimes to fulfil the petition of those whom He singularly loves, that He may fulfil it otherwise with something more helpful to the salvation of the petitioner, as we read in 2 Cor. xii, 7-9; and the Lord says to some: Ye know not what ye ask (Matt. xx, 22). Therefore Augustine says (Ep. ad Paulin. et Theras.): "The Lord is good in often not giving what we will, to give instead what we should prefer."

CHAPTER XCVII—How the Arrangements of Providence follow a Plan

GOD by His providence directs all things to the end of the divine goodness, not that anything accrues as an addition to His goodness by the things that He makes, but His aim is the impression of the likeness of His goodness so far as possible on creation. But inasmuch as every created substance must fall short of the perfection of the divine goodness, it was needful to have diversity in things for the more perfect communication of the divine goodness, that what cannot perfectly be represented by one created exemplar, might be represented by divers such exemplars in divers ways in a more perfect manner. Thus man multiplies his words to express by divers expressions the conception of his mind, which cannot all be put in one word. And herein we may consider the excellence of the divine perfection shown in this, that the perfect goodness which is in God united and simple, cannot be in creatures except according to diversity of modes and in many subjects. Things are different by having different forms, whence they take their species. Thus then the end of creation furnishes a reason for the diversity of forms in things. From the diversity of forms follows a difference of activities, and further a diversity of agents and patients, properties and accidents.

Evidently then it is not without reason that divine providence distributes to creatures different accidents and actions and impressions and allocations. Hence it is said: The Lord by wisdom hath founded the earth, hath established the heavens in prudence. By his wisdom the depths have broken out, and the clouds grow thick with dew (Prov. iii, 19, 20).

As it is necessary for one wishing to build a house to look out for timber, but his looking out for pitch-pine (ligna abietina) depends on his mere will, not on his plan of building a house; so it is necessary for God to love His own goodness, but it does not thence necessarily follow that He should wish to have that goodness represented by creatures, since the divine goodness is perfect without that. Hence the bringing of creatures into being depends on the mere will of God, although it is done in consideration of the divine goodness. Supposing however that God wishes to communicate His goodness by way of similitude as far as possible, it logically follows thence that there should be creatures of different sorts: but it does not follow of necessity that creatures should be of this or that grade of perfection, or exist in this or that number. But supposing that it is in the divine will to wish this number in creation, and this grade of perfection in each creature, it thence follows logically that creation be in such and such form, and such and such matter; and so of further consequences. Manifestly then providence disposes of things according to a certain plan, and yet this plan presupposes the divine will.

What has been said shuts out two errors, the error of those who believe that all things follow mere will without reason, which is the error of sundry Doctors of the Mohammedan law, as Rabbi Moses says; according to whose teaching, the only difference between fire warming and fire freezing is God's so willing the former alternative; and again the error is shut out of those who say that the order of causes springs from divine providence by way of necessity.

There are certain words of Holy Scripture which appear to put down all things to the mere will of God. Their meaning is not to take away all rational character from the dispensations of Providence, but to show that the will of God is the first principle of all things. Such texts are: All things, whatsoever he hath willed, the Lord hath done (Ps. cxxxiv, 6:) Who can say to him, Why doth thou so? (Job ix, 12:) Who resisted his will? (Rom. ix, 19.) And Augustine (De Trin.III:) "Nothing but the will of God is the prime cause of health and sickness, of rewards and punishments, of graces and recompenses."

Thus in answer to the question, Why? asked of any natural effect, we can render a reason from some proximate cause, yet so that we reduce all things to the prime cause. Thus if it is asked why wood gets hot in presence of fire, it is answered [etc., etc., in terms of Aristotelian physics], and so on till we come to the will of God [who willed to create matter and energy, such as we know them, from the beginning]. Hence whoever answers the question, why the wood got hot, Because God has willed it so, answers appropriately, if he intends to carry back the question to the prime cause; but inappropriately, if he intends to exclude all other causes.

CHAPTER XCIX—*God can work beyond the Order laid down for Creatures, and produce Effects without Proximate Causes*

SINCE accidents follow upon the substantial principles of the thing, he who immediately produces the substance of a thing must be able immediately to work in the thing whatever effects follow upon substantial existence. But God by creation has brought all things immediately into being. He can therefore immediately move anything to any effect without intermediate causes.

But if any one says that, once God has fixed an orderly course of events, He cannot change it without changing Himself; and that He would change Himself, if ever He worked in the world to the production of effects apart from their own proper causes, such a saying may be refuted by a study of nature. For the orderly course of events fixed by God, if we look at it as it obtains in creation, will be found to hold for the most part, but not everywhere or always: for sometimes, although in a minority of cases, the thing turns out otherwise, either for lack of power in the agent, or for indisposition of the matter, or from some *vis major* supervening. Yet not on that account does the law of providence fail or suffer change: for it comes under providence that the natural course of things, instituted to hold usually, should sometimes fail. If therefore by the action of some created power the natural course of events may be altered from the usual to the unusual, and that without any alteration of divine providence, much more may the divine power sometimes do a thing, without prejudice to its own providence, beyond the course assigned to natural events by God. This God does at times to manifest His power: for there is no better way of manifesting the subjection of all nature to the divine will than by something being done at times beyond the course of nature: for thereby it appears that the course of events proceeds from Him, and is not of necessity of nature, but through free will. Nor should this be accounted a frivolous reason to allege, that God works some effects in nature to the end of manifesting Himself to human minds, since it has been shown that all the material creation is subordinated to serve the end of intellectual nature, while the end of intellectual nature itself is the knowledge of God. No wonder then if some change is wrought in corporeal substance to afford intelligent nature a knowledge of God.

CHAPTER C—That the things which God does beyond the Order of Nature are not contrary to Nature

SINCE God is prime agent, all things inferior to Him are as His instruments. But instruments are made to serve the end of the prime agent, according as they are moved by Him: therefore it is not contrary to, but very much in accordance with, the nature of the instrument, for it to be moved by the prime agent. Neither is it contrary to nature for created things to be moved in any way whatsoever (qualitercunque) by God: for they were made to serve Him.

4. The first measure of every being and of every nature is God, seeing that He is the first being and canse of being to all. And since everything must be judged by

its measure, that must be called 'natural' to a thing whereby it is conformed to its measure, or standard. That then will be natural to a thing, which has been put into it by God. Therefore, though something further be impressed upon a thing, making it otherwise than as it was before, that is not against nature.

5. All creatures stand to God as the products of art to the artist (B. II, Chap. XXIV). Hence all nature may be called an artistic product of divine workmanship (artificiatum divinae artis). But it is not contrary to the notion of workmanship for the artist to work something to a different effect in his work, even after he has given it the first form. Neither then is it contrary to nature if God works something in natural things to a different effect from that which the ordinary course of nature involves.

Hence Augustine says: "God, the Creator and Founder of all natures, does nothing contrary to nature, because to every creature that is natural which He makes so, of whom is all measure, number and order of nature.

## CHAPTER CI—Of Miracles

CHAPTER 101—THINGS that are done occasionally by divine power outside of the usual established order of events are commonly called miracles (wonders). We wonder when we see an effect and do not know the cause. And because one and the same cause is sometimes known to some and unknown to others, it happens that of the witnesses of the effect some wonder and some do not wonder: thus an astronomer does not wonder at seeing an eclipse of the sun, at which a person that is ignorant of astronomy cannot help wondering. An event is wonderful relatively to one man and not to another. The absolutely wonderful is that which has a cause absolutely hidden. This then is the meaning of the word 'miracle,' an event of itself full of wonder, not to this man or that man only. Now the cause absolutely hidden to every man is God, inasmuch as no man in this life can mentally grasp the essence of God (Chap. XLVII). Those events then are properly to be styled miracles, which happen by divine power beyond the order commonly observed in nature.

Of these miracles there are several ranks and orders. Miracles of the highest rank are those in which something is done by God that nature can never do. Miracles of the second rank are those in which God does something that nature can do, but not in that sequence and connexion. Thus it is a work of nature that an animal should live, see and walk: but that it should live after death, see after blindness, walk after lameness, these things nature is powerless to effect, but God sometimes brings them about miraculously. A miracle of the third rank is something done by God, which is usually done by the operation of nature, but is done in this case without the working of natural principles, as when one is cured by divine power of a fever, in itself naturally curable, or when it rains without any working of the elements.

## CHAPTER CII—That God alone works Miracles

WHAT is entirely subject to established order cannot work beyond that order. But every creature is subject to the order which God has established in nature. No creature therefore can work beyond this order, which working beyond the order of nature is the meaning of working miracles.

2. When any finite power works the proper effect to which it is determined, that is no miracle, though it may surprise one who does not understand the operation. But the power of every creature is limited to some definite effect, or effects. Whatever therefore is done by the power of any creature cannot properly be called a miracle. But what is done by the power of God, infinite and incomprehensible, is properly a miracle.

3. Every creature in its action requires some subject to act upon: for it belongs to God alone to make a thing out of nothing (B. II, Chap. XXI). But nothing that requires a subject for its action can act except to the production of those effects to which that subject is in potentiality: for the work of action upon a subject is to educe that subject from potentiality to actuality. As then a creature can never create, so it can never act upon a thing except to the production of that which is in the potentiality of that thing. But in many miracles done by divine power a thing is done, which is not in the potentiality of that upon which it is done, as in the raising of the dead. Hence it is said of God: Who doth great wonderful works alone (Ps. cxxxv, 4).

CHAPTER CIII—How Separately Subsisting Spirits work certain Wonders, which yet are not true Miracles

IT was the theory of Avicenna that matter is far more obedient to spiritual agencies than to the action of contraries in nature. Hence he goes on to say that upon the suggestion of these spiritual agents there sometimes follows an effect in the lower world, such as rain, or the cure of some sick person, without the coming in of any intermediate corporeal agency. He instances the change wrought in the body by the mere suggestion of a strong impression of phantasy, as when one walking upon a plank set aloft easily falls, because his fear pictures a fall to him, whereas he would not fall if the same plank were laid on the ground, giving him no occasion to fear. Again it is notorious that upon the mere suggestion of the soul the body grows hot, as in desire or anger, or is chilled, as in fear. Sometimes too a strong suggestion brings on an illness, a fever, or even leprosy. Thereupon Avicenna says that if the soul is pure, not subject to bodily passions, and strong in its suggestive power, not only its own body will obey its suggestion, but even foreign bodies, even to the healing of the sick upon suggestion made by it. And this he thought to be the cause of the evil eye (fascinationis), that any soul having a strong affection of malevolence is capable of making a noxious impression on another, particularly on a child, who for the tenderness of his constitution is readily susceptible of such impressions. Hence he concludes that much more does an effect in this lower world follow upon the suggestion of pure spirits, without the action of any bodily agent. And this position tallies well enough with his other theories: for he supposes that all substantial forms in this lower world are effluxes from a pure spirit, and that bodily agents do no more than prepare the matter to receive the impression of the separately subsisting spiritual agent. But this is not true according to the doctrine of Aristotle, who proves that such forms as are in matter arise from other forms which are also in matter, for thus is maintained the likeness between maker and made.

    The fact is, a created spirit has no power of its own to induce any form upon corporeal matter otherwise than by setting some body into local motion. This much is in the power of a created spirit, to make a body obey it to the extent of moving locally. So by moving a body locally an angel can employ natural agents to the production of certain effects. But such action is not miraculous, properly speaking. Hence it remains true that created spirits do not work miracles of their own power. But there is nothing against their working miracles inasmuch as they work in the power of God, as appears from the fact that one choir of angels is especially told off, as Gregory says, to work miracles. Gregory further says that some saints sometimes work miracles by an act of power, and not merely by intercession.

CHAPTER CIV—That the Works of Magicians are not due solely to the Influence of the Heavenly Spheres

It would be superfluous to translate this chapter. The one point of interest which it contains is the enumeration of wonders ascribed to magicians in the thirteenth century. Such wonders are answers given about the whereabouts of things stolen, about buried treasures, about future events, also about points of science: speaking apparitions: statues that move and speak: locks opening on a person's mere approach: people becoming invisible. St Thomas writes: "If any one says that such apparitions are not in the external sense but are simply imaginary, that explanation has its difficulties: for no one takes imaginary forms for true ones except in cases of alienation of the mind from exterior impressions: only when the natural judgement of sense is impaired can phantoms be attended to as though they were realities: but these conversations and apparitions occur to men who have the full use of their external senses." He mentions "statues made by the necromantic art," but does not explicitly refer to that evocation of the spirits of the departed, which is the presence of modern spiritualism.

CHAPTER CV—Whence the performances of Magicians derive their Efficacy

MAGICIANS in their performances use certain words with a meaning to the production of definite effects. Now a word, as meaning something, has no power except from some understanding, the understanding either of him who utters the word or of him to whom it is uttered: from the understanding of the utterer, in the case where a word is of such power that by the idea which it contains it is apt to produce real effects, the idea being applied to the production of those effects by the ministry of the voice: from the understanding of the person addressed, in the case when the hearer is induced to do something by the reception into his understanding of the idea conveyed by the word. Now it cannot be said that those words, uttered by magicians with a meaning, have their efficacy from the understanding of him who utters them. For, since power follows upon essence, difference of power argues a difference of essential principle. But we find the condition of the understanding of men generally to be such that it is more true to say that its cognition is caused by things than that any idea which it conceives can be the cause of things. If then there are any men who by words expressive of the concept of their understanding can change things one into another, and do that by power of their own (res possint transmutare propria virtute), they must be beings of another species from ordinary mortals, and cannot be called men in the sense in which others are men (dicentur aequivoce homines). The alternative is to suppose that such effects are accomplished by the understanding of some person, to whom the speech of him who utters such words is addressed. This supposition has its confirmation in the fact that the expressions which magicians use consist of invocations, entreaties, adjurations, or even commands, as of one person talking with another.

Besides, in the ceremonies of this art they employ certain characters and geometrical figures. But a figure is no principle of action, imparted or received: or else mathematical drawings would be active and passive. Matter therefore cannot be disposed by geometrical figures to the reception of any natural effect. It follows that these figures are not used as disposing causes, but as signs. Now we use signs only to address other intelligent beings. Magical arts therefore owe their efficacy to some intelligence, to whom the speech of the magician is addressed, — as is also shown by the sacrifices, prostrations, and other rites employed, which can be nothing else but signs of reverence paid to some intelligent nature.

CHAPTER CVI—That the Subsistent Intelligence, which lends Efficacy to Magical Performances, is not Good in both Categories of Being

IT remains to be further investigated, what that intelligent nature is, by whose power these operations are carried into effect. To begin with, it is apparent that it is no good and praiseworthy nature. For it is not the behavior of an intelligence well-disposed to lend countenance to acts contrary to virtue. But that is what is done by magical arts: they usually serve to bring about adulteries, thefts, killing, and the like evil practices. Hence they who use such arts are called 'evil practitioners' (malefici).

3. The working of a benignant intelligence is to bring men to the proper good things of men, which are the good things of reason: but to draw men away from those good things, and allure them to trifles, is the conduct of an intelligence of a perverse bent. Now by these magical arts men make no profit in the good things of reason, which are sciences and virtues, but only in such trifles as the finding of things stolen, the catching of robbers, and the like.

4. There seems to be a certain grimace and character of unreasonableness attaching to the proceedings of the aforesaid arts. Thus they require an agent who abstains from sexual intercourse, and yet they are frequently employed for the procurement of sexual intercourse in its illicit forms.

6. As it belongs to the good to lead on to goodness, one might expect any right-minded intelligence to lead on to truth, truth being the proper good of the understanding. But the proceedings of magicians are generally of a character to mock men and deceive them.

8. It is not the way of a rightly ordered intelligence, supposing it to be a superior being, to take orders from an inferior; or, supposing it to be an inferior, to suffer itself to be entreated as though it were a superior being. But magicians invoke those whose assistance they use, with supplication, as though they were superior beings; and then, when they have come, they command

them as though they were inferiors.

### CHAPTER CVII—That the Subsistent Intelligence, whose aid is employed in Magic, is not Evil by Nature

WHATEVER is in things must be either cause or caused: otherwise it would not be in relation with other things. The subsistent beings in question then are either causes only or they are also caused. If they are causes only, evil cannot be cause of anything except incidentally (Chap. XIV); and everything incidental must be reducible to that which is ordinary: therefore there must be something in them prior to the evil that is there, something whereby they are causes. But that which is prior in everything is its nature and essence. Therefore these subsistent beings are not evil in their nature. The same conclusion follows if they are things caused. For no agent acts except with some intention of good: evil therefore cannot be the effect of any cause except incidentally. But what is caused incidentally only cannot be by nature, since every nature has a regular and definite mode of coming into being.

4. Nothing can exist unless it has existence from the first being, and the first being is the sovereign good (B. II, Chap. XV). But since every being, as such, acts to the production of its own likeness, all things that come of the first being must be good.

7. Since the will tends to good grasped by the understanding, and finds therein its natural and proper

object and end, it is impossible for any subsistent intelligence to have by nature a bad will, unless the understanding in it naturally is mistaken in its judgement of what is good. But no understanding can be so mistaken: for false judgements in acts of the understanding are like monsters in the physical universe, which are not according to nature, but out of the way of nature: for the good of the understanding and its natural end is the knowledge of truth.

This is also confirmed by the authority of Holy Scripture: for it is said, Every creature is good (1 Tim. iv, 4): God saw all things that he had made, and they were very good (Gen. i, 31).

Hereby is excluded the error of the Manicheans, who suppose that these subsistent intelligences, commonly called demons or devils, are naturally evil.

Porphyry tells in his Letter to Anebo that there is a certain kind of spirits who make it their business to listen to magicians, a kind naturally deceitful, assuming every form, personating gods [angels] and men and souls of the departed; and that this kind of being it is which makes all these appearances for better or for worse: for the rest, that this kind of spirit renders no assistance towards anything that is really good, but on the contrary is the author of evil counsel, and accuses and hampers and envies the earnest votaries of virtue, and is full of hastiness and pride, rejoices in the smell of burnt meats, and is captivated by flatteries. The only thing to quarrel with in this account is his saying that such malice is in these spirits "naturally."

CHAPTER CIX—That in Spirits there may be Sin, and how

AS there is an order in active causes, so also in final causes, requiring that the secondary end should be subordinate to the primary, as the secondary agent depends on the primary. Now every will naturally wishes that which is the proper good of the person willing, namely, his own perfect well-being; and the will cannot possibly will ought to the contrary of this. If we can find a voluntary agent, whose good is a final end, such as not to be contained under the order leading to any other end, but rather all other ends being contained in the order leading up to it, — in such a voluntary agent there can be no fault of the will. Such a voluntary agent is God, whose being is sovereign goodness, which is the final end. In God then there can be no fault of the will. But in any other voluntary agent, whose proper good must necessarily be contained in the order leading to some other good, a sin of the will may occur, — considering the agent as he is in his own nature. In every voluntary agent there is a natural inclination to will and love his own perfect well-being, and that to such an extent that he cannot will the contrary. But a created agent has no natural endowment of so subordinating his own well-being to another end than himself as to be incapable of swerving from that end: for the higher end does not belong to the creature's own nature, but to a superior nature. It is left therefore to the decision of his own will to subordinate his proper wellbeing to a higher end. Sin therefore might have found place in the will of a pure spirit in this way, — that he did not refer his own good and well-being to the final end, but made that good his end and adhered to it accordingly. And because rules of conduct necessarily are taken from the end in view, it followed as a matter of course that the said spirit arranged his other elections according to that same object (ex re ipsa) in which he had placed his last end. Hence his will was not regulated by any higher will, a position of independence proper to God alone. In this sense we must understand the saying that he aimed at equality with God [cf. Isai. xiv, 13], not that he ever expected his goodness to equal the divine goodness: such a thought could never have occurred to his mind. But to wish to rule others, and not to have one's own will ruled by any superior, is to wish to be in power and cease to be a subject; and that is the sin of pride. Hence it is aptly said that the first sin that a spirit committed was pride. But because once error has been committed in regard to a first principle, a varied and manifold course of error is bound to ensue, so from the spirit's first inordination of will there followed manifold other sin in his will, such as hatred of God for withstanding his pride and justly chastising his offence, envy against man, and the like.

Further we may note that when any one's proper good is subordinate to several higher powers, it is open to a voluntary agent to withdraw himself from his subordination to one superior, and not relinquish his subordination to another, be that other the superior or the inferior of the first. Thus a soldier, being subordinate at once to the king and to the general of the army, may direct his will to the good of the general and not to the good of the king, or the other way about. If the general withdraws from his allegiance to the king, the will of the soldier, withdrawing from the will of the general and directing his affection to the king, will be good; and the will of the soldier, following the general's will against the will of the king, will be evil. Now not only are pure spirits subordinate to God, but also one of them is subordinate to another from first to last (B. II, Chap. XCV). And because in any voluntary agent, short of God, there may be sin in his will, if we consider him as left to his own nature, possibly one of the higher angels, or even the very highest of all, committed a sin in his will. And this is probable enough, that the sinner was highest of them all: for he would not have made his own good estate the final end of his acquiescence, had not his goodness been very perfect. Some of the lower angels then of their own will may have subordinated their good to [thrown in their lot with] that leader, and so have withdrawn their allegiance from God, and sinned as he did: while others, observing due regard to God in the motion of their will, rightly withdrew from their subordination to the sinner, although he was higher than they in the order of nature.

This is the difference between man and a pure spirit, that in the one being of man there are several appetitive faculties, one subordinate to another: this is not the case in pure spirits, although one of them is under another. But in man, however the inferior appetite may swerve from due subordination, any sin that occurs occurs in his will. As then it would be a sin in pure spirits for any inferior amongst them to swerve from due subordination to a superior, while that superior remained in subordination to God; so in the one person of man sin may occur in two ways: in one way by the human will not subordinating its own good to God, and that sin man has in common with the pure spirit; in another way by the good of the lower appetite not being regulated according to the higher, as when the pleasures of the flesh, to which the concupiscible appetite tends, are willed not in accordance with reason; and this sin does not occur in pure spirits.

CHAPTERS CVIII, CX—Arguments seeming to prove that Sin is impossible to Spirits, with Solutions of the same

ARG. 1. Every other cognitive faculty but the understanding makes use of living bodily organs. In pure spirits therefore it is impossible for there to be any cognitive faculty but the understanding; and whatever they take cognizance of, they have understanding of. But in so far as one has understanding, one does not err: for all error springs from lack of understanding. Therefore there can be no error in the apprehension of these spirits. But without such error there can be no sin in the will: because the will always tends to good as apprehended: hence unless there he a mistake in the apprehension of good, there can be no sin in the will.

Arg. 2. In us there occurs sin of the will in respect of matters about which we have true knowledge of their general bearings, but on a particular point our judgement is hampered by some passion fettering the reason. But these passions cannot be in spiritual beings, because such passions belong to the sensitive part, and that has no action without a bodily organ. Having therefore a right knowledge in general, the will of a pure spirit cannot tend to evil by any defend of knowledge in particular.

Arg. 3. No cognitive faculty is deceived about its own proper object, but only about some object foreign to it: thus sight is not deceived in judging of colors, but when a man undertakes by sight to judge of tastes, then deception occurs. Now the proper object of understanding is the essence of a thing. No deception then is incident to the apprehension of understanding, so long as it fixes upon the pure quiddities of things: but all intellectual deception, we may think, arises from the forms of things apprehended coming to be mixed up with phantasms, as in our experience. But such a mode of cognition does not obtain in pure spirits, since phantasms cannot be without a body. To pure spirits therefore no error in cognition can possibly be incident, and consequently no sin in the will.

Reply to Arguments 1, 2, 3. We are not obliged to say that there was any error in the understanding of a pure spirit, in the shape of a false judgement, judging that to be good which is not good: the mistake, such as it was, lay in not attending to the higher good, to which the spirit's private good ought to have been referred: the reason of which inattention [read inconsideration is ratio] may have been the inward turning of the will upon the spirit's private good: for it is open to the will to turn more or less of its affection upon this object or upon that.

Arg. 5. Since appetite or desire tends to nothing but its own proper good, it seems impossible for desire to go astray in the case when the person desiring has one only definite good to desire. The reason why sin is incident to our desire is the composition of our nature, a compound of the spiritual and the corporeal, occasioning a multiplicity of things to be good for us, one thing being good for us in mind and another in body. Of this variety of good things the less important has to be subordinated to the more important. Hence sin of the will arises in us when we neglect that order, and go after what is good for us under a certain qualification, discarding what is good for us absolutely. But in pure spirits there is no such composition, no diversity of things good for them; nay, all their good is intellectual. Hence it seems they are incapable of sin in the will.

Reply. The angel who sinned did not go after any other good than the one good that was proper to him: but his sin lay in this, that he dropped the higher good to which he should have subordinated himself As we sin by pursuing the lower goods of the body away from the order of reason, so the devil sinned by not referring his own excellence to the excellence of God.

Arg. 6. In us, sin of the will arises out of excess or defect, while virtue lies in the mean between them. But pure spirits can pursue only intellectual good things, in which things no excess is possible, for of themselves they are in the mean between excess and defect, as truth is in the mean between two errors.

Reply. The devil passed the mean of virtue inasmuch as he did not submit himself to a superior order; and thus he gave himself more than his due, and to God less than His due.

CHAPTER CXII—That Rational Creatures are governed by Providence for their own sakes, and other Creatures in reference to them

THE very condition of intellectual nature, whereby it is mistress of its own acts, requires the care of Providence, providing for it for its own sake: while the condition of other creatures, that have no dominion over their own act, indicates that care is taken of them not for themselves, but for their subordination to other beings. For what is worked by another is in the rank of an instrument: while what works by itself is in the rank of a prime agent. Now an instrument is not sought for its own sake, but for the use of the prime agent: hence all diligence of workmanship applied to instruments must have its end and final point of reference in the prime agent. On the other hand all care taken about a prime agent, as such, is for its own sake.

2. What has dominion over its own act, is free in acting. For he is free, who is a cause to himself of what he does: whereas a power driven by another under necessity to work is subject to slavery. Thus the intellectual nature alone is free, while every other creature is naturally subject to slavery. But under every government the freemen are provided for their own sakes, while of slaves this care is taken that they have being for the use of the free.

3. In a system making for an end, any parts of the system that cannot gain the end of themselves must be subordinate to other parts that do gain the end and stand in immediate relation to it. Thus the end of an army is victory, which the soldiers gain by their proper act of fighting: the soldiers alone are in request in the army for their own sakes; all others in other employments in the army, such as grooms or armourers, are in request for the sake of the soldiers. But the final end of the universe being God, the intellectual nature alone attains Him in Himself by knowing Him and loving Him (Chap. XXV). Intelligent nature therefore alone in the universe is in request for its own sake, while all other creatures are in request for the sake of it.

6. Everything is naturally made to behave as it actually does behave in the course of nature. Now we find in the actual course of nature that an intelligent subsistent being converts all other things to his own use, either to the perfection of his intellect, by contemplating truth in them, or to the execution of works of his power and development of his science, as an artist develops the

conception of his art in bodily material; or again to the sustenance of his body, united as that is to an intellectual soul.

Nor is it contrary to the conclusion of the aforesaid reasons, that all the parts of the universe are subordinate to the perfection of the whole. For that subordination means that one serves another: thus there is no inconsistency in saying that unintelligent natures serve the intelligent, and at the same time serve the perfection of the universe: for if those things were wanting which subsistent intelligence requires for its perfection, the universe would not be complete.

By saying that subsistent intelligences are guided by divine providence for their own sakes, we do not mean to deny that they are further referable to God and to the perfection of the universe. They are cared for for their own sakes, and other things for their sake, in this sense, that the good things which are given them by divine providence are not given them for the profit of any other creature: while the gifts given to other creatures by divine ordinance make for the use of intellectual creatures.

Hence it is said: Look not on sun and moon and stars besides, to be led astray with delusion and to worship what the Lord thy God hath created for the service of all nations under heaven (Deut. iv, 19): Thou hast subjected all things under his feet, sheep and all oxen and the beasts of the field (Ps. viii, 8).

Hereby is excluded the error of those who lay it down that it is a sin for man to kill dumb animals: for by the natural order of divine providence they are referred to the use of man: hence without injustice man uses them either by killing them or in any other way: wherefore God said to Noe: As green herbs have I given you all flesh

(Gen. ix, 3). Wherever in Holy Scripture there are found prohibitions of cruelty to dumb animals, as in the prohibition of killing the mother-bird with the young (Deut. xxii, 6, 7), the object of such prohibition is either to turn man's mind away from practicing cruelty on his fellow-men, lest from practicing cruelties on dumb animals one should go on further to do the like to men, or because harm done to animals turns to the temporal loss of man, either of the author of the harm or of some other; or for some ulterior meaning, as the Apostle (1 Cor. ix, 9) expounds the precept of not muzzling the treading ox.

CHAPTER CXIII—That the acts of the Rational Creature are guided by God, not merely to the realization of the Specific Type, but also to the realization of the Individual

EVERYTHING is reckoned to exist for the sake of its activity, activity being the final perfection of a thing. Thus then everything, so far as it comes under divine providence, is guided by God to its proper act. But a rational creature subject to providence is governed and provided for as an individual for its own sake, not merely for the sake of the species, as is the case with other perishable creatures (Chap. CXII). Thus then rational creatures alone are guided by God to their acts, not merely specific but individual.
2. Whatever things are guided in their acts only in what appertains to the species, such things have not the choice of doing or not doing: for what is consequent upon the species is common and natural to all individuals contained under the species; and what is natural is not in our power. If then man were guided in his acts only to the

extent of fitting him for his species, he would have no choice of doing or not doing, but would have to follow the natural inclination common to the whole species, as happens in all irrational creatures.

3. In whatsoever beings there are found actions over and above such as fall in with the common inclination of the species, such beings must be regulated by divine providence in their actions with some guidance beyond that which is extended to the species. But in the rational creature many actions appear, which the inclination of the species is not sufficient to account for, as is shown by their being not alike in all, but various in various individuals.

4. The rational creature alone is capable of being guided to its acts not merely specifically but individually: for by the gift of understanding and reason it is able to discern the diversity of good and evil according as is befitting to diverse individuals, times and places.

5. The rational creature is not only governed by divine providence, but is also capable to some extent of grasping the notion of providence, whereas other creatures share in providence merely by being subject to providence. Thus the rational creature is partaker in providence, not merely by being governed, but by governing: for it governs itself by its own acts, and also other beings. But every lower providence is subject to the supreme providence of God. Therefore the government of the acts of the rational creature, in so far as they are personal acts, belongs to divine providence.

6. The personal acts of the rational creature are properly the acts that come from a rational soul. Now the rational soul is capable of perpetuity, not only in the species, as other creatures are, but also in the individual.

The acts therefore of the rational creature are guided by divine providence, not only as they belong to the species, but also as they are personal acts.

CHAPTER CXIV—That it was necessary for a Law to be given to Man by God

THE acts of irrational creatures, as they belong to the species, are guided by God according to a natural inclination, consequent upon the nature of the species. Therefore, over and above that, there must be given to men something to guide them in their personal acts, and that we call 'law.'

3 and 4. To them is a law fittingly given, who know what they are about, and have the alternative of doing a thing or leaving it undone. But that is proper to the rational creature only. Therefore the rational creature alone is conceptible of law.

Hence it is said: I will give my law in their hearts (Jer. xxx, 33): I will write for him my manifold laws (Osee viii, 12).

CHAPTER CXV—That the main purpose of the Divine Law is to subordinate Man to God

THE end which God intends is Himself.

2. The end of every human creature is to adhere to God, for in that his happiness consists.

4. That should be the main purpose of a law, from which the law derives its efficacy. But the law given by God has efficacy among men from the fact that man is suited to God. This therefore ought to be the chief precept

in the divine law, that the human mind should adhere to God.

Hence it is said: *And now, Israel, what doth the Lord thy God ask of thee but that thou fear the Lord thy God and walk in his ways, and love him and serve the Lord thy God with thy whole heart and thy whole soul?*(Deut. x, 12.)

CHAPTER CXVI—That the End of the Divine Law is the Love of God

THE main intention of the divine law is that man should adhere to God; and man adheres to God chiefly by love. There are two powers whereby man may cleave to God, his understanding and his will. By the lower faculties of his soul man cannot cleave to God, but adheres to lower things. Now the adhesion that is of the understanding is completed by that which is of the will: for by the will man comes to rest in what the understanding apprehends. The will cleaves to a thing either through love or through fear, but in different ways. When it adheres to a thing through fear, it adheres for the sake of something else, namely, to avoid an evil threatening it, if it does not adhere: but when it adheres to a thing through love, it adheres for the thing's own sake. But what is for its own sake carries the day over what is only for the sake of something else. Therefore the adhesion of love to God is the chief way of adhering to Him, and is the point principally intended in the divine law.

2. The end of every law, and particularly of the divine law, is to make men good. Now a man is called good from having a good will: for the will it is which

reduces to act whatever good there is in the man: but the will is good by willing good, and particularly the chief good, which is the end: the more then the will wills this good, the better the man is. Therefore the will of the sovereign good, which is God, is what most of all makes men good, and is principally intended in the divine law.

3. The law aims at making men virtuous: but it is a condition of virtue that the virtuous person should act firmly and with pleasure; and love it is that best makes us do a thing firmly and with delight. Therefore it is said: The end of the commandment is charity (1 Tim. i, 5): The greatest and first commandment is, Thou shalt love the Lord thy God (Matt. xxii, 37, 38).

CHAPTER CXVII—That by the Divine Law we are directed to the Love of our Neighbor

THERE should be a union of affection among those who have one common end: but men share in the one common last end of happiness, to which they are ordained of God; and therefore they should be united in mutual love.

2. Whoever loves another, must in consequence also love those whom that other loves and who are united with him. But men are loved by God, seeing that for them He has prepared the enjoyment of Himself as their last end. Therefore as one is a lover of God, so must he also be a lover of his neighbor.

3. Since man is naturally a social animal, he needs to be helped by other men to gain his proper end; and this is most aptly done by mutual love prevailing amongst men.

4. To attend to divine things, a man needs

tranquility and peace. Now the things that might trouble peace are most effectually taken away by mutual love. Since then the law of God orders men to attend to divine things, mutual love amongst men must necessarily be a provision of the divine law.

5. The divine law is given to man to bear out the natural law. But it is natural to all men to love one another: a sign of this is the fact that by a sort of natural instinct man helps any man, even a stranger, in necessity, as by calling him back from a wrong turn that he may have taken on his way, lifting him up from a fall, and the like, as though every man were kinsman and friend of every other man.

Hence it is said: This is my commandment, that ye love one another (John xv, 12): This commandment we have of God, that he who loves God does love also his brother (1 John iv, 21): The second commandment is, thou shalt love thy neighbor as thyself (Matt. xxii, 39).

CHAPTER CXVIII—That by Divine Law men are obliged to a Right Faith

AS sight by the bodily eye is the principle of the bodily passion of love, so the beginning of spiritual love must be the intellectual vision of some object of the same. But the vision of that spiritual object of understanding, which is God, cannot be had at present by us except through faith, because God exceeds our natural reason, especially if we consider Him in that regard under which our happiness consists in enjoying Him.

2. The divine law directs man to be entirely subject to God. But as man will is subjected to God by loving Him, so his understanding is subjected to Him by

believing Him, — but not by believing anything false, because no falsehood can be proposed to man by God, who is the truth: hence he who believes anything false does not believe God.

3. Whoever holds an erroneous view about a thing, touching the essence of the thing, does not know the thing. Thus if any one were to fix on the notion of irrational animal, and take that to be man, he would not know man. The case would be otherwise, if he was mistaken only about some of the accidents of man. But in the case of compound beings, though he who errs about any of the essentials of a thing does not know the thing, absolutely speaking, still he knows it in a sort of a way: thus he who thinks man to be an irrational animal knows him generically: but in the case of simple beings this cannot be, — any error shuts out entirely all knowledge of the thing. But God is to the utmost degree simple. Therefore whoever errs about God does not know God. Thus he who believes God to be corporeal has no sort of knowledge of God, but apprehends something else instead of God. Now as a thing is known, so is it loved and desired. He then who errs concerning God, can neither love Him nor desire Him as his last end. Since then the divine law aims at bringing men to love and desire God, that same law must bind men to have a right faith concerning God.

Hence it is said: Without faith it is impossible to please God (Heb. xi, 6); and at the head of all other precepts of the law there is prescribed a right faith in God: Hear, O Israel: the Lord thy God is one Lord (Deut. vi, 4).

## CHAPTER CXIX—That by certain Sensible Rites our mind is directed to God

BECAUSE it is connatural to man to gather his knowledge through the senses, and most difficult for him to transcend sensible things God has provided for man that even in sensible things there should be made for him a commemoration of things divine. To this end sensible sacrifices have been instituted, which man offers to God, not as though God needed them, but to bring home to man the lesson that he ought to offer himself and all he has to God, his end, Creator, Ruler, and Lord of all. There are also exercised upon man certain hallowings through certain sensible things, whereby man is washed, or anointed, or given to eat and drink, along with the utterance (prolatione) of audible words, to represent to man by these sensible signs the augmentation of spiritual gifts wrought in him from without, namely, by God, whose name is expressed in audible words. Also certain sensible rites are performed by men, not to rouse God to action, but to prompt themselves to divine service. Of this nature are prostrations, genuflections, vocal cries and chants: which things are not done as though God had need of them, who knows all, even the affection of the mind, — whose will is unchangeable (Chap. XCV), and who moreover does not accept the movement of the body for its own sake: but we do these things on our own behalf, that by these sensible rites our intention may be directed to God and our affection inflamed. At the same time also we hereby make profession of God being author of our soul and body, in that we pay Him acts of homage spiritual and bodily.

Hence it is not surprising that the [Manichean] heretics, who say that God is not the author of our body, blame these bodily observances being paid to God. In which censure they evidently fail to remember that they themselves are men, not seeing that sensible representations are necessary to us for inward knowledge and affection. For it is experimentally shown that our soul is excited by bodily acts to think and feel: hence we properly use such acts to raise our mind to God.

In the payment of these bodily observances the cult, or worship, of God is said to consist. For we are said to cultivate those objects to which we pay attention by our works. Now we busy ourselves in paying attention to the things of God, not as though we were of service to Him, as is the case when we are said to tend, or cultivate, other things by our attentions, but because such actions are of service to ourselves, enabling us to come nearer to God. And because by inward acts we go straight to God, therefore it is by inward acts properly that we worship God: nevertheless outward acts also belong to the cult, or worship, of God, inasmuch as by such acts our mind is raised to God, as has been said.

Hence the worship of God is also called religion, because by such acts a man in some sort binds (ligat) himself, that his thought may not wander astray from God; and also because by a sort of natural instinct he feels himself bound (obligatum) to God, that in such manner as he can he should pay reverence to Him from whom is the origin of his being and of all his good.

Hence also religion has received the name of piety, for piety is that whereby we pay due honor to parents: hence aptly the honor paid to God, parent of all, is taken to be a part of piety, and they who oppose the worship of God are called impious.

But because not only is God cause and origin of our being, but our whole being is in His power, and all that is in us is His due, and thereby He is truly our Lord and Master, therefore what we perform in honor of God is called service. Now God is our master not by accident, as one man is another's master, but by nature; and therefore the service that we owe to God is quite different from that whereby we are accidentally subject to a man, the dominion of man over man being partial, and derivative from God. Hence the service especially due to God is called among the Greeks latria.

CHAPTER CXX—That the Worship of Latria is to be paid to God alone

THERE have been some who have thought that this worship should be paid not only to the first principle of all things, but also to all creatures that are above men. Hence, while considering God to be the one prime and universal principle of all things, they have still thought it right to pay latria, first after God, to the subsistent intelligences in the heavens, which they also called gods, whether they existed entirely apart from bodies or were the souls of spheres or stars. Secondly, also to certain subsistent intelligences which they believed to be united to bodies of air, and called them genii (daimones): because they believed them to be above men, as a body of air is above a body of earth, they insisted that these intelligences also were to be worshipped by men with divine worship, and in comparison with men they said that they were gods, as being intermediate between men and gods. And because they believed that the souls of good men, by the fact of their separation from bodies, passed to a higher state than the state of the present life, they considered that divine worship should be paid also to the souls of the dead, whom they called ἥρωες, or manes. Some again, taking God to be the soul of the universe, have believed that the worship proper to Godhead is to be paid to the whole universe and to all its parts, not however for the sake of the material part, but for the sake of the soul, which they said was God, as honor is paid to a wise man, not for his body but for his mind. Some again used to say that even things naturally below man still should be worshipped by man with divine honors, inasmuch as some portion of the power of a higher nature is communicated to them. Hence, believing that certain images made by man were receptive of supernatural power, either from the influence of the heavenly bodies or from the presence of Spirits within them, they said that such images should receive divine worship, and they called those images gods: on which account themselves were called 'idolaters,' because they paid the worship of latria to idols and images.

    1. But it is irrational in men who posit one only separate first principle, to pay divine worship to another. For we pay worship to God, not as though He needed it, but to strengthen in ourselves by sensible signs a true opinion about God. Now the opinion that God is one, exalted above all, cannot be strengthened in us by sensible signs except by our paying him some separate and peculiar tribute, which we call divine worship. Evidently then true opinion about the one principle is weakened, if divine worship is paid to several.

    2. This exterior worship is necessary for man, to the end that man's soul may conceive a spiritual reverence for God. But custom goes a long way in moving the mind of man: for we are more easily moved to that to which we are accustomed. Now the custom among

men is that the honor that is paid to him who holds the highest place in the commonwealth, as to the king or emperor, is paid to none other. Therefore there should be a worship that is paid to none other than the one principle of the universe; and that we call the worship of latria.

3. If the worship of latria is due to another merely because he is superior, and not because he is supreme, it would follow that one man should pay latria to another man, and one angel to another angel, seeing that among men, and also among angels, one is superior to another. And since among men he who is superior on one point is inferior on another, it would follow that men should interchange latria in their mutual dealings, which is absurd.

4. Man ought to pay God something special in recognition of the special benefit of his creation; and that is the worship of latria.

5. Latria means service, and service is due to the master. Now he is properly and truly called master, who lays down to others precepts of conduct, and himself takes a precept of conduct from none: for he who executes the arrangement of a superior is rather minister than master. But God's providence disposes all things to their due actions: hence in Holy Writ the angels and the heavenly bodies are said to minister both to God, whose ordinance they execute, and to us, to whose benefit their actions tend. Therefore the worship of latria, due to the sovereign master, is to be paid only to the sovereign principle of the universe.

6. Among all acts of latria, a unique rank belongs to sacrifice: for genuflections, prostrations and other such marks of honor may be paid even to man, although with another intention than they are paid to God: but no one

ever thought to offer sacrifice except to him whom he regarded as God, or affected so to regard. The outward rite of sacrifice represents the inward true sacrifice, whereby the human mind offers itself to God, as to the principle of its creation, the author of its activity, the term of its happiness. Therefore to God alone should man offer sacrifice and the worship of latria, and not to any created spirits whatsoever.

Hence it is said: *He shall be slain who offers sacrifice to any gods but to the Lord alone* (Exod. xxii, 20): *The Lord thy God shalt thou adore, and him only shalt thou serve* (Deut. vi, 13). And because it is an undue thing for the worship of latriato be paid to any other than the first principle of all things, and only an evil-minded rational creature will incite others to undue acts; evidently men have been set on to the aforesaid undue worships by the instigation of devils, who have presented themselves to men to be adored in place of God, seeking divine honor. Hence it is said: *All the gods of the heathen are devils* (Ps. xcv, 5): *The things which the heathen sacrifice, they sacrifice to devils, and not to God* (1 Cor. x, 20).

CHAPTER CXXI—That the Divine Law directs man to a Rational Use of Corporeal and Sensible Things

AS man's mind may be raised to God by corporeal and sensible things, provided that they are duly used to show reverence to God, so also the undue use of them either totally withdraws the mind from God, fixing the final intention of the will upon inferior things, or clogs the mind's aspiration after God, making it take unnecessary interest in such things. Now the divine law is given for this end chiefly, to lead man to cling to God. It is a function therefore of divine law to direct man in his affection for and use of corporeal and sensible things.

2. As man's mind is subordinate to God, so his body is subordinate to his soul, and his lower powers to his reason. It belongs therefore to divine providence, the plan of which, as proposed by God to man, is the divine law, to see that all things keep their order. Therefore that divine law must so direct man as that his lower powers shall be subject to his reason, and his body to his soul, and exterior things shall serve his necessity.

4. Every lawgiver must comprise in his legislation those enactments without which the law could not be observed. Now law being set over reason, man could not follow the law unless all other things belonging to man were subjected to reason. Hence it is said: Your reasonable service (Rom. xii, i); and, This is the will of God, your sanctification (1 Thess. iv, 9). Hereby is excluded the error of such as say that those acts alone are sinful, whereby our neighbor is either hurt or shocked.

CHAPTER CXXII—Of the reason for which Simple Fornication is a Sin by Divine Law, and of the Natural Institution of Marriage

HENCE appears the folly of those who say that simple fornication is not a sin. For they say: Given a woman free from a husband, and under no control of father or any other person, if any one approaches her with her consent, he does her no wrong, because she is pleased so to act, and has the disposal of her own person: nor does he do any wrong to another, for she is under no one's control: therefore there appears no sin. Nor does it seem to be a sufficient answer to say that she wrongs God, for

God is not offended by us except by what we do against our own good (Chap. CXXI): but it does not appear that this conduct is against man's good: hence no wrong seems to be done to God thereby. In like manner also it does not appear a sufficient answer, that wrong is thereby done to one's neighbor, who is scandalized: for sometimes a neighbor is scandalized by what of itself is not a sin, in which case the sin is only incidental: but the question is not whether fornication is a sin incidentally, but whether it is a sin ordinarily and in itself.

We must seek a solution from what has been said before: for it has been said (Chapp. XVI, LXIV) that God has care of everything according to that which is good for it. Now it is good for everything to gain its end, and evil for it to be diverted from its due end. But as in the whole so also in the parts, our study should be that every part of man and every act of his may attain its due end. Now though the semen is superfluous for the preservation of the individual, yet it is necessary to him for the propagation of the species: while other excretions, such as excrement, urine, sweat, and the like, are needful for no further purpose: hence the only good that comes to man of them is by their removal from the body. But that is not the object in the emission of the semen, but rather the profit of generation, to which the union of the sexes is directed. But in vain would be the generation of man unless due nurture followed, without which the offspring generated could not endure. The emission of the semen then ought to be so directed as that both the proper generation may ensue and the education of the offspring be secured.

Hence it is clear that every emission of the semen is contrary to the good of man, which takes place in a way whereby generation is impossible; and if this is done on purpose, it must be a sin. I mean a way in which generation is impossible in itself as is the case in every emission of the semen without the natural union of male and female: wherefore such sins are called 'sins against nature.' But if it is by accident that generation cannot follow from the emission of the semen, the act is not against nature on that account, nor is it sinful; the case of the woman being barren would be a case in point.

Likewise it must be against the good of man for the semen to be emitted under conditions which, allowing generation to ensue, nevertheless bar the due education of the offspring. We observe that in those animals, dogs for instance, in which the female by herself suffices for the rearing of the offspring, the male and female stay no time together after the performance of the sexual act. But with all animals in which the female by herself does not suffice for the rearing of the offspring, male and female dwell together after the sexual act so long as is necessary for the rearing and training of the offspring. This appears in birds, whose young are incapable of finding their own food immediately they are hatched: for since the bird does not suckle her young with milk, according to the provision made by nature in quadrupeds, but has to seek food abroad for her young, and therefore keep them warm in the period of feeding, the female could not do this duty all alone by herself: hence divine providence has put in the male a natural instinct or standing by the female for the rearing of the brood. Now in the human species the female is clearly insufficient of herself for the rearing of the offspring, since the need of human life makes many demands, which cannot be met by one parent alone. Hence the fitness of human life requires man to stand by woman after the sexual act is done, and not to go off at once and form connexions with any one he meets, as is the way with fornicators. Nor is this reasoning traversed by the fact of some particular woman having wealth and power enough to nourish her offspring all by herself: for in human acts the line of natural rectitude is not drawn to suit the accidental variety of the individual, but the properties common to the whole species.

A further consideration is, that in the human species the young need not only bodily nutrition, as animals do, but also the training of the soul. Other animals have their natural instincts (suas prudentias) to provide for themselves: but man lives by reason, which [read quam] takes the experience of a long time to arrive at discretion. Hence children need instruction by the confirmed experience of their parents: nor are they capable of such instruction as soon as they are born, but after a long time, the time in fact taken to arrive at the years of discretion. For this instruction again a long time is needed; and then moreover, because of the assaults of passion, whereby the judgement of prudence is thwarted, there is need not of instruction only, but also of repression. For this purpose the woman by herself is not competent, but at this point especially there is requisite the concurrence of the man, in whom there is at once reason more perfect to instruct, and force more potent to chastise. Therefore in the human race the advancement of the young in good must last, not for a short time, as in birds, but for a long period of life. Hence, whereas it is necessary in all animals for the male to stand by the female for such time as the father's concurrence is requisite for bringing up of the progeny, it is natural for man to be tied to the society of one fixed woman for a long period, not a short one. This social tie we call marriage. Marriage then is natural to man, and an irregular connexion outside of marriage is contrary to the good of man; and therefore fornication must be sinful.

Nor yet should it be counted a slight sin for one to procure the emission of the semen irrespective of the due purpose of generation and rearing of issue, on the presence that it is a slight sin, or no sin at all, to apply any part of one's body to another use than that to which it is naturally ordained, as if, for example, one were to walk on his hands, or do with his feet something that ought to be done with his hands. The answer is that by such inordinate applications as those mentioned the good of man is not greatly injured: but the inordinate emission of the semen is repugnant to the good of nature, which is the conservation of the species. Hence, after the sin of murder, whereby a human nature already in actual existence is destroyed, this sort of sin seem to hold the second place, whereby the generation of human nature is precluded.

The above assertions are confirmed by divine authority. The unlawfulness of any emission of semen, upon which offspring cannot be consequent, is evident from such texts as these: Thou shalt not lie with mankind as with womankind: Thou shalt not lie with any beast (Levit. xviii, 22, 23): Nor the effeminate, nor sodomites, shall possess the kingdom of God (1 Cor. vi, 10). The unlawfulness of fornication and of all connexion with any other woman than one's own wife is clear from Deut. xxiii, 17:There shall be no whore among the daughters of Israel, nor whoremonger among the sons of Israel: Keep thyself from all fornication, and beyond thine own wife suffer not the charge of knowing another(Job. iv, 13): Fly fornication (1 Cor. vi, 18).

Hereby is refuted the error of those who say that there is no more sin in the emission of the sementhan in the ejection of other superfluous products from the body.

CHAPTER CXXIII—That Marriage ought to be Indissoluble

LOOKING at the matter rightly, one must see that the aforesaid reasons not only argue a long duration for that natural human partnership of male and female, which we call marriage, but further imply that the partnership ought to be lifelong. 1. Property is a means to the preservation of human life. And because natural life cannot be preserved in one and the same person of the father living on for all time, nature arranges for its preservation by the son succeeding his father in likeness of species: wherefore it is appropriate that the son should succeed his father in his property. It is natural therefore that the father's interest in his son should continue to the end of his life, and that father and mother should dwell together to the end.

2. Woman is taken into partnership with man for the need of childbearing: therefore when the fertility and beauty of woman ceases, there is a bar against her being taken up by another man. If then a man, taking a woman to wife in the time of her youth, when beauty and fertility wait upon her, could send her away when she was advanced in years, he would do the woman harm, contrary to natural equity.

3. It is manifestly absurd for the woman to be able to send away the man, seeing that woman is naturally subject to the rule of man, and it is not in the power of a

subject to run away from control. It being then against the order of nature for the woman to be allowed to desert the man, if the man were allowed to desert the woman, the partnership of man and woman would not be on fair terms, but would be a sort of slavery on the woman's side.

4. Men show a natural anxiety to be sure of their own offspring; and whatever stands in the way of that assurance runs counter to the natural instinct of the race. But if the man could send away the woman, or the woman the man, and form a connexion with another, certainty as to parentage would be difficult, when a woman had intercourse first with one man and then with another.

5. The greater the love, the more need for it to be firm and lasting. But the love of man and woman is counted strongest of all; seeing that they are united, not only in the union of the sexes, which even among beasts makes a sweet partnership, but also for the sharing in common of all domestic life, as a sign whereof a man leaves even father and mother for the sake of his wife (Gen. ii, 24). It is fitting therefore for marriage to be quite indissoluble.

6. Of natural acts, generation alone is directed to the good of (the specific) nature: for eating and the separation from the body of other excretions concern the individual, but generation has to do with the preservation of the species. Hence, as law is instituted for the common good, the function of procreation ought to be regulated by laws divine and human. Now the laws laid down ought to proceed on the basis of the dictate of nature (ex naturali instinctu), if they are human laws, as in the exact sciences every human discovery takes its origin from principles naturally known: but if they are divine laws, they not only develop the dictate of nature, but also make up the

deficiency of what nature dictates, as dogmas divinely revealed surpass the capacity of natural reason. Since then there is in the human species a natural exigency for the union of male and female to be one and indivisible, such unity and indissolubility must needs be ordained by human law. To that ordinance the divine law adds a supernatural reason, derived from the significancy of marriage as a type of the inseparable union of Christ with His Church, which is one as He is one. Thus then irregularities in the act of generation are not only contrary to the dictate of nature, but are also transgressions of laws divine and human: hence on this account any irregular behavior in this matter is even a greater sin than in the matter of taking food or the like. But since all other factors in human life should be subordinate to that which is the best thing in man, it follows that the union of male and female must be regulated by law, not from the mere point of view of procreation, as in other animals, but also with an eye to good manners, or manners conformable to right reason, as well for man as an individual, as also for man as a member of a household or family, or again as a member of civil society. Thus understood, good manners involve the indissolubility of the union of male and female: for they will love one another with greater fidelity, when they know that they are indissolubly united: each partner will take greater care of the things of the house, reflecting that they are to remain permanently in possession of the same things: occasions of quarrels are removed, that might otherwise arise between the husband and the wife's relations, if the husband were to divorce his wife; and thus affinity becomes a firmer bond of amity: also occasions of adultery are cut off, occasions which would readily offer themselves, if husband could divorce his wife, or wife her husband.

Hence it is said: But I say to you that whoever putted away his wife, except for fornication, and married another, committed adultery; and he that married her that is put away, committed adultery (Matt. xix, 9): But to them that are united in marriage, it is not I that give commandment, but the Lord, that the wife depart not from her husband (1 Cor. vii, 10).

Divorce was reckoned an impropriety also among the ancient Romans, of whom Valerius Maximus (De memor. dictis, II, 1) relates that they believed that the marriage tie ought not to be broken off even for barrenness.

Hereby the custom is banned of putting away wives, which however in the Old Law was permitted to the Jews for their hardness of heart, because they were prone to the killing of their wives: so the less evil was permitted to keep out the greater.

CHAPTER CXXIV—That Marriage ought to be between one Man and one Woman ONE general reason holds for all animals, which is this, that every animal desires free enjoyment of the pleasure of sexual union as of eating: which freedom is impeded by there being either several males to one female, or the other way about: and therefore animals fight alike for food and for sexual jealousy. But in men there is a special reason, inasmuch as man naturally desires to be sure of his own offspring. But here a difference comes in. Both of the above mentioned reasons hold for the case of the cohabitation of one female with several males: but the second reason does not hold against the cohabitation of one male with several females, — I mean certainty in point of parentage is not in that case prevented. But the first reason makes against it: for as the free enjoyment of the female is taken from the male, if the female has another partner, so the same free enjoyment is taken from the female, if the male has more than one partner.

2. In every species of animal in which the sire takes any interest in the offspring, one male keeps company with one female only, as in all birds that rear their young in common: for one male could not avail for several females as a helper in the rearing of their progeny: whereas in animals in which the males take no interest in the offspring, one male consorts with several females promiscuously, and the female with several males, as appears in dogs, poultry, and the like. But the male's interest in the offspring is greater in the human species than in any other.

3 and 4. The reason why a wife is not allowed more than one husband at a time is because otherwise paternity would be uncertain. If then while the wife has one husband only, the husband has more than one wife, there will not be a friendship of equality on both sides, friendship consisting in a certain equality. There will not be the friendship of a free man with a free woman, but a sort of friendship of a slave with her master. The husband might well be allowed a plurality of wives, if the understanding were allowable, that the friendship of each with him was not to be that of a free woman with a free man but of a slave with her master. And this is borne out by experience: for among men that keep many wives the wives are counted as menials.

5. From one man having several wives there arises discord at the domestic hearth, as experience shows. Hence it is said: They shall be two in one flesh(Gen. ii,

24).

## CHAPTER CXXV—That Marriage ought not to take place between Kindred

SINCE in marriage there is a union of different persons, those persons who ought to reckon themselves as one because of their being of one stock, are properly excluded from intermarrying, that they may love one another more ardently on the mere ground of their common origin.

2. Since the intercourse of man and wife carries with it a certain natural shame, those persons should be prevented from such intercourse who owe one another a mutual reverence on account of the tie of blood. And this is the reason touched on in Leviticus xviii.

3. Excessive indulgence in sexual pleasures makes for the corruption of good manners: for such pleasures of all others most absorb the mind and hinder the right exercise of reason. But such excessive indulgence would ensue, if the intercourse of the sexes were allowed among persons who must necessarily dwell under the same roof, where the occasion of such intercourse could not be withdrawn.

5. In human society the widening of friendships is of the first importance. That is done by the marriage tie being formed with strangers.

It is to be observed that as that inclination is 'natural,' which works upon objects as they usually occur, so law too is framed for what usually happens. Thus it is no derogation from the reasons above alleged, that in some particular case the venture may turn out otherwise: for the good of the individual ought to be overlooked in view of the good of the many, since the good of the multitude is ever more divine than the good of the individual. Lest however any particular complaint might remain wholly without remedy, there rests with legislators and others on like footing authority to dispense in a general enactment so far as is necessary in a particular case. If the law is human, a dispensation may be given by men possessed of power like to that which made the law. If the law is a divine enactment, a dispensation may be given by divine authority, as in the Old Law a dispensatory indulgence seems to have been granted for plurality of wives, and for concubines, and divorce.

CHAPTER CXXVI—That not all Sexual Intercourse is Sin

THE members of the body being the instruments of the soul, the end of every member is the use of it, as in the case of any other instrument. But there are members of the body the use of which is for the intercourse of the sexes: that therefore is their end. But that which is the end of any natural thing cannot be in itself evil, because the things of nature are ordinances of divine providence. Therefore the intercourse of the sexes cannot be in itself evil.
3. Natural inclinations are put into things by God, who is the prime mover of all. Therefore it is impossible for the natural inclination of any species to be directed to an object in itself evil. But in all full-grown animals there is a natural inclination to sexual union, which union

therefore cannot be in itself evil.

4. That without which something good and excellent cannot be, is not in itself evil. But the perpetuity of the species in animals is not preserved except through generation, which is of sexual intercourse.

Hence it is said: She sinned not, if she marry (1 Cor. vii, 36).

Hereby is excluded the error of those who totally condemn marriage, which some do because they believe that temporal things proceed not from a good but from an evil principle.

CHAPTER CXXVII—That of no Food is the Use Sinful in itself

EVERYTHING is done rationally, when it is directed according to its due bearing upon a due end. But the due end of the taking of food is the preservation of the health by nourishment. Therefore whatever food can serve that end, may be taken without sin.

2. Of no thing is the use evil in itself unless the thing itself be evil in itself. But no food is in its nature evil; because everything is in its nature good (Chap. VII); albeit some particular food may be evil to some particular person, inasmuch as it makes against his bodily health. Therefore of no food, considered as such and such a thing, is the partaking a sin in itself: but it may be a sin, if a person uses it irrationally and not to his health.

3. To apply things to the purpose for which they exist is not in itself evil. But plants exist for the sake of animals, some animals for the sake of others, and all for the sake of man (Chap. LXXXI). Therefore to use either plants, or the flesh of animals, either for eating, or for any

other purpose for which they are useful to man (vel ad quidquid aliud sunt homini utilia), is not in itself a sin.

4. The defect which makes sin redounds from soul to body, but not backwards from body to soul: for by sin we mean a disorder of the will. But articles of food concern the body immediately, not the soul. Therefore the taking of various foods cannot be in itself a sin, except in so far as it is inconsistent with rectitude of will. And that may come to be in several ways: in one way by some inconsistency with the proper end of food, as when for the pleasure of eating one uses food that disagrees with health either in kind or in quantity. Another way would be when the food becomes not the condition of him who eats it, or of the society in which he lives, as when one is more nice in his food than his means will allow, or violates the social conventions of those with whom he sits at table. A third way would be in the case of certain foods prohibited by some special law: thus in the Old Law sundry meats were forbidden for what they signified; and in Egypt of old the eating of beef was prohibited, lest agriculture should suffer; and again there is the case of rules prohibiting the use of certain foods in order to check the lower appetites.

Hence the Lord says: Not what entered in at the mouth defiles a man (Matt. xv, 11). Since eating and the intercourse of the sexes are not things in themselves unlawful, and exterior possessions are necessary for getting food, for rearing and supporting a family, and other bodily wants, it follows that neither is the possession of wealth in itself unlawful, provided the order of reason be observed, — I mean, provided the man possesses justly the things that he has, and does not fix the final end of his will in them, and uses them duly for his own and others' profit.

Hereby is excluded the error of some, who, as Augustine says, "most arrogantly called themselves Apostolics, because they did not receive into their communion married men and proprietors, such as are many monks and clerks whom the Catholic Church now contains: these people are heretics, because, separating themselves from the Church, they think that there is no hope for other persons who make use of what they do without" (De haeresibus, c. 40).

CHAPTER CXXVIII—How the Law of God relates a man to his Neighbor

OF all things that man makes use of, the chief are other men. Man is naturally a social animal, needing many things that the individual cannot procure by himself. The divine law therefore must needs instruct man to live according to the order of reason in his relations with other men.

2. The end of the divine law is to bring man to cleave to God. Now man is aided thereto by his fellow-man, as well in point of knowledge as in point of affection: for men help one another in the knowledge of the truth, and one incites another to good and restrains him from evil. Hence it is said: Iron is sharpened by iron, and man sharpens the face of his friend (Prov. xxvii, 17): Better two together than one,etc. (Eccles iv, 9-12).

There is then orderly concord amongst men, when to each there is rendered his own, which is the act of justice; and therefore it is said: The work of justice is peace (Isa. xxxii, 17). To the observance of this justice man is inclined both by an interior and an exterior principle. By an interior principle, in so far as a man has a will to observe the precepts of the divine law, which is done by his bearing love to God and to his neighbor: for whoever loves another renders him his due spontaneously and with pleasure, and even acts more by liberality: hence the whole fulfilment of the law hinges upon love (Rom. xiii, 10: Matt. xxii, 40). But because some are not so inwardly disposed as to do of their own accord what the law commands, they have to be dragged by an exterior force to the fulfilment of the justice of the law; and so they fulfil the law under fear of penalties, not as freemen but as slaves. Hence it is said: When thou shalt do thy judgements upon the earth by punishing the wicked, the inhabitants of earth shall learn justice (Isa. xxvi, 9). Others are so disposed as to do of their own accord what the law bids them. They are a law to themselves, having charity, which bends their wills in place of a law to generous conduct. There was no need of an exterior law being enacted for them: hence it is said: The law was not made for the just, but for the unjust: which is not to be taken to mean that the just are not bound to fulfil the law, as some have misunderstood the text, but that the just are inclined of themselves to do justice even without a law.

CHAPTER CXXIX—That the things commanded by the Divine Law are Right, not only because the Law enacts them, but also according to Nature

BY the precepts of the divine law the human mind is subordinated to God, and all the rest of man is subordinated to reason. But this is just what natural order requires, that the inferior be subject to the superior. Therefore the things commanded by the divine law are in themselves naturally right.

2. Divine providence has endowed men with a natural tribunal of reason (naturale judicatorium rationis), to be the ruling principle of their proper activities. But natural principles are ordained to natural purposes. There are certain activities naturally suited to man, and these activities are in themselves right, and not merely by positive law.

3. Where there is a definite nature, there must be definite activities proper to that nature: for the proper activity of every nature is consequent upon the nature. Now it is certain that men's nature is definite. There must therefore be certain activities that in themselves befit man.

4. Wherever a thing is natural to any one, any other thing also is natural, without which the first thing cannot be had, for nature fails not in necessities. But it is natural to man to be a social animal. Those things therefore naturally befit man, without which the maintenance of human society would be impossible. Such things are the securing to every man of his own, and abstinence from wrongdoing. Some points therefore of human conduct are naturally right.

5. The use of lower creatures to meet the need of human life is a natural property of man. Now there is a certain measure in which the use of the aforesaid creatures is helpful to human life. If this measure is transgressed, as in the disorderly taking of food, it results in harm to man. There are therefore certain human acts naturally appropriate, and others naturally inappropriate.

6. In the natural order man's body is for his soul, and the lower powers of the soul for reason. It is therefore naturally right for man so to manage his body and the

lower faculties of his soul as that the act and good of reason may least of all be hindered, but rather helped. Mismanagement in this regard must naturally be sinful. We count therefore as things naturally evil carousings and revellings and the disorderly indulgence of the sexual instinct, whereby the act of reason is impeded and subjected to the passions, which do not leave the judgement of the reason free.

7. To every man those things are naturally befitting, whereby he tends to his natural end; and the contraries are naturally unbefitting. But God is the end to which man is ordained by nature (Chap. CXV). Those things therefore are naturally right, whereby man is led to the knowledge and love of God; and the contraries are naturally evil for man.

Hence it is said: The judgements of the Lord are righteous, having their justification in themselves (Ps. xviii, 10).

Hereby is excluded the tenet of those who say that things just and right are the creation of positive law.

CHAPTER CXXX—That the Divine Government of Men is after the manner of Paternal Government

THE father has care of the child, not only in his relations with other men, as the king has care of him, but also in his individual concerns, as has been shown above of God (Chap. XCIII). And this with good reason, for a parent is like God in giving natural origin to a human being. Hence divine and paternal government extend to the individual, not merely as a member of society, but as a person subsisting in his own nature by himself. The two governments differ however in this, that paternal government can extend only to the things that appear in man externally, but divine government reaches also to interior acts and dispositions. For no man can take cognizance of things hidden from him: the secrets of hearts are hidden from men, though open to God (B. I, Chap. LIX). God therefore takes account of man not only as to his exterior behavior, but also as to his inward affections, what he means to do, and what he intends to gain by doing it. Of such points man takes no cognizance, except so far as by outward acts the inward disposition is shown.

Every one has care of things according as they belong to him: for solicitude about things that are no affair of yours is blamed as meddlesomeness. But one man belongs to another's charge otherwise than as he belongs to God. One man belongs to another either by natural origin and bodily descent, or by some combination in external works. But man belongs to God inasmuch as he has his origin from Him, which origin means a certain likeness to God: for every being acts to the production of its own likeness. Now man has more of the likeness of God in his soul than in his body, and most of all in his mind. Clearly therefore, in the origin of man as coming from God, the main thing intended is the mind, and for the mind's sake the other (sentient) parts of the soul are produced by God; and for the soul the body is produced: so God's principal care is for the mind of man, — first, for the mind; then for the other parts of the soul, and after them for the body. Hence it is by the mind that man attains his last end, which is human happiness (Chap. XXXVII). Other things in man serve as instruments for the securing of happiness. Hence we may observe that human government takes cognizance of interior acts so far as they are directed to external conduct and are thereby unfolded to view: but God contrariwise takes cognizance of external conduct so far as it points to interior dispositions, particularly in regard of the mind, whereby man is capable of happiness, — human happiness consisting, as has been said, in the fruition of God. The whole care therefore that God has of man is in view of preparing his mind for the fruition of God, whereunto the mind is prepared by faith, hope and charity: for by faith man's mind is disposed to recognize God as a Being above himself: by hope it is strengthened to reach out to Him and see in Him man's true good: by charity it fixes upon Him so as immovably to adhere to Him. All things that God requires of man in this life are referable to these three virtues.

Hence it is said: And now, Israel, what doth the Lord thy God ask of thee, except that thou fear the Lord thy God and walk in his ways? (Deut. x, 12.) Now there remain faith, hope and charity, these three (1 Cor. xiii, 13).

But because the human mind is naturally more imperfect than other intellectual natures; and the more perfect a thing is, the more energy it shows in tending to its end; it appears that the human mind is naturally weaker in tending to God, the end of all, than are the higher minds of the angels. This weakness shows itself on two points. First, in the deficiency of intellectual power in the human soul, as compared with higher intelligences, so that it cannot go straight to intellectual truth as it is in itself (Chapp. XLI, CXIX). Secondly, in the obstacles that keep it back from throwing itself with all its force upon God; obstacles on the part of the body, which claims care for sustenance and repose; and again obstacles on the part of the lower powers of the soul, inasmuch as the excitements of phantasy and the perturbations of passion trouble that interior peace, which is so necessary for the mind freely to throw itself upon God. These obstacles cannot be wholly removed by man from his path, so long as he lives in this mortal body: for he has to attend to the things necessary for this mortal life, and is thereby hindered from always actually tending to God. But the aforesaid hindrances should be so far got under that there should be in man's mind an intention at least, directed to God without interruption; and the more the mind can be even actually fixed on God, the more perfect will man's life be, as keeping nearer to its last end. And this actual fixing of the mind upon God will go to strengthen the intention directed towards Him, which intention must needs come to naught unless at times the mind be fixed upon Him actually. All the precepts and counsels therefore of the divine law go to furnish man with aids for fixing his mind on God and removing obstacles to such attention.

For both these purposes man needs to live at peace and concord with his fellow-men. For man needs to be aided by man, as well to the preservation of life and limb, as also to the end that one man may inflame and incite and instruct another to yearn after God. In the absence of peace and concord, man's mind must be disquieted by contentions and fighting, and hindered from aspiring to God. And therefore the divine law has made provision for the preservation of peace and concord amongst men by the practice of justice. It commands that to every man be rendered his due, as honor to parents: that none be harmed or hindered in the enjoyment of the good that belongs to him, whether by word, — hence the prohibition of false witness, — or by deed touching his own person, — hence the prohibition of murder, — or by deed touching a person allied to him, — hence the prohibition of adultery, or by deed touching his property, — hence the prohibition of theft. And because God takes cognizance not only of the public but also of the domestic behavior of men, the divine law has forbidden neglect of wife, servants, etc., which is no concern of human law.

But it is not enough for peace and concord to be preserved among men by precepts of justice, unless there be a further consolidation of mutual love. Justice provides for men to the extent that one shall not get in the way of another, but not to the extent of one helping another in his need. One may happen to need another's aid in cases in which none is bound to him by any debt of justice, or where the person so bound does not render any aid. Thus there came to be need of an additional precept of mutual love amongst men, so that one should aid another even beyond his obligations in justice.

Hence it is said: His commandment we have received, that whoever loves God should also love his brother (1 John iv, 21): This is my commandment, that ye love one another as I have loved you (John xv, 12).

It is evident that love suffices for the fulfilment of the works of justice. Hence it is said: Love is the fulfilment of the law(Rom. xiii, 10): to commend which fulfilment there are given us precepts and counsels of God concerning works of mercy, love and succor of enemies, and the like deeds of kindness, which overflow and run over the measures of justice.

But because the aforesaid precepts of justice require their completion in the love of one's neighbor, and that depends on the love of God; and when love is gone, and faith and charity are also gone, the human mind cannot duly tend to God; it follows that the observance of the precepts of the aforesaid virtues is necessarily required of man, and by the neglect of them man is entirely thrown out of his subordination to God. Now human life takes its denomination from the end to which it is directed. They who constitute their last end in pleasures are said to lead a life of pleasure. They who constitute their last end in the contemplation of truth are said to lead a contemplative life: hence whosoever constitute their last end in the enjoyment of God, their life is an adherence to God, which is absolutely the life of man, for to that end man is naturally ordained (Chap. XXXVII). On other ends man's life is dependent only in a qualified sense, inasmuch as such ends are not imposed on man by nature, but by his own choice. Death then being the opposite of life, it is a sort of death to a man to drop out of the order which has its last term in God. Hence the sins whereby a man breaks away from such order are called 'mortal,' or 'deadly' sins; and those instructions of the law whereby men are held to their engagements of justice, charity, hope, and faith, are called 'commandments,' or 'prohibitions,' because they are to be of necessity observed.

As one necessary condition for the flight of the mind to God is peace with neighbors, with whom man has to live in society and be aided by them, so another necessary condition is peace and good order of the elements within man himself. We observe that there are two ways in which the free flight of the mind to God may be hindered. One way is by the intensification of the acts of the lower powers. When one power comes vigorously into action, it draws to itself the interest of man, which cannot be scattered over many objects simultaneously: hence another power must be either stopped from acting or have its activity diminished. By the lower powers I mean the sentient powers, as well apprehensive, namely, the external and internal senses, the phantasy and other attendant powers, as also appetitive, as the irascible and concupiscible faculties. Hence when there is strong delight in sense, or much excitement of phantasy, or an inclination of the concupiscible or of the irascible faculty to their several objects, the mind must necessarily be impeded in its act of ascent to God.

In another way the movement of the mind to God may be hindered on the part of the mind itself, by its occupation with other things: for one power cannot be in perfect activity over several objects simultaneously. But since the mind at times uses the inferior powers as obedient instruments, and can occupy itself with several objects, when they all bear upon one and all help to apprehend that one, we must understand that the mind is then only hindered from its flight to God by the lower powers, or by its own occupation with other objects, when those powers or those objects bear not at all on the mind's movement to God: otherwise, far from being hindrances, they may be positive helps to the free flight of man's mind to his Creator.

Indeed man cannot altogether avoid occupying his mind about other things, by the fact that he must be solicitous about the necessaries of his bodily life. There are however among men various degrees of this solicitude. The first degree of solicitude extends just so far as the common measure of human life requires. It involves the providing of necessaries for self, wife, children, and other persons belonging to oneself according to one's state. This degree of solicitude is lawful, and may be said to be connatural to man.

The second degree is reached when a man is more solicitous about the aforesaid things of the body than the common measure of human life requires according to his state, without however this solicitude going so far as to withdraw him from his subordination to God, or making him transgress the commandments of justice and charity. There is evidently sin in this, since the man exceeds his proper measure; yet not mortal sin, since he undertakes nothing contrary to the precepts of justice and charity. His sin is called 'venial,' as being readily 'pardonable,' — as well because, for one who keeps his face set towards his last end, any error that he may make is easily put straight, — thus in speculative sciences anyone who has a true conception of principles may thereby easily correct such errors as he may fall into in drawing conclusions; and the end in view in the things of action is like the first principle in things of speculation, — as also because to one steady in friendship any delinquency is readily forgiven, — as also because it is no easy matter absolutely to observe due measure and exceed in nothing. Hence whoever does not cast away from his heart the rule of reason, which is laid down by the end in view, even though he does not altogether observe rectitude in the things which have to be regulated by that rule, is not overmuch to be blamed, but deserves pardon.

The third degree is when the solicitude for temporals grows so great as to withdraw the soul from subordination to God, and bring it to transgress the commandments of justice and charity, faith and hope, without which man's mind cannot remain in due relation with God; and this is manifest mortal sin.

The fourth degree is when contrariwise man's solicitude for worldly things stops short of the common measure of human life. If this is owing to remissness and flabbiness of mind, or to any undue eagerness, it is to be held for a base proceeding: for the transgression of the golden mean in either direction is blameworthy. But if lower things are neglected that better things may be attended to, to wit, that the mind may take a free flight to the things of God, this is a virtue more perfect than human. To teach man such perfection, there have not been given him commandments, but rather counsels to draw him forth and incite him.

CHAPTER CXXXI—Of the Counsels that are given in the Divine Law

BECAUSE the best part for man is to fix his mind on God and divine things, and it is impossible for man to busy himself with intense ardor in a number of different directions, there are given in the divine law counsels for enabling the human mind to take a more free flight to God. These counsels withdraw men from the occupations of the present life, so far as is possible for men still living on earth. Such withdrawal is not so necessary to justice as that justice cannot be without it: for virtue and justice is not done away with by man's making use of corporeal and earthly things according to the order of reason: therefore these admonitions of the divine law are called counsels, and not commandments, inasmuch as they advise a man to drop things less good for things that are better.

Human solicitude busies itself about the common measure of human life in three chief particulars. First, about one's own person, what one is to do or where to live; secondly, about persons related to oneself, especially wife and children; thirdly, about the procurement of exterior things, needful for the support of life. For cutting off solicitude about exterior things there is given in the divine law the counsel of poverty, which prompts to the casting away of the things of this world. Hence the Lord says: If thou wilt be perfect, go, sell what thou hast and give to the poor, and come, follow me (Matt. xix, 21). For cutting off solicitude about wife and children there is given man the counsel of virginity, or continence. Hence it is said: About virgins I have no commandment of the Lord, but I give a counsel; and, adding the reason of this counsel, he continues: He that is without a wife is solicitous for the things of the Lord, how he may please God; but he that is with a wife is solicitous for the things of the world, how he may please his wife, and is divided (1 Cor. vii, 25-33). For cutting off man's solicitude even about himself there is given the counsel of obedience, whereby a man commits the disposal of his acts to his superior. Therefore it is said: Obey your superiors and be subject to them, for they watch as having to render an account of your souls (Heb. xiii, 17).

Because the highest perfection of human life consists in the mind of man being detached from other things and fixed on God, and the three counsels aforesaid seem singularly to dispose the mind to this detachment, we may see in them proper adjuncts of a state of perfection, not that they themselves constitute perfection, but inasmuch as they are dispositions to perfection, which consists in the union of the detached soul with God. This is expressly shown in the words of our Lord counselling poverty: If thou wilt be perfect, go, sell what thou hast, and give to the poor, and follow me, — where He places the perfection of life in the following of Him.

They may also be called effects and signs of perfection. For when the mind is strongly possessed with love and desire of anything, it thereupon counts other things as quite secondary: so from man's mind being carried with fervent love and desire to divine things, wherein its perfection consists, the consequence is a casting off of all that might retard its movement to God, — care of property, affection for wife and children, and even love of one's own self. This is signified by the words of Scripture: If a man shall give the whole substance of his house in exchange for love, he will account it nothing (Cant. viii, 7): Having found one precious pearl, he went and sold all that he had, and acquired it (Matt. xiii, 46): the advantages that I had I considered as dirt, that I might gain Christ (Philip. iii, 8).

Since then the three counsels aforesaid are dispositions to perfection, and effects of perfection, and signs of the same, they who make the three corresponding vows to God are properly said to be in a state of perfection. The perfection to which they dispose the mind consists in the free converse of the soul with God. Hence they who make profession of the aforesaid vows are called 'religious,' as dedicating themselves and all that is theirs to God by a manner of sacrifice, extending to property by poverty, to the body by continence, and to the will by obedience: for religion consists in the worship of God (Chap. CXIX).

CHAPTERS CXXXII, CXXXV—Arguments against Voluntary Poverty, with Replies

THERE have been found persons to condemn voluntary poverty, thereby going against the teaching of the gospel, Of these Vigilantius was the first. He has had imitators, men making themselves out to be doctors of the law, not understanding either what they say or about what they affirm (1 Tim. i, 7). They have been led by these and the like reasons.

Arg. 1. Animals that cannot find the necessaries of life at any time of the year, have a natural instinct for gathering such necessaries at a time when they can be found, and laying them up, as we see in bees and ants. But men need many things for the preservation of their life, which cannot be found any time. Therefore man has a natural tendency to gather together and lay up such things, and it is against the law of nature to scatter them again.

Reply. Still it is not necessary for everyone to be busy with this task of gathering: as even among bees not all have the same duty, some gather honey, others make cells out of wax, — to say nothing of the queen-bees being exempt from all such occupations. And so it must be with men: for many things being necessary to human life, for which one man by himself cannot suffice, different functions have to be undertaken by different men, — some have to labor in the fields, some to tend cattle, and some to build. And because human life needs not only corporal but also spiritual aids, some have to devote themselves to spiritual things for the benefit of the rest; and these persons should be set free from the care of temporals.

Arg. 2. As everyone is bound by natural law to preserve his life, so also his exterior substance, as being the means whereby life is preserved.

Reply. For them who relinquish temporal things

there still remains every likelihood and hope of finding the sustenance necessary for life, either through their own labor, or the benefactions of others, whether in the shape of possessions held in common or of food daily given: for what we can do through our friends, in a manner we can do of ourselves, as the Philosopher says (Eth. Nic.VIII, xi).

Arg. 3. Man is by nature a social animal. But society cannot be maintained among men except on a system of mutual aid. To take their part in this system of aid they render themselves incapable, who fling away their exterior substance.

Reply. It is a greater thing to aid another in spirituals than in temporals, spiritual things being the more necessary to the end of final happiness. Hence he who by voluntary poverty strips himself of the ability to aid others in temporals, in order to the acquirement of spiritual good, whereby he may aid others to better advantage, does nothing against the good of human society.

Arg. 4. If it is an evil thing to have worldly substance, a good thing to rid neighbors of evil, and an evil thing to lead them into evil, it follows that to give any of the substance of this world to a needy person is evil, and to take away such substance from him who has it is good: which is absurd. It is therefore a good thing to have worldly substance, and to fling it entirely away by voluntary poverty is evil.

Reply. Wealth is a good thing for man, so far as it is directed to rational good, but not in itself: hence poverty may very well be better than wealth, if by poverty man finds his way to a more perfect good.

Arg.5. Occasions of evil are to be shunned. But

poverty is an occasion of evil, leading men on to thefts, flatteries, perjuries, and the like.

Reply. Neither riches, nor poverty, nor any other exterior condition is of itself the good of man. Such things are good only as tending to the good of reason. Hence vice may arise out of any of them, when they are not turned to man's use according to the rule of reason. Still not for that are they to be accounted simply evil, but only the abuse of them is evil.

Arg. 6. Virtue, lying in the mean, is spoilt by either extreme. There is a virtue called liberality, which consists in giving where one should give, and holding one's hand where one should hold it. On the side of defect is the vice of stinginess, which holds its hand in all cases indiscriminately. On the side of excess is the vice of lavish giving away of everything, as is done by those who embrace voluntary poverty, a vice akin to prodigality.

Reply. The golden mean is not determined according to quantity of exterior goods, but according to the rule of reason. Hence sometimes it happens that what is extreme in quantity of some exterior commodity is the mean according to the rule of reason. There is none who tends to great things more than the magnanimous man, or who in expenditure surpasses the munificent, or princely man. The rule of reason does not measure the mere quantity of commodity employed, but the condition of the person and his intention, fitness of place, time, and the like, also many conditions of virtue. Therefore one does not run counter to virtue by voluntary poverty, even though one abandon all things. Nor is this an act of prodigality, seeing that it is done with a due end and other due conditions. To expose oneself to death, under due conditions, is an act of fortitude and a virtue: yet that is going far beyond the abandonment of one's possessions.

CHAPTERS CXXXIII, CXXXVI—Of various Modes of Living adopted by the Votaries of Voluntary Poverty

FIRST MODE. The first mode is for the possessions of all to be sold, and all to live in common on [the capital fund accumulated by] the price, as was done under the Apostles at Jerusalem: As many as had possessions in lands or houses sold them, and laid the price at the feet of the Apostles, and division was made to each according to the need of each (Acts iv, 34, 35).

Criticism. It is not easy to induce many men with great possessions to take up this mode of life; and if the amount realized out of the possessions of a few rich is divided among many recipients, it will not last long.

Reply. This mode will do, but not for a long time. And therefore we do not read of the Apostles instituting this inode of living when they passed to the nations among whom the Church was to take root and endure.

Second Mode. To have possessions in common, sufficient to provide for all members of the community out of what the property brings in, as is done in most monasteries.

Criticism. Earthly possessions breed solicitude, as well for the gathering in of the returns as also for the defense of them against acts of fraud and violence; and this solicitude is all the greater as greater possessions are required for the support of many. In this way then the end of voluntary poverty is defeated, at least in the case of many, who have the procuratorship of these possessions. Besides, common possession is wont to be a source of discord.

Reply. The administration of these common possessions may be left to the care of one or a few persons, and the rest remain without solicitude for temporals, free to attend to spiritual things. Nor do they who undertake this solicitude for others lose any of the perfection of their life: for what they seem to lose by defect of quiet they recover in the service of charity, in which perfection consists. Nor is there any loss of concord by occasion of this mode of common possessions. For they who adopt voluntary poverty ought to be persons who despise temporal things; and such persons are not the men to quarrel over temporals.

Third mode. To live by the labor of one's hands, as St Paul did and advised others to do. *We have not eaten bread of any one for nothing, but in labor and fatigue, night and day working, not to be a burden to any of you: not that we had not authority to act otherwise, but to present ourselves to you as a model for you to imitate: for when we were with you, we laid down to you the rule, if any man not work, neither let him eat* (2 Thess. iii, 8-10).

Criticism. It seems folly for one to abandon what is necessary, and afterwards try to get it back again by labor. Moreover, whereas the end of the counsel of voluntary poverty is the readier following of Christ in freedom from worldly solicitudes, earning one's livelihood by one's own labor is a matter of more anxiety than living on the possessions which one had before, especially if they were a modest competency. And the

Lord seems to forbid manual labor to His disciples in the text: Behold the fowls of the air, for they sow not, neither do they reap: consider the lilies of the field how they grow, they labor not, neither do they spin (Matt. vi, 26, 28). Moreover this mode of living is inadequate. Many desire a perfect life, who have not the capacity for earning their livelihood by labor, not having been brought up thereto: also there is the possibility of sickness. And no little time must be spent in labor to suffice for earning a livelihood: many spend their whole time in labor, and yet can scarcely live. Thus the votaries of voluntary poverty will be hindered from study and spiritual exercises; and their poverty will be more of a hindrance than a help to the perfection of their life.

Reply. In the case of rich men, their possessions involve solicitude in getting them or keeping them; and the heart of the owner is drawn to them; inconveniences which do not happen to one whose sole object is to gain his daily bread by the labor of his hands. Little time is sufficient, and little solicitude is necessary, for gaining by the labor of one's hands enough to support nature: but for gathering riches and superfluities, as craftsmen in the world propose, much time has to be spent and much solicitude shown. Our Lord in the Gospel has not forbidden labor of the hands, but anxiety of mind about the necessaries of life. He did not say, Do not labor, but, Be not solicitous. And this precept He enforces by an argument from less to greater. For if divine providence sustains birds and lilies, which are of inferior condition, and cannot labor at those works whereby men get their livelihood, much more will it provide for men, who are of worthier condition, and to whom it has given ability to win their livelihood by their own labors. It is the exception for a man not to be able to win enough to live upon by the labor of his hands; and an institution is not to be rejected for exceptional cases. The remedy is, for him whose labor is not enough to keep him, to be helped out either by others of the same society, who can make more by their labor than is necessary for them, or by others who are well off. Nor need those who are content with little spend much time in seeking a livelihood by the labor of their hands: so they are not much hindered from spiritual works, especially as in working with their hands they can think of God and praise Him.

Fourth mode. To live on the alms contributed by others, who retain their wealth. This seems to have been the method observed by our Lord: for it is said that sundry women followed Christ, and ministered to him out of their means (Luke viii, 2, 3).

Criticism. It seems irrational for one to abandon his own and live on an other's property, — or for one to receive of another and pay him back nothing in return. There is no impropriety in ministers of the altar and preachers, to whom the people are indebted for doctrine and other divine gifts, receiving support at their hands: for the laborer is worthy of his hire, as the Lord says (Matt. x, 10); and the Apostle, the Lord hath ordained that they who preach the gospel should live by the gospel(1 Cor. ix, 14). But it is an apparent absurdity for these persons who minister to the people in no office to receive the necessaries of life from the people. Others moreover, who through sickness and poverty cannot help themselves, must lose their alms through these professors of voluntary poverty, since men neither can nor will succor a great multitude of poor. Moreover independence of spirit is particularly requisite for perfect virtue: otherwise men easily become partakers in other people's sins, either by expressly consenting to them, or by palliating or dissembling them. But this method of life is a great drawback to such independence, for a man cannot but shrink from offending one by whose patronage he lives. Moreover the necessity of exposing one's necessities to others, and begging relief, renders mendicants objects of contempt and dislike, whereas persons who take up a perfect life ought to be reverenced and loved. But if anyone will praise the practice of begging as conducive to humility, he seems to talk altogether unreasonably. For the praise of humility consists in despising earthly exaltation, such as comes of riches, honors, fame, but not in despising loftiness of virtue, for in that respect we ought to be magnanimous. That then would be a blameworthy humility, for the sake of which any one should do anything derogatory to loftiness of virtue. But the practice of begging is so derogatory, as well because it is more virtuous to give than to receive, as also because there is a look of filthy lucre about it.

Reply. There is no impropriety in him being supported by the alms of others, who has abandoned his own possessions for the sake of something that turns to the profit of others. Were this not so, human society could not go on. If everyone busied himself only about his own affairs, there would be no one to minister to the general advantage. The best thing then for human society (hominum societati) is that they who neglect the care of their own interests to serve the general advantage, should be supported by those whose advantage they serve. Therefore do soldiers live on pay provided by others, and civil rulers are provided for out of the common fund. But they who embrace voluntary poverty to follow Christ, certainly abandon what they have to serve the common advantage, enlightening the people by wisdom, learning and example, or sustaining them by their prayer and intercession. Hence there is nothing base in their living on what they get from others, seeing that they make a greater return, receiving temporals and helping others in spirituals. Hence the Apostle says: Let your abundance in temporals supply their want, that their abundance in spirituals also may supply your want (2 Cor. viii, 14: cf. Rom. xv, 27). For he who abets another becomes a partner in his work, whether for good or evil. By their example other men become less attached to riches, seeing them abandon riches altogether for the sake of perfection. And the less one loves riches, the more ready will he be to make distribution of his riches in other's need: hence they who embrace voluntary poverty are useful to other poor people, provoking the rich to works of mercy by word and example. Nor do they lose their liberty of spirit for the little they receive from others for their sustenance. A man does not lose his independence except for things that become predominant in his affections: for things that a man despises, if they are given to him, he does not lose his liberty. Nor is there any unseemliness in their exposing their necessities, and asking what they need either for themselves or others. The Apostles are read to have done so (2 Cor. viii, ix). Such begging does not render men contemptible, if it is done moderately, for necessaries, not for superfluities, without importunity, and with due regard to the conditions of the persons asked, and place and time. There is no shadow of disgrace about such begging, though there would be, if it were done with importunity or without discretion.

There is, no doubt, a certain humiliation in

begging, as having a thing done to you is less honorable than doing it, and receiving than giving, and obeying royal power than governing and reigning. The spontaneous embracing of humiliations is a practice of humility, not in any and every case, but when it is done for a needful purpose: for humility, being a virtue, does nothing indiscreetly. It is then not humility but folly to embrace any and every humiliation: but where virtue calls for a thing to be done, it belongs to humility not to shrink from doing it for the humiliation that goes with it, for instance, not to refuse some mean service where charity calls upon you so to help your neighbor. Thus then where begging is requisite for the perfection of a life of poverty, it is a point of humility to bear this humiliation. Sometimes too, even where our own duty does not require us to embrace humiliations, it is an act of virtue to take them up in order to encourage others by our example more easily to bear what is incumbent on them: for a general sometimes will do the office of a common soldier to encourage the rest. Sometimes again we may make a virtuous use of humiliations as a medicine. Thus if any one's mind is prone to undue self-exaltation, he may with advantage make a moderate use of humiliations, either self-imposed or imposed by others, so to check the elation of his spirit by putting himself on a level with the lowest class of the community in the doing of mean offices.

Fifth mode. There have also been some who said that the votaries of a perfect life should take no thought either for begging or laboring or laying up anything for themselves, but should expend their sustenance from God alone, according to the texts, Be not solicitous, and, Take no thought for the morrow (Matt. vi, 25, 34).

Criticism. This seems quite an irrational

proceeding. For it is foolish to wish an end and omit the means ordained to that end. Now to the end of eating there is ordained some human care of providing oneself with food. They then who cannot live without eating ought to have some solicitude about seeking their food. There follows also a strange absurdity: for by parity of reasoning one might say that he will not walk, or open his mouth to eat, or avoid a stone falling, or a sword striking him, but expect God to do all, which is tantamount to tempting God.

Reply. It is quite an irrational error to suppose that all solicitude about making a livelihood is forbidden by the Lord. Every action requires care: if then a man ought to have no solicitude about temporal things, it follows that he should do nothing temporal, which is neither a possible nor a reasonable course. For God has prescribed to every being actions according to the peculiarity of its nature. Man, being made up of a nature at once spiritual and corporeal, must by divine ordinance exercise bodily actions; and at the same time have spiritual aims; and he is the more perfect, the more spiritual his aims are. But it is not a mode of perfection proper to man to omit bodily action: bodily actions serve necessary purposes in the preservation of life; and whoever omits them neglects his life, which he is bound to preserve. To look for aid from God in matters in which one can help oneself by one's own action, and so to leave that action out, is a piece of folly and a tempting of God: for it is proper to the divine goodness to provide for things, not immediately by doing everything itself, but by moving other things to their own proper action (Chap. LXXVII). We must not then omit the means of helping ourselves, and expect God to help us in defect of all action of our own: that is inconsistent with the divine ordinance and with His goodness.

But because, though it rests with us to act, still that our actions shall attain their due end does not rest with us, owing to obstacles that may arise, the success that each one shall have in his action comes under divine arrangement. The Lord then lays it down that we ought not to be solicitous for what does not belong to us, that is, for the success of our actions: but He has not forbidden us to be solicitous about what does belong to us, that is, for the work which we ourselves do. It is not then to act against the precept of the Lord, to feel solicitude for the things which have to be done; but he goes against the precept, who is solicitous for what may turn out even when (etiam si) he does all that is in his power to do, and takes due precautions beforehand (praemittat) to meet the contingency of such untoward events.

When that is done, we ought to hope in God's providence, by whom even the birds and herbs are sustained. To feel solicitude on such points seems to appertain to the error of the Gentiles who deny divine providence. Therefore the Lord concludes that we should take no thought for the morrow(Matt. vi, 34), by which He has not forbidden us to lay up betimes things needful for the morrow; but He forbids that solicitude about future events which goes with a sort of despair of the divine assistance, as also the allowing of the solicitude that will have to be entertained to-morrow to come in before its time perversely to-day: for every day brings its own solicitude; hence it is added, Sufficient for the day is the evil thereof.

CHAPTER CXXXIV—In what the Good of Poverty consists

LET us observe in riches what is to be thought of poverty. Exterior riches are necessary to the good of virtue inasmuch as by them we support the body and succor other people. Means to an end must derive their goodness from the end. Exterior riches therefore must be some sort of a good to man, still not a principal but a secondary good: for the principal good is the end, — other things are good as subordinate to the end. Therefore it has been held that the virtues are the greatest of good things to man, and exterior riches the least. Now the means to any end must be checked by the requirements of that end. Riches therefore are so far forth good as they make for the exercise of virtue. But if that measure is exceeded, and the exercise of virtue impeded by them, they are no longer to be counted among good but among evil things. Hence it comes about that the possession of riches is a good thing for some men, who turn them to a virtuous use; and an evil thing for other men, who thereby are withdrawn from virtue, either by excessive solicitude or excessive affection for their wealth, or by elation of mind thence arising.

But there are virtues of the active life and virtues of the contemplative life; and these two orders of virtues make use of riches in different ways. The contemplative virtues need riches solely for the sustenance of nature: the active virtues as well for this purpose as also for the further purpose of helping a neighbor. Hence the contemplative life is more perfect in this, that it requires fewer earthly aids, its attention being wholly given to divine things. Hence the Apostle says: Having food, and wherewith to be clothed, with these let us be content (1 Tim. vi, 8).

Poverty then is praiseworthy, inasmuch as it delivers a man from the vices in which some men are entangled by riches. Again, inasmuch as it removes the solicitude that goes with wealth, it is useful to some persons, namely, to those who have the gift of occupying themselves with better things; but hurtful to others, who, set free from this solicitude, busy themselves about worse things. But in so far as poverty takes away the good that comes of riches, namely, the helping of other people, and hinders self-support, it is simply an evil, except in so far as the loss of the power of helping neighbors in temporals may be compensated by the advantage of a free attention to divine and spiritual things. But the good of one's own subsistence is so necessary, that the lack of it can be compensated by no other good: for on the offer of no other good should a man deprive himself of the means of supporting his own life. Poverty therefore is praiseworthy, when it delivers a man from earthly cares, and he thereby arrives to give his mind more freely to divine and spiritual things, yet so that he retains the means of lawful self-support, whereunto not much provision is requisite. And the less solicitude any method of poverty involves, the more praiseworthy is that poverty. But poverty is not more praiseworthy, the greater it is: for poverty is not good in itself, but only inasmuch as it removes from a man's path the obstacles of his freely applying himself to spiritual things: hence the measure of such removal of obstacles is the measure of the goodness of poverty. And this is a general principle with respect to all creatures: they are good only in so far as they lead to virtue, not in themselves.

CHAPTER CXXXVII—Arguments against

Perpetual Continence, with Replies

ARG. 1. The good of the species is more godlike than the good of the individual. He then who abstains altogether from the act whereby the species is perpetuated, sins more than he would by abstaining from the act whereby the individual is preserved, namely, eating and drinking.

Reply. Things that belong to the necessity of the individual stand on a different footing from things that belong to the necessity of the community. In the necessities of the individual, individual provision must be made: everyone must make use of meat and drink. But in the necessities of the community it is neither needful nor possible for the office of meeting such needs to be assigned to every individual. Many things are necessary to a multitude of men, which no one individual can attend to: therefore there must be different offices for different persons, as in the body the several members have their several functions. Since then procreation is not a necessity of the individual, but a necessity of the species, there is no need for all men to be procreants; but some men may abstain, and devote themselves to other offices, as to the life of a soldier or a contemplative.

Arg. 2. By divine ordinance there are given to man members apt for procreation, and a force of appetite inciting him thereto: whoever then altogether abstains from procreation seems to resist the ordinance of God.

Reply. Divine providence gives to man endowments necessary for the species as a whole: still there is no call upon every individual man to make use of every one of these endowments. Thus man has a building capacity and a fighting capacity: yet all men need not be builders or soldiers; neither need every one apply himself to procreation.

Arg. 3. If it is good for one man to lead a life of continence, it is better for many so to do, and the best thing of all would be for all to do it: so the human race would become extinct.

Reply. From things necessary to the community, though it be better for individuals to abstain, when one is given to better things, still it is not good for all to abstain. This is apparent in the order of the universe. Though a pure spirit is better than a bodily substance, still that would not be a better but a more imperfect universe, in which there were pure spirits alone. Though the eye is better than the foot, it would not be a perfect animal that had not both eye and foot. So neither would the state of the commonwealth of mankind be perfect, unless there were some applied to acts of procreation, and others abstaining from such acts and given to contemplation.

Arg. 4. Chastity, like other virtues, lies in the mean. Therefore he acts against virtue, who altogether abstains from the gratification of his appetites.

Reply. This objection has been already solved in treating of poverty (Chapp. CXXXII, CXXXV, Arg. 6). Irrational abstinence from all [lawful] sexual pleasures is called the vice of insensibility: but a rational abstinence [from all even lawful forms of such gratification] is a virtue exceeding the common measure of man, for it puts man in some sort of participation of the likeness of God. Hence virginity is said to be allied to angels.

But though we say in general that it is better for one individual to observe continence than to use marriage, it may very well be that for some other individual the second course is the better. Hence the Lord says: Not all men take this word: whoever can take, let him take (Matt. xix, 11, 12).

## CHAPTER CXXXIX—Against those who find fault with Vows

SOME have taken it for a folly to bind oneself by vow to obey another, or to observe any practice: for there is more of virtue in a good act as there is more of freedom: hence the praiseworthiness of virtuous acts seems to be diminished by their being done under necessity of obedience or vow.

But these cavilers seem to be ignorant of the nature of necessity. For there is a twofold necessity: a necessity of constraint, and this diminishes the praiseworthiness of virtuous acts, as telling against their voluntariness: for that is done under constraint, which is contrary to the will. There is again a necessity springing out of interior inclination; and this, far from diminishing, increases the credit of a virtuous act: for it makes the will tend to the act of virtue all the more earnestly. For evidently, the more perfect the habit of virtue is, with all the more force does it urge the will to the act of virtue and leaves it less chance of swerving. Nay, if it attains to the highest pitch of perfection, it induces a sort of necessity of well-doing, as will appear in the case of the Blessed, who cannot sin (B. IV, Chap. XCII); nor yet is there anything thereby lost either to the freedom of the wilt or to the goodness of the act. There is another necessity derived from the bearing of the means on the end in view, as when it is said to be necessary for one to find a ship in order to cross the sea. But neither does this necessity diminish the freedom of the will or the goodness of the acts: nay rather, for one to act as doing something necessary to an end is in itself praiseworthy, and all the more praiseworthy the better the end. But it will be seen that the necessity of observing what one has vowed to observe, or obeying the superior under whom one has placed oneself, is not a necessity of constraint: nor again is it a necessity arising out of interior inclination, but out of the bearing of means on the end: for it is necessary for the votary to do this or that, if the vow is to be fulfilled, or the obedience kept. Since then these are praiseworthy ends, inasmuch as they are acts whereby a man submits himself to God, the aforesaid necessity takes off nothing from the praise of virtue.

From yet another point of view the fulfilment of a vow, or of a superior's commands, for God's sake, is worthy of greater praise or reward. For as one act may be an act of two vices, in that the act of one vice is directed to the end of another vice, e.g., when one steals to commit fornication, in which case the act is specifically one of avarice, but intentionally one of lust,— so in the same way the act of one virtue may be directed to the act of another virtue, as when one gives for charity, in which case the act is specifically one of liberality, but finally one of charity: such an act is more praiseworthy for the greater virtue of charity than for liberality: hence, though the liberality come to fall short, the act will be more praiseworthy, inasmuch as it is referred to charity, and worthy of greater reward, than if it were done with greater liberality, but not in view of charity. Let us suppose then a man doing some act of virtue, say, fasting, or restraining his sexual passion: if he does this without a vow, it will be an act of chastity, or abstinence: but if he does it under a vow, it is further referable to another virtue, that virtue to which it belongs to vow and pay one's vows to God, which is called the virtue of religion, a higher virtue than chastity, or abstinence, as putting us in a right relation with God. The act of abstinence therefore, or continence, will be more praiseworthy inasmuch as it is done under vow, even though the doer of it does not take so much delight in his abstinence, or continence: that deficiency is made up by his taking delight in a higher virtue, which is religion.

If any one does anything for God, he offers the act to God, such as it is: but if he does it under a vow, he offers to God not only the act but also the power: thus he clearly has the intention of rendering to God some greater service. Therefore his act will be the more virtuous by reason of the greater good intended, even though another shows himself more fervent in the execution.

Moreover, the will that goes before a deed, virtually endures throughout the whole course of the doing of it; and renders it praiseworthy, even when the agent in the execution of his work is not thinking of the purpose for which he began: for it is not necessary for him who has undertaken a journey for God's sake, to be actually thinking of God at every step of the journey. But clearly he who has vowed to do a thing has willed it more intensely than another who simply has a purpose of doing it; because he has not only willed to do it, but also has willed to fortify himself against failing to do it. This original earnestness of will renders the fulfilment of the vow, with more or less of earnestness, praiseworthy, even when the will is not actually fixed on the work, or is fixed on it but languidly. Thus what is done under vow is more praiseworthy than what is done without vow, other conditions however being equal.

### CHAPTER CXL—That neither all Good Works nor all Sins are Equal

COUNSELS are not given except of the better good. But in the divine law there are given counsels of poverty and continency: these then are better than the use of matrimony and the possession of temporal estate, which things however are quite consistent with virtuous action.

2. Acts are specified by their objects. The better therefore the object, the more virtuous will be the act according to its species. But the end is better than the means thereto; and in the category of means the better is that which comes nearer to the end. Therefore among human acts that is the best, which tends straight to God, the last end; and after that, an act is better in its species according as its object is nearer to God.

3. Good is in human acts according as they are regulated by reason. But some acts come nearer to reason than others: acts which are acts of reason itself have more of the good of reason in them than the acts of the lower powers commanded by reason.

4. The commandments of the law are best fulfilled by love (Chap. CXXVIII). But one man may do his duty out of greater love than another.

6. The better act is the act of the better virtue. But one virtue is better than another: thus munificence is

better than liberality, and high-souled conduct in a high position (magnanimitas) than decency in a lowly state (moderantia, i.e., μετριότης).

Hence it is said: He who joined his virgin in marriage doth well: but he who joined her not doth better (1 Cor. vii, 38).

By the same reasons it appears that not all sins are equal: for one sin goes wider of the last end than another sin, is a greater perversion of the order of reason, and does greater harm to one's neighbor. Hence it is said: Thou hast done more wicked things than they in all thy ways (Ezech. xvi, 47).

But there may seem to be some reason in the position that all virtuous acts are equal, if we consider that every virtuous act is directed to a final good: hence, if there is the same final good for all virtuous acts, they must all be equally good. — It is to be replied that, though there is one final end of goodness, nevertheless there is a difference of degree in the good things that are referred to that end, some of them being better than others and nigher to the last end. Hence there will be degrees of goodness in the will and its acts according to the diversity of good objects to which the will and its acts are terminated, though the ultimate end be the same.

Or again it may be argued that all sins are equal, because sin in human acts comes solely of overpassing the rule of reason: but he overpasses the rule of reason who swerves from it in a small matter, equally with him who swerves from it in a great one; just as, if a line be drawn, not to be overstepped, it comes to the same thing in court whether the trespasser has overstepped it little or much; or as a boxer is cast, once he has gone outside the limits of the ring, little or much: so then, once a man has overstepped the bounds of reason, the amount of his transgression makes no difference. On careful consideration, however, it appears that in all cases where perfection and goodness consists in a certain conformity to measure, the evil will be the greater, the greater the departure from that due conformity. Thus health consists in a due blending of humors, and beauty in a due proportion of features and limbs, and truth in a conformity of thought or speech to fact. The greater the unevenness of humors, the greater the sickness: the greater the incongruity of features or limbs, the greater the ugliness; and the greater the departure from truth, the greater the falsehood: thus the reckoning is not so false that brings in 5 for 3 as that which brings in 100 for 3. But the good of virtue consists in a certain conformity to measure: for virtue is a mean, according to due limitation under the circumstances, between contrary vices. Wickedness then is greater, the further it is out of this harmony. Nor is transgressing the limits of virtue like transgressing bounds fixed by a court. For virtue being of itself good, the transgression of it is of itself evil; and therefore the greater the departure from virtue, the greater the evil. But the transgression of a limit fixed by a court is not of itself evil, but only accidentally so, inasmuch as it is forbidden. But in these accidental connexions, though the being of one thing at all follows upon another's being at all, it does not follow that the being of the one thing in a higher degree follows upon the other's coming to be in a higher degree. Thus if a white body is musical, it does not follow that the whiter the body, the more musical: but it does follow that if whiteness is distinctive of vision, a stronger whiteness wilt be more distinctive.

    A noteworthy difference between sins is that

between mortal and venial sin. A mortal sin is one that deprives the soul of spiritual life. The essence of spiritual life consists in two things, according to the likeness of natural life. Just as the body lives naturally by its union with the soul, which is the principle of life; and again, quickened by the soul, the body moves of itself, while a dead body either remains immovable, or is moved only by an exterior power: so is man's will alive, when conjoined by a right intention with its last end, which is its object and, as it were, its form; and in thus cleaving by love to God and to its neighbor, it is moved by an interior principle of action. But when a right intention of the last end and love is gone, the soul is, as it were, dead, and no longer moves of itself to do any right actions, but either wholly gives over doing them, or is led to do them only by an exterior principle, to wit, the fear of punishment. Whatever sins therefore stand not with a right intention of the last end and love, are mortal sins: but, so long as these finalities are attended to, any deficiency in point of right order of reason will not be a mortal sin, but venial.

CHAPTER CXLI—That a Man's Acts are punished or rewarded by God

TO him it belongs to punish or reward, to whom it belongs to lay down the law. But it belongs to divine providence to lay down the law for men (Chap. CXIV): therefore also to punish or reward.

2. Whenever there is due order to an end, that order must lead to the end, and departure from that order must shut out the end: for things that are according to an end derive their necessity from the end, in such way that they must be, if the end is to follow, and while they are

without impediment, the end ensues. But God has imposed upon men's acts an order in respect of their final good. If then that order is duly laid down, it must be that they who walk according to it shall gain their final good, that is, be rewarded, and they who depart from that order by sin shall be shut out from their final good, that is, punished.

3. As physical things are subject to the order of divine providence, so also human acts. In regard to both the one and the other the due order may be observed, or it may be transgressed. But there is this difference, that the observation or transgression of the due order lies in the power of the human will, but not in the power of physical things. As then in physical things, when due order is observed in them, there follows of natural necessity their preservation and good, but their destruction and evil when the due and natural order is departed from; so in human things it needs must be that when a man voluntarily observes the order of law by Heaven imposed upon him, he gains good, not of necessity, but by the dispensation of the ruler, — that is to say, he gains reward; and conversely, when the order of law is neglected, he comes to evil, that is to say, is punished.

4. It is part of the perfection of God's goodness to have no part of nature in disorder. Hence we see in the physical world that every evil is part of an orderly arrangement to some good, as the killing of the sheep is the feeding of the wolf. Since then human acts are subject to the order of divine providence as well as physical events, the evil that happens in human acts must lead up in an orderly way to good. But this is most aptly brought about by the punishment of sins: for thus excesses beyond the due amount are embraced under the order of justice,

which restores equality. Man exceeds the due degree and proper amount by preference of his own will to that of God, satisfying himself against the ordinance of God: this inequality is removed by his being compelled to suffer something against his will according to the same ordinance.

6. Divine providence has arranged things so that one shall profit another. But it is most fitting for man to be advanced to his final good as well by the good as by the evil of his fellow man, being excited to do well by seeing well-doers rewarded, and withheld from evil-doing by seeing evil-doers punished. Hence it is said: *I am the Lord thy God . . . . visiting the iniquities of the fathers upon the children . . . . and doing mercy a thousand fold upon them that love me and keep my commandments* (Exod. xx, 5, 6): *Thou wilt render to every one according to his works* (Ps. lxi, 13): *To them who, according to patience in good work, seek glory and honor and incorruption, life everlasting: but to them who . . . . obey not the truth, but give credit to iniquity, wrath and indignation* (Rom. ii, 7, 8).

CHAPTER CXLII—Of the Difference and Order of Punishments

EVIL is the privation of good: hence the order and difference of punishments must be according to the difference and order of good things. The chief good and final end of man is happiness: the higher good for him then is that which comes nearer to this end. Coming nearest to it of all is virtue, and whatever else advances man to good acts leading to happiness: next is a due disposition of reason and of the powers subject to it: after that, soundness of bodily health, which is necessary to unfettered action: lastly, exterior goods, as accessory aids to virtue. The greatest punishment therefore for man will be exclusion from happiness: after that, the privation of virtue, and of any perfection of supernatural (supernaturalium) powers in his soul for doing well: then the disorder of the natural powers of his soul: after that, the harm of his body; and finally the taking away of exterior goods.

But because it belongs to the idea of pain not only that it should be a privation of good, but also that it should be contrary to the will, and not every man's will esteems goods as they really are, but sometimes the privation of the greater good is less contrary to the will, and therefore seems less of a punishment, it so comes about that the majority of men, esteeming sensible and corporeal things more and knowing them better than the good things of the intellect and the spirit, dread corporeal penalties more than spiritual ones: thus in their estimation the order of punishments is the very reverse of that aforesaid. With them, injuries to the body and losses of exterior things make the greatest punishment: but as for disorder of the soul and loss of virtue and forfeiture of the enjoyment of God, in which the final happiness of man consists, all this they count little or nothing. Hence it is that they do not consider the sins of men to be punished by God, because they see usually sinners enjoying good health and the blessings of exterior fortune, of which sometimes virtuous men are deprived. This ought not to appear surprising to persons who look straight at the facts. For since all exterior things are referable to things interior, and the body to the soul, exterior and corporeal good things are really good for man in so far as they turn to the good of reason within him; and turn to his evil so far as they hinder that good of reason. Now God, the disposer of all things, knows the measure of human virtue: hence He sometimes supplies a virtuous man with corporeal and exterior good things to aid his virtue, and does him a favor in so doing: sometimes again He withdraws the aforesaid things, considering them to be an obstacle to man's virtue and enjoyment of God. Where they are such an obstacle, exterior good things turn to a man's prejudice, and the loss of them to his gain. If then punishment in every case means the infliction of some evil, and it is not an evil for a man to be deprived of exterior and corporeal good things so far as is conducive to his advancement in virtue, such deprivation will not be a punishment to a virtuous man: on the other hand a real punishment to the wicked will be the concession to them of exterior goods, whereby they are incited to evil. Hence it is said: *The creatures of God are turned to hate, and to a temptation to the souls of men, and a trap for the feet of the unwise* (Wisd. xiv, 11). But because it is of the notion of punishment not only to be an infliction of evil, but further an evil contrary to the will, the loss of corporeal and exterior goods, even when it makes for advancement in virtue and not for evil, is called punishment by a stretch of language, inasmuch as it is contrary to the will.

CHAPTER CXLIII—*That not all Punishments nor all Rewards are Equal*

AS there are degrees in virtuous actions and in sins (Chap. CXL), so there must be degrees of rewards and punishments: for so the equality of distributive justice requires, that unequal returns be made for unequal services.

Hence it is said: According to the measure of the sin shall also be the measure of the stripes (Deut. xxv, 2).


CHAPTER CXLIV—Of the Punishment due to Mortal and Venial Sins respectively in regard to the Last End

MAN may sin in either of two ways, either so that the intention of his mind be quite turned away from subordination to God, the final good, and that is a mortal sin: or otherwise so that, while the mind's intention remains fixed on the final end, some obstacle is put in the way to retard its free movement to the end, and that is a venial sin. As then the difference of punishments must be according to the difference of sins, it follows that whoever sins mortally must have for his punishment to be cast out from the attainment of his end; but he who sins venially is punished, not by being cast out, but by being retarded or experiencing difficulty in gaining his end; for so the equality of justice is preserved, in that as man, by sinning [venially], voluntarily turns aside from his end, so in suffering punishment, against his will, he should be impeded in the gaining of that end.

3. When any one attains a good thing that he was not intending, that is by luck and chance. If then he whose intention is turned away from the last end were to gain that last end, it would be by luck and chance, — which is an absurd thing to suppose, seeing that the last end is a good of intelligence, and luck and chance are inconsistent with intelligent action, because chance events come about

without the direction of intelligence: it is absurd then to suppose intelligence gaining its end by an unintelligent method. He then will not gain his end, who by sinning mortally has his intention turned away from his last end.

5. In an orderly course of means leading up to an end such a relation obtains that, if the end is or is to be, the means thereto must be: if the means to the end are not forthcoming, neither will the end be forthcoming: for if the end could be secured without the means to the end being taken, it would be labor lost to seek the end by the taking of such means. But it is by arts of virtue, the chief element in which is an intention of the due end, that man attains to his last end and happiness (Chap. CXLI). Whoever then acts against virtue, and turns his back on his last end, it is proper for him to suffer deprivation of that end.

Hence it is said: Depart from me, all ye workers of iniquity (Matt. vii, 23).

CHAPTER CXLV—That the Punishment whereby one is deprived of his Last End is Interminable

THERE is no privation except of that which naturally belongs to the subject: a puppy at birth cannot be said to lie under any privation of sight. But man is not apt to attain his last end in this life (Chap. XLVIII). Therefore any privation of such end must come as a punishment after this life. But after this life there remains to man no ability of gaining his last end, since it is through the body that he gains perfection alike in knowledge and in virtue. And once the soul is separated from the body, it returns not again to this state of receiving perfection from the body, as we have argued above (B. II, Chap. LXXXIII) against the advocates of the transmigration of souls (transcorporationem ponentes). Whoever then incurs this punishment must be deprived of his last end, and remain eternally deprived of it.

3. Natural equity seems to require everyone to be deprived of the good against which he takes action, as thereby he renders himself unworthy of that good. Hence by process of civil justice whoever offends against the commonwealth is deprived of the society of the commonwealth altogether, either by death or by perpetual banishment. Nor is the time taken by his offence considered, but the power against which he has offended. He then who sins against his last end and against charity, which is the foundation of the society of the Blessed and of wayfarers on the road to Blessedness, ought to be punished eternally, though his sin took only a short space of time.

4. In the divine judgement the will is taken for the deed: because as men see what is done outwardly, so does God view the hearts of men. But whoever for the sake of some temporal good has turned himself away from the final end, which is possessed forever, has preferred the temporal enjoyment of that good to the eternal enjoyment of the last end: much more then, it clearly appears, would he have willed the enjoyment of that temporal good for all eternity. Therefore according to the divine judgement he ought to be punished as though he had gone on sinning for eternity. And beyond question, for eternal sin eternal punishment is due.

Hence it is said: These shall go into everlasting punishment, but the just into life everlasting (Matt. xxv, 46).

Hereby is excluded the error of them who say that

the punishment of the wicked will at some time come to an end. This position seems to have had its foundation in the position of certain philosophers who said that all punishments were purgatorial, and consequently at some time terminable. And this position seems plausible, as well by the custom of mankind, for human laws inflict penalties as means and in a manner medicines for the amendment of vices; as also by reason, for if punishment were inflicted, not for the sake of something else, but for its own sake, it would follow that the authority punishing took delight in punishments for their own sake, which is inconsistent with the goodness of God: it needs must be then that punishment is inflicted for the sake of something else, and no more suitable end appears than the amendment of vices. There seems therefore reason for saying that all punishments are purgatorial, and consequently terminable, since whatever is matter of purgation is accidental in regard of the creature, and can be removed without consumption of its substance.

In reply it must be allowed that punishments are inflicted by God, not for their own sake, as though God took delight in them, but for the sake of something else, namely, in view of the order which He wishes to impose on creatures, in which order the good of the universe consists (B. II, Chap. XLV). The order of the universe requires all things to be dispensed by God in due proportion, in weight, number, and measure (Wisd. xi, 21). But as rewards answer proportionably to virtuous actions, so punishments to sins; and to some sins everlasting punishments are proportionable. God then inflicts eternal punishments on some sins, that the due order may be observed in things, which order proves His wisdom.

But even though one were to allow that all punishments are applied to the amendment of vices, and to no other purpose, not on that account are we obliged to suppose that all punishments are purgatorial and terminable. For even by human laws some men are punished by death, not for their amendment, but for the amendment of others: hence it is said: For the scourging of the pestilent man, the fool shall be wiser (Prov. xix, 25). Sometimes also human laws drive men out of the State into perpetual banishment, that the State may be purer by being rid of them: hence it is said: Cast out the scorner, and the quarrel will go out with him, and suits and brow- beatings will cease (Prov. xxii, 10). Even then though punishments be employed only for the reformation of manners, it may very well be that by the judgement of God some men ought to be forever separated from the society of the good and eternally punished, that by the fear of everlasting punishment men may cease to sin, and the society of the good may be the purer for their separation, as it is said: There shall not enter therein anything unclean, or making abomination or lying (Apoc. xxi, 27).

CHAPTER CXLVI—That Sins are punished also by the experience of something Painful

PUNISHMENT ought to be proportionate to the fault. But in a fault not only is there an aversion of the mind from the last end, but also an undue conversion of it to other objects as ends. Not only then should the sinner be punished by exclusion from the end, but also by other things turning to his pain.

2. No one is afraid to lose what he does not desire

to gain. They then who have their will turned away from their last end, have no fear of being shut out from it. Consequently that mere exclusion would not be enough to call them off from sinning. Some other punishment then must be employed, which sinners may fear.

3. One who puts to undue use the means to a certain end, not only is deprived of the end, but incurs some other hurt besides. Thus inordinate taking of food not only does not bring health, but further induces sickness. But whoever sets up his rest in creatures does not use them as he ought: he does not refer them to their last end. Not only then ought he to be punished by going without happiness, but also by experiencing some pain from creatures.

Hence divine Scripture not only threatens sinners with exclusion from glory, but also with affliction in other ways. *Depart from me, ye cursed, into everlasting fire* (Matt. xxv, 41). *He shall rain nets on sinners: fire and brimstone and the breath of stormy winds shall be the portion of their cup* (Ps. x, 7).

CHAPTER CXLVII—That it is Lawful for judges to inflict Punishments

MEN who on earth are set over others are ministers of divine providence. But it is the order of providence that the wicked be punished.

4. Good stands in no need of evil, but the other way about (Chap. XI). Whatever then is of necessity for the preservation of good, cannot be of itself evil. But for the preservation of concord among men it is necessary for penalties to be inflicted on the wicked.

5. The common good is better than the good of the

individual. Therefore some particular good must be withdrawn for the preservation of the common good. But the life of certain pestilent fellows is a hindrance to the common good, that is, to the concord of human society. Such persons therefore are to be withdrawn by death from the society of men.

Hence the Apostle says: He beareth not the sword in vain (Rom. xiii, 4: cf. 1 Pet. ii, 14).

Hereby is excluded the error of those who say that corporal punishments are unlawful, and quote in support of their error such texts as, Thou shalt not kill(Exod. xx, 13): Let both grow until the harvest(Matt. xiii, 30). But these are frivolous allegations. For the same law which says, Thou shalt not kill, adds afterwards: Thou shalt not suffer poisoners (maleficos, φαρμακούς) to live (Exod. xxii, 18). And as for both growing until the harvest, how that is to be understood appears from what follows: lest perchance in gathering the tares ye root out along with them the wheat also: in this passage then the killing of the wicked is forbidden where it cannot be done without danger to the good, as happens when the wicked are not yet clearly marked off from the good by manifest sins, or when there is ground for apprehension that the wicked may involve many good men in their ruin.

The fate of the wicked being open to conversion so long as they live does not preclude their being open also to the just punishment of death. Indeed the danger threatening the community from their life is greater and more certain than the good expected by their conversion. Besides, in the hour of death, they have every facility for turning to God by repentance. And if they are so obstinate that even in the hour of death their heart will not go back upon its wickedness, a fairly probable reckoning may be made that they never would have returned to a better mind.

## CHAPTER CXLVIII—That Man stands in need of Divine Grace for the Gaining of Happiness

IT has already been shown (Chapp. CXI–CXIII) that divine providence disposes of rational creatures otherwise than of other things, inasmuch as their nature stands on a different footing from that of others. It remains to be shown that also in view of the dignity of their end divine providence employs a higher method of government in their regard. Their nature clearly fits them for a higher end. As being intelligent, they can attain to intelligible truth, which other creatures cannot. So far as they attain this truth by their own natural activity, God provides for them otherwise than for other creatures, giving them understanding and reason, and further the gift of speech, whereby they can aid one another in the knowledge of truth. But beyond this, the last end of man is fixed in a certain knowledge of truth which exceeds his natural faculties, so that it is given to him to see the First Truth in itself. To creatures lower than man it is not given to arrive at an end exceeding the capacities of their natures. In view of this end, a method of government must be found for man, different from that which suffices for the lower creation. For the means must be proportionate to the end: if then man is ordained to an end transcending his natural capacities, he must be furnished with some supernatural assistance from heaven, enabling him to tend to that end.

2. A thing of inferior nature cannot be brought to that which is proper to a superior nature except by the virtue and action of the said superior nature. Thus the moon, which has no light of its own, is made luminous by the virtue and action of the sun. But to behold the First Truth as it is in itself so transcends the capacity of human nature as to be proper to God alone (Chap. LII). Therefore man needs help of God to arrive at such an end.

5. There are many impediments in the way of man's arriving at his end. He is impeded by the weakness of his reason, which is easily dragged into error, and so erring he is thrown off the right way of arriving at his end. He is impeded by the passions of the sensitive portion of his nature, and by the tastes which drag him to sensible and inferior things. The more he clings to such things, the further he is separated from his last end: for these things are below man, whereas his end is high above him. He is impeded also very frequently by infirmity of body from the performance of the acts of virtue which carry him on to his end. Man therefore needs the divine assistance, lest with such impediments in his way, he fail altogether in the gaining of his last end.

Hence it is said: No man can come to me, unless the Father, who hath sent me, draw him (John vi, 44): As the branch cannot bear fruit of itself unless it abide in the vine, so neither can ye unless ye abide in me (John xv, 4).

Hereby is excluded the error of the Pelagians, who said that man could merit the glory of God by sheer free will of his own.

CHAPTER CXLIV—That the Divine Assistance does not compel a Man to Virtue

DIVINE providence provides for all things according to their mode of existence (Chap. LXXIII, n. 2). But it is proper to man and to every rational creature to act voluntarily and to be master of his own acts; and compulsion is contrary to voluntariness.

3. It is by will that man is directed to a final end: for the good and the final end is the object of will. And the divine assistance is vouchsafed us for this special purpose, that we may attain to our final end. That aid therefore does not exclude the act of our will: on the contrary, it is precisely the act of our will that the divine assistance produces in us: hence the Apostle says: It is God who worked in us both to will and to act according to the good will (Phil. ii, 13). But compulsion defeats in us the act of the will: for we do that under compulsion of which we will the contrary.

4. Man arrives at his last end by acts of virtue. But acts done under compulsion are not acts of virtue, for in virtue the chief thing is choice.

Hence it is said: Consider that to-day the Lord hath put forth in thy sight life and good, and on the other hand death and evil, that thou mayest love the Lord thy God and walk in his ways. But f thy heart is turned away, and thou wilt not hear, etc. (Deut. xxx, 15-18): Before man is life and death, good and evil: what pleases him shall be given to him (Ecclus xv, 18).

CHAPTER CL—*That Man cannot Merit beforehand the said Assistance*

EVERYTHING stands as matter to that which is above itself. Now matter does not move itself to its own perfection, but must be moved by another. Man then does not move himself to the gaining of the divine assistance, which is above him, but rather he is moved by God to the gaining of it. But the motion of the mover precedes the motion of the thing moved, alike in the order of thought and in the order of causation. The divine assistance therefore is not given to us because we are advanced to receive it by our good works; but rather we are proficient in good works because we are forestalled by the divine assistance.

Hence it is said: Not by the works of justice that we have done, but according to his own mercy he hath saved us (Tit. iii, 5): It is not of him that willed, nor of him that runneth, but of God that showed mercy (Rom. ix, 16): because man needs must be forestalled by the divine assistance for purposes both of willing well and doing well. As the victory is attributed to the general, which is won by the labor of the soldiers, so such expressions as the above are not to be taken as exclusive of the free choice of the will, according to the misconstruction which some have put upon them, as though man were not master of his own acts, interior and exterior, but they show that man is under God. Again it is said: Turn us, O Lord, to thee, and we shall be turned (Lament. v, 21): which shows that our turning, or conversion, is anticipated by the aid of God converting us. Still we read, as spoken in the person of God: Turn ye to me, and I will turn to you (Zach. i, 3); not that the work of God in us does not go before our conversion; but the meaning is that the conversion, whereby we turn to God, is aided also by His subsequent aid, strengthening it to arrive to effect, and securing it that it may reach its due term.

Hereby is excluded the error of the Pelagians, who

said that the divine assistance is given us in consideration of our deservings; and that, while the beginning of our justification is of ourselves, the consummation of it is of God.

CHAPTER CLI—That the aforesaid Assistance is called 'Grace,' and what is the meaning of 'Grace constituting a State of Grace'

BECAUSE what is given to another without any previous deserts of his is said to be given gratis, and because the divine aid given to man anticipates all human deserving, it follows that this aid is given to man gratis, and therefore is aptly called by the name of 'grace.' Hence the Apostle says: If by grace, it is not now of works, otherwise grace is no more grace (Rom. xi, 6).

There is also another reason why the aforesaid assistance of God has received the name of 'grace.' One person is said to be 'in the good graces' of another, because he is well loved by him. Now it is of the essence of love that he who loves should wish good and do good to him whom he loves. God indeed wishes and does good to all His creatures, for the very being of the creature and its every perfection is of God willing and working it (B. I, Chapp. XXIX, XXX: B. II, Chap. XV): hence it is said: Thou loves all things that are, and hates none of the things that thou hast made (Wisd. xi, 25). But a special tie of divine love is observable in connexion with those to whom He renders assistance, enabling them to attain the good which transcends the order of their nature, namely, the perfect fruition, not of any created good, but of God's own self. This assistance then is aptly called 'grace,' not only because it is given 'gratis,' but also because by this assistance a man comes to be, by a special prerogative, 'in the good graces' of God.

This grace, in the man in the state of grace, must be a form and perfection of him who has it.

1. That whereby a man is directed to an end must be in continual relation with him: for the mover works change continually until the body moved attains the term of its motion. Since then man is directed to his last end by the assistance of divine grace, he must continually enjoy this assistance until he arrives at the end. But that would not be if the assistance were afforded him only as a sort of motion or passion, and not as a form abiding and, as it were, resting in him: for the movement and passion would not be in the man, except when his attention was being actually turned to the end, as is not the case continually, which is evident most of all in men asleep. Therefore the grace that puts a man in the state of grace is a form and perfection abiding in man, even when he is not actively engaged.

2. The love of God is causative of the good that is in us, as the love of man is called forth and caused by some good that is in the object of his love. But man is excited to special love by some special good pre-existent in the object. Therefore where there is posited a special love of God for man, there must consequently be posited some special good conferred by God on man. Since then the grace that constitutes the State of grace denotes a special love of God for man, there must be likewise denoted some special goodness and perfection thereby existing in man.

3. Everything is ordained to an end suited to it according to the character of its form: for of different

species there are different ends. But the end to which man is directed by the assistance of divine grace is something above human nature. Therefore there must be superadded to man some supernatural form and perfection, whereby he may be aptly ordained to the aforesaid end.

4. Man ought to arrive at his last end by dint of activities of his own. Now everything is active in virtue of some form of its own. In order then that man may be brought to his last end by activities of his own, there must be superadded to him some form, to validate his activities for the gaining of his last end.

5. Divine providence provides for all according to the mode of their nature. But it is a mode proper to man to require for the perfection of his actions, over and above his natural powers, certain perfections in the shape of habits, whereby he may do good, and do it well, connaturally, readily, and pleasantly. Therefore the aid of grace, given man by God for arriving at his last end, implies some form and perfection intrinsic to man.

Hence in Scripture the grace of God is spoken of as light: Ye were once darkness, but now light in the Lord (Eph. v, 8). The perfection whereby man is led on to his final end in the vision of God is appropriately termed light, light being the principle of vision.

Hereby is set aside the opinion of some who say that the grace of God is no positive quality in man (nihil in homine ponit), as no positive quality is ascribed to the courtier who is said to be in the good graces of the King, but rather to the King who has an affection for him. We see how this mistake arose, from failing to observe the difference between divine love and human love: for divine love is causative of the good that it loves in another, but not so human love.

## CHAPTER CLII—That the Grace which constitutes the State of Grace causes in us the Love of God

THE grace which constitutes the state of grace is an effect of God's love. But the proper effect of God's love in man is to make man love God: for the chief effort of the lover is laid out in drawing the beloved to the love of him; and unless that succeeds, the love must be broken off.

2. There must be some union between those who have one end in view, as citizens in one State, and soldiers ranked together on the battlefield. But the final end to which man is led by the assistance of divine grace is the vision of God as He essentially is, which is proper to God Himself; and so God shares this final good with man. Man then cannot be led on to this end unless he is united with God by conformity of will, the proper effect of love: for it belongs to friends to like and dislike together, and to rejoice and grieve together. The grace then that constitutes the state of grace renders man a lover of God, as he is thereby guided to an end shared with him by God.

3. The grace that constitutes the state of grace must principally perfect the heart. But the principal perfection of the heart is love. The proof of that is, that every motion of the heart starts from love: for no one desires, or hopes, or rejoices, except for some good that he loves; nor loathes, nor fears, nor is sad, or angry, except about something contrary to the good that he loves.

4. The form whereby a thing is referred to any end assimilates that thing in a manner to the end: thus a body

by the form of heaviness acquires a likeness and conformity to the place to which it naturally moves. But the grace that constitutes the state of grace is a form referring man to his last end, God. By grace then man attains to a likeness of God. And likeness is a cause of love.

5. A requisite of perfect work is that the work be done steadily and regularly. That is just the effect of love, which makes even hard and grievous tasks seem light. Since then the grace that constitutes the state of grace goes to perfect our works, the said grace must establish the love of God within us.

Hence the Apostle says: The charity of God is spread abroad in our hearts by the Holy Ghost who is given to us (Rom. v, 5).

CHAPTER CLIII—That Divine Grace causes in us Faith

THE movement of grace, guiding us to our last end, is voluntary, not violent (Chap. CXLIX). But there can be no voluntary movement towards an object unless the object be known. Therefore grace must afford us a knowledge of our last end. But such knowledge cannot be by open vision in our present state (Chap. XLVIII): therefore it must be by faith.

2. In every knowing mind, the mode of knowledge follows the mode of nature: hence an angel, a man, and a dumb animal have different modes of knowledge according to their differences of natures. But, for the gaining of his last end, man has a perfection superadded to him, over and above his nature, namely, grace. Therefore there must also be superadded to him a

knowledge, over and above his natural knowledge, and that is the knowledge of faith, which is of things not discerned by natural reason.

3. As when wood is first warmed by fire, the fire does not take kindly to the wood; but finally, when the wood is all ablaze, the fire becomes as it were connatural to the wood and a part of its very being: or as when a pupil is taught by a master, he must, to start with, take in the ideas of the master, not as understanding them of himself, but in the spirit of one ready to accept on another's word things beyond his capacity; and so in the end, when his education is advanced, he will be able to understand those things: in like manner, before we arrive at our final end, which is the clear vision of the First Truth as it is in itself, the intellect of man must submit to God in readiness to take His word; and that submission and readiness to believe is the work of divine grace.

4. See further, B. I, Chapp. IV, V.

Hence the Apostle says: *By grace ye are saved through faith; and that not of yourselves, for it is the gift of God* (Eph. ii, 8).

Hereby is refuted the error of the Pelagians, who said that the beginning of faith in us was not of God, but of ourselves.

CHAPTER CLIV—*That Divine Grace causes in us a Hope of future Blessedness*

IN every lover there is caused a desire of union with his loved one, so far as may be: hence it is most delightful to live in the society of those whom one loves. As then by grace man is made a lover of God, there must be caused in him a desire of union with God, so far as may be. But faith, which is caused of grace, declares the possibility of a union of man with God in perfect fruition, wherein blessedness consists. Consequently the desire of this fruition follows upon the love of God. But desire is a troublesome thing, without hope of attainment. It was proper therefore that in men, in whom the love of God and faith in Him was caused by grace, there should be caused also the hope of attaining to future blessedness.

3. Virtue, the way to blessedness, is paved with difficulties: hence the need of hope.

4. No one stirs to reach an end, which he reckons it impossible to compass.

Hence it is said: *He hath regenerated us unto a living hope* (1 Pet. i, 3): *In hope we are saved* (Rom. viii, 24).

## CHAPTER CLV—Of Graces given gratuitously

SINCE the things done by God are done in order (Chapp. LXXVII–LXXX), a certain order had to be followed in the manifestation of the truths of faith, so that some should receive those truths immediately from God, others receive of them, and so in order even to the last. The invisible good things, the vision of which makes the happiness of the blessed, and which are the objects of faith, are first revealed by God to the blessed angels by open vision: then by the ministry of angels they are manifested by God to certain men, not by open vision, but by a certitude arising from divine revelation. This revelation is made by an inner light of the mind, elevating the mind to see such things as the natural light of the understanding cannot attain to. As the natural light of the understanding renders a man certain of what he observes by that light, so does this supernatural light convey certainty of the objects which it reveals: for we cannot securely publish to others what we are not certain of ourselves. This light, which inwardly enlightens the mind, is sometimes borne out by other aids to knowledge, as well exterior as interior. There may be formed by divine power some utterance, or locution, heard by the external senses. Or it may be an inner locution, caused by God, and perceived by phantasy. Or there may be bodily appearances, external and visible, formed by God. Or such corporeal appearance may be inwardly depicted in phantasy. By these means, aided by the light inwardly impressed on his mind, man receives a knowledge of divine things. Hence, without the inner light, these aids are insufficient for the knowledge of divine things; whereas the inner light is sufficient of itself without them.

Now because those who receive a revelation from God ought in the order of divine enactment to instruct others, there needed to be further communicated to them the grace of speech. Hence it is said: The Lord hath given me a learned tongue (Isai. l, 4): I will give you speech and wisdom, which all your adversaries shall not be able to withstand and gainsay (Luke xxi, 15). Hence also the gift of tongues (Acts ii, 4).

But because any announcement put forth requires confirmation before it can be received, — unless indeed it is self-evident, and the truths of faith are not evident to human reason, — there was need of something to confirm the announcements of the preachers of the faith. But, inasmuch as they transcend reason, they could not be confirmed by any demonstrative process of reasoning from first principles. The means therefore to show that the announcements of these preachers came from God was the evidence of works done by them such as none other than God could do, healing the sick, and other miracles. Hence the Lord, sending his disciples to preach, said: Heal the sick, raise the dead, cleanse lepers, cast out devils (Matt. x, 8); and, They going forth preached everywhere, the Lord working withal, and confirming their words by the signs that followed.

In the aforesaid effects of grace we observe a certain difference. Though the name of 'grace' applies to them all, inasmuch as they are given 'gratuitously' without any preceding merit, nevertheless the working of love alone has a further claim to the name of 'grace,' as constituting the subject in 'the state of grace,' or in 'the good graces of God' (gratum Deo facit): for it is said: I love them that love me (Prov. viii, 17). Hence faith and hope and other means to the last end may be in sinners, who are not in the grace of God: love alone is the proper gift of the just, because he who abides in charity abides in God, and God in him (1 John iv, 16).

There is another difference to be observed in these workings of grace, and it is this, that some of them are necessary for a whole lifetime, as believing, hoping, loving, and obeying the commandments of God, without which things salvation is impossible; and for these effects there must be in man certain habitual perfections, that he may be able to act according to them as occasion requires.342Other effects of grace are necessary, not for a whole lifetime, but at certain times and places, as working of miracles, or foretelling of future events. To these effects habitual perfections are not given, but certain impressions are made by God, which cease when the act ceases, and have to be repeated when the act is repeated. Thus prophets in every revelation are illumined with a new light; and in every working of miracles there must be a fresh putting into operation of divine power.

## CHAPTER CLVI—That Man needs the Assistance of Divine Grace to persevere in Good

THE power of free will regards matters of election: but a matter of election is some particular thing to be done; and a particular thing to be done is what is here and now: but perseverance is not a matter of present and immediate conduct, but a continuance of activity for all time: perseverance therefore is an effect above the power of free will, and therefore needing the assistance of divine grace.

3. Though man is master of his act, he is not master of his natural powers; and therefore, though he is free to will or not will a thing, still his willing cannot make his will in the act of willing adhere immovably to the thing willed or chosen. But the immovable adherence of the will to good is requisite for perseverance: perseverance therefore is not in the power of free will.

Hence it is said: He who hath begun a good work in you will perfect it unto the day of Christ Jesus(Philip. i, 6): The God of all grace, who hath called us to his eternal glory in Christ Jesus, himself will perfect us through some little suffering, confirm and establish us(1 Pet. v, 10). There are also found in Holy Scripture many prayers for perseverance: e.g., Perfect my steps in thy ways, that my footsteps may not slip (Ps. xvi, 5); and especially that petition of the Lord's Prayer, Thy kingdom come: for the kingdom will not come for us unless we persevere in good.

Hereby is refuted the error of the Pelagians, who said that free will is sufficient for man for his perseverance in good, and that there is no need of the assistance of grace for the purpose.

As free will is not sufficient for perseverance in good without the help of God given from without, so neither is any infused habit. For in the state of our present life the habits infused into us of God do not totally take away from our free will its fickleness and liability to evil, although they do to some extent establish the free will in good. And therefore, when we say that man needs the aid of grace for final perseverance, we do not mean that, over and above the habitual grace first infused into him for the doing of good acts, there is infused into him another habitual grace enabling him to persevere; but we mean that, when he has got all the gratuitous habits that he ever is to have, man still needs some aid of divine providence governing him from without.

CHAPTER CLVII—That he who falls from Grace by Sin may be recovered again by Grace

IT belongs to the same power to continue and to repair after interruption, as is the case with the powers of nature in regard of bodily health. But man perseveres in good by the aid of divine grace: therefore, if he has fallen by sin, he may be recovered by help of the same grace.

2. An agent that requires no predisposition of its subject, can imprint its effect on its subject, howsoever disposed. But God, requiring no predisposition of the subject of His action, when the subject is corporeal, — as

when He gives sight to the blind, or raises the dead to life, — does not require any previous merit either in the will for the conferring of His grace, which is given without merits (Chap. CXLIX). Therefore even after a man has fallen from grace by sin, God can confer on him the grace that puts the recipient in the state of grace, whereby sins are taken away.

5. In the works of God there is nothing in vain, as neither in the works of nature, for nature has this prerogative of God. Now it would be in vain for anything to move with no chance of arriving at its term. Whatever naturally moves to a certain end, must be somehow competent to get there. But after a man has fallen into sin, so long as the state of this life lasts, there remains in him an aptitude of being moved to good, shown by such signs as desire of good and grief at evil. Therefore there is some possibility of his return to good.

6. There exists in nature no potentiality, which cannot be reduced to act by some natural active power. Much less is there in the human soul any potentiality, which is not reducible to act by the active power of God. But even after sin there still remains in the human soul a potentiality of good, because the natural powers, whereby the soul is related to its proper good, are not taken away by sin.

Therefore it is said: Though your sins be as scarlet, they shall be made white as Snow (Isai. i, 18): Charity covered all sins (Prov. x, 12). Nor do we ask of the Lord in vain, Forgive us our trespasses.

Hereby is refuted the error of the Novatians, who said that man cannot obtain pardon for sins committed after baptism.

## CHAPTER CLVIII—That Man cannot be delivered from Sin except by Grace

BY mortal sin man is turned away from his last end. And to that last end he is set on his way only by grace.

2. Offence is removed only by love. But by mortal sin man quarrels with God: for it is said that God 'hates' sinners, inasmuch as He is minded to deprive them of the last end, which He has in preparation for them who love Him. Man then cannot rise from sin except by grace, whereby friendship is established between God and man.

Hence it is said: It is I who blot out thine iniquities for my own sake (Isai. xliii, 25).

Hereby is refuted the error of the Pelagians, who said that man can rise from sin by free will.

## CHAPTER CLIX—How Man is delivered from Sin

BECAUSE man cannot return to one opposite without retiring from the other, to return to the state of righteousness he must withdraw from sin, whereby he had declined from righteousness. And because it is chiefly by the will that man is set on the way to his last end, or turned away therefrom, he must not only withdraw from sin in exterior act by ceasing to sin, but he must further withdraw in will, that so he may rise again by grace. Now withdrawal of the will from sin means at once repentance for the past and a resolution to avoid sin in future. For if a man did not purpose to cease from sin, sin as it is in itself (or sin in general) would not be contrary to his will. If he were minded to cease from sin, but had no sorrow for sin past, that same particular sin of which he was guilty would not be against his will. Now the will must withdraw from sin by taking the course contrary to that which led it into sin. But it was led into sin by appetite and delight in inferior things. Therefore it must withdraw from sin by certain penal inflictions. As delight drew it to consent to sin, so these inflictions strengthen it in abomination of sin.

When then man by grace has obtained pardon for his sin and has been restored to the state of grace, he still remains bound by God's justice to some punishment for his sin. If of his own will he exacts this punishment of himself, he is thereby said to 'make satisfaction' to God, inasmuch as by punishing himself for his sin he fulfils with labor and pain the order instituted of heaven, which order he had transgressed by sinning and following his own will. But if he does not exact this punishment of himself it will be inflicted by God, since the domain of divine providence cannot be suffered to lie in disorder. The punishment in that case will not be called 'satisfactory,' since it will not be of the choice of the sufferer, but it will be called 'purificatory,' or 'purgatorial,' because he will be purified and purged by another punishing him; and so whatever was inordinate in him will be brought back to due order. Hence the Apostle says: If we were to judge ourselves, we should not be judged: but while we are judged, we are chastised by the Lord, that we may not be condemned with this world (1 Cor. xi, 31).

Nevertheless, in the process of conversion, the disgust for sin and the fixing of the affections on God may be so intense as that there shall remain no outstanding liability to punishment. For the punishment which one suffers after the forgiveness of sin is necessary to bring the mind to cleave more firmly to good, — punishments being medicines, — as also for the observance of the order of justice in the punishment of the sinner. But love of God, especially when it is vehement and strong, is sufficient to establish man's mind in good; and intense disgust for a past fault carries with it great sorrow for the same. Hence by the vehemence of the love of God and hatred for sin there is excluded any further need of satisfactory or purgatorial punishment. And though the vehemence be not so great as totally to bar the punishment, nevertheless, the greater the vehemence, so much less of punishment will suffice.

But what we do through our friends we are reckoned to do of ourselves, inasmuch as friendship makes two one in heart, and this is especially true of the love of charity: therefore, as a man may make satisfaction to God of himself, so also may he do it through another, especially in case of necessity: for the punishment which his friend suffers on his account he reckons as his own punishment; and thus punishment is not wanting to him in that he has compassion for the sufferings of his friend, and that all the more for his being the cause of his friend's suffering. And again the affection of charity in him who suffers for his friend makes his satisfaction more acceptable to God than it would be if he were suffering for his own doings: for the one is an effort of spontaneous charity, the other an acquiescence in necessity. Hence we learn that one man may make satisfaction for another, provided both of them be in charity. Hence the saying of the Apostle: Bear you one another's burdens, and so ye shall fulfil the law of Christ (Gal. vi, 2).

CHAPTER CLX—That it is reasonably reckoned a Man's own Fault if he be not converted to God, although he cannot be converted without Grace

SINCE no one can be set on the way to his last end without the aid of divine grace, or without it have the necessary means of reaching that end, as are faith, hope, love and perseverance, some might think that man is not to blame for being destitute of these gifts, especially seeing that he cannot merit the assistance of divine grace, nor be converted to God unless God convert him: for none is responsible for that which depends on another. But allow this, and many absurdities follow. It follows that the man who has neither faith nor hope nor love of God, nor perseverance in good, still does not deserve punishment: whereas it is expressly said: He that believeth not the Son shall not see life, but the wrath of God abides on him (John iii, 36). And since none reaches the end of happiness without the aforesaid endowments, it would follow further that there are some who neither attain to happiness nor yet suffer punishment of God: the contrary whereof is shown from what will be said to all present at the judgement of God: Come .... possess ye the kingdom prepared for you, or, Depart .... into everlasting fire(Matt. xxv, 34-41).

To solve this doubt, we must observe that though one can neither merit divine grace beforehand, nor acquire it by movement of his free will, still he can hinder himself from receiving it: for it is said of some: They have said unto God, 'Depart from us, we will not have the knowledge of thy ways'(Job xxi, 14). And since it is in the power of free will to hinder the reception of divine grace or not to hinder it, not undeservedly may it be reckoned a man's own fault, if he puts an obstacle in the way of the reception of grace. For God on His part is ready to give grace to all men: He wills all men to be saved and to come to the knowledge of the truth (1 Tim. ii, 4). But they alone are deprived of grace, who in themselves raise an obstacle to grace. So when the sun lights up the world, any evil that comes to a man who shuts his eyes is counted his own fault, although he could not see unless the sunlight first came in upon him.

CHAPTER CLXI—That a Man already in Mortal Sin cannot avoid more Mortal Sin without Grace354

WHEN it is said that it is in the power of free will to avoid putting obstacles to grace, that saying is to be understood of those in whom the natural faculty is unimpaired by sin. But if the will has fallen into evil courses by some previous inordinate act, it will not be altogether in its power to avoid putting obstacles in the way of grace. For though for some momentary occasion it may abstain from some particular act of sin by its own power, nevertheless, if left long to itself, it will fall into sin; and by sin an obstacle is put to grace. For when the mind of man turns aside from the state of righteousness, it clearly puts itself out of relation with its due end. Thus what ought to be the prime object of its affections, as being its last end, comes to be less loved than that other object to which it has inordinately turned, making of it another last end. Whatever in such a posture of the mind occurs to fit in with the inordinate end, however inconsistent with the due end, will be chosen, unless the will be brought back to due order, so as to prefer the due end to all others, and that is an effect of grace. But the choice of anything inconsistent with the last end puts an obstacle in the way of grace, as grace goes to turn one in the direction of the end. Hence after sin a man cannot abstain from all further sin before by grace he is brought back to due order.

Moreover, when the mind is inclined to a thing, it is no longer impartial between two alternatives. And that to which the mind is more inclined it chooses, unless by a rational discussion, not unattended with trouble, it is withdrawn from taking that side: hence sudden emergencies afford the best sign of the inward bent of the mind. But it is impossible for the mind of man to be so continually watchful as rationally to discuss whatever it ought to do or not to do. Consequently the mind will at times choose that to which it is inclined by the present inclination: so, if the inclination be to sin, it will not stand long clear of sin, thereby putting an obstacle in the way of grace, unless it be brought back to the state of righteousness.

Further we must consider the assaults of passion, the allurements of sense, the endless occasions of evil-doing, the ready incitements of sin, sure to prevail, unless the will be withheld from them by a firm adherence to the last end, which is the work of grace.

Hence appears the folly of the Pelagian view, that a man in sin can go on avoiding further sins without grace. On the contrary the Lord bids us pray: Lead us not into temptation, but deliver us from evil.

But though persons in sin cannot of their own power help putting obstacles in the way of grace, unless they be forestalled by some aid of grace, still this lack of power is imputable to them for a fault, because it is left behind in them by a fault going before; as a drunken man is not excused from murder, committed in drunkenness, when he gets drunk by fault of his own. Besides, though this person in sin has it not in his unaided power altogether to avoid sin, still he has power here and now to avoid this or that sin: hence whatever he commits, he voluntarily commits, and the fault is imputed to him not undeservedly.

CHAPTER CLXII—That some Men God delivers from Sin, and some He leaves in Sin

THOUGH the sinner raises an obstacle to grace, and by the exigence of the order of things ought not to receive grace, nevertheless, inasmuch as God can work setting aside the connatural order of things, as when He gives sight to the blind, or raises the dead, He sometimes out of the abundance of His goodness forestalls by the assistance of His grace even those who raise an obstacle to it, turning them away from evil and converting them to good. And as He does not give sight to all the blind, nor heal all the sick, that in those whom He heals the work of His power may appear, and in the others the order of nature may be observed, so He does not forestall by His aid all who hinder grace, to their turning away from evil and conversion to good, but some He so forestalls, wishing in them His mercy to appear, while in others He would have the order of justice made manifest. Hence the Apostle says: God, though willing to show his wrath, and to make his power known, endured with much longsuffering vessels of wrath, fitted for destruction, that he might show forth the riches of his glory upon the vessels of mercy, which he hath prepared unto glory(Rom. ix, 22, 23).

But when, of men who are enthralled in the same sins, God forestalls and converts some, and endures, or permits, others to go their way according to the order of things, we should not enquire the reason why He converts these and not those: for that depends on His sheer will, just as from His sheer will it proceeded that, when all things were made out of nothing, some things were made in a position of greater advantage than others (digniora). Hence again the apostle says: Hath not the potter power over the clay, to make of the same lump one vessel unto honor and another unto dishonor? (Rom. ix, 21.)

Hereby is refuted the error of Origen, who said that the reason why some were converted to God, and not others, was to be sought in divers works that their souls had done before they were united with their bodies, a theory already set aside (B. II, Chapp. XLIV, LXXXIII).

## CHAPTER CLXIII—That God is Cause of Sin to no Man

THOUGH there are some sinners whom God does not convert to Himself, but leaves them in their sins according to their deserts, still He does not induce them to sin.

1. Men sin by deviating from God their last end. But as every agent acts to its own proper and befitting end, it is impossible for God's action to avert any from their ultimate end in God.

2. Good cannot be the cause of evil, nor God the cause of sin.

3. All the wisdom and goodness of man is derived from the wisdom and goodness of God, being a likeness

thereof. But it is repugnant to the wisdom and goodness of man to make any one to sin: therefore much more to divine wisdom and goodness.

4. A fault always arises from some defect of the proximate agent, not from any defect of the prime agent. Thus the fault of limping comes from some defect of the shin-bone, not from the locomotor power, from which power however is whatever perfection of movement appears in the limping. But the proximate agent of human sin is the will. The sinful defect then is from the will of man, not from God, who is the prime agent, of whom however is whatever point of perfect action appears in the act of sin.

Hence it is said: *Say not, He himself hath led me astray: for he hath no use for sinful men: He hath commanded none to do impiously, and he hath not given to any man license to sin* (Ecclus xv, 12, 21): *Let none, when he is tempted, say that he is tempted by God: for God tempted no man to evil* (James i, 13).

Still there are passages of Scripture, from which it might seem that God is to some men the cause of sin. Thus it is said: *I have hardened the heart of Pharaoh and his servants*(Exod. x, 1): *Blind the heart of this people, and make its ears dull, and close its eyes, lest perchance it see with its eyes, and be converted, and I heal it: Thou hast made us wander from thy ways: Thou hast hardened our heart, that we should not fear thee*(Isai. vi, 10: lxiii, 17): *God delivered them over to a reprobate sense, to do those things which are not seemly*(Rom. i, 28). All these passages are to be understood as meaning that God does not bestow on some the help for avoiding sin which He bestows on others. This help is not merely the infusion of grace, but also an exterior guardianship, whereby the occasions of sin are providentially removed from a man's path. God also aids man against sin by the natural light of reason, and other natural goods that He bestows on man. When then He withdraws these aids from some, as their conduct deserves that he should, according to the exigency of His justice, He is said to harden them, or to blind them.

## CHAPTER CLXIV—Of Predestination, Reprobation, and Divine Election

SINCE it has been shown that by the action of God some are guided to their last end with the aid of grace, while others, bereft of that same aid of grace, fall away from their last end; and at the same time all things that are done by God are from eternity foreseen and ordained by His wisdom, as has also been shown, it needs must be that the aforesaid distinction of men has been from eternity ordained of God. Inasmuch therefore as He has from eternity pre-ordained some to be guided to the last end, He is said to have 'predestined' them. Hence the Apostle says: Who hath predestined us to the adoption of sons, according to the purpose of his will (Eph. i, 5). But those to whom from eternity He has arranged not to give grace, He is said to have 'reprobated,' or 'hated,' according to the text: I have loved Jacob, and hated Esau (Malach. i, 2). In point of this distinction, inasmuch as some He has reprobated and some He has predestined, we speak of the divine 'election,' of which it is said: He hath elected us in him before the constitution of the world(Eph. i, 4). Thus it appears that predestination and election and reprobation is a part of divine providence, according as by the said providence men are guided to their last end. And it may be shown that predestination and election do not induce necessity, by the same arguments whereby it was shown that divine providence does not take away contingency from creation (Chap. LXXII).

But that predestination and election have no cause in any human merits may be shown, not only by the fact that the grace of God, an effect of predestination, is not preceded by any merits, but precedes all merit, but also by this further fact, that the divine will and providence is the first cause of all things that are made. Nothing can be cause of the will and providence of God; although of the effects of providence, and of the effects of predestination, one effect may be cause of another. *For who hath first given to him, and recompense shall be made him? For if him and by him and in him are all things: to him be glory forever, Amen* (Rom. xi, 35, 36).

## BOOK IV
## OF GOD IN HIS REVELATION

### CHAPTER I—Preface1

LO, *these things that have been said are but a part of his ways; and whereas we have heard scarce one little drop of his speech, who shall be able to look upon the thunder of his greatness?* (Job xxvi, 14.) It is the nature of the human mind to gather its knowledge from sensible things; nor can it of itself arrive at the direct vision of the divine substance, as that substance is in itself raised above all sensible things and all other beings to boot, and beyond all proportion with them. But because the perfect good of man consists in his knowing God in such way as he can, there is given man a way of ascending to the knowledge of God, to the end that so noble a creature should not seem to exist altogether in vain, unable to attain the proper end of his existence. The way is this, that as all the perfections of creatures descend in order from God, who is the height of perfection, man should begin from the lower creatures, and ascend by degrees, and so advance to the knowledge of God. Of this descent of perfections from God there are two processes. One is on the part of the first origin of things: for the divine wisdom, to make things perfect, produced them in order that the universe might consist of a complete round of creatures from highest to lowest. The other process belongs to the things themselves: for, as causes are nobler than effects, the first and highest products of causation, while falling short of the First Cause, which is God, nevertheless are superior to the effects which they themselves produce; and so on in order, until we come to the lowest of creatures. And because in that 'roof and crown of all things' (summo rerum vertice), God, we find the most perfect unity; and everything is stronger and more excellent, the more thoroughly it is one; it follows that diversity and variety increase in things, the further they are removed from Him who is the first principle of all. Therefore the process of derivation of creatures from their first principle may be represented by a sort of pyramid, with unity at the apex, and the widest multiplicity at the base. And thus in the diversity of things there is apparent a diversity of ways, beginning from one principle and terminating in different terms. By these ways then our understanding can ascend to God.

But the weakness of our understanding prevents us from knowing these ways perfectly. Our knowledge begins with sense; and sense is concerned with exterior accidents (phenomena), which are of themselves sensible, as color, smell, and the like. With difficulty can our mind penetrate through such exterior phenomena to an inner knowledge of things, even where it perfectly grasps by sense their accidents. Much less will it be able to attain to a comprehension of the natures of those objects of which we perceive only a few phenomena by sense; and still less of those natures no accidents of which lie open to sense, but certain effects which they produce, inadequate to their power, enable us to recognize them. But even though the very natures of things were known to us, still we should have but slight knowledge of their order, of their mutual relations, and direction by divine providence to their final end, since we cannot penetrate the plan of Providence. The ways themselves then being so imperfectly known to us, how shall we travel by them to any perfect knowledge of the First Beginning of all things, which transcends all created ways and is out of all proportion with them? Even though we knew the said ways perfectly, we should still fall short of perfect knowledge of their origin and starting-point.

Feeble and inadequate then being any knowledge to which man could arrive by these ways, God has revealed to men facts about Himself which surpass human understanding; in which revelation there is observed an order of gradual transition from imperfect to perfect. In man's present state, in which his understanding is tied to sense, his mind cannot possibly be elevated to any clear discernment of truths that surpass all proportions of sense: in that state the revelation is given him, not to be understood, but to be heard and believed. Only when he is delivered from the thralldom of sensible things, will he be elevated to an intuition of revealed truth. Thus there is a threefold knowledge that man may have of divine things. The first is an ascent through creatures to the knowledge of God by the natural light of reason. The second is a descent of divine truth by revelation to us; truth exceeding human understanding; truth accepted, not as demonstrated to sight, but as orally delivered for belief. The third is an elevation of the human mind to a perfect insight into things revealed.

This triple knowledge is suggested by the text above quoted from Job. These things that have been said are but a part of his ways, applies to that knowledge whereby our understanding ascends by way of creatures to a knowledge of God. And because we know these ways but imperfectly, that is rightly put in, but a part, for we know in part (1 Cor. xiii, 9). The next clause, and whereas we have heard scarce one little drop of his speech, refers to the second knowledge, whereby divine truths are revealed for our belief by means of oral declaration: for faith is hearing, and hearing by the word of Christ (Rom. x, 17). And because this imperfect knowledge is an effluent from that perfect knowledge whereby divine truth is seen in itself, — a revelation from God by the ministry of angels, who see the face of the Father (Matt. xviii, 10), 10 he rightly terms it a drop, as it is written: In that day the mountains shall drop sweetness (Joel iii, 18). But because revelation does not take in all the mysteries which the angels and the rest of the blessed behold in the First Truth, there is a meaning in the qualification, one little drop: for it is said: Who shall magnify him as he is from the beginning? many things are hidden greater than these, for we see but a few of his works (Ecclus xliii, 35): I have many things to say to you, but ye cannot hear them now (John xvi, 2). These few points that are revealed to us are set forth under similitudes and obscurities of expression, so as to be accessible only to the studious, hence the expressive addition, *scarce*, marking the difficulty of the enquiry. The third clause, *who shall be able to look upon the thunder of his greatness?* points to the third knowledge, whereby the First Truth shall be known, not as believed, but as seen: for *we shall see him as he is* (1 John iii, 2). No little fragment of the divine mysteries will be perceived, but the Divine Majesty itself, and all the perfect array of good things: hence the Lord said to Moses: *I will show thee all good* (Exod. xxxiii, 19). Rightly therefore we have in the text the words *look upon his greatness*. And this truth shall not be proposed to man under the covering of any veils, but quite plain: hence the Lord says to His disciples: *The hour cometh, when I will no longer speak to you in proverbs, but will tell you openly of my Father* (John xvi, 25): hence [the] word *thunder* in the text, indicative of this plain showing.

The words of the above text are adapted to our purpose: for whereas in the previous books we have spoken of divine things according as natural reason can arrive through creatures to the knowledge of them, — but that imperfectly, according to the limitations of the author's capacity, so that we can say with Job: *Lo, these things that have been said are but a part of his ways*; it remains now to treat of truths divinely revealed for our belief, truths transcending human understanding. And the words of the text are a guide to our procedure in this matter. As we have *scarce heard the truth* in the statements of Holy Scripture, those being as it were one little drop coming down to us, and no man in this life can *look upon the thunder of his greatness*, our method will be as follows. Taking as first principles the statements of

Holy Scripture, we will endeavor to penetrate their hidden meaning to the best of our ability, without presuming to claim perfect knowledge of the matter. Our proofs will rest on the authority of Holy Scripture, not on natural reason: still it will be our duty to show that our assertions are not contrary to natural reason, and thereby defend them against the assaults of unbelievers. And since natural reason ascends by creatures to the knowledge of God, while the knowledge of faith descends by divine revelation from God to us, and it is the same way up and down, we must proceed in these matters of supra-rational belief by the same way in which we proceeded in our rational enquiries concerning God. Thus we shall treat first of the supra-rational truths that are proposed for our belief concerning God Himself, as the confession of the Trinity [Chapp. I - XXVI: cf. I, Chap. IX: this answers to Book I]. Secondly, of the supra-rational works done by God, as the work of the Incarnation and its consequences [Chapp. XXVII - LXXVIII: answering to Book II]. Thirdly, of the supra-rational events expected at the end of human history, as the resurrection and glorification of bodies, the everlasting bliss of souls, and events therewith connected [Chapp. LXXIX - XCVII: answering to Book III].

### CHAPTER II—Of Generation, Paternity, and Sonship in God

WE find in the New Testament frequent attestations that Jesus Christ is the Son of God: Matt. xi, 27: Mark i, 1: John iii, 35: v, 21: Rom. i, 1: Heb. i, 1. And the same, though more rarely, in the Old Testament: Prov. xxx, 4: Ps. ii, 7: Ps. lxxxviii, 27. On the two last passages we must understand that as some expressions in the context may suit David, others not at all, these words are spoken of David and Solomon, according to the custom of Scripture, as prefiguring someone else, in whom all that is said is fulfilled.

And because the names of 'Father' and 'Son' are consequent upon some generative process, Scripture has not omitted to speak of divine generation, Ps. ii, 7: Prov. viii, 24, 25: John i, 14, 18: Heb. i, 6.1

CHAPTER III—That the Son of God is God

WE must not however fail to observe that divine Scripture uses the above names also to denote the creation of things: thus it is said: Who is the father of rain? or who hath begotten the drops of dew? From whose womb hath ice gone forth, and who hath begotten the frost from heaven? (Job xxxviii, 28.) Lest then by these names of paternity, sonship, and generation, nothing further should be understood than an act of creative energy, Scripture has further not failed to call Him God also, whom it has named Son and Begotten, — John i, 1, 14: Titus iii, 11: Ps. xliv, 7, 8[Heb. i, 8, 9]: Isa. ix, 6. And that Jesus Christ is the Son of God, Peter confessed, Matt. xvi, 16.

CHAPTERS IV, IX—The Opinion of Photinus touching the Son of God, and its rejection2

IT is customary in Scripture for those who are justified by divine grace to be called sons of God, — John i, 12: Rom. viii, 1: 1 John iii, 1: and begotten of God, James i, 1: 1 John iii, 9; and, what is more wonderful, even the name of Godhead is ascribed to them, Exod. vii,

1: Ps. lxxxi, 6: John x, 35. Going upon this usage, some wrong-headed men took up the opinion that Jesus Christ was a mere man, that His existence began with His birth of the Virgin Mary, that He gained divine honors above the rest of men through the merit of His blessed life, that like other men He was the Son of God by the Spirit of adoption, and by grace was born of God, and by a certain assimilation to God is called in the Scriptures God, not by nature, but by some participation in the divine goodness, as is also said of the saints, 2 Pet. i, 4. And this position they endeavored to confirm by authority of Holy Scripture: All power is given to me in heaven and on earth (Matt. xxviii, 18): but, say they, if He were God before all time, He would not have received power in time. Also it is said of the Son that He was made of the seed of David according to the flesh, and predestinated the Son of God in power (Rom. i, 3, 4): but what is made and predestinated is not eternal. Again the text, He was made obedient unto death, even the death of the cross: wherefore hath God exalted him, and given him the name that is above every name(Phil. ii, 8, 9), seems to show that by merit of His obedience and suffering He was granted divine honors and raised above all. Peter too says: Let all the House of Israel most certainly know that this Jesus, whom ye have crucified, God hath made Lord and Christ (Acts ii, 36). He seems then to have become God in time, not to have been born so before all ages. They also allege in support of their opinion those texts of Scripture which seem to point to defect in Christ, as that He was carried in woman's womb (Luke i, 42: ii, 5), that He grew in age (Luke ii, 52), that He suffered hunger (Luke iv, 2) and fatigue (John iv, 6), and was subject to death, that he continually advanced (Luke ii, 40, 52), that He confessed

He did not know the day of judgement (Mark xiii, 32), that He was stricken with fear of death (Luke xxii, 42, 44), and other weaknesses inadmissible in one who was God by nature.

But careful study of the words of Holy Scripture shows that there is not that meaning in them which these Photinians have supposed. For when Solomon says: The abysses as yet were not, and I (Wisdom) was already conceived (Prov. viii, 24), he sufficiently shows that this generation took place before all corporeal things. And though an endeavor has been to wrest away these and other testimonies by saying that they are to be understood of predestination, in the sense that before the creation of the world it was arranged that the Son of God should be born of the Virgin Mary, not that her Son existed before the world; nevertheless the words which follow show that He was before Mary not only in predestination, but really. For it follows: When he weighed the foundations of the earth, I was with him arranging all things: but if He had existed in predestination only, He could have done nothing. This conclusion may be drawn also from the Evangelist John: for, that none might take as referring to predestination the words, In the beginning was the Word, he adds: All things were made by him, and without him was made nothing: which could not be true, had He not real existence before the world was. Likewise from the texts John iii, 13: vi, 38, it appears that He had real existence ere He descended from heaven. Besides, whereas according to the above-mentioned position, a man by the merit of His life was advanced to be God, the Apostle contrariwise declares that, being God, He was made man: Being in the form of God, he thought it no robbery, etc. (Phil. ii, 6.) Again, among the rest who had the grace of God, Moses had it abundantly, of whom it is said: The Lord spoke to Moses face to face, as a man is wont to speak to his friend (Exod. xxxiii, 11). If then Jesus Christ were only called 'Son of God' by reason of the grace of adoption, as is the, case with other Saints, Moses might be called 'Son of God' on the same title as Christ, allowing all the while that Christ was endowed with more abundant grace: for among the rest of the saints one is filled with greater grace than another, and still they are all called 'Sons of God.' But Moses is not called 'Son' on the same title as Christ: for the Apostle distinguishes Christ from Moses as the son from the servant: Moses indeed was faithful in his house as a servant: but Christ as the Son in his own house (Heb. iii, 5).

The like argument may be gathered from many other places of Scripture, where Christ is styled 'Son of God' in a singular manner above others, as at His baptism, This is my beloved Son(Matt. iii, 17); or where He is called 'the Only-begotten,' — The Only-begotten Son, who is in the bosom of the Father, he hath declared(John i, 18): for were He Son in a general way, as others are, He could not be called 'Only-begotten': sometimes too He is designated as 'First-born,' to show that there is a derivation of sonship from Him to others: To be made conformable to the image of his Son, that he may be the first-born among many brethren (Rom. viii, 29): God hath sent his Son, that we might receive the adoption of sons(Gal. iv, 4: which texts show that He, by the likeness of whose Sonship others are called sons, is Son Himself after another way than they.

Furthermore, in the Holy Scriptures some works are set down as so peculiarly proper to God as to be never attributable to anyone else, e.g., the sanctification of souls and the forgiveness of sins: for it is said, I am the Lord who sanctify you (Levit. xx, 8): I am he who blot out thy sins for mine own sake (Isai. xliii, 25). Yet both these works Scripture attributes to Christ, Heb. ii, 11: xiii, 12. He declared of Himself that He had the power of forgiving sins, and proved His assertion by a miracle (Matt. ix, 1-8); and the angel foretold of Him that He should save his people from their sins (Matt. i, 21). Christ therefore as sanctifier and forgiver of sins is not called 'God' in the same sense as others are called 'gods,' who are sanctified and whose sins are forgiven, but as one having the power and nature Godhead.

As for those testimonies of Scripture whereby the Photinians endeavored to show that Christ is not God by nature, they do not serve their purpose: for we confess in Christ the Son of God after the Incarnation two natures, a human and a divine: hence there are predicated of Him at once attributes proper to God, by reason of His divine nature, and attributes seeming to involve some defect, or shortcoming, by reason of His human nature. Thus His saying, All power is given to me, does not mean that He then received the power as a new thing to Him, but that the power, which, the Son of God had enjoyed from all eternity, had now begun to appear in the same Son made man, by the victory which He had gained over death by rising again.3Hereby it is also clear that Peter's saying (Acts ii, 36) of God having made him[Jesus] Lord and Christ, is to be referred to the Son in His human nature, in which He began to have in time what in His nature He had from eternity.

Nor does the Apostle (Rom. i, 3) say absolutely that the Son was 'made,' but that He was made of the seed of David according to the flesh by the assumption of human nature. Hence the following words, predestinated Son of God, apply to the Son in His human nature: for that union of human nature with the Son of God, which made it possible man to be called Son of God, was not due to any human merits, but to the grace of God predestinating.

CHAPTER V—Rejection of the Opinion of Sabellius concerning the Son of God

BECAUSE it is a fixed idea in the mind of all who think rightly of God, that there can be but one God by nature, some, conceiving from the Scriptures the belief that Christ is truly and by nature God and the Son of God, have confessed that Christ, the Son of God, and God the Father are one God; and yet have not allowed that there was any 'God the Son,' so called according to His nature from eternity, but have held that God received the denomination of Sonship from the time that He was born of the Virgin Mary. Thus all things that Christ suffered in the flesh they attributed to God the Father. This was the opinion of the Sabellans, who were also called 'Patripassians,' because they asserted that the Father had suffered, and that the Father Himself was Christ. The peculiarity of this doctrine was the tenet that the term 'Son of God' does not denote any existing Person, but a property supervening upon a pre-existing Person.

The falsity of this position is manifest from Scripture authority. For Christ in the Scriptures is not only called the Son of the Virgin, but also the Son of God. But it cannot be that the same person should be son of himself, or that the same should give existence and receive it. We observe also that after the Incarnation the

Father gives testimony of the Son: *This is my beloved Son* (Matt. iii, 17): thereby pointing to His person. Christ therefore is in person other than His Father.

CHAPTER VI—*Of the Opinion of Arius concerning the Son of God*

WHEREAS it is not in accordance with sacred doctrine to say, with Photinus, that the Son of God took His beginning from Mary; or, with Sabellius, that the eternal God and Father began to be the Son by taking flesh; there were others who took the view, which Scripture teaches, that the Son of God was before the Incarnation and even before the creation of the world; but because the Son is other than the Father, they accounted Him to be not of the same nature with the Father: for they could not understand, nor would they believe, that any two beings, distinct in person, had the same essence and nature. And because, according to the doctrine of faith, alone of natures the nature of God the Father is believed to be eternal, they believed that the nature of the Son was not from eternity, although the Son was before other creatures. And because all that is not eternal is made out of nothing and created by God, they declared that the Son of God was made out of nothing and is a creature. But because they were driven by the authority of Scripture to call the Son also God, they said that He was one with God the Father, not by nature, but by a union of wills, and by participation in the likeness of God beyond other creatures. Hence, as the highest creatures, the angels are called in Scripture 'gods' and 'sons of God,' — e.g., *Where werst thou, when the morning stars praised me,* and all the sons of God shouted for joy?(Job xxxviii, 4-7): God stood in the assembly of gods(Ps. lxxxi, 1): — they considered that He should be called 'Son of God' and 'God' pre-eminently above others, inasmuch as through Him the Father created every other creature.

## CHAPTER VII—Rejection of Arius's Position

HOLY Scripture calls Christ 'Son of God' and the angels 'sons of God,' yet not in the same sense. To which of the angels did he ever say: Thou art my Son, this day have I begotten thee? (Heb. i, 5). 2. If Christ were called 'Son' in the same sense as all the angels and saints, He would not be Only-begotten, however much, for the excellence of His nature above the rest, He might be called first-born(Ps. lxxxviii, 27). But the Scripture declares Him to be the Only-begotten (John i, 14).

5. Of whom is Christ according to the flesh, who is over all things, God blessed forever (Rom. ix, 5):10Expecting the blessed hope and coming of the glory of the great God and our Savior Jesus Christ (Tit. ii. 13): I will raise up to David a just branch, and this is what they shall call him, the Lord our just one (Jerem. xxiii, 5, 6), where in the Hebrew we find the tetragrammaton, the name of God alone.

7. No creature receives the whole fullness of the divine goodness: but in Christ there dwells all the fullness of the Godhead (Col. ii, 9).

8. An angel's mind falls far short of the divine mind: but the mind of Christ in point of knowledge does not fall short of the divine mind: for in Him are hidden all treasures of wisdom and knowledge(Col. ii, 3).

9. All things whatsoever that the Father hath are mine; All mine are thine, and thine are mine (John xvi,

15: xvii, 10). [Cf. Luke xv, 31.] Therefore there is the same essence and nature of the Father and the Son.

10. In Phil. ii, 7, 8, by the form of God is understood no other than the nature of God, as by the form of a servant is understood no other than human nature.

11. The Jews sought to kill him because he said that God was his Father, making himself equal to God (John v, 18). This is the narrative of the evangelist, whose testimony is true (John xix, 35): nor is it doubtful to any Christian but that what Christ said of Himself is true.

13. No created substance represents God in His substance: for whatever appears of the perfection of any creature is less than what God is: hence through no creature can the essence of God be known. But the Son represents the Father; for the Apostle says of Him that He is the image of the invisible God (Col. i, 15). And lest He should be accounted an image falling short of and failing to represent the essence of God; or an image whence the essence of God could not be known, even as man is said to be the image of God (1 Cor xi, 7), He is declared to be a perfect image, representing the very substance of God, the splendor of his glory, and figure of his substance (Heb. i, 3).

19. Our final happiness is in God alone; and to Him alone the honor of latriais to be paid (B. III, Chap. CXX). But our happiness is in God the Son: This is life everlasting, that they know thee, and him whom thou hast sent, Jesus Christ (John xvii, 3). And it is said: That all may honor the Son, as they honor the Father (John v, 23); and again, Adore him, all ye angels (Ps. xcvi, 8), which the Apostle (Heb. i, 6) quotes as applying to the Son.

Taught by these and similar evidences of Holy

Scripture, the Catholic Church confesses Christ to be the true and natural Son of God, co-eternal and equal with the Father; true God, of the same essence and nature with the Father; begotten, not created, nor made. Hence it appears that the faith of the Catholic Church alone truly confesses generation in God, referring the generation of the Son to the fact of His receiving the divine nature of the Father. Other teachers heretically refer this generation to a nature extraneous to Godhead, — Photinus and Sabellius to a human nature; Arius not to a human indeed, but still to a created nature, more honorable than other creatures. Arius further differs from Sabellius and Photinus in asserting that this generation was before the creation of the world, while they say that it was not before the Virgin birth. Sabellius however differs from Photinus in this, that Sabellius confesses Christ to be true God by nature, which neither Photinus nor Arius confesses; but Photinus says that He was a mere man, Arius that He was a sort of compound super-excellent creature, at once divine and human. Photinus and Arius confess that the person of the Father and of the Son is different, which Sabellius denies. The Catholic faith therefore, taking the middle course (media via incedens) confesses, with Arius and Photinus against Sabellius, that the person of the Father and of the Son is different, the Son being begotten, the Father absolutely unbegotten; but with Sabellius against Photinus and Arius, that Christ is true God by nature, and of the same nature with the Father, — albeit not of the same person. Hence we gather some inkling of the truth of the Catholic position: for to the truth, as the Philosopher says, even false opinions testify; whereas false opinions are at variance, not only with the truth, but with one another.

## CHAPTER VIII—Explanation of the Texts which Arius used to allege for himself

THAT they may know thee, the only true God(John xvii, 3) is not to be taken to mean that the Father alone is true God, as though the Son were not true God, but that the one sole true Godhead belongs to the Father, without however the Son being excluded from it. Hence John, interpreting these words of the Lord, attributes to the true Son both these titles which here our Lord ascribes to His Father: That we may know the true God, and be in his true Son Jesus Christ: this is the true God and life everlasting (1 John v, 20). But even though the Son had confessed that the Father alone is true God, He should not for that be understood Himself as Son to be excluded from Godhead; for since the Father and the Son are one God, whatever is said of the Father by reason of His Divinity is as though it were said of the Son, and conversely. Thus the Lord's saying: No one knoweth the Son but the Father, nor does anyone know the Father but the Son(Matt. xi, 27), is not to be understood as excluding the Father from knowledge of Himself, or the Son either.

2. In the text, Whom in his own time he will show forth, who is blessed and alone powerful, King of Kings and Lord of Lords(1 Tim.. vi, 15), it is not the Father that is named, but that which is common to the Father and the Son. For that the Son also is King of Kings and Lord of Lords, is manifestly shown in the text: He was clad in a garment sprinkled with blood, and his name was called, the Word of God: and he hath on his garment and on his thigh written, King of Kings and Lord of Lords(Apoc. xix, 13, 16).

3. The sense of the text, the Father is greater than I

(John xiv, 28), is taught us by the Apostle (Phil. ii, 6). For since 'greater' is relative to 'less,' this must be understood of the Son according as He is made less; and He was made less in His taking the form of a servant, yet withal being equal to God the Father in the form of God. And no wonder if on this account the Father is said to be greater than Him, since the Apostle says that He was even made less than the angels: *That Jesus, who was made a little less than the angels, we have seen crowned with glory and honor for his suffering of death*(Heb. ii, 9.: cf. Ps. viii, 4-6).

4. *Then the Son also himself shall be subject to him who subjected to him all things.*14The context here shows that this is to be understood of Christ as man: for as man He died, and as man He rose again: but in His divinity, *doing all things that the Father does* (John v, 19), He too has subjected to Himself all things: for *we look for a Savior, the Lord Jesus Christ, who will reform the body of our lowliness, made conformable to the body of his glory, by the act of his power of subjecting all things to himself*(Phil. iii, 20).

5. By the Father being said to give to the Son (John iii, 35: Matt. xi, 27), nothing else is understood than the generation of the Son, whereby the Father has given the Son His own nature And this may be gathered from the consideration of that which is given: for the Lord says: *That which my Father hath given me is greater than all*(John x, 29): where that which is greater than all is the divine nature, wherein the Son is equal to the Father.

6. Hence it appears how the Son is said to be taught (John v, 20: xv, 15), although He is not ignorant. It has been shown above that, in God, understanding and being are the same (B. I, Chap. XLV): hence the

communication of the divine nature is also a communication of intelligence. But a communication of intelligence may be called a 'showing,' or 'speaking,' or 'teaching.' By the fact, then, of the Son having received the divine nature of His Father at His birth, He is said to have 'heard' from His Father, or the Father to have 'shown' Him: not that the Son was in ignorance before, and afterwards the Father taught Him: for the Apostle confesses Christ the power of God and wisdom of God (1 Cor. i, 24); and wisdom cannot be ignorant, or power weak.

7. The text, The Son cannot do anything of himself (John v, 19), argues no weakness in the Son; but since with God to act is no other thing than to be, it is here said that the Son cannot act of Himself, but has His action of the Father, as He cannot be of Himself, but only of the Father. Were He to be 'of Himself,' He could not be the Son. But because the Son receives the same nature that the Father has, and consequently the same power, therefore though He neither is 'of Himself' (a se) nor acts of Himself, still He is 'by Himself' (per se) and acts by Himself, since He at once is by His own nature, which He has received from the Father, and acts by His own nature received from the Father. Hence, to show that though the Son does not act 'of Himself,' nevertheless He acts 'by Himself,' the verse goes on: Whatsoever things he (the Father) doeth, these the Son also doeth in like manner.

8. All the texts about the Father giving commandment to the Son, and the Son obeying the Father, or praying to the Father, are to be understood of the Son as He is subject to His Father, which is only in point of the humanity which He has assumed (John xiv, 31: xv, 10: Phil. ii, 8), as the Apostle shows (Heb. v, 7:

Gal. iv, 4).

10. His saying, To sit on my right or left hand is not mine to give you, but to them for whom it is prepared(Matt. xx, 23), does not show that the Son has no power of distributing the seats in heaven, or the participation of life everlasting, which He expressly says does belong to Him to bestow: I give them life everlasting(John x, 27); and again it is said: The Father hath given all judgement to the Son(John v, 22): He will set the sheep on his right hand and the goats on his left(Matt. xxv, 33): it belongs then to the power of the Son to set any one on His right or on His left, whether both designations mark different degrees of glory; or the one refers to glory, the other to punishment. We must look to the context, whereby it appears that the mother of the sons of Zebedee rested on some confidence of kindred with the man Christ. The Lord then by His answer did not mean that it was not in His power to give what was asked, but that it was not in His power to give to them for whom it was asked: for it did not belong to Him to give inasmuch as He was the Son of the Virgin, but inasmuch as He was the Son of God; and therefore it was not His to give to any for their connexion with Him according to fleshly kindred, as He was the Son of the Virgin, but it belonged to Him as Son of God to give to those for whom it was prepared by His Father according to eternal predestination.

11. Nor from the text: Of that day and hour no one knoweth, no, not the angels of heaven, nor the Son, but my Father alone(Mark xiii, 32):19can it be understood that the Son did not know the hour of His coming, seeing that in Him are hidden all treasures of wisdom and knowledge(Col. ii, 3), and seeing that He perfectly knows

that which is greater still, namely, the Father (Matt. xi, 2720 but the meaning is that the Son, as a man in His place amongst men, behaved Himself after the manner of one ignorant in not revealing that day to His disciples. For it is a usual mode of speaking in Scripture for God to be said to know a thing, if He makes it known: thus, *Now I know that thou fears the Lord* (Gen. xxii, 12), means 'I have made it known.' And contrariwise the Son is said not to know that which He does not make known to us.

CHAPTER 12—How the Son of God is called the Wisdom of God

WISDOM in man is a habit whereby our mind is perfected in the knowledge of the highest truths: such are divine truths. Wisdom in God is His knowledge of Himself. But because He does not know Himself by any presentation of Himself other than His essence, and His act of understanding is His essence, the wisdom of God cannot be a habit, but is the very essence of God. But the Son of God is the Word and Concept of God understanding Himself. The Word of God, thus conceived, is properly called 'begotten Wisdom': — hence the Apostle names Christ *the wisdom of God* (1 Cor. i, 24). This Word of wisdom, conceived in the mind, is a manifestation of the wisdom of the mind which thereby understands: as in us acts are a manifestation of habits. Also the divine wisdom is called 'light,' as consisting in a pure act of knowledge; and the manifestation of light is the brightness thence proceeding: the Word of divine wisdom therefore is fittingly called the 'brightness of light,' according to the text: *being the brightness of his glory* (Heb. i, 3). But though the Son, or

Word of God, is properly called 'conceived wisdom,' nevertheless the name of Wisdom, when used absolutely, must be common to the Father and the Son; since the wisdom that is resplendent through the Word is the essence of the Father, and the essence of the Father is common to Him with the Son.

CHAPTER XVII—That the Holy Ghost is true God

A TEMPLE is consecrated to none but God: hence it is said: The Lord in his holy temple (Ps. x, 5). But there is a temple appointed to the Holy Ghost, as it is said: Know you not that your members are the temple of the Holy Ghost? (i Cor. vi, 19.) The Holy Ghost then is God, particularly since our members, which the text says are the temple of the Holy Ghost, are the members of Christ: for the writer had said before: Know you not that your bodies are the members of Christ? (v.15.) Seeing that Christ is true God, it would be inappropriate for the members of Christ to be the temple of the Holy Ghost, unless the Holy Ghost were God.

2. The service of latria (B. III, Chap. CXX) is paid by holy men to God alone (Deut. vi, 13). But holy men pay that service to the Holy Ghost: for it is said: We who serve the Spirit as God (qui spiritui Deo servimus. — Phil. iii, 3). And though some manuscripts have, We who serve in the spirit of the Lord (qui spiritu Domini servimus [showing the reading θεοῦ]), yet the Greek manuscripts and the more ancient Latin ones have, We who serve the Spirit as God (qui spiritui Deo servimus); and from the Greek itself [λατρεύοντες] it appears that this is to be understood of the service of latria, which is

due to God alone.

3. To sanctify men is a work proper to God: I am the Lord who sanctify you (Levit. xxii, 9). But it is the Holy Ghost who sanctifies, according to the words of the Apostle: Ye are washed and sanctified and justified, in the name of our Lord Jesus Christ and in the Spirit of our God(1 Cor. vi, 11).

4. As the life of the body is by the soul, so the soul's life of justice is by God: hence the Lord says: As the living Father hath sent me, and I live by the Father, so whosoever eateth me, the same shall also live by me (John vi, 58). But such life is by the Holy Ghost; hence it is added: It is the Spirit that giveth life (John vi, 63): and the Apostle says: If with the spirit ye mortify the deeds of the flesh, ye shall live (Rom. viii, 18).

7. The Spirit searches all things, even the profound things of God. For what man knoweth the things of a man but the spirit of man that is in him? So the things also that are of God no man knoweth but the Spirit of God (1 Cor. ii, 10, 11). But to comprehend all the profound things of God is not given to any creature: for no one knoweth the Son but the Father, nor doth anyone know the Father but the Son (Matt. xi, 27); and in the person of God it is said, My secret to me ( Isai. xxiv, 16). Therefore, the Holy Ghost is, not a creature.

8. According to the above comparison, the Holy Ghost is to God as a man's spirit to man. But a man's spirit is intrinsic to man, not of a foreign nature, but part of him. Therefore the Holy Ghost is not of a nature extrinsic to Deity.

11. Evidently from Holy Scripture it was God who spoke by the prophets, as it is said: I will hear what the Lord God speaketh in me (Ps. lxxxiv, 9). But it is equally

evident that the Holy Ghost spoke in the prophets: *The Scripture must be fulfilled, which the Holy Ghost foretold by the mouth of David* (Acts i, 16). *The holy men of God spoke, inspired by the Holy Ghost* (2 Pet. i, 21). Clearly then the Holy Ghost is God.

17. The Holy Ghost is expressly called God in the text: *Ananias, why hath Satan tempted thy heart to lie to the Holy Ghost? . . . . Thou hast not lied to men, but to God* (Acts. v, 3, 4).

23. *Now there are diversities of graces, but the same Spirit. And there are diversities of ministries, but the same Lord. And there are diversities of operations, but the same God, who worked all in all. . . . But all these things one and the same Spirit worked, dividing to everyone according as he will* (1 Cor. xii, 4, 5, 6, 11). This text clearly declares the Holy Ghost to be God, as well by saying that the Holy Ghost works what it has previously said that God works, as also by the declaration of His working according to the arbitrement of His own will.

CHAPTER XVIII—That the Holy Ghost is a Subsistent Person

BUT inasmuch as some have maintained that the Holy Ghost is not a subsistent Person, but is either the divinity of the Father and the Son (cf. St Aug. de haeresibus, n. 52), or some accidental perfection of the mind given us by God, as wisdom, or charity, or other such created accidents, we must evince the contrary.

1. Accidental forms do not properly work, but the subject that has them works according to the arbitrement of his own will: thus a wise man uses wisdom when he wills. But the Holy Ghost works according to the

arbitrement of His own will (1 Cor. xii, 11).

2. The Holy Ghost is not to be accounted an accidental perfection of the human mind, seeing that He is the cause of such perfections: for *the charity of God is spread abroad in our hearts by the Holy Ghost who is given to us* (Rom. v, 5): *To one is given by the Spirit the utterance of wisdom, to another the utterance of knowledge according to the same Spirit* (1 Cor. xii, 8).

3. The Holy Ghost proceeds from the Father and receives from the Son (John xv, 26: xvi, 14): which cannot be understood of the divine essence.

4. Scripture speaks of the Holy Ghost as of a subsistent Person: *The Holy Ghost said to them: Set aside for me Barnabas and Saul for the work unto which I have taken them: . . . . and they, sent by the Holy Ghost, went* (Acts xiii, 2, 4): *It hath seemed good to the Holy Ghost and us* (Acts xv, 28).

5. The Father and the Son being subsistent Persons and of divine nature, the Holy Ghost would not be numbered with them (Matt. xxviii, 19: 2 Cor. xiii, 13: 1 John v, 7) were He not a Person subsistent in the divine nature.

CHAPTER XX—Of the Effects which the Scriptures attribute to the Holy Ghost in respect of the whole Creation

THE love wherewith God loves His own goodness is the cause of the creation of things (B. I, Chap. LXXXVI); and it is laid down that the Holy Ghost proceeds as the love wherewith God loves Himself. Therefore the Holy Ghost is the principle of the creation of things; and this is signified in Ps. ciii, 30: *Send forth* thy spirit and they shall be created. Again, as the Holy Ghost proceeds as love, and love is an impulsive and motor power, the motion that is from God in things is appropriately attributed to the Holy Ghost. But the first motion, or change, coming from God in things is the production of the diversity of species from matter created formless (ex materia creata informi species diversas produxit). This work the Scripture attributes to the Holy Ghost: The Spirit of God moved over the waters (Gen. i, 2) By the waters Augustine wishes to be understood primordial matter. The Spirit of the Lord is said to move over them, not as being in motion on Himself, but as the principle of motion. The government of creation also is fitly assigned to the Holy Ghost, as government is the moving and directing of things to their proper ends. And because the governing of subjects is an act proper to a lord, lordship too is aptly attributed to the Holy Ghost: the Spirit is Lord (1 Cor. iii, 17).

Life also particularly appears in movement. As then impulse and movement by reason of love are proper to the Holy Spirit, so too is life fitly attributed to Him, as it is said: It is the Spirit that quickened (John vi, 64: 2 Cor. iii, 6).

CHAPTER XXI—Of the Effects attributed to the Holy Ghost in Scripture in the way of Gifts bestowed on the Rational Creature

SINCE the Father, Son and Holy Ghost have the same power, as they have the same essence, everything that God works in us must be by the efficient causation of Father, Son and Holy Ghost together. But the word of wisdom, sent us by God, whereby we know God, is properly representative of the Son; and the love, wherewith we love God, is properly representative of the Holy Ghost. Thus the charity that is in us, though it is the effect of Father, Son and Holy Ghost, is in a certain special aspect said to be in us through the Holy Ghost. But since divine effects not only begin by divine operation, but are also sustained in being by the same, and nothing operates where it is not, it needs must follow that wherever there is any effect wrought by God, there is God Himself who works it. Hence, since the charity wherewith we love God is in us through the Holy Ghost, the Holy Ghost Himself must be in us, so long as charity is in us. Know you not that ye are the temple of God, and the Holy Ghost dwelled in you? (1 Cor. iii, 16.) And through the Holy Ghost the Father and Son also dwell in us. Hence the Lord says: We will come to him, and take up our abode with him (John xiv, 23). Cf. 1 John iv, 13, 16.

It is a point of friendship to reveal one's secrets to one's friend: for as friendship unites affections, and makes of two as it were one heart, a man may well seem not to have uttered beyond his own heart what he has revealed to his friend. Hence the Lord says to His disciples: I will not call you servants, but friends, because all things that I have heard from my Father I have made known to you (John xv, 15). Since then by the Holy Ghost we are constituted friends of God, the revelation of divine mysteries to men is fittingly said to take place through the Holy Ghost: To us God has revealed them through the Holy Ghost (1 Cor. ii, 10). Besides the revealing of one's secrets to one's friend, which is part of the union of affections that goes with friendship, there is a further requisite of the same union, to share one's possessions with one's friend, according to 1 John iii, 17. And therefore all the gifts of God are said to be given us by the Holy Ghost (1 Cor. xii, 7-11). And by such gifts of the Spirit we are conformed to God, and by Him rendered apt to the performance of good works, and our way is thereby paved to happiness: which three effects the Apostle declares: God hath anointed us, and sealed us, and given the pledge of the Spirit in our hearts (2 Cor. i, 21, 22: cf. Eph. i, 13, 14). The sealing may be taken to imply the likeness of conformity to God: the anointing, the fitting of man to do perfect acts: the pledge, the hope whereby we are set on the way to the heavenly inheritance of life everlasting.

And because good will towards a person leads at times to the adoption of him as a son, that so the inheritance may belong to him, the adoption of the sons of God is properly attributed to the Holy Ghost: Ye have received the spirit of adoption of sons, wherein we cry, Abba, Father (Rom. viii, 15).

Again, by admission to friendship all offence is removed. Since then we are rendered sons of God through the Holy Ghost, through Him also our sins are forgiven us by God; and therefore the Lord says: Receive ye the Holy Ghost: whose sins ye shall forgive, they are forgiven them (John xx, 22). And therefore forgiveness is denied to them who blaspheme against the Holy Ghost (Matt. xii, 31), as to persons who have not that whereby man attains the forgiveness of his sins.

CHAPTER XXII—Of the Effects attributed to the Holy Ghost in the attraction of the Rational Creature to God

IT is a mark of friendship to take delight in the

company of one's friend, to rejoice at what he says and does, and to find in him comfort and consolation against all troubles: hence it is in our griefs especially that we fly to our friends for comfort. Since then the Holy Ghost renders us friends of God, making Him to dwell in us and we in Him, we have through the same Holy Spirit joy in God and comfort under all the adversities and assaults of the world: hence it is said: *Give me back the joy of thy salvation, and strengthen me with thy guiding Spirit*(Ps. l, 14): *The kingdom of God is justice and peace and joy in the Holy Ghost* (Rom. xiv, 17): *The Church had peace, and was edified, walking in the fear of the Lord, and filled with the consolation of the Holy Ghost*(Acts ix, 31).

Another mark of friendship is to fall in with a friend's wishes. Now God's wishes are unfolded to us by His commandments, the keeping of which therefore is part of our love of God : *If ye love me, keep my commandments* (John xiv, 15). As then we are rendered lovers of God by the Holy Ghost, by Him we are also led to fulfil God's commandments: *Whosoever are led by the Spirit of God, the same are the sons of God* (Rom. viii, 14). But it is a noteworthy point that the sons of God are led by the Holy Ghost, not as bondsmen, but as free. He is free, who is a cause unto himself; and we do that freely which we do of ourselves, that is, of our own willing; but what we do against our will, we do, not freely, but after the manner of bondsmen. The Holy Ghost then, rendering us lovers of God, inclines us to act of our own will, freely, out of love, not as bondsmen prompted by fear. *Ye have not received the spirit of bondage again in fear, but ye have received the spirit of adoption as sons* (Rom. viii, 15). True good being the object of the will, whenever a man turns away from true good under the influence of passion or ill habit, and so is swayed by a power foreign to his proper self, he in that respect behaves like a bondsman. On the other hand, if we consider his act as a genuine act of his will, inclined to what is good for him in his own eyes, although not really good, he acts freely in thus following passion or corrupt habit. But again he acts like a bondsman, if, while the volition of fancied good just mentioned remains, he nevertheless abstains from what he wills for fear of the law enacted to the contrary. Since then the Holy Ghost inclines the will by love to true good, its natural object, He takes away alike the servitude whereby, a slave to passion and sin, man acts against the due order of his will, and that other servitude whereby man acts according to the law, but against the motion of his will, like a slave of the law and no friend to it. Hence the Apostle says: Where the Spirit of the Lord is, there is liberty (2 Cor. iii, 17): If ye are led by the Spirit, ye are not under the law (Gal. v, 18)

CHAPTER XXIII—Replies to Arguments alleged against the Divinity of the Holy Ghost

CHAP. XVI. It was the position of Arius that the Son and Holy Ghost were creatures, the Son however being greater than the Holy Ghost, and the Holy Ghost being His minister, even as he said the Son was to the Father. After Arius came Macedonius, who was orthodox on the point of the Father and Son being of one and the same substance, but refused to believe the same of the Holy Ghost, and said that He was a creature.

Chap. XXIII. 2. He shall not speak of himself but whatsoever things he shall hear, he shall speak (John xvi, 13). Since all the knowledge and power and action of God is the essence of God, all the knowledge and power and action of the Son and of the Holy Ghost is from another; but that of the Son is from the Father only, that of the Holy Ghost from the Father and the Son. To hear then, on the part of the Holy Ghost, signifies His taking knowledge, as He takes essence, from the Father and the Son.

3. The Son of God is said to have been sent in this sense, that He appeared to man in visible flesh; and, thus came to be in the world in a new way, in which He had not been before, namely, visibly, although He had always been there invisibly as God. And the Son's doing this came to Him of His Father: hence in this respect He is said to be 'sent' by the Father. In like manner the Holy Ghost too appeared visibly both in the appearance of a dove over Christ in His baptism, and in fiery tongues over the Apostles; and though He did not become a dove or fire, still He appeared under such visible appearances as signs of Himself. And thus He too came to be in a new way in the world, visibly; and this He had of the Father and of the Son, hence He is said to be 'sent' by the Father and the Son, which does not imply inferiority in Him, but procession. There is yet another way in which the Holy Ghost is said to be sent, and that invisibly. The Son proceeds from the Father as the knowledge wherewith God knows Himself; and the Holy Ghost proceeds from Father and Son as the love wherewith God loves Himself. Hence when through the Holy Ghost one is made a lover of God, the Holy Ghost is an indweller in him; and thus He comes to be in a new way in man, in point of the new special effect of His indwelling in man. Now that the Holy Ghost works this effect in man, comes to Him of the Father and the Son; and therefore He is said to be

invisibly sent by Father and Son.

4. Nor is the Holy Ghost excluded from the Divinity by the occasional mention of the Father and the Son without the Holy Ghost (Matt. xi, 27: John xvii, 3: Rom. i, 7: 1 Cor. viii, 6): for hereby the Scripture silently intimates that whatever attribute of divinity is predicated of one of the three, must be understood of them, all, seeing that they are one God. God the Father can never be taken to be without the Word and without Love; and the Word and Love cannot be taken to be without the Father. Hence it is said of the Son: No one knoweth the Father but the Son (Matt. xi, 27): so it is also said of the Holy Ghost: The things that are of God, none knoweth but the Spirit of God (1 Cor. ii, 11): though it is certain that neither the Father nor the Son is excluded from this knowledge of divine things.

7. Habitually in Holy Scripture the language of human passion is applied to God (B. I, Chapp. LXXXIX–LXCI). Thus it is said: The Lord was angered in fury against his people (Ps. cv, 40): for He punishes, as men in anger do: hence it is added: And gave them over into the hands of the Gentiles. So in the text, Sadden not the Holy Spirit of God (Eph. iv, 30), the Holy Ghost is said to be saddened, because He abandons sinners; as men, when they are saddened and annoyed, forsake the company of them that annoy them.

8. Another customary phraseology of Holy Scripture is the attributing of that to God, which He produces in man. So it is said: The Spirit himself asked for us with unspeakable groanings (Rom. viii, 26): because He makes us ask, for He produces in our hearts the love of God, whereby we desire to enjoy Him and ask according to our desire.

9. Since the Holy Ghost proceeds as the love wherewith God loves Himself; and since God loves with the same love Himself and other beings for the sake of His own goodness (B. I Chapp. LXXV, LXXVI); it is clear that the love wherewith God loves us belongs to the Holy Ghost. In like manner also the love wherewith we love God. In respect of both these loves the Holy Ghost is well said to be given. In respect of the love wherewith God loves us, He may be said to be given, in the sense in which one is said to give his love to another, when he begins to love him. Only, be it observed, there is no beginning in time for God's love of any one, if we regard the act of divine will loving us; but the effect of His love is caused in time in the creature whom He draws to Himself. Again, in respect of the love wherewith we love God, the Holy Ghost may be said to be given us, because this love is produced in us by the Holy Ghost, who by reason of this love dwells in us, and so we possess Him and enjoy His support. And since the Holy Ghost has it of the Father and the Son that He is in us and is possessed by us, therefore He is aptly said to be given us by the Father and the Son. Your Father from heaven will give the good Spirit to them that ask him (Luke xi, 13; cf. Acts v, 32: John xv, 26). Nor does this argue Him to be less than the Father and the Son, but only to have His origin from them.

11. It is reasonable that in the case of the divine nature alone nature should be communicated in more modes than the one mode of generation. In God alone act and being are identical: hence since there is in God, as in every intelligent nature, both intelligence and will, alike that which proceeds in Him as intelligence, to wit, the Word, and that proceeds in Him as love and will, to wit,

Love, must have divine being and be God; thus as well the Son as the Holy Ghost is true God.

CHAPTER XXIV—That the Holy Ghost proceeds from the Son

IF any man have not the Spirit of Christ, he is not of him (Rom. viii, 9). These words of the Apostle show that the same Spirit is of the Father and of the Son: for the text alleged follows upon these words immediately preceding: *If so be that the Spirit of God dwell in you.* Now it cannot be said that the Holy Ghost is the Spirit merely of the man Christ (Luke iv, 3): for from Gal. iv, 6, *Since ye are sons, God hath sent the Spirit of his Son into your hearts,* it appears that the Holy Ghost makes sons of God inasmuch as He is the Spirit of the Son of God, — sons of God, that is to say, by adoption, which means assimilation to Him who is Son of God by nature. For so the text has it: *He hath predestined (them) to become conformable to the image of his Son, that he may be the first-born among many brethren* (Rom. viii, 29). But the Holy Ghost cannot be called the Spirit of the Son of God except as taking His origin from Him: for this distinction of origin is the only one admissible in the Godhead.

2. The Holy Ghost is sent by the Son: *When the Paraclete cometh, whom I will send you from the Father* (John xv, 26). Now the sender has some authority (*auctoritatem*) over the sent. We must say then that the Son has some authority in respect of the Holy Ghost. Now that cannot be an authority of dominion, superiority, or seniority: it can only be an authority in point of origin. So

then the Holy Ghost is from the Son. But if anyone will have it that the Son also is sent by the Holy Ghost, according to the text (Luke iv, 18) where the Lord said that the saying of Isaias (lxi, 1) was fulfilled in Him: *The Spirit of the Lord is upon me: to preach glad tidings to the poor he hath sent me*: we must observe that it is in respect of the nature which He has assumed that the Son is said to be sent by the Holy Ghost [cf. Acts x, 38]: but the Holy Ghost has assumed no such nature, that the Son in point thereof should send Him or have authority regarding Him.

3. The Son says of the Holy Ghost: *He shall glorify me, because he shall receive of mine* (John xvi, 14). Now it cannot be maintained that He shall receive that which belongs to the Son, namely, the divine essence, but not receive it of the Son, but only of the Father: for it follows, *All things whatsoever that the Father hath are mine: therefore did I say to you that he shall receive of mine*: for if all things that the Father has belong to the Son, the authority of the Father, whereby He is the principle of the Holy Ghost, must belong likewise to the Son.

7. The Son is from the Father, and so too is the Holy Ghost. The Father then must be related to the Son and to the Holy Ghost as a principle to that which is of the principle. Now He is related to the Son in the way of paternity, but not so to the Holy Ghost, otherwise the Holy Ghost would be the Son. There must then be in the Father another relation, which relates Him to the Holy Ghost; and that relation is called 'spiration.' In like manner, as there is in the Son a relation which relates Him to the Father, and is called 'filiation,' there must be in the Holy Ghost too a relation which relates Him to the Father, and is called 'procession.' And thus in point of the origin

of the Son from the Father there are two relations, one in the originator, the other in the originated, namely, paternity and filiation; and other two in point of the origin of the Holy Ghost, namely spiration and procession. Now paternity and spiration do not constitute two persons, but belong to the one person of the Father, because they are not opposed one to the other. Neither then would filiation and procession constitute two persons, but would belong to one person, but for the fact of their being opposed one to the other. But it is impossible to assign any other opposition than that which is in point of origin. There must then be an opposition in point of origin between the Son and the Holy Ghost, so that one is from the other.

10. If the rejoinder is made that the processions of Son and Holy Ghost differ in principle, inasmuch as the Father produces the Son by mode of understanding, as the Word, and produces the Holy Ghost by mode of will, as Love, the opponent must go on to say that according to the difference of understanding and will in God the Father there are two distinct processions and two distinct beings so proceeding. But will and understanding in God the Father are not distinguished with a real but only with a mental distinction (B. I, Chapp. XLV, LXXIII). Consequently the two processions and the two beings so proceeding must differ only by a mental distinction. But things that differ only by a mental distinction are predicable of one another: thus it is true to say that God's will is His understanding, and His understanding is His will. It will be true then to say that the Holy Ghost is the Son, and the Son the Holy Ghost, which is the impious position of Sabellius. Therefore, to maintain the distinction between Holy Ghost and Son, it is not enough to say that the Son proceeds by mode of understanding

and the Holy Ghost by mode of will, unless we further go on to say that the Holy Ghost is of the Son.

13. The Father and the Son, being one in essence, differ only in this, that He is the Father, and He the Son. Everything else is common to Father and Son. But being the origin of the Holy Ghost lies outside of the relationship of paternity and filiation: for the relation whereby the Father is Father differs from the relation whereby the Father is the origin of the Holy Ghost. Being the origin then of the Holy Ghost is something common to Father and Son.

CHAPTER XXVI—That there are only Three Persons in the Godhead, Father and Son and Holy Ghost

FROM all that has been said we gather that in the divine nature there subsist three Persons, Father, Son, and Holy Ghost; and that these three are one God, being distinct from one another by relations alone. The Father is distinguished by the relation of paternity and by being born of none: the Son is distinguished from the Father by the relationship of filiation: the Father and Son from the Holy Ghost by spiration; and the Holy Ghost from the Father and the Son by the procession of love whereby He proceeds from both. Besides these three Persons it is impossible to assign in the divine nature any fourth Person.

1. The three divine Persons, agreeing in essence, can be distinguished only by the relation of origin. These relations of origin cannot obtain in respect of any process tending to things without, as whatever proceeded without would not be co-essential with its origin; but the process must all stay within. Now such a process, abiding within

its origin, is found only in the act of understanding and will.36Hence the divine persons cannot be multiplied except in accordance with the requirements of the process of understanding and will in God. But in God there can be but one process of understanding, seeing that His act of understanding is one, simple, and perfect, whereby, understanding Himself, He understands all other things; and so there can be in God only one procession of the Word. In like manner the process of love must be one and simple, because the divine will also is one and simple, whereby in loving Himself God loves all other things. There can therefore be in God but two Persons proceeding: one by way of understanding, as the Word, or Son; the other by way of love, as the Holy Ghost: there is also one Person not proceeding, namely, the Father. There can only therefore be three Persons in the Trinity.

2. The divine Persons must be distinguished according to their mode of procession. Now the mode of personal procession can be but threefold. There may be a mode of not proceeding at all, which is proper to the Father; or of proceeding from one who does not proceed, which is proper to the Son; or of proceeding from one who does proceed, which is proper to the Holy Ghost. It is impossible therefore to assign more than three Persons.

3. If any objicient says that, the Son being perfect God, there is in Him perfect intellectual power, whereby He can produce a Word; and in like manner the Holy Ghost, being infinite goodness, which is a principle of communication, must be able to communicate the divine nature to another divine person, he should take note that the Son is God as begotten, not as begetting; hence the power of understanding is in Him as in one proceeding as a Word, not as in one producing a Word. In like manner

the Holy Ghost being God as proceeding, there is in Him infinite goodness as in a person receiving, not as in one communicating infinite goodness to another. The whole fullness of Godhead then is in the Son, numerically the same as in the Father, but with a relation of birth, as it is in the Father with a relation of active generation. If the relation of the Father were attributed to the Son, all distinction would be taken away: for the divine Persons are distinguished one from another solely by their mutual relations. And the like argument holds of the Holy Ghost.

A likeness of the divine Trinity is observable in the human mind. That mind, by actually understanding itself, conceives its 'word' in itself, which 'word' is nothing else than what is called the 'intellectual expression (intentio intellecta, cf. B. I, Chap. LIII) existing in the mind; which mind, going on to love itself, produces itself in the will as an object loved. Further it does not proceed, but is confined and complete in a circle, returning by love to its own substance, whence the process originally began by formation of the 'intellectual expression' of that substance. There is however a process going out to exterior effects, as the mind for love of itself proceeds to some action beyond itself. Thus we remark in the mind three things: the mind itself, whence the process starts within its own nature; the mind conceived in the understanding; and the mind loved in the will. And so we have seen that there is in the divine nature a God unbegotten, the Father, the origin of the entire procession of Deity; and a God begotten after the manner of a 'word' conceived in the understanding, namely, the Son; and a God proceeding by mode of love, who is the Holy Ghost: beyond Him there is no further procession within the divine nature, but only a proceeding to exterior effects.

But the representation of the divine Trinity in us falls short, in regard of Father, Son and Holy Ghost being one nature, and each of them a perfect Person. Hence there is said to be in the mind of man the 'image' of God: Let us make man to our image and likeness (Gen. i, 26). But as for the irrational creation, on account of the remoteness and obscurity of the representation as found in them, there is said to be the 'foot-print' of the Trinity, but not the 'image' (vestigium, non imago).

CHAPTER XXVII—Of the Incarnation of the Word according to the Tradition of Holy Scripture

OF all the works of God, the mystery of the Incarnation most transcends reason. Nothing more astonishing could be imagined as done by God than that the true God and Son of God should become true man. To this chief of wonders all other wonders are subordinate. We confess this wonderful Incarnation under the teaching of divine authority, John i, 14: Phil. ii, 6-11. The words of our Lord Jesus Christ Himself also declare it, in that sometimes He says of Himself humble and human things, e.g., The Father is greater than I (John xiv, 28): My soul is sorrowful even unto death(Matt. xxvi, 38): which belonged to Him in the humanity which He had assumed: at other times lofty and divine things, e.g., I and the Father are one(John x, 30): All things that the Father hath are mine(John xvi, 15): which attach to Him in His divine nature. And the actions that are recorded of Him show the same duality of nature. His being stricken with fear, sadness, hunger, death, belongs to His human nature: His healing the sick by His own power, His raising the dead and effectually commanding the elements, His casting out of devils, forgiving of sins, His rising from the dead when He willed, and finally ascending into heaven, show the power of God that was in Him.

CHAPTER XXVIII—Of the Error of Photinus concerning the Incarnation

PHOTINUS and others pretend that the divinity was in Christ, not by nature, but by a high degree of participation in divine glory, which He had merited by His works. But on this theory it would not be true that God had taken flesh so as to become man, but rather that a fleshly man had become God. It would not be true that the Word was made flesh (John i, 14), but that flesh had been made the Word. Kenosis and coming down would not be predicable of the Son of God, but rather glorification and being lifted up would be predicated of man. It would not be true that, being in the form of God, he emptied [ἐκένωσεν] himself, taking the form of a servant (Phil. ii, 6), but only the exaltation of man to divine glory would be true, of which presently we read, wherefore hath God exalted him. It would not be true, I descended from heaven (John vi, 38), but only, I ascend to my Father (John xx, 17): notwithstanding that Holy Scripture joins both assertions together: None ascended into heaven but he who descended from heaven, the Son of man, who is in heaven (John iii, 13): He who descended, the same also ascended above all the heavens (Eph. iv, 10). Nor would it be true to say of the Son that He was sent by the Father, or that He went out from the Father to come into the world, but only that He went to the Father, although He Himself makes the two declarations together: I go to him who sent me: I went out from the Father, and came into the world; and again I leave the world and go unto the Father (John xvi, 5, 28).

CHAPTER XXIX—Of the Error of the Manicheans concerning the Incarnation

THE Manicheans said that the Son of God took not a real but an apparent body; and that the things which He did as man, — being born, eating, drinking, walking, suffering, and being buried, — were not done in reality, but in show. To begin with, this theory robs Scripture of all authority. For since a show of flesh is not flesh, nor a show of walking walking, the Scripture lies when it says, The Word was made flesh, if the flesh was only apparent: it lies when it says that Jesus Christ walked, ate, was dead and buried, if these things happened only in fantastic appearance. But if even in a small matter the authority of Holy Scripture is derogated from, no point of our faith can any longer remain fixed, as our faith rests on the Holy Scripture, according to the text, These things are written that ye may believe (John xx, 31).

Someone may say that the veracity of Holy Scripture in relating appearance for reality is saved by this consideration, that the appearances of things are called figuratively and in a sense by the names of the things themselves, as a painted man is called in a sense a man. But though this is true, yet it is not the way of Holy Scripture to give the whole history of one transaction in this ambiguous way, without there being other passages of Holy Scripture from whence the truth may be manifestly gathered. Otherwise there would follow, not the instruction but the deception of men: whereas the Apostle says that whatsoever things are written, are written for our instruction (Rom. xv, 4); and that all Scripture, divinely inspired, is useful for teaching and instructing (2 Tim. iii, 16). Besides, the whole gospel narrative would be poetical and fabulous, if it narrated appearances of things for realities, whereas it is said: We have not been led by sophisticated fables in making known to you the power of our Lord Jesus Christ (2 Peter i, 16). Wherever Scripture has to tell of appearances, it gives us to understand this by the very style of the narrative, e.g., the apparition of the three men to Abraham, who in them adored God and confessed the Deity (Gen. xviii). As for the visions of the imagination (imaginarie visa) seen by Isaias, Ezechiel, and other prophets, they originate no error, because they are not narrated as history, but as prophetic pictures: still there is always something put in to show that it is but an apparition (Isai. vi, 1: Ezech. i, 4: viii, 3).

When divine truths are conveyed in Scripture under figurative language, no error can thence arise, as well from the homely character of the similitudes used, which shows that they are but similitudes; as also because what in some places is hidden under similitudes, in others is revealed by plain speaking. But there is no Scripture authority to derogate from the literal truth of all that we read about the humanity of Christ. When the Apostle says: God sent his Son in the likeness of sinful flesh (Rom. viii, 3): he does not say, in the likeness flesh, but adds sinful, since Christ had true flesh, but not sinful flesh, there being no sin in Him; but His flesh was like sinful flesh, inasmuch as He had flesh liable to suffering, as man's flesh was rendered liable by sin. So the expression, made in the likeness of men(Phil. ii, 7), conveys no idea of illusion: that is shown by what follows, taking the form of a servant, where 'form' is clearly put for 'nature,' as the adjoining clause shows, being in the form of God: for it is not supposed that Christ was God only in resemblance.

Moreover there are passages in which Holy Scripture expressly bars the suspicion of Christ being a mere appearance, Matt. xiv, 26, 27: Luke xxiv, 37-39: Acts x, 40, 41: and St John's words, What was from the beginning, what we have heard, what we have seen with our eyes, what we have looked upon, and our hands have handled, of the word of life (1 John i, 1). In fact, if Christ had not a real body, He did not really die; neither therefore did he really rise again: And if Christ be not risen again, then is our preaching vain, and your faith is also vain, yea and we are found false witnesses of God, because we have given testimony of God that he hath raised up Christ, whom he hath not raised up [if He never really died] (1 Cor. xv, 14, 15).

CHAPTERS XXXII, XXXIII—Of the Error of Arius and Apollinaris concerning the Soul of Christ

ARIUS held that Christ had no soul, but assumed flesh alone, to which the Divinity stood in the place of a soul. In this he was followed by Apollinaris. Apollinaris however was brought to confess that Christ had a sensitive soul; but he averred that the Divinity stood to that sensitive soul in place of mind and intellect (S. Aug. de haeresibus, 55).

1. It is impossible for the Word of God to be the

form of a body.

2. Take away what is of the essence of man, and a true man cannot remain. But manifestly the soul is the chief constituent of the essence of man, being his form. If Christ then had not a soul, He was not true man, though the Apostle calls Him such: *One mediator between God and men, the man Christ Jesus* (1 Tim. ii, 5).

4. What is generated of any living being cannot be called its offspring, unless it come forth in the same species. But if Christ had no soul, He would not be of the same species with other men: for things that differ in 'form' cannot be of the same species. At that rate Christ could not be called the Son of Mary, or she His mother: which however is asserted in Scripture (Luke i, 43: ii, 33: John xix, 25).

5. Express mention is made of the soul of Christ, Matt. xxvi, 8: John x, 18: xii, 27.

9. The body stands to the soul as matter to form, and as the instrument to the prime agent. But matter must be proportionate to form, and the instrument to the prime agent. Therefore according to the diversity of souls there must also be a diversity of bodies. And this is apparent even to sense: for in different animals we find different arrangements of limbs, adapted to different dispositions of souls. If then in Christ there were not a soul such as our soul, neither would He have had limbs like the limbs of man.

CHAPTER XXXIV—Of the Error of Theodore of Mopsuestia concerning the Union of the Word with Man

BY the foregoing chapters it appears that neither was the divine nature wanting to Christ, as Photinus said;

nor a true human body, according to the error of the Manicheans; nor again a human soul, as Arius and Apollinaris supposed. These three substances then meet in Christ, the Divinity, a human soul, and a true human body. It remains to enquire, according to the evidence of Scripture, what is to be thought of the union of the three. Theodore of Mopsuestia, then, and Nestorius, his follower, brought out the following theory of this union.

They said that a human soul and a human body were naturally united in Christ to constitute one man of the same species and nature with other men; and that in this man God dwelt as in His temple by grace, as He does in other holy men. Hence He said Himself: Dissolve this temple, and in three days I will raise it up: which the Evangelist explains: He spoke of the temple of his body (John ii, 19). Hereupon there followed a union of affections between the Man Christ and God, the Man adhering with hearty good will to God, and God willingly accepting Him, as He says Himself: He that sent me is with me; and he hath not left me alone, because I do always the things that are pleasing to him(John viii, 29): giving us to understand that the union of that Man with God is as the union of which the Apostle speaks: He that adheres to God, is one spirit(1 Cor. vi, 17). And as by this union the names that properly apply to God are transferred to men, so that they are called gods, and sons of God, and lords, and holy ones, and christs, as appears by divers passages of Scripture (e.g., Pss. lxxxi, civ); so are divine names duly applied to the Man Christ, and by reason of the indwelling of God and the union of affections with Him He is called God, and Son of God, and Lord, and Holy One, and Christ. Moreover, because in that Man there was greater fullness of grace than in other holy men, He was above others the temple of God, and more closely united with God in affection, and shared the divine names by a peculiar privilege of His own; and for this excellence of grace He was put in participation of divine honor and dignity, and has come to be adored along with God. And thus one is the person of the Word of God, and another the person of that Man who is adored along with God. Or if there is said to be one person of them both, that will be by reason of the aforesaid union of affections, on the strength of which that Man and the Word of God will be one person, in the same way in which it is said of husband and wife that they are no more two, but one flesh (Matt. xix, 6). And because such a union does not authorize us to predicate of the one whatever can be predicated of the other — for not whatever is true of the husband is true of the wife, or vice versa, — therefore in the case of the union of the Word with that Man this Nestorian doctrine has it we should not fail to notice how the properties of that Man, belonging to His human nature, cannot fitly be predicated of the Word of God, or God. Thus it is proper to that Man to have been born of a Virgin, to have suffered, died, and been buried: all of which things, Nestorians say, are impossible to predicate of God, or of the Word of God. But because there are some names which, while applying to God in the first place, are communicated to man in a sense, as Christ, Lord, Holy One, or even Son of God, they see no difficulty in terms expressive of the above incidents of humanity being united as predicates with these names. So they think it proper to say that 'Christ,' 'the Lord of glory,' 'the Saint of saints,' or even 'the Son of God,' was 'born of a virgin,' 'suffered,' 'died,' and 'was buried.' Therefore they say that the Blessed Virgin should not be called 'mother of God,' or 'of the Word of God,' but 'mother of Christ.'

1. Any thoughtful person may see that this theory cannot stand with the truth of the Incarnation. The theory holds that the Word of God was united with the Man Christ only by the indwelling of grace and consequent union of wills. But the indwelling of the Word of God in man does not mean the Word of God being Incarnate: for the Word of God and God Himself dwelt in all the saints from the beginning of the world, according to the text: Ye are the temple of the living God, as God says: I will dwell in them (2 Cor vi, 16: Levit. xxvi, 12). But this indwelling cannot be called an incarnation: otherwise God must have become incarnate frequently from the beginning of the world. Nor is it enough to constitute an incarnation, if the Word of God and God dwelt in the Man Christ with more abundant grace: for greater and less do not make a difference of species in point of union.

3. Everything that is made anything is that which it is made, as what is made man is man, and what is made white is white. But the Word of God has been made man (John i, 14). Therefore the Word of God is man. But, of two things differing in person, or suppositum, the one cannot possibly be predicated of the other. When it is said 'Man is an animal,' that self-same being which is an animal is man. When it is said, 'Man is white,' some particular man himself is pointed at as being white, although whiteness is beyond the essential notion of humanity. But in no way can it be said that Socrates is Plato, or any other of the individuals either of the same or of a different species. If then the Word has been made flesh, that is, man, it is impossible for there to be two persons, one of the Word, the other of the Man.

4. No one would say, 'I am running,' when someone else was running, except perhaps figuratively, meaning that another was running in his place. But that man who is called Jesus (John ix, 11) says of Himself, Before Abraham was, I am (John viii, 58); I and the Father are one (John x, 30); and sundry other phrases, manifestly proper to the divinity of the Word. Therefore the person of that Man speaking is the person of the Son of God.

6. To ascend into heaven is clearly an attribute of Christ as man, who in their sight was taken up (Acts i, 9). And to descend from heaven is an attribute of the Word of God. But he who descended, the same is he that hath ascended (Eph. iv, 10).

11. Though a man be called 'Lord' by participation in the divine dominion, still no man, nor any creature whatever, can be called 'the Lord of glory': because the glory of happiness to come is something which God alone by nature possesses, others only by the gift of grace: hence it is said: The Lord of mighty deeds, he is the king of glory (Ps. xxiii, 10). But, had they known, never could they have crucified the Lord of glory (1 Cor. ii, 8). It is true then to say that God was crucified.

12. Scripture attributes suffering and death to the only-begotten Son of God: He spared not his own Son, but gave him up for us all (Rom. viii, 32): God so loved the world as to give his only begotten Son (John iii, 16: cf. verse 1and Rom. v, 8).

17. The word was made flesh (John i, 14). But the Word was not flesh except of a woman. The Word then was made of a woman (Gal. iv, 4), — of a Virgin Mother, for a Virgin is the Mother of the Word of God.

19. Phil. ii, 5-11. If with Nestorius we divide

Christ into two — into the Man, who is the Son of God by adoption, and the Son of God by nature, who is the Word of God, — this passage cannot be understood of the Man. That Man, if he be mere man, was not, to begin with, in the form of God so as afterwards to come to be in the likeness of men, but rather the other way about, being man, He became partaker of the Deity, in which participation He was not emptied, but exalted. It must then be understood of the Word of God, that He was, to begin with, from eternity in the form of God, that is, in the nature of God, and afterwards emptied himself by being made in the likeness of men. That emptying cannot be understood to mean the mere in dwelling of the Word of God in the man Christ Jesus. For from the beginning of the world the Word of God has dwelt by grace in all holy men, yet not for that is it said to be emptied: for God's communication of His goodness to creatures is no derogation from Himself but rather an exaltation, inasmuch as His pre-eminence appears by the goodness of creatures, and all the more the better the creatures are. Hence if the Word of God dwelt more fully in the Man Christ than in other saints, there was less emptying of the Word in His case than in the case of others. Evidently then the union of the Word with human nature is not to be understood to mean the mere indwelling of the Word of God in that Man, but the Word of God truly being made man. Thus only can that emptying be said to take place; the Word of God being said to be emptied, that is made small, not by any loss of His own greatness, but by the assumption of human littleness.

24. The man Christ, speaking of Himself, says many divine and supernatural things, as, I will raise him up at the last day (John vi, 40): I give them life

everlasting (John x, 28). Such language would be the height of pride, if the speaker were not Himself God, but only had God dwelling in him. And still Christ says of Himself: Learn of me, because I am meek and humble of heart (Matt. xi, 29).

26. In him all things were made (Col. i, 16) is said of the Word of God; and first-born of the dead (ib. 18) is said of Christ; in such context as to show that the Word of God and Christ are one and the same person.

27. The same conclusion appears in 1 Cor. viii, 6: And one Lord Jesus Christ, by whom are all things.

The opinion of Nestorius on the mystery of the Incarnation differs little from the opinion of Photinus. Both asserted that the man Christ was God only through the indwelling of grace. Photinus said that Christ merited the name and glory of Godhead by His passion and good works. Nestorius avowed that He had this name and glory from the first instant of His conception on account of the full and ample indwelling of God in Him. But concerning the eternal generation of the Word they differ considerably; Nestorius confessing it, Photinus denying it entirely.

## CHAPTER XXXV—Against the Error of Eutyches

EUTYCHES, to save the unity of person in Christ against Nestorius, said that in Christ there was only one nature. He went on to explain how before the union there were two distinct natures, one divine and one human; but in the union they both met so as to form one. He said then that the person of Christ was of two natures, but did not subsist in two natures. The falsity of this statement is apparent on many counts.

1. In Christ Jesus there was a Body, and a natural Soul, and the Divinity. The Body of Christ, even after the union, was not the Divinity of the Word: for the Body of Christ, even after the union, was passible, visible to bodily eyes, and distinct in lineaments and limbs, all of which attributes are alien to the Divinity of the Word. In like manner the Soul of Christ after union was distinct from the Divinity of the Word, because the Soul of Christ, even after the union, was affected by the passions of sadness and grief and anger (Mark iii, 5: xiv, 34), which again can in no way be adapted to the Divinity of the Word. But soul and body make up human nature. Thus then, even after union, there was a human nature in Christ, other than the Divinity of the Word, which is the divine nature.

2. Being in the form of God, he took the form of a servant (Phil. ii, 6, 7). It cannot be said that the form of God and the form of a servant are the same, for nothing takes that which it already has. In Eutyches's view, Christ having already the form of God, could not have taken the form of a servant, the two being the same. Nor can it be said that the form of God in Christ was changed by the union, for so Christ after the union would not be God. Nor again can it be said that the form of the servant was mingled with the form of God, for mingled elements do not remain entire, but both are partially changed: hence it should not be said that He had taken the form of a servant, but something of that form. Thus the Apostle's words must mean that in Christ, even after union, there were two forms, therefore two natures.

3. If we suppose a blending of both natures, divine and human, neither would remain, but some third thing;

and thus Christ would be neither God nor man. Eutyches then cannot be understood to mean that one nature was made out of the two. He can only mean that after union only one of the natures remained. Either then in Christ only the divine nature remained, and what seemed in Him human was merely phenomenal, as the Manicheans said; or the divine nature was changed into a human nature, as Apollinaris said: against both of whom we have argued above (Chapp. XXIX, XXXI).

5. When one nature is constituted of two permanent components, these components are either bodily parts, like the limbs of an animal, a case not in point here, or they are matter and form, like body and soul: but God is not matter, nor can He stand to any matter in the relation of form. Therefore in Christ, true God and true Man, there cannot be one nature only.

7. Where there is no agreement in nature, there is no specific likeness. If then the nature of Christ is a compound of divine and human, there will be no specific likeness between Him and us, contrary to the saying of the Apostle: He ought in all things to be made like to his brethren (Heb. ii, 17).

9. Even this saying of Eutyches seems inconsistent with the faith, that there were two natures in Christ before the union: for as human nature is made up of body and soul, it would follow that either the soul, or the body of Christ, or both, existed before the Incarnation, which is evidently false.

CHAPTER XXXVI—Of the Error of Macarius of Antioch, who posited one Operation only and one Will only in Christ

TO every nature there is a proper activity: for the form is the principle of activity, and different natures have different forms and different acts. If then in Christ there is only one operation, there must be in Him only one nature: but to hold that is the Eutychian heresy.

2. There is in Christ a perfect divine nature, whereby He is consubstantial with the Father; and a perfect human nature, whereby He is of one species with us. But it is part of the perfection of the divine nature to have a will (B. I, Chap. LXXII); and part of the perfection of human nature to have a will, whereby a man is capable of free choice. There must therefore be two wills in Christ.

3. If in Christ there is no other will than the will of the Word, by parity of reasoning there can be in Him no understanding but the understanding of the Word: thus we are brought back to the position of Apollinaris (Chap. XXXII).

4. If there was only one will in Christ, that must have been the divine will: for the Word could not have lost the divine will, which he had from eternity. But it does not belong to the divine will to merit. Thus then Christ would have merited neither for Himself nor for us by His passion, contrary to the teaching of the Apostle: He was made obedient unto death, therefore hath God exalted him (Phil. ii, 8, 9).

6. In one ordinary man, though he be one in person, there are nevertheless several appetites and operations according to different natural principles. In his rational part there is in him will: in his sensible part there is in him an irascible [θυμός] and a concupiscible appetite [ἐπιθυμητικόν]: and again there is physical tendency following upon physical powers. In like manner he sees

with the eye, hears with the ear, walks with the foot, speaks with the tongue, and understands with the mind, all so many different activities. And the reason is, because activities are not only multiplied according to difference of active subjects, but also according to the difference of the principles whereby one and the same subject works, from which principles also the activities derive their species. But the divine activity differs much more from the human than the natural principles of human nature from one another. There is therefore a difference of will and a difference of operation between the divine and the human nature in Christ, although Christ Himself is one in both natures.

7. The authority of Scripture shows plainly two wills in Christ: Not to do my will, but the will of Him that sent me (John vi, 38): Not my will but thine be done (Luke xxii, 42). These texts show that Christ had a will of His own, besides the will of His Father. On the other hand there was a will common to Him with the Father: for Father and Son have one will, as they have one nature. There are then in Christ two wills.

8. And in like manner of operations, or activities, — there was in Christ one operation common to Him with the Father, of which He says: Whatsoever things the Father doeth, the same the Son doeth also(John v, 19); and there was in Him another operation which attached not to the Father, as sleeping, hungering, eating, and the like things that Christ did or suffered in His humanity, as the Evangelists record (Mark iv, 38; xi, 12; ii, 16).

Monothelism appears to have sprung from the inability of its authors to distinguish between what is absolutely one and what is one in subordination to another. They saw that the human will in Christ was altogether subordinate to the divine will, so that Christ willed nothing with His human will otherwise than as the divine will predisposed Him to will. In like manner Christ wrought nothing in His human nature either in doing or in suffering, except what the divine will arranged, according to the text, *I do ever the things that are pleasing to him* (John viii, 29). The human operation of Christ gained a divine efficacy by His union with the Divinity, in consequence of which everything that He did or suffered made for salvation: wherefore Dionysius calls the human activity of Christ 'theandric.' Seeing then that the human will and operation of Christ was subordinate to the divine, with a subordination that never failed, they [the Monothelites] judged that there was only one will and operation in Christ; although it is not the same thing to be one by subordination and one absolutely.

CHAPTER XXXIX—The Doctrine of Catholic Faith concerning the Incarnation

ACCORDING to the tradition of Catholic faith we must say that in Christ there is one perfect divine nature, and a perfect human nature, made up of a rational soul and human flesh; and that these two natures are united in Christ, not by mere indwelling of the one in the other, or in any accidental way, as a man is united with his garment, but in unity of one person. For since Holy Scripture without any distinction assigns the things of God to the Man Christ, and the things of the Man Christ to God, He must be one and the same person, of whom both varieties of attributes are predicable. But because opposite attributes are not predicable of one and the same subject in the same respect, and there is an opposition between the divine and human attributes that are predicated of Christ, — as that He is passible and impassible, dead and immortal, and the like, — these divine and human attributes must be predicated of Christ in different respects. If we consider that of which these opposite attributes are predicated, we shall find no distinction to draw, but unity appears there. But considering that according to which these several predications are made, there we shall see the need of drawing a distinction. Since that according to which divine attributes are predicated of Christ is different from that according to which human attributes are predicated of Him, we must say that there are in Him two natures, unamalgamated and unalloyed. And since that of which these human and divine attributes are predicated is one and indivisible, we must say that Christ is one person, and one suppositum, supporting a divine and a human nature.

Thus alone will divine attributes duly and properly be predicated of the Man Christ, and human attributes of the Word of God. Thus also it appears how, though the Son is incarnate, it does not follow that the Father or the Holy Ghost is incarnate: for the incarnation does not have place in respect of that unity of nature wherein in the three Persons agree, but in respect of person and suppositum, wherein the three Persons are distinct. Thus as in the Trinity there is a plurality of persons subsisting in one nature, so in the mystery of the Incarnation there is one person subsisting in a plurality of natures.

CHAPTER XLI—Some further Elucidation of the Incarnation

EUTYCHES made the union of God and man a

union of nature: Nestorius, a union neither of nature nor of person: the Catholic faith makes it a union of person, not of nature. To forestall objections, we need to form clear notions of what it is to be united 'in nature,' and what it is to be united 'in person.'

Those things then are united 'in nature,' which combine to constitute the integrity of some specific type, as soul and body are united to constitute the specific type of 'animal.' Once a specific type is set up in its integrity, no foreign element can be united with it in unity of nature without the breaking up of that specific type.55But what is not of the integrity of the specific type is readily found in some individual contained under the species, as whiteness and clothedness in Socrates or Plato. All such non-specific attributes are said to be united 'in unity of suppositum,' or in the case of rational beings, 'in unity of person,' with the individual.

Now some have reckoned the union of God and man in Christ to be after the manner of things united 'in unity of nature.' Thus Arius and Apollinaris and Eutyches. But that is quite an impossibility. For the nature of the Word is a sovereignly perfect whole from all eternity, incapable of alteration or change: nothing foreign to the divine nature, — no human nature, nor any element of human nature, — can possibly come to thrust itself into that unity. Others saw the impossibility of this position, and turned aside in the contrary direction. Whatever is added to any nature without belonging to the integrity of the same, may be reckoned to be either an accident, as whiteness and music, or to stand in an accidental relation to the subject, as a ring, a dress, a house. Considering then that human nature is added to the Word of God without belonging to the integrity of His nature, these [Nestorians] thought that the union of this supperadded human nature with the Word was merely accidental. Manifestly, it could not be in the Word as an accident, for God is not susceptible of accidents; and besides human nature itself stands in the category of substance, and cannot be an accident of anything. The alternative which they embraced was to conclude that the human nature stood in an accidental relation with the Word. Nestorius then laid it down that the human nature stood to the word in the relation of a temple to the Deity whose temple it was; and that union with human nature meant a mere indwelling of the Word in that nature. And because a temple has its individuality apart from him that dwells in it, and the individuality proper to human nature is personality, it followed that the personality of the human nature was one, and the personality of the Word another; and thus the Word and the Man were two persons: all which conclusion has been set aside by our previous arguments.

We must therefore lay it down that the union of the Word with the Man was such, that neither was one nature compounded out of two; nor was the union of the Word with human nature like the union of a substance with something exterior to it and standing in an accidental relation to it, like the relation of a man to his garment and his house: but the Word must be considered to subsist in human nature as in a nature made properly its own, so that that Body is truly the Body of the Word of God, and that Soul the Soul of the Word of God, and the Word of God truly is man. And though such union cannot be perfectly explained by mortal man, still we will endeavor, according to our capacity and ability, to say something towards the building up of faith and the defense of this mystery of faith against unbelievers.

In all creation there is nothing so like this union as the union of soul and body. So the Athanasian Creed has it: "As the rational soul and flesh is one man, so God and man is one Christ." But whereas the rational soul is united with the body, (a) as form with matter, (b) as chief agent with instrument (B. II, Chapp. LVI, LVII); this comparison cannot hold in respect of the former mode of union, for so we should be brought round to the [Eutychian] conclusion, that of God and man there was made one nature. We must take the point of the comparison then to be the union of soul with body as of agent with instrument. And with this the sayings of some ancient Doctors agree, who have laid it down that the human nature in Christ is an instrument of His divinity, as the body is an instrument of the soul. The body and its parts, as instruments of the soul, come in a different category from exterior instruments. This axe is not my own proper instrument as is this hand. With this axe many men may work: but this hand is set aside for the proper activity of this soul. Therefore the hand is a tool conjoined with and proper to him that works with it: but the axe is an instrument extrinsic to the workman and common to many hands. Thus then we may take it to be with the union of God and man. All men stand to God as instruments wherewith He works: For he it is that worked in us to will and accomplish on behalf of the good will (Phil. ii, 13). But other men stand to God as extrinsic and separate instruments. God moves them, not merely to activities proper to Himself, but to activities common to all rational nature, such as understanding truth, loving goodness, and working justice. But human nature has been taken up in Christ to work as an instrument proper to God alone, such works as cleansing of sins, illumination of the mind by grace, and introduction to everlasting life. The human nature therefore of Christ stands to God as an instrument proper and conjoined, as the hand to the soul.

The aforesaid examples however are not alleged as though a perfect likeness were to be looked for in them. We must understand how easy it was for the Word of God to unite Himself with human nature in a union far more sublime and intimate than that of the soul with any 'proper instrument.'

CHAPTER XL, XLIX—Objections against the Faith of the Incarnation, with Replies

ARG. 1. If God has taken flesh, He must be either changed into a body, or be some power resident in a body.

Reply1. The Incarnation does not mean either the conversion of the Word into flesh, or the union of the Word with a human body as the form of the same.

Arg.2. If the person of the Word of God acquires a new subsistence in a human nature, it must undergo a substantial change, as everything is changed that acquires a new nature.

Reply2. The change is not in the Word of God, but in the human nature assumed by the Word.

Arg.3. If the personality of the Word of God has become the personality of a human nature, it follows that since the Incarnation the Word of God has not been everywhere, as that human nature is not everywhere.

Reply 3. Personality does not extend beyond the bounds of that nature from which it has its subsistence. But the Word of God has not its subsistence from its human nature, but rather draws that human nature to its own subsistence or personality: for it does not subsist through it, but in it.

Arg. 4. One and the same thing has only one quiddity, substance, or nature. It seems impossible therefore for one person to subsist in two natures.

Reply 4. The assertion is true, if you speak of the nature whereby a thing has being, absolutely speaking; and so, absolutely speaking, the Word of God has being by the divine nature alone, not by the human nature. But by the human nature it has being as Man.

Arg. 8. Soul and body in Christ are of not less potency than they are in other men. But their union in other men constitutes a person: therefore also in Christ.

Reply 8. The human soul and body in Christ being drawn into the personality of the Word, and not constituting another person besides the person of the Word, does not mark a diminution of potency, but a greater excellence. Everything is better for being united to what is more excellent than itself, better than it was, or would be, if it stood by itself.

Arg. 10. This man, who is Christ, considered merely as made up of soul and body, is a substance: but not a universal, therefore a particular substance: therefore a person.

Reply 10. Yes, He is a person, but no other person than the person of the Word: because the human nature has been so assumed by the person of the Word that the Word subsists as well in the human as in the divine nature: but what subsists in human nature is 'this man': therefore the Word Himself is spoken of61when we say 'this Man.'

Arg. 11. If the personality of the divine and human nature in Christ is the same, divine personality must be part of the notion of the Man who is Christ. But it is not part of the notion of other men. Therefore the application of the common term 'man' to Christ and to other men is an instance of the use of the same term not in the same sense; and thus He will not be of the same species with us.

Reply11. Variation of the sense of a term comes from diversity of form connoted, not from diversity of person denoted. The term 'man' does not vary in sense by denoting sometimes Plato, sometimes Socrates. The term 'man' then, whether used of Christ or of other men, always connotes the same form, that is, human nature, and is predicated of them all in the same sense. But the denotation varies in this that, as taken for Christ, the term denotes an uncreated person; but as taken for other men, a created person.

CHAPTER XLIV—That the Human Nature, assumed by the Word, was perfect in Soul and Body in the instant of Conception

THE Word of God took a body through the medium of a rational soul: for the body of man is not more assumable by God than other bodies except for the rational soul. The Word of God then did not assume a body without a rational soul. Since then the Word of God assumed a body from the first instant of conception, in that very instant the rational soul must have been united with the body.

4. The body which the Word assumed was formed from the first instant of conception, because it would have been against the fitness of things for the Word of God to have assumed anything that was formless. Moreover the soul, like any other natural form, requires its proper

matter. Now the proper matter of the soul is an organized body: for "the soul is the actualization of an organic, natural body, that is in potentiality to life." If then the soul was united with the body from the first instant of conception, the body must needs have been organized and formed from the first instant of conception. Moreover in the order of the stages of generation the organization of the body precedes the introduction of the rational soul: hence, positing the latter, we must posit the former stage also. But increase in quantity up to the due measure may very well be subsequent to the animation of the body. Thus then, concerning the conception of the Man assumed, we must think that in the very instant of conception His body was organized and formed, but had not as yet its due quantity.

CHAPTER XLV—That Christ was born of a Virgin without prejudice to His true and natural Humanity

GOD'S power being infinite, and all other causes deriving their efficacy from that, any effect produced by any cause may be produced by God without aid of that cause, and yet be of the same species and nature as though it had been produced in the ordinary way. As then the natural power of the human semen produces a true man, having the species and nature of a man, so the divine power, which has given that power to the semen, may produce the effect of that power, without calling the cause into activity, and so constitute a true man, having the species and nature of a man. Nor is anything lost to the dignity of the Mother of Christ by the virgin conception and birth: there is nothing in that to prevent her being called the Mother of the Son of God: for by the working of divine power she supplied the matter physically requisite for the generation of the body of Christ: which is all that a mother need do.

CHAPTERS XLVI, XLVII—That Christ was conceived by the Holy Ghost

THOUGH every divine activity, whereby anything is done in creatures, is common to the entire Trinity, nevertheless the formation of the body of Christ is appropriately attributed to the Holy Ghost: for in Scripture every grace is wont to be attributed to the Holy Ghost, since what is given gratuitously is reckoned to be bestowed out of the love of the giver; and there is no greater grace bestowed on man than his coming to be united with God in union of person. Still the Holy Ghost cannot be called the father of Christ in His human generation; because the Holy Ghost did not produce the human nature of Christ out of His own substance, but merely by an exertion of His power.

CHAPTER LIV—Of the Incarnation as part of the Fitness of Things

BY the fact of God having willed to unite human nature to Himself in unity of person, it is plainly shown to men that man can be intellectually united with God and see Him with an immediate vision. It was therefore very fitting for God to assume human nature, thereby to lift up man's hope to happiness. Hence since the Incarnation men have begun to aspire more after happiness, as Christ Himself says: I have come that they may have life and have it more abundantly (John x, 10).

2. Although in certain respects man is inferior to some other creatures, and in some respects is likened to the very lowest, yet in respect of the end for which he is created nothing is higher than man but God alone: for in God alone does the perfect happiness of man consist. This dignity of man, requiring to find happiness in the immediate vision of God, is most aptly shown by God's immediate assumption of human nature. The Incarnation has borne this fruit, visible to all eyes, that a considerable portion of mankind has abandoned the worship of creatures, trampled underfoot the pleasures of the flesh, and devoted itself to the worship of God alone, in whom alone it expects the perfect making of its happiness, according to the admonition of the Apostle: Seek the things that are above (Col. iii, 1).

3. Since the perfect happiness of man lies in a knowledge of God beyond the natural capacity of any created intelligence (B. III, Chap. LII), there was wanted for man in this life a sort of foretaste of this knowledge to guide him to the fullness of it; and that foretaste is by faith (B. III, Chapp. XL, CLIII). But this knowledge of faith, whereby a man is guided to his last end, ought to be of the highest certitude: to which perfect certitude man needed to be instructed by God Himself made man. So it is said: No man hath seen God ever: the only begotten Son, who is in the bosom of the Father, he hath told us (John i, 18): For this I was born, and for this I came into the world to give testimony to the truth (John xviii, 37). Thus we see that since the Incarnation of Christ men have been instructed more evidently and surely in the

knowledge of God, according to the text: The earth is filled with the knowledge of the Lord (Isai. xi, 9).

4. Since the perfect happiness of man consists in the enjoyment of God, it was requisite for man's heart to be disposed to desire this enjoyment. But the desire of enjoying anything springs from the love of it. Therefore it was requisite for man, making his way to perfect happiness, to be induced to love God. Now nothing induces us to love any one so much as the experience of his love for us. Nor could God's love for man have been more effectually demonstrated to man than by God's willing to be united with man in unity of person: for this is just the property of love, to unite the lover with the loved.

5. Friendship resting on a certain equality, persons very unequal cannot be conjoined in friendship. To promote familiar friendship then between man and God, it was expedient that God should become man, "that while we know God in visible form, we may thereby be borne on to the love of His invisible perfections" (Mass of Christmas Day).

6. For the strengthening of man in virtue it was requisite that he should receive doctrine and examples of virtue from God made man, since of mere men even the holiest are found at fault sometimes. I have given you an example, that as I have done so ye also do (John xiii, 15).

8. The tradition of the Church teaches us that the whole human race has been infected by sin. And it is part of the order of divine justice that sin should not be forgiven without satisfaction. But no mere man was able to satisfy for the sin of all mankind, since every mere man is something less than the whole multitude of mankind. For the deliverance then of mankind from their common

sin, it was requisite for one to make satisfaction, who was at once man, so that satisfaction should be expected of him, and something above man, so that his merit should be sufficient to satisfy for the sin of the whole human race. Now in the order of happiness there is nothing greater than man but God alone: for though the angels are higher in condition of nature, they are not higher in respect to their final end, because they are made happy with the same happiness as man. It was needful therefore for man's attainment of happiness that God should become man, to take away the sin of the world (John i, 29: Rom. iv, 25: v, 18: Heb. ix, 28).

CHAPTER LV—Points of Reply to Difficulties touching the Economy of the Incarnation

WE must bear in mind that, so immovable is the divine goodness in its perfection, that nothing is lost to God, however near any creature is raised to Him: the gain is to the creature.

3. Man being a compound of a spiritual and a corporeal nature, and thereby, we may say, occupying the borderland of two natures, all creation seems to be interested in whatever is done for man's salvation. Lower corporeal creatures make for his use, and are in some sort of subjection to him: while the higher spiritual creation, the angelic, has in common with man its attainment of the last end. This argues a certain appropriateness in the universal Cause of all creatures taking to Himself in unity of person that creature whereby He is more readily in touch with all the rest of creation.

4. Sin in man admits of expiation, because man's choice is not immovably fixed on its object, but may be

perverted from good to evil, and from evil brought back to good; and the like is the case of man's reason, which, gathering the truth from sensible appearances and signs, can find its way to either side of a conclusion. But an angel has a fixed discernment of things through simple intuition; and as he is fixed in his apprehension, so is he fixed also in his choice. Hence he either does not take to evil at all; or if he does take to evil, he takes to it irrevocably, and his sin admits of no expiation. Since then the expiation of sin was the chief cause of the Incarnation, it was more fitting for human nature than for angelic nature to be assumed by God.

7. Though all created good is a small thing, compared with the divine goodness, still there can be nothing greater in creation than the salvation of the rational creature, which consists in the enjoyment of that divine goodness. And since the salvation of man has followed from the Incarnation of God, it cannot be said that that Incarnation has brought only slight profit to the world. Nor need all men be saved by the Incarnation, but they only who by faith and the sacraments of faith adhere to the Incarnation.

8. The Incarnation was manifested to man by sufficient evidences. There is no more fitting way of manifesting Godhead than by the performance of acts proper to God. Now it is proper to God to be able to change the course of nature (naturae leges), by doing something above that nature of which Himself is the author. Works overriding the ordinary course of nature (opera quae supra leges naturae fiunt) are the aptest evidences of divine being. Such works Christ did; and by these works He argued His Divinity. When asked, Art thou he that is to come? He replied, The blind see, the

lame walk, the lepers are cleansed, the deaf hear, the dead rise again (Luke vii, 22). And if it be said that the same miracles have been wrought by others, we must observe that Christ worked them in a very different and more divine way. Others are said to have wrought miracles by prayer, but Christ wrought them by command, as of His own power. And He not only wrought them Himself, but He gave to others the power of working the same and even greater miracles; and they worked them at the mere invocation of the name of Christ. And not only corporal miracles, but spiritual miracles, were wrought through Christ and at the invocation of His name: the Holy Ghost was given, hearts were set on fire with divine love, minds were suddenly instructed in the knowledge of divine things, and the tongues of the simple were rendered eloquent to propose the divine truth to men (Heb. ii, 3, 4).

9. Human nature is so conditioned as not to be apt to be led to perfection at once; but it must be led by the hand through stages of imperfection, so to arrive at perfection at last, as we see in the training of children. If great and unheard-of truths were proposed to a multitude, they would not grasp them immediately: their only chance is to become accustomed to such truths by mastering lesser truths first. Thus it was fitting for the human race to receive their first instruction in the things of salvation by light and rudimentary lessons (levia et minora documenta), delivered by the patriarchs, the law and the prophets; and that finally in the consummation of ages the perfect doctrine of Christ should be set forth on earth. When the fullness of time was come, God sent his Son (Gal. iv, 4). The law was our paedagogue unto Christ, but now we are no longer under a paedagogue (Gal. iii, 24, 25).

12. It was not expedient for the Incarnate God in this world to live in wealth and high honor: first, because the object of His coming was to withdraw the minds of men from their attachment to earthly things, and to raise them to things heavenly, for which purpose He found it necessary to draw men by His example to a contempt of riches: secondly, because if He had abounded in riches, and had been set in some high position, His divine doings would have been ascribed rather to secular power than to the virtue of the Divinity. This indeed forms the most efficacious argument of His Divinity, that without aid of secular power He has changed the whole world for the better.

13. God's commandment to men is of works of virtue; and the more perfectly any one performs an act of virtue, the more he obeys God. Now of all virtues charity is the chief: all others are referred to it. Christ's obedience to God consisted most of all in His perfect fulfilment of the act of charity: for greater charity than this no man hath, that a man lay down his life for his friends (John xv, 13).

15. Though God has no wish for the death of men, yet He has a wish for virtue; and by virtue man meets death bravely, and exposes himself to danger of death for charity. Thus God had a wish for the death of Christ, inasmuch as Christ took upon Himself that death out of charity, and bravely endured it.

17. It is well said that Christ wished to suffer the death of the cross in order to give an example of humility. The virtue of humility consists in keeping oneself within one's own bounds, not reaching out to things above one, but submitting to one's superior. Thus humility cannot befit God, who has no superior, but is above all.

Whenever anyone subjects himself out of humility to an equal or any inferior, that is because he takes that equal or inferior to be his superior in some respect. Though then the virtue of humility cannot attach to Christ in His divine nature, yet it may attach to Him in his human nature. And His divinity renders His humility all the more praiseworthy: for the dignity of the person adds to the merit of humility; and there can be no greater dignity to a man than his being God. Hence the highest praise attaches to the humility of the Man God, who, to wean men's hearts from worldly glory to the love of divine glory, chose to endure a death of no ordinary sort, but a death of the deepest ignominy.

19. It was necessary for Christ to suffer (Luke xxiv, 46), not only to afford an example of braving death for the love of truth, but also for the expiation of the sins of other men; which expiation He made by His own sinless Self choosing to suffer the death due to sin, and so satisfying for others by taking on Himself the penalty due to others. And though the sole grace of God is sufficient for the forgiveness of sins, nevertheless in the process of that forgiveness something is required on his part to whom the sin is forgiven, namely, to offer satisfaction to him whom he has offended. And because men could not do this for themselves, Christ did it for all, suffering a voluntary death for charity.

20. Although when it is a question of punishing sins, he must be punished who has sinned, nevertheless, when it is a question of making satisfaction, one may bear another's penalty. When punishment is inflicted for sin, his iniquity is put into the scale who has sinned: but when satisfaction is made by the offender's voluntary taking upon himself a penalty to appease him whom he has

offended, account is taken in that case of the affection and good will of him who makes the satisfaction. And this appears best in the case of one taking upon himself a penalty instead of another, and God accepting the satisfaction of one for another (B. III, Chap. CLIXad fin.)

25. Though the death of Christ is sufficient satisfaction for original sin, there is nothing incongruous in the miseries consequent upon original sin remaining in all men, even in those who are made partakers of the redemption of Christ. It was a fit and advantageous arrangement for the punishment to remain after the guilt was taken away: — first, for the conformity of the faithful with Christ, as of members with their head, that as Christ endured many sufferings, so His faithful should be subject to sufferings, and so arrive at immortality, as the Apostle says: If we suffer with him, so that we be glorified with him(Rom. viii, 17): — secondly, because if men coming to Christ gained immediate exemption from death and suffering, many men would come rather for these corporal benefits than for spiritual goods, contrary to the intention of Christ, who came into the world to draw men from the love of corporal things to spiritual things: — thirdly, because this sudden impassibility and immortality would in a manner compel men to receive the faith of Christ, and so the merit of faith would be lost.

26. Each individual must seek the remedies that make for his own salvation. The death of Christ is a universal cause of salvation, as the sin of the first man was a universal cause of damnation. But there is need of a special application to each individual for the individual to share in the effect of a universal cause. The effect of the sin of our first parent reaches each individual through his carnal origin. The effect of the death of Christ reaches

each individual by his spiritual regeneration, whereby he is conjoined and in a manner incorporated with Christ.

CHAPTER L—That Original Sin is transmitted from our First Parent to his Posterity

THIS expressly appears from the words of the Apostle: As by one man sin came into the world, and by sin death, so death passed on to all men, seeing that all have sinned (Rom. v, 12). It cannot be said that by one man sin entered into the world by way of imitation, because in that interpretation sin would have reached only to those who imitate the first man in sinning; and since by sin death came into the world, death would reach only those who sin in the likeness of the first man that sinned. But to exclude this interpretation the Apostle adds: Death reigned from Adam to Moses even over those who did not sin in the likeness of the transgression of Adam. The Apostle's meaning therefore was not that by one man sin entered into the world in the way of imitation, but in the way of origin. Moreover, the common custom of the Church is to administer baptism to new-born children. But there would be no purpose in such administration, unless there were sin in them. If it is said that the purpose of infant baptism is not the cleansing of sin, but the arriving at the kingdom of God, the saying is nonsensical. They who say so, appeal to our Lord's words: Unless a man be born again of water and the Holy Ghost, he cannot enter into the kingdom of God (John iii, 5). The fact is, no one is excluded from the kingdom of God except for some fault. For the end of every rational creature is to arrive at happiness; which happiness can be only in the kingdom of God; which kingdom again is nothing else than the organized society of those who enjoy the vision of God, in which true happiness consists (B. III, Chap. LXIII). But nothing fails to gain its end except through some fault or flaw. If then unbaptized children cannot arrive at the kingdom of God, we must say that there is some fault, flaw, or sin in them.

CHAPTERS LI, LII—Arguments against Original Sin, with Replies

CHAP. LII — Before dealing with objections, we must premise that there are apparent in mankind certain probable signs of original sin, as we can argue fault from penalty. Now the human race generally suffers various penalties, corporal and spiritual. Among corporal penalties the chief is death, to which all the others lead up, as hunger, thirst, and the like. Among spiritual penalties the chief is the weak hold that reason takes of man, so that man with difficulty arrives at the knowledge of truth, easily falls into error, and cannot altogether surmount his bestial appetites, but often has his mind clouded by them. Someone may say that these defects, corporal and spiritual, are not penal, but natural. But looking at the thing rightly, and supposing divine providence, which to all varieties of perfection has adapted subjects apt to take up each variety, we may form a fairly probable conjecture that God, in uniting the higher nature of the soul to the lower nature of the body, had the intention that the former should control the latter; and further intended to remove, by His special and supernatural providence, any impediment to such control arising out of any defect of nature. Thus, as the rational soul is of a higher nature than the body, it might be supposed that such would be the terms of the union of the soul with the body, that nothing could possibly be in the body contrary to the soul whereby the body lives; and in like manner, as reason in man is associated with sensitive appetite and other sensitive powers, it might be expected that reason would not be hampered by those sensitive powers, but rather would rule them. In accordance with these natural anticipations, we lay it down, according to the doctrine of faith, that the original constitution of man was such that, so long as his reason was subject to God, his lower faculties served him without demur, and no bodily impediment could stand in the way of his body obeying him, God and His grace supplying whatever was wanting in nature to the achievement of this result. But when his reason turned away from God, his lower powers revolted from reason; and his body became subject to passions contrary to the [rational] life that is by the soul. Thus then, though it may be admitted that these defects are natural, if we look at human nature on its lower side; nevertheless, if we consider divine providence and the dignity of the higher portion of human nature, we have a fairly probable ground for arguing that these defects are penal. Thus we may gather the inference [a priori] that the human race must have been infected with some sin from its first origin. Now we may answer the arguments to the contrary.

Arg.1. The son shall not bear the iniquity of his father (Ezech. xviii, 20).

Reply1. There is a difference between what affects one individual and what affects the nature of a whole species: for by partaking in the species many men are as one man, as Porphyry says. The sin then that belongs to one individual is not imputable to another individual, unless he sins too, because the one is personally distinct from the other. But any sin touching the specific nature itself may without difficulty be propagated from one to another, as the specific nature is imparted by one to others [by generation]. Since sin is an evil of rational nature, and evil is a privation of good, we must consider of what good the privation is, in order to decide whether the sin in question belongs to our common nature, or is the particular sin of a private individual. The actual sins then, that are commonly committed by men, take away some good from the person of the sinner, such as grace and the due order of the parts of his soul: hence they are personal, and not imputable to a second party beyond the one person of the sinner. But the first sin of the first man not only robbed the sinner of his private and personal good, namely, grace and the due order of his soul, but also took away a good that belonged to the common nature of mankind. According to the original constitution of this nature, the lower powers were perfectly subject to reason, reason to God, and the body to the soul, God supplying by grace what was wanting to this perfection by nature. This benefit, which by some is called 'original justice,' was conferred on the first man in such sort that it should be propagated by him to posterity along with human nature. But when by the sin of the first man reason withdrew from its subjection to God, the consequence was a loss of the perfect subjection of the lower powers to reason, and of the body to the soul, — and that not only in the first sinner, but the same common defect has come down to posterity, to whom original justice would otherwise have descended. Thus then the sin of the first man, from whom, according to the doctrine of faith, all other men are descended, was at once a personal sin, inasmuch as it deprived that first man of his own private good, and also a sin of nature (peccatum naturale), inasmuch as it took away from that man, and consequently from his posterity, a benefit conferred upon the whole of human nature. This defect, entailed upon other men by their first parent, has in those other men the character of a fault, inasmuch as all men are counted one man hy participation in a common nature. This sin is voluntary by the will of our first parent, as the action of the hand has the character of a fault from the will of the prime mover, reason. In a sin of nature different men are counted parts of a common nature, like the different parts of one man in a personal sin.

Arg.5. What is natural is no sin, as it is not the mole's fault for being blind.

Reply 5. The defects above mentioned are transmitted by natural origin, inasmuch as nature is destitute of the aid of grace, which had been conferred upon nature in our first parent, and was meant to pass from him to posterity along with nature; and, inasmuch as this destitution has arisen from a voluntary sin, the defect so consequent comes to bear the character of a fault. Thus these defects are at once culpable, as referred to their first principle, which is the sin of Adam; and natural, as referred to a nature now destitute [of original justice].

Arg.6. A defect in a work of nature happens only through defect of some natural principle.

Reply6. There is a defect of principle, namely, of the gratuitous gift bestowed on human nature in its first creation; which gift was in a manner 'natural,' not that it was caused by the principles of nature, but because it was given to man to be propagated along with his nature.

Arg.9. The good of nature is not taken away by sin: hence even in devils their natural excellences remain.

Therefore the origin of human generation, which is an act of nature, cannot have been vitiated by sin.

Reply9. By sin there is not taken away from man the good of nature which belongs to his natural species, but a good of nature which was superadded by grace.

10. The gift, not belonging to the essence of the species, was nevertheless bestowed by God gratuitously on the first man, that from him it might pass to the entire species: in like manner the sin, which is the privation of that gift, passes to the entire species.

11. Though by the sacraments of grace one is so cleansed from original sin that it is not imputed to him as a fault, — and this is what is meant by saying that he is personally delivered from that sin, — yet he is not altogether healed; and therefore by the act of nature [i.e., of generation] original sin is transmitted to his posterity. Thus then in the human procreant, considered as a person, there is no original sin; and there may very well be no actual sin in the act of procreation: still, inasmuch as the procreant is a natural principle of procreation, the infection of original sin, as regards the nature, remains in him and in his procreative act.

### CHAPTER LVI—Of the Need of Sacraments

THE death of Christ is the universal cause of man's salvation: but a universal cause has to be applied to particular effects. Thus it was found necessary for certain remedies to be administered to men by way of bringing Christ's death into proximate connexion with them. Such remedies are the Sacraments of the Church. And these remedies had to be administered with certain visible signs: — first, because God provides for man, as for other beings, according to his condition; and it is the condition of man's nature to be led through sensible things to things spiritual and intelligible: secondly, because instruments must be proportioned to the prime cause; and the prime and universal cause of man's salvation is the Word Incarnate: it was convenient therefore that the remedies, through which that universal cause reaches men, should resemble the cause in this, that divine power works invisibly through visible signs.

Hereby is excluded the error of certain heretics, who wish all visible sacramental signs swept away; and no wonder, for they take all visible things to be of their own nature evil, and the work of an evil author (B. III, Chap. XV).

These visible sacramental signs are the instruments of a God Incarnate and Crucified (instrumenta Dei incarnati et passi).

CHAPTER LVII—Of the Difference between the Sacraments of the Old and of the New Law

THESE Sacraments, having their efficacy from the Passion of Christ, which they represent, must fall in and correspond with the salvation wrought by Christ. Before the Incarnation and Passion of Christ this salvation was promised, but not accomplished: it was wrought by the Incarnation and Passion of the Word. Therefore the Sacraments that preceded the Incarnation of Christ must have been such as to signify and promise salvation: while the Sacraments that follow the Passion of Christ must be such as to render salvation to men, and not merely show it forth by signs.

This avoids the error of the Jews, who believe that

the sacred rites of the Law must be observed forever, because they were instituted by God, who repents not and changes not. There is no change or repentance about an arrangement, which arranges for different things to be done according to the fitness of different times; as the father of a family gives different commands to his son in his nonage and when he is come of age. Still more irrational was the error of those who said that the rites of the Law were to be observed along with the Gospel; an error indeed which is self-contradictory: for the observance of the Gospel rites is a profession that the Incarnation and the other mysteries of Christ are now accomplished; while the observance of the rites of the Law is a profession that they are still to be fulfilled.

CHAPTER LVIII—Of the Number of the Sacraments of the New Law

THE remedies that provide for spiritual life are marked off, one from another, according to the pattern of corporal life. Now in respect of corporal life we find two classes of subjects. There are some who propagate and regulate corporal life in others, and some in whom corporal life is propagated and regulated. To this corporal and natural life three things are ordinarily necessary, and a fourth thing incidentally so. First, a living thing must receive life by generation or birth. Secondly, it must attain by augmentation to due quantity and strength. The third necessity is of nourishment. These three, generation, growth, and nutrition, are ordinary necessities, since bodily life cannot go on without them. But because bodily life may receive a check by sickness, there comes to be incidentally a fourth necessity, the healing of a living thing when it is sick. So in spiritual life the first thing is spiritual generation by Baptism: the second is spiritual growth leading to perfect strength by the Sacrament of Confirmation: the third is spiritual nourishment by the Sacrament of the Eucharist: there remains a fourth, which is spiritual healing, either of the soul alone by the Sacrament of Penance, or of the soul first, and thence derivatively, when it is expedient, of the body also, by Extreme Unction. These Sacraments then concern those subjects in whom spiritual life is propagated and preserved. Again, the propagators and regulators of bodily life are assorted according to a twofold division, namely, according to natural origin, which belongs to parents, and according to civil government, whereby the peace of human life is preserved, and that belongs to kings and princes. So then it is in spiritual life: there are some propagators and conservators of spiritual life by means of spiritual ministration only, and to that ministration belongs the Sacrament of Order: there are others who propagate and preserve at once corporal and spiritual life together, and that is done by the Sacrament of Matrimony, whereby man and woman come together to raise up issue and educate their children to the worship of God.

## CHAPTER LIX—Of Baptism

THE generation of a living thing is a change from not living to life. Now a man is deprived of spiritual life by original sin; and whatever sins are added there to go still further to withdraw him from life. Baptism therefore, or spiritual generation, was needed to serve the purpose of taking away original sin and all actual sins. And because the sensible sign of a Sacrament must be suited to represent the spiritual effect of the Sacrament, and the washing away of filth is done by water, therefore Baptism is fittingly conferred in water sanctified by the word of God. And because what is brought into being by generation loses its previous form and the properties consequent upon that form, therefore Baptism, as being a spiritual generation, not only takes away sins, but also all the liabilities contracted by sins, — all guilt and all debt of punishment: therefore no satisfaction for sins is enjoined on the baptized.

With the acquisition of a new form there goes also the acquisition of the activity consequent upon that form; and therefore the baptized become immediately capable of spiritual actions, such as the reception of the other Sacraments. Also there is due to them a position suited to the spiritual life: that position is everlasting happiness: and therefore the baptized, if they die fresh from baptism, are immediately caught up into bliss: hence it is said that baptism opens the gate of heaven.

One and the same thing can be generated only once: therefore, as Baptism is a spiritual generation, one man is to be baptized only once. The infection that came through Adam defiles a man only once: hence Baptism, which is directed mainly against that infection, ought not to be repeated. Also, once a thing is consecrated, so long as it lasts, it ought not to be consecrated again, lest the consecration should appear to be of no avail: hence Baptism, as it is a consecration of the person baptized, ought not to be repeated.

## CHAPTER LX—Of Confirmation

THE perfection of spiritual strength consists in a

man's daring to confess the faith of Christ before any persons whatsoever, undeterred by any shame or intimidation. This Sacrament then, whereby spiritual strength is conferred on the regenerate man, constitutes him a champion of the faith of Christ. And because those who fight under a Prince wear his badge, persons confirmed are signed with the sign of Christ, whereby He fought and conquered. They receive this sign on their foreheads, to signify that they do not blush publicly to confess the faith of Christ. The signing is done with a composition of oil and balsam, called 'chrism,' not unreasonably. By the oil is denoted the power of the Holy Ghost, whereby Christ is termed 'anointed' [Acts ii, 36: x, 38] and from Christ [χριστός, anointed] 'Christians' have their name, as soldiers serving under Him. In the balsam, for its fragrance, the good name is shown, which they who live among worldly people should have, to enable them publicly to confess the name of Christ, to which end they are brought forth from the remote confines of the Church to the field of battle. Appropriately too is this Sacrament conferred by bishops only, who are the generals of the Christian army: for in secular warfare it belongs to the general to enroll soldiers: thus the recipients of this Sacrament are enrolled in a spiritual warfare, and the bishop's hand is imposed over them to denote the derivation of power from Christ.

## CHAPTER LXI—Of the Eucharist

BECAUSE spiritual effects are produced on the pattern of visible effects, it was fitting that our spiritual nourishment should be given us under the appearances of those things that men commonly use for their bodily nourishment, namely bread and wine. And for the further correspondence of spiritual signs with bodily effects, in the spiritual regeneration of Baptism the mystery of the Word Incarnate is united with us otherwise than as it is united in this Sacrament of the Eucharist, which is our spiritual nourishment. In Baptism the Word Incarnate is only virtually contained, but in the Sacrament of the Eucharist we confess Him to be contained substantially, as nourishment must be substantially united with the nourished.

And because the completion of our salvation was wrought by Christ's passion and death, whereby His Blood was separated from His Body, therefore the Sacrament of His Body is given us separately under the species of bread, and His Blood under the species of wine.

CHAPTER LXIII—Of the Conversion of Bread into the Body of Christ

IT is impossible for the true Body of Christ to begin to be in this Sacrament by local motion, because then it would cease to be in heaven, upon every consecration of this Sacrament; as also because this Sacrament could not then be consecrated except in one place, since one local motion can only have one terminus; also because local motion cannot be instantaneous, but takes time. Therefore its presence must be due to the conversion of the substance of bread into the substance of His Body, and of the substance of wine into the substance of His Blood. This shows the falseness of the opinion of those who say that the substance of bread co-exists with the substance of the Body of Christ in this Sacrament; also of those who say that the substance of bread is annihilated. If the substance of bread co-exists with the Body of Christ, Christ should rather have said, Here is my Body, than, This is my Body. The word here points to the substance which is seen, and that is the substance of bread, if the bread remain in the Sacrament along with the Body of Christ. On the other hand it does not seem possible for the substance of bread to be absolutely annihilated, for then much of the corporeal matter of the original creation would have been annihilated by this time by the frequent use of this mystery: nor is it becoming for anything to be annihilated in the Sacrament of salvation.

We must observe that the conversion of bread into the Body of Christ falls under a different category from all natural conversions. In every natural conversion the subject remains, and in that subject different forms succeed one another: hence these are called 'formal conversions.' But in this conversion subject passes into subject, while the accidents remain: hence this conversion is termed 'substantial.' Now we have to consider how subject is changed into subject, a change which nature cannot effect. Every operation of nature presupposes matter, whereby subjects are individuated; hence nature cannot make this subject become that, as for instance, this finger that finger. But matter lies wholly under the power of God, since by that power it is brought into being: hence it may be brought about by divine power that one individual substance shall be converted into another pre-existing substance. By the power of a natural agent, the operation of which extends only to the producing of a change of form and presupposes the existence of the subject of change, this whole is converted into that whole with variation of species and form. So by the divine power, which does not presuppose matter, but produces it, this matter is converted into that matter, and consequently this individual into that: for matter is the principle of individuation, as form is the principle of species. Hence it is plain that in the change of the bread into the Body of Christ there is no common subject abiding after the change, since the change takes place in the primary subject [i.e., in the matter], which is the principle of individuation. Yet something must remain to verify the words, This is my body, which are the words significant and effective of this conversion. But the substance does not remain: we must say therefore that what remains is something beside the substance, that is, the accident of bread. The accidents of bread then remain even after the conversion.

This then is one reason for the accident of bread remaining, that something may be found permanent under the conversion. Another reason is this. If the substance of bread was converted into the Body of Christ, and the accidents of bread also passed away, there would not ensue upon such conversion the being of the Body of Christ in substance where the bread was before: for nothing would be left to refer the Body of Christ to that place. But since the dimensions of bread (quantitas dimensiva panis), whereby the bread held this particular place, remain after conversion, while the substance of bread is changed into the Body of Christ, the Body of Christ comes to be under the dimensions of bread, and in a manner to occupy the place of the bread by means of the said dimensions.

CHAPTER LXIV—An Answer to Difficulties raised in respect of Place

IN this Sacrament something is present by force of conversion, and something by natural concomitance. By force of conversion there is present that which is the immediate term into which conversion is made. Such under the species of bread is the Body of Christ, into which the substance of bread is converted by the words, This is my body. Such again under the species of wine is the Blood of Christ, when it is said, This is the chalice of my blood. By natural concomitance all other things are there, which, though conversion is not made into them, nevertheless are really united with the term into which conversion is made. Clearly, the term into which conversion of the bread is made is not the Divinity of Christ, nor His Soul: nevertheless the Soul and the Divinity of Christ are under the species of bread, because of the real union of them both with the Body of Christ. If during the three days that Christ lay dead this Sacrament had been celebrated, the Soul of Christ would not have been under the species of bread, because it was not really united with His Body: nor would His Blood have been under the species of bread, nor His Body under the species of wine, because of the separation of the two in death. But now, because the Body of Christ in its nature is not without His Blood, the Body and Blood are contained under both species; the Body under the species of bread by force of conversion, and the Blood by natural concomitance; and conversely under the species of wine.

Hereby we have an answer to the difficulty of the incommensurateness of the Body of Christ with the space taken up by the bread. The substance of the bread is converted directly into the substance of the Body of Christ: but the dimensions of the Body of Christ are in the Sacrament by natural concomitance, not by force of conversion, since the dimensions of the bread remain. Thus then the Body of Christ is not referred to this particular place by means of its own dimensions, as though commensurate room had to be found for them, but by means of the dimensions of the bread, which remain, and for which commensurate room is found.

And so of the plurality of places. By its own proper dimensions the Body of Christ is in one place only; but by means of the dimensions of the bread that passes into it, the Body of Christ is in as many places as there are places in which the mystery of this conversion is celebrated, — not divided into parts, but whole in each: for every consecrated bread is converted into the whole Body of Christ.

CHAPTER LXV—The Difficulty of the Accidents remaining

IT cannot be denied that the accidents of bread and wine do remain, as the infallible testimony of the senses assures us. Nor is the Body and Blood of Christ affected by them, since that could not be without change in Him, and He is not susceptible of such accidents. It follows that they remain without subject. Nor is their so remaining an impossibility to the divine power. The same rule applies to the production of things and to their conservation in being. The power of God can produce the effects of any secondary causes whatsoever without the causes themselves, because that power is infinite, and supplies to all secondary causes the power in which they act: hence it can preserve in being the effects of secondary causes without the causes. Thus in this Sacrament it preserves the accident in being, after removing the substance that preserves it.

CHAPTER LXVI—What happens when the Sacramental Species pass away

FOR the removal of this doubt there has been invented a famous theory (famosa positio), which is held by many. They say that when this Sacrament comes to be changed in the ordinary process of digestion or to be burnt, or otherwise destroyed, the accidents are not converted into substance, but there returns by miracle the substance of bread that had been before, and out of that are generated the products into which this Sacrament is found to turn. But this theory cannot stand at all. It seems better to say that in the consecration there is miraculously conferred upon the accidents the power of subsistence, which is proper to substance: hence they can do all things, and have all things done to them, that the substance itself could do, or have done to it, if it were there: hence without any new miracle they can nourish, or be reduced to ashes, in the same mode and order as if the substance of bread and wine were there.

CHAPTER LXVII—Answer to the Difficulty raised in respect of the Breaking of the Host

IT has been said above (Chap. LXIV) that the substance of the Body of Christ is in this Sacrament by virtue of the Sacrament [Sacramental words]: but the dimensions of the Body of Christ are there by the natural concomitance which they have with the substance. This is quite the opposite way to that in which a body naturally is in place. A body is in place by means of its dimensions, by which it is made commensurate with its place.

But substantial being and quantitative being do not stand in the same way related to that in which they are. Quantitative being is in a whole, but is not whole in each part: it is part in part, and whole in the whole. But substantial being is whole in the whole, and whole in every part of the same, as the whole nature and species of water is in every drop of water, and the whole soul in every part of the body. Since then the Body of Christ is in the Sacrament by reason of its substance, into which the substance of bread is changed, while the dimensions of bread remain, — it follows that as the whole species of bread was under every part of its (visible) dimensions, so the whole Body of Christ is under every part of the same. The breaking then (of the Host) does not reach to the Body of Christ, as though the Body of Christ were subjected to that breaking: its subject is the dimensions of bread, which remain.

## CHAPTER LXVIII—The Explanation of a Text

NOR is there anything contrary to the tradition of the Church in the word of the Lord saying to the disciples, who seemed scandalized: *The words that I have spoken to you are spirit and life* (John vi, 63). He did not thereby give them to understand that His true flesh was not delivered to be eaten by the faithful in this Sacrament, but that it was not delivered to be eaten in the way of ordinary flesh, taken and torn with the teeth in its own proper appearance, as food usually is; that it is received in a spiritual way, not in the usual way of fleshly food.

CHAPTER LXIX—Of the kind of Bread and Wine that ought to be used for the Consecration of this Sacrament

THOSE conditions must be observed which are essential for bread and wine to be. That alone is called wine, which is liquor pressed out of grapes: nor is that properly called bread, which is not made of grains of wheat. Substitutes for wheaten bread have come into use, and shave got the name of bread; and similarly other liquors have come into use as wine: but of no such bread other than bread properly so called, or wine other than what is properly called wine, could this Sacrament possibly be consecrated: nor again if the bread and wine were so adulterated with foreign matter as that the species should disappear. A valid Sacrament may be consecrated irrespectively of varieties of bread and wine, when the varieties are accidental, not essential. The alternative of leavened or unleavened bread is an instance of such accidental variety; and therefore different churches have different uses in this respect; and either use may be accommodated to the signification of the Sacrament. Thus as Gregory says in the Register of his Letters: "The Roman Church offers unleavened bread, because the Lord took flesh without intercourse of the sexes: but other Churches offer leavened bread, because the Word of the Father, clothed in flesh, is at once true God and true man." Still the use of unleavened bread is the more congruous, as better representing the purity of Christ's mystical Body, the Church, which is figured in a secondary way (configuratur) in this Sacrament, as the text has it: Christ our Passover is sacrificed: therefore let us feast in the unleavened bread of sincerity and truth(1 Cor. v, 7, 8).

This shuts out the error of some heretics who say that this Sacrament cannot be celebrated in unleavened bread: a position plainly upset by the authority of the gospel, where we read (Matt. xxvi, 17: Mark xiv, 12: cf. Luke xxii, 7) that the Lord ate the Passover with His disciples, and instituted this Sacrament, on the first day of the azymes, at which time it was unlawful for leavened bread to be found in the houses of the Jews (Exod. xii, 15); and the Lord, so long as He was in the world, observed the law. It is foolish then to blame in the use of the Latin Church an observance which the Lord Himself adhered to in the very institution of this Sacrament.

CHAPTER LXX—That it is possible for a man to sin after receiving Sacramental Grace

St Thomas, characteristically, proves his thesis by four a prior arguments, and one of testimonies from Scripture. We may rest satisfied with the one too common argument of experience. He continues: "Hereby is excluded the error of certain heretics (St Jerome, Contra Jovin.Chap. XXXI, says it was an error of Jovinian), that man, after receiving the grace of the Holy Ghost, cannot sin; and that if he sins, he never had the grace of the Holy Ghost." The only possibility of heresy in such a plain matter is by taking sanctifying grace to consist in nothing else than election and predestination to glory (cf. B. III, Chap. CLXIV). In the tautological sense that all whom God foresees in the ranks of the Blessed will be finally Blessed, it is true to say that 'once elect, always elect.'

But it would be heresy to say that sin is never imputed to the elect. Oliver Cromwell, dying, asked a minister, whether it was possible to fall from grace. The Calvinist minister at his bedside said that it was not possible. "Then," said the dying man, "I am safe, for I was in grace once." How did he know that? Was it provable from a baptismal register? Not to a Calvinist. St Thomas concludes the chapter thus: "The text 1 John iii, 6, 9, means that anyone who is adopted as a son, or born again as a son of God, receives gifts of the Holy Ghost, which of themselves are powerful enough to keep the man from sin, nor can he sin so long as he lives according to them: he may however act contrary to them, and by sinning depart from them. He that is born of God, cannot sin, in the same way that 'warm water cannot chill one,' or 'the just man never acts unjustly,' to wit, in so far as he is just." In other words, the text holds good in sensu composito, not in sensu diviso.

CHAPTER LXXI—*That a man who sins after the Grace of the Sacraments may be converted to Grace*

HEREBY is excluded the error of the Novatians, who denied pardon to sinners after baptism. They took occasion of their error from the text: It is impossible for those who have been once enlightened [φωτισθέντας, baptized], and have tasted the heavenly gift, and have been made partakers of the Holy Ghost .... and have fallen, to be again renewed [ἀνακαινίζειν, renovari, Vulg.] unto penance (Heb. vi, 4, 6). But the sense is plain from the immediate context: crucifying to themselves again the Son of God, and making him a mockery. There is denied to them then that renewal unto penance, whereby a man is crucified along with Christ, which is by baptism: for as many of us as have been baptized in Christ Jesus, have been baptized in his death (Rom. vi, 3, 6: Gal. ii, 19, 20: v, 24). As then Christ is not to be crucified again, so he who sins after baptism is not to be baptized again. Hence the Apostle does not say that it is impossible for such persons to be reclaimed, or converted, to penance, but that it is impossible for them to be renewed[ἀνακαινίζειν], renovation being the effect usually ascribed to baptism, which is called the laver of regeneration and renewal [ἀνακαινώσεως] (Titus iii, 5).

CHAPTER LXXII—Of the need of the Sacrament of Penance, and of the Parts thereof

THE Sacrament of Penance is a spiritual cure. As sick men are healed, not by being born again, but by some reaction (alteratio) set up in their system; so, of sins committed after baptism, men are healed by the spiritual reaction of Penance, not by repetition of the spiritual regeneration of Baptism. Now a bodily cure is sometimes worked entirely from within by the mere effort of nature; sometimes from within and from without at the same time, when nature is aided by the benefit of medicine. But the cure is never wrought entirely from without: there still remain in the patient certain elements of life, which go to cause health in him. A spiritual cure cannot possibly be altogether from within, for man cannot be set free from guilt but by the aid of grace (B. III, Chap. CLVII). Nor can such a cure be altogether from without, for the restoration of mental health involves the setting up of orderly motions in the will. Therefore the spiritual restoration, effected in the Sacrament of Penance, must be wrought both from within and from without. And that happens in this way.

The first loss that man sustains by sin is a wrong bent given to his mind, whereby it is turned away from the unchangeable good, which is God, and turned to sin. The second is the incurred liability to punishment (B. III, Chapp.CXLI–CXLVI). The third is a weakening of natural goodness, rendering the soul more prone to sin and more reluctant to do good. The first requisite then of the Sacrament of Penance is a right ordering, or orientation of mind, turning it to God and away from sin, making it grieve for sin committed, and purposing not to commit it in future. All these things are of the essence of Contrition. This re-ordering of the mind cannot take place without charity, and charity cannot be had without grace (B. III, Chap. CLI). Thus then Contrition takes away the offence of God, and delivers from the liability of eternal punishment, as that liability cannot stand with grace and charity: for eternal punishment is in separation from God, with whom man is united by grace and charity.

This re-ordering of the mind, which consists in Contrition, comes from within, from free will aided by divine grace. But because the merit of Christ, suffering for mankind, is the operative principle in the expiation of all sins (Chap. LV), a man who would be delivered from sin must not only adhere in mind to God, but also to the mediator between God and men, the man Christ Jesus (1 Tim. ii, 5), in whom is given remission of all sins. For spiritual health consists in the turning of the mind and heart to God; which health we cannot gain otherwise than through the physician of our souls Jesus Christ, who saves his people from their sins (Matt. i, 21); whose merit is sufficient for the entire taking away of all sins, since He it is that taketh away the sins of the world (John i, 29). Not all penitents however perfectly gain the effect of remission; but each one gains it in so much as he is united with Christ suffering for sins. Our union with Christ in baptism comes not of any activity of our own, as from within, because nothing begets itself into being; it is all of Christ, who hath regenerated us unto living hope(1 Peter i, 3): consequently the remission of sins in baptism is by the power of Christ, uniting us to Himself perfectly and entirely; the result being that not only is the impurity of sin taken away, but also all liability to sin is entirely cancelled, — always excepting the accidental case of those who gain not the effect of the Sacrament, because they are not sincere in approaching it. But in this spiritual cure (the Sacrament of Penance), it is our own act, informed with divine grace, that unites us with Christ. Hence the effect of remission is not always gained totally by this union, nor do all gain it equally. The turning of mind and heart to God and to detestation of sin may be so vehement as to gain for the penitent a perfect remission of sin, including at once purification from guilt and a discharge of the entire debt of punishment. But this does not always occur. Sometimes, though the guilt is taken away and the debt of eternal punishment cancelled, there still remains some obligation of temporal punishment, to save the justice of God, which redresses fault by punishment.

But since the infliction of punishment for fault requires a trial, the penitent who has committed himself to Christ for his cure must await the judgement of Christ in the assessment of his punishment. This judgement Christ exercises through His ministers, as in the other Sacraments. No one can give judgement upon faults that he is ignorant of. Therefore a second part of this Sacrament is the practice of Confession, the object of which is to make the penitent's fault known to Christ's minister. The minister then, to whom Confession is made, must have judicial power as vice-regent of Christ, who is appointed judge of the living and of the dead (Acts x, 42). There are two requisites of judicial power, authority to investigate the offence, and power to acquit (potestas absolvendi) or condemn. This science of discerning and this power of binding or loosing are the two keys of the Church, which the Lord committed to Peter (Matt. xvi, 19). He is not to be understood to have committed them to Peter for Peter to hold them alone, but that through him they might be transmitted to others; or else the salvation of the faithful would not be sufficiently provided for. These keys have their efficacy from the Passion of Christ, whereby Christ has opened to us the gate of the heavenly kingdom. As then without Baptism, in which the Passion of Christ works, there can be no salvation for men, — whether the Baptism be actually received, or purposed in desire, when necessity, not contempt, sets the Sacrament aside; so for sinners after Baptism there can be no salvation unless they submit themselves to the keys of the Church either by actual Confession and undergoing of the judgement of the ministers of the Church, or at least by purposing so to do with a purpose to be fulfilled in seasonable time: because there is no other name under heaven given to men, whereby we are to be saved (Acts iv, 12).

Hereby is excluded the error of certain persons, who said that a man could obtain pardon of his sins without confession and purpose of confession; or that the prelates of the Church could dispense a sinner from the obligation of confession. The prelates of the Church have no power to frustrate the keys of the Church, in which their whole power is contained; nor to enable a man to obtain forgiveness of his sins without the Sacrament which has its efficacy from the Passion of Christ: only Christ, the institutor and author of the Sacraments, can do that. The prelates of the Church can no more dispense a man from confession and absolution in order to remission of sin than they can dispense him from baptism in order to salvation.

But this is a point to observe. Baptism may be efficacious to the remission of sin before it is actually received, while one purposes to receive it: though afterwards it takes fuller effect in the gaining of grace and the remission of guilt, when it actually is received. And sometimes the very instant of baptism is the instant of the bestowal of grace and the remission of guilt where it was not remitted before. So the keys of the Church work their effect in some cases before the penitent actually places himself under them, provided he have the purpose of placing himself under them. But he gains a fuller grace and a fuller remission, when he actually submits himself to the keys by confessing and receiving absolution. And the case is quite possible (nihil prohibet) of a person at confession receiving grace and the forgiveness of the guilt of sin by the power of the keys in the very instant of absolution [i.e., not before then]. Since then in the very act of confession and absolution a fuller effect of grace and forgiveness is conferred on him who by his good purpose had obtained grace and remission already, we clearly see that by the power of the keys the minister of the Church in absolving remits something of the temporal punishment which the penitent still continued to owe after his act of contrition. He binds the penitent by his injunction to pay the rest. The fulfilment of this injunction is called Satisfaction, which is the third part of Penance, whereby a man is totally discharged from the debt of punishment, provided he pays the full penalty due. Further than this, his weakness in spiritual good is cured by his abstaining from evil things and accustoming himself to good deeds, subduing the flesh by fasting, and improving his relations with his neighbor by the bestowal of alms upon those neighbors from whom he had been culpably estranged.

Thus it is clear that the minister of the Church in the use of the keys exercises judicial functions. But to none is judgement committed except over persons subject to his court. Hence it is not any and every priest that can absolve any and every subject from sin: priest can absolve that subject only over whom he is given authority.

CHAPTER LXXIII—Of the Sacrament of Extreme Unction

BY dispensation of divine justice, the sickness of the soul, which is sin, sometimes passes to the body. Such bodily sickness is sometimes conducive to the health of the soul, where it is borne humbly and patiently and as a penance whereby one may make satisfaction for sin. Sometimes again sickness injures spiritual well-being by hindering the exercise of virtues. It was fitting therefore to have a spiritual remedy, applicable to sin precisely in this connexion of bodily sickness being a consequence of sin. By this spiritual remedy bodily sickness is sometimes cured, when it is expedient for salvation. This is the purpose of the Sacrament of Extreme Unction, of which

St James speaks (James v, 14, 15). Nor is the Sacrament useless, even though bodily health does not ensue upon its reception: for it is directed against other consequences of sin, as proneness to evil and difficulty in doing good, infirmities of soul which have a closer connexion with sin than bodily infirmity. Negligence, the various occupations of life, and the shortness of time, prevent a man from perfectly remedying the above defects by penance. Thus this Sacrament is a wholesome provision for completing the sinner's cure, delivering him from his debt of temporal punishment, and leaving nothing in him at the departure of his soul from his body to hinder his reception into glory.

This Sacrament is not to be given to all sick persons, but only to such as seem to be near to death from sickness. If they recover, this Sacrament may be administered to them again, if they are again reduced to the like state. For the unction of this Sacrament is not an unction of consecration, like the unction of Confirmation, the ablution of Baptism, and certain other unctions, which are never repeated, because the consecration always remains so long as the thing consecrated lasts: but the anointing in this Sacrament is for healing, and a healing medicine ought to be given again and again as often as the sickness recurs.

Though some are in a state near to death without sickness, as are persons condemned to death, and they would need the spiritual effects of this Sacrament, still this Sacrament is not to be given to them, but only to the sick, since it is given under the form of bodily medicine, and bodily medicine is not proper except for one bodily sick. For in the administration of Sacraments their signification must be observed.

Oil is the special matter of this Sacrament, because it is of efficacy for bodily healing by mitigation of pains, as water, which washes bodies, is the matter of the Sacrament in which spiritual cleansing is performed. And as bodily healing must go to the root of the malady, so this unction is applied to those parts of the body from which the malady of sin proceeds, as are the organs of sense.

And because through this Sacrament sins are forgiven, and sin is not forgiven except through grace, clearly grace is conferred in this Sacrament. Nor is a bishop necessary to give this Sacrament, since the Sacrament does not bestow any excellence of state, as do those Sacraments in which a bishop is the minister. Since however a great abundance of grace, proper to effect a perfect cure, is required in this Sacrament, it is right that many priests should take part in the rite, and that the prayer of the whole Church should help out the effect of this Sacrament: hence James says: Let him bring in the priests of the Church, and the prayer of faith shall save the sick man. If however only one priest be present, he is understood to confer the Sacrament in the power of the whole Church, whose minister he is, and whose person he bears. As in other Sacraments, the effect of this Sacrament may be hindered by the insincerity (fictionem) of the recipient.

## CHAPTER LXXIV—Of the Sacrament of Order

SINCE Christ intended to withdraw His bodily presence from the Church, He needed to institute other men as ministers to Himself, who should dispense the Sacraments to the faithful. Hence He committed to His disciples the consecration of His Body and Blood, saying: Do this in memory of me (Luke xxii, 19). He gave them the power of forgiving sins, according to the text: Whose sins you shall forgive, they are forgiven them (John xx, 23). He enjoined on them the function of baptizing: Go, teach all nations, baptizing them (Matt. xxviii, 19). Now a minister stands to his master as an instrument to a prime agent. An instrument must be proportionate to the agent: therefore the ministers of Christ must be conformable to Him. But Christ, our Lord and Master, by His own power and might worked out our salvation, inasmuch as He was both God and man. As man, He suffered for our redemption: as He was God, His suffering brought salvation to us. The ministers of Christ then must be men, and at the same time have some share in the Divinity (aliquid divinitatis participare) in point of spiritual power: for an instrument too has some share in the power of the prime agent.

Nor can it be said that this power was given to the disciples of Christ not to be transmitted to others. It was given unto edification (2 Cor. xiii, 10), to the building up of the Church, and must be perpetuated so long as the Church needs building up, that is, to the end of the world(Matt. xxviii, 20). And since spiritual effects are transmitted to us from Christ under sensible signs, this power had to be delivered to men under some such signs, — certain forms of words, definite acts, as imposition of hands, anointing, the delivery of a book or chalice, and the like. Whenever anything spiritual is delivered under a corporeal sign, that is called a Sacrament. Thus in the conferring of spiritual power a Sacrament is wrought, which is called the Sacrament of Order. Now it is a point of divine liberality that the bestowal of power should be accompanied with the means of duly exercising that power. But the spiritual power of administering the Sacraments requires divine grace for its convenient exercise: therefore in this Sacrament, as in other Sacraments, grace is bestowed. Among Sacraments the noblest, and that which sets the crown on the rest, is the Sacrament of the Eucharist. Therefore the power of Order must be considered chiefly in relation to this Sacrament: for everything is ruled by the end for which it is made. Now the power that gives perfection, also prepares the matter to receive it. Since then the power of Order extends to the consecration of the Body of Christ and the administration of the same to the faithful, it must further extend to the rendering of the faithful fit and worthy for the reception of that Sacrament. But the believer is rendered fit and worthy by being free from sin: otherwise he cannot be united with Christ spiritually, with whom he is sacramentally united in the reception of this Sacrament. The power of Order therefore must extend to the remission of sins by the administration of those Sacraments which are directed to that purpose, Baptism and Penance.

CHAPTER LXXV—Of the Distinction of Orders

SINCE the power of Order is principally directed to the consecration of the Body of Christ, and its administration to the faithful, and the cleansing of the faithful from sin, there must be some chief Order, the power of which extends chiefly to these objects; and that is the Order of Priesthood. There must be other Orders to serve the chief Order by one way or another preparing its matter; and these are the Orders of Ministers. The power of Priesthood extending to two objects, the consecration of the Body of Christ, and the rendering the faithful by absolution from sin fit to receive the Eucharist, the lower Orders must serve the Priesthood either in both or in one of these respects. The lower Orders serve the Priesthood only in preparing the people [for the Eucharist]. This the Doorkeepers do by shutting out unbelievers from the company of the faithful: the Lectors by instructing the catechumens in the rudiments of the faith, — hence the Scripture of the Old Testament is committed to their reading: the Exorcists by cleansing those who are already instructed, if in any way they are hindered by the devil from the reception of the Sacraments. The higher Orders serve the priestly Order both in the preparation of the people and in the consummation of the Sacrament. Thus the Acolytes have a ministry to exercise over the vessels, other than sacred, in which the matter of the Sacrament is prepared: hence the altar-cruets are delivered to them at their ordination. The Subdeacons have a ministry to exercise over the sacred vessels, and over the arrangement of the matter not yet consecrated. The Deacons have a further ministry over the matter already consecrated, as the deacon administers the Blood of Christ to the faithful. These three Orders of Priests, Deacons and Subdeacons, are called Sacred Orders, because they receive a ministry over sacred things. The higher Orders also serve for the preparation of the people: for to Deacons is committed the publishing of the doctrine of the Gospel to the people: to Subdeacons that of the Apostles: while Acolytes render to both the attendance which conduces to solemnity of teaching, by carrying candles and otherwise serving.

CHAPTER LXXVI—Of the Episcopal Dignity,

and that therein one Bishop is Supreme

THERE must be some power of higher ministry in the Church to administer the Sacrament of Order; and this is the episcopal power, which, though not exceeding the power of the simple priest in the consecration of the Body of Christ, exceeds it in its dealings with the faithful. The presbyter's power is derived from the episcopal; and whenever any action, rising above what is common and usual, has to be done upon the faithful people, that is reserved to bishops; and it is by episcopal authority that presbyters do what is committed to them; and in their ministry they make use of things consecrated by bishops, as in the Eucharist the chalice, altar-stone and palls.

1. Though populations are different in different dioceses and cities, still, as there is one Church, there must be one Christian people. As then in the spiritual people of one Church there is required one Bishop, who is Head of all that people; so in the whole Christian people it is requisite that there be one Head of the whole Church.

2. One requisite of the unity of the Church is the agreement of all the faithful in faith. When questions of faith arise, the Church would be rent by diversity of judgements, were it not preserved in unity by the judgement of one. But in things necessary Christ is not wanting to His Church, which He has loved, and has shed His blood for it: since even of the Synagogue the Lord says: What is there that I ought further to have done for my vineyard and have not done it.?(Isai. v, 4.) We cannot doubt then that by the ordinance of Christ one man presides over the whole Church.

3. None can doubt that the government of the Church is excellently well arranged, arranged as it is by

Him through whom kings reign and lawgivers enact just things (Prov. viii, 15). But the best form of government for a multitude is to be governed by one: for the end of government is the peace and unity of its subjects: and one man is a more apt source of unity than many together.

But if any will have it that the one Head and one Shepherd is Christ, as being the one Spouse of the one Church, his view is inadequate to the facts. For though clearly Christ Himself gives effect to the Sacraments of the Church, — He it is who baptizes, He forgives sins, He is the true Priest who has offered Himself on the altar of the cross, and by His power His Body is daily consecrated at our altars, — nevertheless, because He was not to be present in bodily shape with all His faithful, He chose ministers and would dispense His gifts to His faithful people through their hands. And by reason of the same future absence it was needful for Him to issue His commission to someone to take care of this universal Church in His stead. Hence He said to Peter before His Ascension, Feed my sheep (John xxi, 1) and before His Passion, Thou in thy turn confirm thy brethren (Luke xxii, 32); and to him alone He made the promise, To thee I will give the keys of the kingdom of heaven (Matt. xvi, 19). Nor can it be said that although He gave this dignity to Peter, it does not pass from Peter to others. For Christ instituted His Church to last to the end of the world, according to the text: He shall sit upon the throne of David and in his kingdom, to confirm and strengthen it in justice and judgement from henceforth, now, and forever (Isai. ix, 7). Therefore, in constituting His ministers for the time, He intended their power to pass to posterity for the benefit of His Church to the end of the world, as He Himself says: Lo, I am with you to the end of the world

(Matt. xxviii, 20).

Hereby is cast out the presumptuous error of some, who endeavor to withdraw themselves from obedience and subjection to Peter, not recognizing his successor, the Roman Pontiff, for the pastor of the Universal Church.

CHAPTER LXXVII—That Sacraments can be administered even by Wicked Ministers

NO agent can do anything in what is beyond his competence, unless he gets power from elsewhere: thus the mayor cannot put restraint upon the citizens except in virtue of the power that he receives from the king. But what is done in the Sacraments exceeds human competence. Therefore no one can administer the Sacraments, however good he may be, unless he receives power so to do. But the opposite of goodness is wickedness and sin. Therefore neither by sin is he hindered from the administration of the Sacraments, who has received power to do so.

5. One man cannot judge of the goodness or wickedness of another man: that is proper to God alone, who searches the secrets of hearts. If then the wickedness of the minister could hinder the effect of the Sacrament, it would be impossible for a man to have a sure confidence of his salvation: his conscience would not remain free from the sense of sin. But it is irrational for anyone to have to rest the hope of his salvation on the goodness of a mere man: for it said, Cursed is the man who puts his trust

in man (Jer. xvii, 5). In order then that we may rest the hope of our salvation on Christ, who is God and man, we must allow that the Sacraments work salvation in the power of Christ, whether they be administered by good or evil ministers.

Hence the Lord says: The Scribes and Pharisees have come to sit in the chair of Moses: whatever things therefore they say to you, observe and do: but according to their works do ye not (Matt. xxiii, 2).

Hereby is cast out the error of those who say that all good men can administer the Sacraments, and no bad men.

CHAPTER LXXVIII—Of the Sacrament of Matrimony

THOUGH by the Sacraments men are restored to grace, they are not immediately restored to immortality. Since then the faithful people needs to be perpetuated to the end of the world, this has to be done by generation. Now generation works to many ends: to the perpetuity of the species, to the perpetuity of the political commonwealth, and to the perpetuity of the Church. Hence it comes to be ruled and guided by different powers. As it works to the good of nature in the perpetuity of the species, it is guided to that end by nature so inclining; and in that respect it is called 'a function of nature.' As it works to social and political good, it is subject to the ordinance of the civil law. As it works to the good of the Church, it must be subject to Church government. But the things that are administered to the people by the ministers of the Church, are called Sacraments. Matrimony then, as consisting in the union of male and female, intending to beget and educate offspring to the worship of God, is a Sacrament of the Church. Hence a blessing is pronounced upon it by the ministers of the Church. And as in other Sacraments something spiritual is prefigured by external acts, so in this Sacrament, by the union of male and female, there is figuratively represented the union of Christ with His Church, according to the text of the Apostle (Eph. v, 32). And because the Sacraments effect what they represent (sacramenta efficiunt quod figurant), we must believe that grace is bestowed by this Sacrament on persons marrying, to enable them to have their part in the union of Christ with His Church; and this aid is very necessary for them, that in their application to fleshly and carnal things they may not be sepa rated from Christ and the Church.

Now the figure must correspond to the reality which it signifies. But the union of Christ with His Church is of one Bridegroom with one Bride to be kept forever. For of the Church it is said: One is my beloved, my perfect one (Cant. vi, 8): nor ever shall Christ be parted from His Church: for so He says Himself, Lo, I am with you even to the end of the world (Matt. xxviii, 20); and so the Apostle, We shall be forever with the Lord (1 Thess. iv, 16). Matrimony therefore, as a Sacrament of the Church, must be of one husband with one wife, to continue without separation: this is meant by the faith (or troth), whereby husband and wife are bound to one another. So then there are three goods of matrimony, as it is a Sacrament of the Church: offspring, to be reared and educated to the worship of God: faith, whereby one husband is tied to one wife: and sacramental signification by the indivisible union of the matrimonial connexion, making it a sacred sign of the union of Christ with His

Church.

## CHAPTER LXXIX—That through Christ the Resurrection of our Bodies will take place

AS we have been delivered by Christ from the penalties incurred by the death of the first man; and as by the sin of the first man there has been bequeathed to us not only sin, but also death, which is the punishment of sin; we must by Christ be delivered from both these consequences, both from guilt and from sin (Rom. iv, 12, 17). To show to us both effects in Himself, He chose both to die and to rise again; to die, to deliver us from sin (Heb. ix, 28); to rise again, to deliver us from death (1 Cor. xv, 20) [cf. Rom. iv, 25]. We gather the effect of Christ's death in the Sacraments so far as remission of guilt goes: at the end of the world we shall gain the effect of Christ's resurrection in our deliverance from death.

But some do not believe in the resurrection of the body; and what is said in Scripture on that subject they perversely understand of a spiritual resurrection from the death of sin to grace: which error is reproved by the Apostle in Hymenaeus and Philetus (2 Tim. ii, 16). Moreover the Lord promises both resurrections, when He says: *The hour cometh, and now is, when the dead shall hear the voice of the Son of God, and they that hear shall live*: which refers to the resurrection of souls, then beginning by men beginning to adhere to Christ by faith. But presently He makes explicit promise of a bodily resurrection: *The hour cometh in which all who are in the tombs shall hear the voice of the Son of God*: for manifestly not souls are in the tombs, but bodies. Cf. Job xix, 25.

Reason too gives evident support to the resurrection of the flesh. — 1. The souls of men are immortal (B. II, Chap. LXXIX). But the soul is naturally united with the body, being essentially the form of the body (B. II, Chap. LVII). Therefore it is against the nature of the soul to be without the body. But nothing that is against nature can be lasting. Therefore the soul will not be forever without the body. Thus the immortality of the soul seems to require the resurrection of the body.

2. The natural desire of man tends to happiness, or final perfection (B. III, Chap. XXIV). Whoever is wanting in any point proper to his perfect well-being, has not yet attained to perfect happiness: his desire is not yet perfectly laid to rest. Now the soul separate from the body is in a sense imperfect, as is every part away from its whole, for the soul is part of human nature.

3. Reward and punishment are due to men both in soul and in body. But in this life they cannot attain to the reward of final happiness (B. III, Chap. XLVIII); and sins often go unpunished in this life: nay, here the wicked live and are comforted and set up with riches (Job xxi, 7). There must then be a second union of soul with body, that man may be rewarded and punished in body and in soul.

CHAPTER LXXXI—Some Points of Reply to Difficulties on the Resurrection

IN the first creation of human nature God endowed the human body with an attribute over and above what was due to it by the natural principles of its constitution, namely, with a certain imperishability, to adapt it to its form, that as the life of the soul is perpetual, so the body might perpetually live by the soul. Granting that this imperishability was not natural in regard of the active principle, still it may be called natural in regard of the end, taking the end of matter to be proportioned to its natural form. When then, contrary to the order of its nature, the soul turned away from God, there was withdrawn from the body that God-given constitution which made it proportionate to the soul; and death ensued. Considering then how human nature actually was constituted to begin with, we may say that death is something which has accidentally supervened upon man through sin. This accident has been removed by Christ, who by the merit of His passion and death has destroyed death. Consequently that same divine power, which originally endowed the body with incorruption, will restore the body again from death to life.

    None of the essential elements in man is altogether annihilated in death. The rational soul, the 'form' of man, remains after death. The matter also remains, which was subject to that form. So by the union of numerically the same soul with numerically the same matter, numerically the same man will be restored.

    What does not bar numerical unity in a man while he lives on uninterruptedly, clearly can be no bar to the identity of the risen man with the man that was. In a man's body while he lives, there are not always the same parts in respect of matter, but only in respect of species. In respect of matter there is a flux and reflux of parts: still that fact does not bar the man's numerical unity from the beginning to the end of his life. We have an example in a fire, which, while it goes on burning, is called numerically one, because its species remains, though the wood is burnt out and fresh wood supplied. So it is in the human body: for the form and species (kind) of the several parts continues unbroken throughout life, but the matter of the parts is dissolved by the natural heat, and new matter accrues by nourishment. But the man is not numerically different by the difference of his component parts at different ages, although it is true that the material composition of the man at one stage of his life is not his material composition at another. So then, for numerically the same man to rise again, it is not requisite for all the material that ever entered into his composition throughout the whole course of his life to be gathered together and resumed, but just so much of it as suffices to make up his proper bulk and stature. We may expect that to be resumed by preference, which was more perfect in the species and form of humanity. If anything was wanting to his due stature, either through untimely death or mutilation, divine power will supply that from elsewhere. Nor will this supplementary matter mar the personal identity of the risen body: for even in the workmanship of nature addition is made from without to the stature of a boy without prejudice to his identity: for the boy and the adult is numerically the same man.

The resurrection is natural in respect of its end and term, inasmuch as it is natural to the soul to be united to the body: but its efficient cause is not any agency of nature, but the divine power alone.

All men will rise again, though not all have adhered by faith to Christ, or have received His Sacraments. For the Son of God assumed human nature, in order to restore it: the defect of nature then shall be made good in all, inasmuch as all shall return from death to life: but the defect shall not be perfectly made good except in such as have adhered to Christ, either by their own act believing in Him, or at least by the Sacrament of faith.

CHAPTER LXXXII—That Men shall rise again Immortal

THAT cannot be said to have been destroyed, which is to go on forever. If then men were to rise again always with the prospect of another death, in no way could death be said to have been destroyed by the death of Christ. But it has been destroyed, — for the present, causally, as was foretold: I will be thy death, O death (Osee xiii, 14): and in the end it shall be destroyed actually: the last enemy to be destroyed is death (1 Cor. xv, 26).

3. The effect is like its cause. But the resurrection of Christ is the cause of our resurrection; and Christ rising from the dead dieth now no more (Rom. vi, 9).

Hence it is said: The Lord shall cast out death for ever (Isa. xxv, 8): Death shall be no more (Apoc. xxi, 24).

Hereby entrance is denied to the error of certain Gentiles of old, who believed that times and temporal events recurred in cycles. For example, in that age one Plato, a philosopher in the city of Athens, and in the school that is called Academic, taught his scholars thus, that in the course of countless revolving ages, recurring at long but fixed intervals, the same Plato, and the same city, and the same school, and the same scholars would recur, and so would be repeated again and again in the course of countless ages. As for the text: What is that has been? That same that shall be. There is nothing new under the sun: nor can anyone say, Lo, this is fresh: for it hath already gone before in the ages that have preceded us (Eccles i, 9): it is to be understood of events like in kind, but not in number.


CHAPTER LXXXIII—That in the Resurrection there will be no use of Food or Intercourse of the Sexes

WHEN our perishable life is over, those things which serve the needs of a perishable existence must also come to an end. One such thing is food, which serves to supply the waste of the body.

The use of the intercourse of the sexes is for generation. If then such intercourse is to continue after the resurrection, unless it is to continue to no purpose, many men will come to exist after the resurrection, who did not exist before.

But if any one says that in the risen Saints there will be use of food and sexual intercourse, not for the preservation of the individual and of the species, but solely for the pleasure that goes with such acts, to the end that no pleasure may be lacking in man's final reward, — such a saying is fraught with many absurdities. In the first place, the life of the risen Saints will be better ordered than our present life. But in this present life it is a disorderly and vicious thing to make use of food and procreation solely for pleasure, and not for the need of sustaining the body or rearing children. For the pleasures that attend such actions are not the ends of those actions, but rather the action is the end and purpose of the pleasure, nature having arranged for pleasure as a concomitant of such actions, lest for the labor that goes with them animals should desist from these actions necessary to nature, as they certainly would desist, were they not enticed by pleasure. It is therefore a perversion of order and an indecency for actions to be done solely for the pleasure that goes with them (B. III, Chap. XXVII). This then shall nowise be the case with the risen Saints, whose life we must assume to be a life of perfect order and propriety. Moreover the notion is ridiculous of seeking bodily pleasures, common to us with brute animals, where there are in view the highest delights, shared with the angels, in the vision of God (B. III, Chap. LI). Hence the Lord says: In the resurrection they shall neither marry nor be given in marriage, but shall be as the angels of God (Matt. xxii, 30).

As for the alleged example of Adam, the perfection of Adam was personal, but human nature was not yet entirely perfect, as the race of mankind was not yet multiplied. Adam then was constituted in the perfection proper to the origin of the human race, for the multiplication of which he needed to beget children, and consequently to make use of food. But the maturity of the risen state is when human nature shall have come to its full perfection, and the number of the elect shall be complete. Then shall generation no more have place, nor the use of food. Therefore the immortality and incorruption of the risen Saints shall be different from that which was in Adam. The immortality and incorruption of the risen Saints will consist in their being incapable of death, or of the dissolution of any part of their bodily frame. The immortality of Adam consisted in his being capable of immortality, provided he did not sin, and capable of death, if he did sin; and this was secured, not by the prevention of all bodily waste in him, but by the aid of food to counteract an entire dissolution.

The Scripture texts that seem to promise the use of food after the resurrection, are to be understood in a spiritual sense. What is said in the Apocalypse, xx, 4, of the thousand years, is to be understood of the resurrection of souls rising from sin, — cf. Eph. v, 14, Rise from the dead, and Christ shall enlighten thee; and the thousand years means the whole period of Church history, during which the martyrs reign with Christ, and the other saints, as well in that kingdom of God which is the Church on earth, as in the heavenly country of departed souls.

Hence we may finally conclude that all the activities of the active life shall cease, as they all bear upon the use of food, and the getting of children, and other necessities of a perishable existence. Alone left in the risen Saints shall be the occupation of the contemplative life: wherefore it is said of the contemplative Mary: Mary hath chosen the better part, which shall not be taken from her (Luke x, 42).

CHAPTER LXXXIV—That Risen Bodies shall be of the same Nature as before

SOME have supposed that in the resurrection our bodies are transformed into spirit, because the Apostle says: There is sown an animal body, there shall rise a spiritual body (1 Cor. xv, 40). And the text, Flesh and blood shall not possess the kingdom of God (1 Cor. xv, 50), has prompted the conjecture that risen bodies shall not have flesh and blood. But this is a manifest error.

1. Our resurrection shall be on the model of the resurrection of Christ, who will reform the body of our humiliation, so that it shall become conformable to the body of his glory (Phil. iii, 21). But Christ after His

resurrection had a body that could be felt and handled, as He says: Feel and see, because a spirit hath not flesh and bones as you see me to have (Luke xxiv, 39): in like manner therefore also other risen men.

5. For numerically the same man to rise again, his essential parts must be numerically the same. If then the body of the risen man shall not consist of these muscles and these bones of which it is now composed, the risen man will not be numerically the same.

6. The supposition of the body passing into a spirit is altogether impossible: for those things only pass into one another which have some matter in common [cf. Chap. LXIII].

7. If the body passes into a spiritual substance, it must either pass into that spiritual substance which is the soul, or into some other. If into that which is the soul, then in the resurrection there will be nothing in man but soul, and he will be exactly as he was before the resurrection. But if into another spiritual substance, then two spiritual substances will be one in nature, which is impossible, since every spiritual substance subsists by itself.

9. He who rises again must be an animal, if he is to be a man.

CHAPTER LXXXV—That the Bodies of the Risen shall be otherwise organized than before

THOUGH the bodies of the risen are to be of the same species with our present bodies, still they will be otherwise organized (aliam dispositionem habebunt); and chiefly in this, that all the bodies of the risen, of good men and evil men alike, will be incorruptible. For that, three reasons may be assigned. First, in respect of the end of the resurrection, which is reward or punishment for the things done in the body; and both the one and the other is to be everlasting (B. III, Chapp. LXII, CXLV). Secondly, in respect of the formal cause of the resurrection, which is the soul. Since the recovery of the body is a provision for the perfection of the soul, it is fitting that the body be organized in such fashion as shall suit the soul (Chap. LXXIX. But the soul is incorruptible, therefore the body shall be restored to it incorruptible. A third reason may be found in the efficient cause of the resurrection. God will restore to life bodies already corrupted and fallen to decay: much more will He be able, once He has restored life to them, to ensure that life abiding in them everlastingly.

This body, now corruptible, will be rendered incorruptible in such sort that the soul shall have perfect control over it, giving it life. Nor shall any foreign power be able to hinder this communication of life. Risen man then shall be immortal, not by taking up another body, that shall be incorruptible, but by his present corruptible body being made incorruptible. *This corruptible mast put on incorruption* (1 Cor. xv, 53). So then that saying, *Flesh and blood shall not possess the kingdom of God* (1 Cor. xv, 50), means that in the risen state the corruption of flesh and blood shall be taken away, while the substance of flesh and blood remains.

CHAPTER LXXXVI—Of the Qualities of Glorified Bodies

BRIGHTNESS. Though by the merit of Christ the defect of nature [i.e., death] is taken away from all, good and bad alike, at the resurrection, there will still remain a difference between the good and bad in their personal attributes. It is of the essence of nature that the human soul be the form of the body, quickening it and preserving it in being; while by personal acts the soul deserves to be raised to the glory of the vision of God, or to be shut out from the order of this glory through its own fault. The bodies of all men alike will be organized as befits the soul, so that the soul shall be an imperishable form giving imperishable being to the body, because to this effect the power of God will entirely subject the matter of the human body to the human soul. But from the brightness and excellence of the soul that is raised to the vision of God, the body, united to such a soul, shall gain a further advantage. It will be entirely subject to the soul, God's power so disposing, not in being only, but in all its actions, experiences, motions and bodily qualities. As then the soul in the enjoyment of the vision of God will be replenished with a spiritual brightness, so by an overflow from soul to body, the body itself, in its way, will be clad in a halo and glory of brightness. Hence the Apostle says: It is sown in dishonor, it shall rise in glory (1 Cor. xv, 43): because our body, which now has no light of its own, shall then be bright and shining, according to the promise: The just shall shine as the sun in the kingdom of their Father (Matt. xiii, 43).

II. Agility. The soul that shall enjoy the vision of God, being conjoined to its last end, will find its desire fulfilled in all things. And because the body moves at the desire of the soul, the body in this case will absolutely obey the beck of the spirit in its every command to move: hence the bodies of the risen will be agile; and this is what the Apostle means, when he says: It is sown in weakness:

it shall rise in power (ib.) We experience weakness in the body, in that it proves incapable of satisfying the soul in the movements and actions which the soul commands. This weakness shall then be entirely removed by virtue overflowing into the body from the soul united to God. Hence it is said of the just that they shall run hither and thither like sparks in a dry bed of reeds (Wisd. iii, 7).

  III. Impassibility. As the soul that enjoys God will have its desire fulfilled in respect of the gaining of all good, so also in respect of the removal of all evil. The body therefore, being made perfect in proportion to the soul, shall be free from all evil, actual and potential. As for actuality, there will be in the risen no corruption, no deformity, no defect. In point of potentiality, the risen Saints will be beyond the possibility of suffering aught that could give them pain: they will thus be impassible. Still this does not bar in them that sensibility which is proper to sentient beings: for they will use the senses to their delight in things that are not inconsistent with their state of incorruption. This impassibility is declared by the Apostle: It is sown in corruption, it shall rise in incorruption.

  IV. Subtlety. As the soul enjoying God shall perfectly adhere to Him, and share in His goodness to the full height of its capacity; so the body shall be perfectly subject to the soul, and share in its attributes so far as possible, in clearness of sense, in seemliness of bodily appetite, and in general perfection of the entire organism: for a natural object is more perfect, the more perfectly its matter is subject to its form. Therefore the Apostle says (1 Cor. xv, 44): There is sown an animal body, there shall rise a spiritual body. The risen body will be spiritual, not as being a spirit, but as being wholly subject to the spirit;

as the present body is called animal, not because it is an animal, but because it is subject to animal appetites and needs food.

It appears by what has been said that the risen body shall be bright and shining, incapable of suffering, moving without difficulty and labor, and most perfectly actuated by its form.

CHAPTER LXXXVIII—Of Sex and Age in the Resurrection

STILL we must not suppose, what some have thought, that female sex has no place in the bodies of the risen Saints. For since resurrection means the reparation of the defects of nature, nothing of what makes for the perfection of nature will be withdrawn from the bodies of the risen. Now among other organs that belong to the integrity of the human body are those which minister to generation as well in male as in female. These organs therefore will rise again in both. Nor is this conclusion impaired by the fact that there will be no longer any use of these organs (Chap. LXXXIII). If that were any ground for their absence from the risen body, all the organs bearing on digestion and nutrition should be absent, for there will not be any use for them either: thus great part of the organs proper to man would be wanting in the risen body. We conclude that all such organs will be there, even organs of which the function has ceased: these will not be there without a purpose, since they will serve to make up the restored integrity of the natural body.

Neither is the weakness of the female sex inconsistent with the perfection of the resurrection. Such weakness is no departure from nature, but is intended by nature. This natural differentiation will argue the thoroughgoing perfection of nature, and commend the divine wisdom that arranges creation in diversity of ranks and orders. Nor is there anything to the contrary in the expression of the Apostle: *Till we all meet and attain to the unity of faith and recognition of the Son of God, even to a perfect man, to the measure of the full stature of Christ*(Eph. iv, 13). This does not mean that in that meeting in which the risen shall go forth to meet Christ in the air every one shall be of the male sex, but it indicates the perfection and strength of the Church, for the whole Church shalt be like a perfect, full-grown man, going out to meet Christ.172

Again, all must rise at the age of Christ, which is the age of perfect manhood, for the sake of the perfection of nature, which is at its best in this age above others.

CHAPTER LXXXIX—Of the quality of Risen Bodies in the Lost

THE bodies of those who are to be lost must be proportionate to their souls. Now the souls of the wicked have a nature which is good, as created by God: but the will in them will be disorderly, falling short of its proper end. Their bodies therefore, so far as nature goes, will be restored to entirety: thus they will rise at a perfect age without any diminution of organs or limbs, and without any defect or detriment, which any malformation or sickness may have brought on. Hence the Apostle says: *The dead shall rise incorrupt* (1 Cor. xv, 52): and that this is to be understood of all men, good and bad alike, is clear from the context. But inasmuch as their soul will have its will turned away from God and deprived of its proper end, their bodies will not be spiritual (1 Cor. xv, 44, in the sense of being wholly subject to the spirit, but rather their soul will be in effect carnal. Nor will their bodies be agile, obeying the soul without difficulty, but rather ponderous and heavy and insupportable to the soul, even as their souls are by disobedience turned away from God. Their bodies will remain liable to suffering, even as now, or more so: they will suffer affliction from sensible things, but not corruption; as their souls will be tormented by the natural desire of happiness made frustrate. Their bodies too will be opaque and darksome, as their souls will be void of the light of divine knowledge. This is the meaning of what the Apostle says, that we shall all rise again, but we shall not all be changed (1 Cor. xv, 51): for the good alone shall be changed to glory, and the bodies of the wicked shall rise without glory.

Some may think it impossible for the bodies of the wicked to be liable to suffering, and yet not liable to disintegration, since every impression suffered, when it goes beyond the common, takes off from the substance: so we see that if a body is long kept in the fire, it will be entirely consumed; and when pain becomes unusually intense, the soul is separated from the body. But all this happens on the supposition of the transmutability of matter from form to form. Now the human body, after the resurrection, will not be transmutable from form to form, either in the good or in the wicked; because in both it will be entirely perfected by the soul in respect of its natural being.

CHAPTER XC—How Incorporeal Subsistent Spirits suffer from Corporeal Fire, and are befittingly punished with Corporeal Punishments

WE must not suppose that incorporeal subsistent spirits, — as the devil, and the souls of the lost before the resurrection, — can suffer from fire any disintegration of their physical being, or other change, such as our perishable bodies suffer from fire. For incorporeal substances have not a corporeal nature, to be changed by corporeal things. Nor are they susceptible of sensible forms except intellectually; and such intellectual impression is not penal, but rather perfective and pleasurable. Nor can it be said that they suffer affliction from corporeal fire by reason of a certain contrariety, as their bodies shall suffer after the resurrection: for incorporeal subsistent spirits have no organs of sense nor the use of sensory powers. Such spirits shall suffer then from corporeal fire by a sort of constriction (alligatio). For spirits can be tied to bodies, either as their form, as the soul is tied to the human body to give it life; or without being the body's form, as magicians by diabolic power tie spirits to images. Much more by divine power may spirits under damnation be tied to corporeal fire; and this is an affliction to them to know that they are tied to the meanest creatures for punishment.

1. Every sin of the rational creature comes of its not submitting in obedience to God. Now punishment ought to correspond and be in proportion to offence, so that the will may be penally afflicted by enduring something the very reverse of what it sinfully loved. Therefore it is a proper punishment for a sinful rational nature to find itself subject by a sort of 'constriction' to bodily things inferior to itself.

2. The pain of sense answers to the offence in respect of its being an inordinate turning to some

changeable good, as the pain of loss answers to the offence in respect of its being a turning away from the Unchangeable Good (B. III, Chap. CXLVI). But the rational creature, and particularly the human soul, sins by inordinate turning to bodily things. Therefore it is a befitting punishment for it to be afflicted by bodily things.

Though the promises in Scripture of corporal rewards, like meat and drink (Isai. xxv, 6: lxv, 13: Luke xxii, 29: Apoc. xxii, 2), for the Blessed, are to be taken in a spiritual sense, nevertheless some corporal punishments, with which the wicked are threatened in Scripture, are to be understood as corporal punishments in the proper sense of the terms used. For though it is not becoming for a higher nature to be rewarded by the use of something inferior to itself: rather its reward should consist in union with something higher than itself: nevertheless the punishment of a superior nature may fittingly consist in its being rated with things inferior to it. Some, however, of the corporeal imagery that we find in Scripture, speaking of the pains of the lost, may very well be interpreted in a spiritual and figurative sense. Thus in the saying, Their worm dieth not (Isai. lxvi, 24: Mark ix, 44), by the worm may be understood the remorse of conscience with which the wicked will be tormented: for it is impossible for a material worm to gnaw a spiritual substance, or so much as the bodies of the damned, which will be imperishable. Weeping and gnashing of teeth too (Matt. xiii, 42) can only be understood metaphorically of subsistent spirits; although in the bodies of the lost after the resurrection the phrase may be taken to have its bodily fulfilment, — not that there can be any flow of tears, for there can be no secretion from such bodies, but the weeping will mean pain of heart, trouble of eyes and head, and such usual accompaniments of weeping.


CHAPTER XCI—That Souls enter upon Punishment or Reward immediately after their Separation from their Bodies

THERE can be no reason for deferring reward or punishment beyond the time at which the soul is first capable of receiving either the one or the other, that is, as soon as it leaves the body.
2. In this life is the state of merit and demerit: hence the present life is compared to a warfare and to the days of a hired laborer: *Man's life is a warfare upon the earth, and his days as those of a day-laborer* (Job vii, 1). But when the state of warfare is over, or the labor of a man hired for the day, then reward or punishment is due at once, according as men have acquitted themselves well or ill in the effort: hence it is said: *The reward of thy hired laborer shall not rest with thee till morning*(Levit. xix, 13).
3. The order of punishment and reward follows that of offence and merit. Now it is only through the soul that merit and demerit appertain to the body: for nothing is meritorious or demeritorious except for being voluntary. Therefore reward and punishment properly pass from the soul to the body, not to the soul for the body's sake. There is no reason therefore why the resumption of bodies should be waited for in the punishing or rewarding of souls: nay, it seems fitting rather that souls, in which fault or merit had a prior place,

should have a priority likewise of punishment or reward.

Hereby is refuted the error of sundry Greeks, who say that before the resurrection of their bodies souls neither mount up to heaven nor are plunged into hell.

But we must observe that there may be some impediment on the part of the good in the way of their souls receiving their final reward in the vision of God immediately upon their departure from the body. To that vision, transcending as it does all natural created capacity, the creature cannot be raised before it is entirely purified: hence it is said that nothing defiled can enter into it(Wisd. vii, 25), and that the polluted shall not pass through it(Isai. xxxv, 8). Now the pollution of the soul is by sin, which is an inordinate union with lower things: from which pollution it is purified in this life by Penance and other Sacraments. Now it happens sometimes that this process of purification is not entirely accomplished in this life; and the offender remains still a debtor with a debt of punishment upon him, owing to some negligence, or distraction, or to death overtaking him before his debt is paid. Not for this does he deserve to be entirely shut out from reward: because all this may happen without mortal sin; and it is only mortal sin that occasions the loss of charity, to which the reward of life everlasting is due. Such persons then must be cleansed in the next life, before entering upon their eternal reward. This cleansing is done by penal inflictions, as even in this life it might have been completed by penal works of satisfaction: otherwise the negligent would be better off than the careful, if the penalty that men do not pay here for their sins is not to be undergone by them in the life to come. The souls then of the good, who have upon them in this world something that needs cleansing, are kept back from their reward, while they endure cleansing purgatorial pains. And this is the reason why we posit a purgatory, or place of cleansing.

CHAPTER XCII—That the Souls of the Saints after Death have their Will immutably fixed on Good

SO long as a soul can change from good to evil, or from evil to good, it is in a state of combat and warfare: it has to be careful in resisting evil, not to be overcome by it, or in endeavoring to set itself free from it. But so soon as the soul is separated from the body, it will be no longer in the state of warfare or combat, but of receiving reward or punishment, according as it has lawfully fought or unlawfully.

3. Naturally the rational creature desires to be happy: hence it cannot will not to be happy: still its will may turn aside from that in which true happiness consists, or, in other words, it may have a perverse will: this comes of the object of true happiness not being apprehended as such, but some other object in its stead, and to this the will inordinately turns, and makes a last end of it: thus he who makes bodily pleasures the end of his existence, counts them best of good things, which is the idea of happiness. But they who are already blessed in heaven apprehend the object of true happiness as making their happiness and last end: otherwise their desire would not be set at rest in that object, and they would not be blessed and happy. The will of the blessed therefore cannot swerve from the object of true happiness.

4. Whoever has enough in what he has, seeks nothing else beyond. But whoever is finally blessed has

enough in the object of true happiness, and therefore seeks nothing that is not in keeping with that object. Now the only way in which the will can be perverse is by willing something inconsistent with the object of true happiness.

5. Sin never befalls the will without some ignorance in the understanding [cf. B. III, Chap. X]: hence it is said, They are mistaken who do evil (Prov. xiv, 22); and the Philosopher says that every evil man is ignorant. But the soul that is truly blessed can in no way be ignorant, since in God it sees all things that appertain to its perfect well-being. In no way then can it have an evil will, especially since that vision of God is always actual.

6. Our soul can err about conclusions before it is brought back to first principles. When the knowledge of conclusions is carried back to first principles, we have scientific knowledge which cannot be false. Now as the principle of demonstration is in abstract sciences, so is the scope, end and aim, in matters of desire. So long then as our will does not attain its final end, it may be perverted, but not after it has arrived at the enjoyment of its final end, which is desirable for its own sake, as the principles of demonstration are self-evident.

CHAPTER XCIII—That the Souls of the Wicked after Death have their Will immutably fixed on Evil

THE very disorder of the will is a punishment and a very great affliction, because insomuch as a person has a disordered will, everything that is done rightly displeases him: thus it will displease the damned to see the will of God fulfilled in all things, that will which they have sinfully resisted.

3. The will is changed from sin to goodness only by the grace of God (B. III, Chapp. CLVII, CLVIII). But as the souls of the good are admitted to a perfect participation in the divine goodness, so the souls of the damned are totally excluded from grace.

4. As the good, living in the flesh, make God the ultimate end of all their doings and desires, so the wicked set up their rest in some undue end which turns them away from God. But the disembodied spirits of the good will immovably cling to the end which they have set before themselves in this life, namely, God. Therefore the souls of the wicked will immovably cling to the end which they too have chosen for themselves. As then the will of the good cannot become evil, so the will of the evil cannot become good.

CHAPTER XCIV—Of the Immutability of the Will of Souls detained in Purgatory

BUT because there are souls which in the instant of their parting do not arrive at happiness, and yet are not damned, we must show that even these souls cannot change their purpose after parting from their bodies; and the proof is this: — the souls of the blessed and of the lost have their will immutably fixed according to the end to which they have adhered. But the souls that carry with them into the next world some matter for purgatory are not ultimately in a different case from the blessed, for they die in charity, whereby we adhere to God as to our last end. Therefore they too will have their will immutably fixed.

CHAPTER XCV—Of the General Cause of Immutability in all Souls after their Separation from the Body

THE end is in matters of desire like the first principles of demonstration in the abstract sciences. These principles are naturally known, and any error concerning them could come only from a perversion of nature [verging on idiocy]: hence a man could not be moved from a true understanding of such principles to a false one, or from a false to a true, except through some change in his nature. It is impossible for those who go wrong over first principles to be brought right by other and more certain principles; or for anyone to be beguiled from a true understanding of such principles by other principles more plausible. So it is in regard of the last end. Everyone has a natural desire of the last end; and the possession of a rational nature, generically as such, carries with it a craving for happiness: but the desire of happiness and the last end in this or that shape and aspect comes from a special disposition of nature: hence the Philosopher says that as the individual is himself, so does the end appear to him. If then the frame of mind under which one desires a thing as his last end is fixed and immovable, the will of such a person is unchangeably fixed in the desire of that end. But these frames of mind, prompting such desires, can be removed from us so long as the soul is united with the body. Sometimes it is an impulse of passion that prompts us to desire a thing as our last end: but the impulse of passion quickly passes away, and with it is removed the desire of that end. In other cases the frame of mind, provocative of such desire, amounts to a habit; and that frame of mind is not so easily got rid of, and the desire of an end thence ensuing is consequently stronger and more lasting: yet even a habit is removable in this life. We have seen then that so long as the frame of mind lasts, which prompts us to desire a thing as our last end, the desire of that particular end is irremovable, because the last end, or whatever be taken for such, is desired above all things else; and no other object of greater desire can ever call us away from the desire of that which we take for our last end. Now the soul is in a changeable state so long as it is united with the body, but not after it is parted from the body. Separated therefore from the body, the soul will be no longer apt to advance to any new end, but must rest for ever in the end already attained. The will then will be immovable in its desire of what it has taken for its last end. But on the last end depends all the goodness or wickedness of the will. Whatever good things one wills in view of a good end, he does well to will them, as he does ill to will anything in view of an evil end. Thus the will of the departed soul is not changeable from good to evil, although it is changeable from one object of volition to another, its attitude to the last end remaining constant.

 Nor is such fixedness of will inconsistent with free will. The act of free will is to choose, and choice is of means to the end, not of the last end. As then there is nothing inconsistent with free choice in our will being immovably fixed in the desire of happiness and general abhorrence of misery, so neither will our faculty of free choice be set aside by our will being resistlessly carried to one definite object as its last end. As at present our common nature is immovably fixed in the desire of happiness in general, so hereafter by one special frame of mind we shall be fixed in the desire of this or that particular object as constituting our last end.

Nor is it to be thought that when souls resume their bodies at the resurrection, they lose the unchangeableness of their will, for in the resurrection bodies will be organized to suit the requirements of the soul (Chapp. LXXXVI, LXXXIX): souls then will not be changed by re-entering their bodies, but will remain permanently what they were.

### CHAPTER CXVI—Of the Last Judgement

THERE is a twofold retribution for the things that a man has done in life, one for his soul immediately upon its separation from the body, another at the resurrection of the body. The first retribution is to individuals severally, as individuals severally die: the second is to all men together, as all men shall rise together. Therefore there must be a twofold judgement: one of individuals, regarding the soul; another a general judgement, rendering to all men their due in soul and body. And because Christ in His Humanity, wherein He suffered and rose again, has merited for us resurrection and life everlasting, it belongs to Him to exercise that judgement whereby risen men are rewarded or punished, for so it is said of Him: He hath given him authority to exercise judgement, because he is the Son of Man (John v, 27). And further, since in the last judgement there will be question of the reward or punishment of persons present in visible bodily shape, it is fitting for that judgement to be a visible process. Hence Christ will take His seat as judge in human shape, so that all can see Him, good and bad. But the vision of His Godhead, which makes men blessed, will be visible only to the good. As for the judgement of souls, that is an invisible process, dealing with invisible beings.


CHAPTER XCVII—Of the State of the World after the Judgement

IT needs must be that the motion of the heavens shall cease; and therefore it is said that time shall be no more (Apoc. x, 6).

A WORD in conclusion from the translator, or restorer. There has been present in my mind throughout my task the figure which I employed in the preface, of the restoration of a thirteenth-century church. I find myself surrounded with débris which I have found it necessary to remove from the structure of the Contra Gentiles: — Ptolemaic astronomy pervading the work even to the last chapter; a theory of divine providence adapted to this obsolete astronomy (B. III, Chapp. XXII, XXIII, LXXXII, XCI, XCII); an incorrect view of motion (B. I, Chap. XIII); archaic embryology (B. II, Chapp. LXXXVI, LXXXIX); total ignorance of chemistry, and even of the existence of molecular physics: deficient scholarship, leading at times to incorrect exegesis (B. IV, Chap. VII, § 5: Chap. XVII, § 2: Chap. XXXIV in Heb. ii, 10): even a theology of grace and the Sacraments that might here and there have expressed itself otherwise had the writer lived subsequently to the Council of Trent and the Baian and Jansenist controversies (B. III, Chap. L): finally, an over-cultivation of genera and species, that is, of logical classification, issuing in a tendency to deductive argument from essences downwards to effects, as though whatever is most valuable in human knowledge could be had by the Aristotelian method of 'demonstration,' with comparatively slight regard to observation and experiment, to critical, historical, and a posterior methods generally.

It may be asked: Seeing that St Thomas is so often at fault in matter where his doctrines have come under the test of modern experimental science and criticism, what confidence can be reposed in him on other points, where his conclusions lie beyond the reach of experience? To a Catholic the answer is simple enough; and it shall be given in St Thomas's own words: "Our faith reposes on the revelation made to the Apostles and Prophets who have written the Canonical Books, not on any revelation that may have been made to other Doctors" (Sum. Theol.I, q. 8 ad 2, — the context is worth reading). Our confidence is limited in conclusions of mere reason, by whomsoever drawn: our confidence is unlimited in matters of faith, as taught by the Church (B. I, Chapp. III–VI). The practical value of the Summa contra Gentiles lies in its exposition of the origin, nature, duty, and destiny of man, according to the scheme of Catholic Christianity. That scheme stands whole and entire in the twentieth century as it stood in the thirteenth: in that, there is nothing to alter in the Contra Gentiles: it is as practical a book as ever it was. The débris are the débris of now worn-out human learning, which St Thomas used as the best procurable in his day, to encase and protect the structure of faith. Or, to express myself in terms of the philosophy of our day, dogma has not changed, but our 'apperception' of it, or the 'mental system' into which we receive it. So the Summa contra Gentiles stands, like the contemporary edifices of Ely and Lincoln: it stands, and it will stand, because it was built by a Saint and a man of genius on the rock of faith.

The Summa contra Gentiles is an historical monument of the first importance for the history of philosophy. In the variety of its contents, it is a perfect encyclopaedia of the learning of the day. By it we can fix the high water mark of thirteenth-century thought: — for it contains the lectures of a Doctor second to none in the greatest school of thought then flourishing, the University of Paris. It is by the study of such books that one enters into the mental life of the period at which they were written; not by the hasty perusal of Histories of Philosophy. No student of the Contra Gentiles is likely to acquiesce in the statement, that the Middle Ages were a time when mankind seemed to have lost the power of thinking for themselves. Mediaeval people thought for themselves, thoughts curiously different from ours, and profitable for us to study.

Lastly, the Summa contra Gentilesis μέγα τεκμήριον— considering the ravages of six and a half centuries of time upon what was once the most harmonious blending of faith with the science of the day, — it is a fact of solemn admonition to all Doctors and Professors of Philosophy and Theology within the Church of Christ, that they should be at least as solicitous as an English Dean and Chapter now are, for the keeping in yearly repair of the great edifice given over to their custody; that they should regard with watchful and intelligent eyes the advance of history, anthropology, criticism and physical science; and that in their own special sciences they should welcome, and make every sane endeavor to promote, what since 1845 has been known as the Development of Doctrine.

www.ingramcontent.com/pod-product-compliance
Lightning Source LLC
Chambersburg PA
CBHW052128070526
44585CB00017B/1746